D1450396

Monmayou
and the
Amazing Care of
Divine Providence

Alain Marie Sauret

Monmayou
and the
Amazing Care of Divine Providence
by
Alain Marie Sauret
Copyright © 2021 Alain Marie Sauret
Designed by James Kent Ridley
Printed in the U.S.A.
Ad Majorem Dei Gloriam

ISBN: 9798488003606

GOODBOOKS MEDIA

3453 Aransas
Corpus Christi, Texas 78411
goodbooksmedia.com

He has given his angels charge over you to guard you in all your ways. These words should fill you with respect, inspire devotion and instill confidence; respect for the presence of angels, devotion because of their loving service, and confidence because of their protection. And so the angels are here; they are at your side, they are with you, present on your behalf. They are here to protect you and to serve you. But even if it is God who has given them this charge, we must nonetheless be grateful to them for the great love with which they obey and come to help us in our great need.

So let us be devoted and grateful to such great protectors; let us return their love and honour them as much as we can and should. Yet all our love and honour must go to him, for it is from him that they receive all that makes them worthy of our love and respect.

We should then, my brothers, show our affection for the angels, for one day they will be our co-heirs just as here below they are our guardians and trustees appointed and set over us by the Father.

St Bernard of Clairvaux

Every endeavor needs time to be conceived, then to sprout and grow ripe for the harvest. The same applies even more so to this account. Since the time I first understood the need of providing the narration as a privileged project until today, a lot of water has flowed under the bridge. Nonetheless, the facts remain and are far more splendid than our best efforts are able to tell.

Pittsburgh,
Sat. 2 Feb. 2019
Feast of the Presentation

Table of Contents

Adrian Monmayou

Tableau # 1
A Phone Call

WE WERE HOME IN PITTSBURGH for a gathering with family and friends, when I received a phone call that would unsettle my mind for several years. It was the evening of my fifty-fourth birthday, on July 19. We were holding a picnic in the back yard with a few neighbors and friends who spoke French. We met in honor of my brother, Jean Marc, who came to visit us with his wife Catherine and their two kids, Carole and Charlie. They'd flown in from Paris. It was an adorable evening, in spite of the troubles we had getting the barbecue going, as we tried to grill steaks and sausages. We were over forty people in the back yard.

Around nine that evening the phone rang.

"The call is for you, daddy," said my middle son, Michel.

Over the phone, my friend Brendan was calling me from Texas. He was trying to say something, but he had just enough time to say, "Oh I only wanted to wish you…"

More than a month had passed since the last time I heard from him. That evening I could hear his voice only in snatches. I guessed the rest of what he wanted to say. However, knowing his Texan cowboy character, I understood that he also was calling me for some other reason than just for wishing me a happy birthday… Nonetheless, it was impossible to hear more than just a few snippets of words at a time connected by long silences and broken pieces of words. Just sounds over the line. Then the phone call dropped.

I tried to call him back immediately, but reached only his answering machine. I left him a message, saying that I regretted that our conversation was interrupted.

I blamed the kids for the bad connection. "*They break everything at home*," I thought, "*plates, doors, wall plaster and chairs. There were every day new things to fix around the house. Now it was even the phone's turn!*"

Notwithstanding, I checked the phone, and it looked normal. I called a friend nearby and asked him to call me back, and the double communication worked fine. "*Maybe the phone wasn't broken, after all.*"

I reviewed my first thought and realized that maybe the connection was a problem with the satellite connecting Pennsylvania and US tropical region. In fact, this wasn't the first time a phone call had broken up with Texas. The same thing had happened days ago during a call with Corpus Christi.

It was a surprise when eight days later Brendan called again. We spoke in French. Brendan was an old friend who I'd met in southeastern France in the Alpine mountains of the Provence area at a hermitage that I used to visit with my children twice a year. This was when my family and I were still living in Rome and I was a civil servant at the Vatican. Besides being a Texan, Brendan was totally fluent in French, which we used to spoke when we met. Additionally, my English was very poor at that time.

"It was not your phone," he said immediately over the line. "There was something or somebody who didn't want me to tell you what happened to me the night before your birthday."

"Who wanted to prevent you telling me what?"

"A certain '*Rapatou*'. He was screaming into the phone. He scared me. This is why I didn't have the courage to call you back too soon."

Being said by a quiet Texas rancher, this was a serious issue.

"*Rapatou*" (we pronounce it Raapaatoo') is the Gascon word to describe some malignant force or essence, as the nickname of the "evil" one. It's somebody who might burn your meal. I didn't react to that much, but instead asked, "And what did he want to prevent you from telling me?"

"I was awaken three times in the night by the same dream. "

I knew the pragmatism of Brendan, and it was difficult to believe

10

that he would give such relevance to a dream. I remained silent for a moment, dazed with a bit of astonishment. But my curiosity was piqued. "*This dream must have been exciting*", I thought. I encouraged him to continue, because he didn't seem willing to say more.

I asked, "Does it happen often for you to have dreams?"

"Usually, Never!" But that night I had four times the same dream, and four times I woke up."

Here, I felt confused since just a moment ago he had said three times, and now he was changing the story to four. This fazed me again, but I decided not to interrupt him. I rose from my bed and moved to the living room where I would not disturb my wife with the noise of the conversation.

"And what did you dream?"

"Oh, I saw a farmer who seemed to be from southern France, maybe from Gascony. I did not know him, but he gave me a message for you."

"A message? And did he say his name?"

"Yes. Let me see… Here it is… He told me; his name is Adrian Monmayou."

"By the name of a dog!" ("*Nom d'un chien !*") I blurted out a common Gascon interjection.

"Pardon? What did you say?"

"Oh nothing, I was thinking."

"And you speak Gascon when you think?" he asked, catching onto the idiom.

"How can you be so sure of his name?" I asked.

"When I woke up in the morning, the first thing I did was write down the name because it was new for me."

"I see. I knew Adrian very well," I said. "He is a very dear old friend. I am very fond of him. He also was an intimate friend of my parents and of many of my siblings. It is seventeen years now that Adrian has died. He was a kind of phenomenon very well known in his area. He surprised everybody at Lunel."

11

"What is Lunel?"

I explained to him that Lunel was a small village near Lafrançaise, between Moissac and Montauban, in the French "Midi" on the North of Toulouse. Lunel is a neighborhood of a few houses held among the hills, dispersed with vineyards and grain fields. These are held in the North of Tarn-et-Garonne department, in southwestern France. Car plates used to end with the number 82. Some people say it is still Gascony over there. The people in that area have a typical Gascon character of eccentricity, creativity, bravery and pride.

"Like the Three Musketeers?" he asked before I could go on.

"Yes, like the three Musketeers who were all Gascons protecting the King in Paris. This was like today when the Swiss guards, who are from Switzerland, protect the Pope in Rome. We see their Gascon character in the novels of Alexandre Dumas, especially in the character of D'Artagnan and…"

"Is Montauban in Gascony?" — For he knew that I grew up in Montauban.

I explained how the borders did not have a precise line. Originally Gascony was simply north of the Basque country, which resides one third in France and two-thirds in Spain. I explained all these things to him because as a Frenchman I felt proud in the distinctions and complexity of my homeland's regions. Brendan listened, knowing he could easily get lost in my detailing. Traditionally the Gascon territory moves from the gulf on the Atlantic Ocean up to the Garonne River. "But the territory is larger than that," I went on.

"Was Cyrano a Gascon?" He was referring to another Musketeer well known for his long nose.

"Yes, he was too!"

A moment of silence followed. I suddenly realized that we had gotten distracted from our original conversation, a typical thing among the Frenchmen of Gascony. It's impossible to talk about anything if you don't talk about wine and food, especially Bordeaux. This is much like talking to a Pittsburgher without somehow talking about the Steelers. Then I got back to him: "And what did Adrian ask you to do?"

Great was my surprise to hear that Adrian was relying on me to carry out a task — which I would have to begin quickly — dealing with an event of which he was a witness. The event took place in Tarn-et-Garonne department from 1947 and up until his death. All happened in the Espis Woods in the Eastern agricultural area of Moissac, at around 30 miles, on the northwestern area of Montauban.

These events shaped the spiritual growth of my parents, of my siblings, the behavior of the whole family and to a large amount of friends. They had a great impact on my own life. We might have to return to this telephone call later and be more specific about the mission with which Adrian asked Brendan to entrust me that night. That dream would awaken my mind to the research that I had done the year before in Montauban and Moissac. It raised to a new level of interest the material that I brought back from France that past Easter.

Many would say that if Adrian wanted to talk to me, he should have done so directly in my own dreams, considering that it was my birthday. Well, probably not. I'm hard of hearing towards some things, and Adrian must have known.

… It was just a free consideration.

I had no picture of Monmayou, then, to check if the countryman that Brendan saw during his sleep was truly Monmayou, and it was

not appropriate during the night to call my sister, Christou, over the phone, and ask if she had a picture of him. It was too early in the morning in France, at that time. I did it later in the day. She replied that maybe she had one and promised to send it to me.

A week later I received the picture of Adrian handling a glass of wine during the cheer-up cocktail, while he was attending her wedding. He was hunched over in the typical bending forward attitude of elder people. I immediately sent it to Brendan.

After a few days he called me: "Yes, I recognize Monmayou in the picture" he said. "The man in the picture is the one I saw in the dreams. However, he was not at all hunched over."

His comment was insightful, for he added, "I understand that in heaven everybody sits upright. Obviously, everyone is well straightened-up over there!"

It made sense.

Now I knew that it was Adrian who spoke to Brendan, and I was wondering how I was supposed to manage in order to fulfill the commitment Monmayou expected.

It took me several months to figure it out.

These pages are, somehow, an answer to his call.

Tableau #2
Gratitude

"WHAT A PARTY!" VITO SAID AT THE END OF THE GET-TO-GETHER. The previous day, he drove all his way from Quebec to attend our family meeting in Pittsburgh. He came with Odile, his wife, to share hope, projects, experiences, concerns, proposals and desire to make our journey on this side of the sea a beautiful adventure under the light of our common ideal: the attempt to make Gospel teachings consistent in our life, or even better, to make them our life.

Nobody knew, over the weekend, about the message I got from Adrian Monmayou.

Actually, even I myself did not know, yet.

For I did receive the information later. When the phone allowed Brendan to tell me.

During the party, Jean-Marc, my brother, told us an interesting tale.

He illustrated the famous story of the sparrow and the crow:

"There was a newborn sparrow on a nest above the road. It was curious to see the world. In its attempts to look beyond its own surroundings, it fell out of the nest. Reaching the road, it was frightened and cold and started to chirp loudly. A caw passed by, felt pity for it, and crapped on it to keep it warm and hidden. As soon as the little bird was able to free its head from the patty of poop, it chirped even more loudly its disappointment. An eagle heard it, and swooped down and snatched it up." And my brother concluded the tale with this surprising teaching: Not all the people who put you in a mess are intending to hurt you, and not all the people who free you from the mud are actually doing so to help you. But above all, the main lesson is: whatever happens to you, be silent and behave."

His words suited Adrian's teaching.

It is always difficult to be at peace in the middle of the many perspectives and many forms of business we address in regular life.

Nonetheless it is what we must be: yes, we must stay always at peace!

Maria and Adrian Monmayou taught me to never complain about injustice, indifference, disrespect and any hardships that surround us, but to immediately address them with respect, care, perseverance, and love.

Chiara Lubich teaches the same: when some difficulty comes, "Never lose time in investigating what it is, where it does come from and why did it happen, etc. Oppositely, we must consider it as a visit of Jesus on the Cross and behave accordingly: with peace and love."

When we do so, all our days are filled with hope, trust, friendship, and become consistent with the teaching of Juan de Yepes: "Where there is no love, put love and you will gather love." Those words of St. John of the Cross confirm the suggestion of psychologist Pierre Daco: "We always suffer in life from what we are capable to change, or to better address. In fact, we usually suffer the missing issues of what we should improve around."

Reflecting now on Jean-Marc's tale, the teaching of such a nice parable reveals to be deeper than it seemed at first … Everything that happens to us is a call from above.

Divine Providence leads us all along during our life, and uses circumstances and people around to do so. During the summer 1949, Chiara Lubich said to her companions that "Everyone is created as a gift to all people around, and all people around are a gift to everyone". Recounting that story, gave me the opportunity to verify the wonderful neighborhood we get from the whole of creation… And the whole of creation follows steps of Divine History.

The person and the family however are so well connected that they move like one.

As an example, our days show post secularism, evidencing the words, which Card. Jean Daniélou wrote in 1962: "Being an atheist today, means being late in history." Our gathering that day marked the enterprise we started on the New Continent, when the whole world, moving to its global entity, needs to get back roots from above and reveal.

All being considered, I have a debt of gratitude to the large number of people who contributed to the story disclosed in the following pages. Directly or indirectly, they show what we are now. Many people are quoted here and there, along the pages. Many more, however, remain in the secret of our excellent relationship. As we can play on piano a four-handed partition, our adventure in the States is the endeavor of several people, including our family, interacting on this side of the seas. Yes, it was an amazing adventure. And it made us fully happy. As far as we still live, it is not done yet.

Later on, wonderful friends concurred to the composition of these pages. I am grateful to all and everyone for enlightening me with their comments, their example, and their friendliness. Such acknowledgement includes first of all my spouse Chiara, our children Marie-Claire, Marie-Thérèse, Marco and Marta, who took part of the edition of these pages, and particularly Michel, who helped me to compose a large number of tableaus and continued to provide his help until the material got some consistency. Then, both of us, we forgot it for a while.

Thanks also to my siblings, Jacqueline, Annie, Marie-Jean, Joseph, Marie-Bénédicte, Jean-Marc, and especially Christou, who provided some irreplaceable pieces. She was familiar with Maria and Adrian Monmayou, with whom she was used to live, when she helped during Vintage season. All the details she gave to me were a kind of challenge, for she had a totally diverse relationship with them. She even disagreed sometimes with my recount of Adrian. Her observations, however, helped me a lot to better understand my own intimacy with Adrian Monmayou.

Many also are the friends we met, here, on the American continent. Without them, we would have been barely able to survivie the challenges we had, almost every day, to address. I like to mention first the hermits of the Eucharist in West Virginia and Texas, all of them, including Patrick and Robert. Then, worthy of notice are the friends of the Focolare living in Chicago, like Gian-Piero, in Washington

D.C., like Patrick, Enrico, Nathan, Ed, Jerry, Nicola, Magdy, and Bill, then in Dallas, like John-Jonathan, and Claudio.

I like to quote Kent, too, from New Moundsville, WV, who gently encouraged me to improve in many ways my habits and behaviors, on this side of the Ocean, in order to make us more appropriate as new settlers on this area. He made me better aware of the culture of this country.

Special thanks go to a few gentlemen, who had a dramatic impact in our lives. I refer to Fr. Higgs, John Connelly, Derek Whordley, David Poecking, Bp. Allen H. Vigneron, Adam J. Card. Maida and his brother, Fr. Ted. Others, who are not quoted, know in their heart the good things we owe them. When we will meet upstairs, in afterlife, it will be the following of a wonderful party.

Vito, whose house in Quebec is the place where I was able to gather the whole story in a manuscript, urged me not to forget the countless followers of Chiara Lubich, members of the Focolare, who always have remained near to us, in spite of the distance overseas, including Pasquale Foresi, whose familiar nickname is Chiaretto, Bruno Venturini, Nuzzomaria, Maras, Peppuccio, Fede, Giancarlo, Jesus, Emmaus, Mario, Marcello, Gustavo, and Luigino… and near to our place Terry and Sam who have been so helpful to us in many ways.

Overall, I say thanks to you, Maria and Adrian Monmayou. And I am, wondering why you took such a pleasure to keep us continually traveling while living on the New Continent: Littleton & Hundred (West Virginia), Pittsburgh (Pennsylvania), Montreal & Chertsey (Quebec), Detroit (Michigan), Corpus Christi & San Antonio (Texas), Wheeling (again in West Virginia), then back to Pittsburgh, then Steubenville (Ohio), and so on…

Our whole story shows how the law of the jungle, which characterizes the surrounding of everybody's life, is always the opportunity of an incredible endeavor. It depends on us to make it a failure or an opportunity, for nothing happens at random. It took a consistent period, and a long series of events for Our Heavenly Father to prepare us with the coming of His Son. All the same, nothing happens to us without the care of Divine Providence. After the Focolare, our spiritual director, who was a hermit in the mountains of Northern Provence, put Chiara and me in contact with the Texan, Fr. Patrick Meaney, who asked me to help him in preparing the statutes of his hermitage community in the U.S.

I composed these constitutions out of my experience with the Focolare Movement, but following scrupulously the words of the co-founder of the Focolare, don Pasquale Foresi, who told me directly: "Do not confuse the two spiritualities, never try to move some member of Catholic Solitudes towards the Focolare and never encourage any member of the Focolare to enter the Catholic Solitudes... I had difficulty at first to understand it. But I did it accurately and later on the light came as it is said in the Gospel: "Who does the truth, comes to the light...." [John 8:32].

I understood that while we need two eyes to see properly, two hands to handle everything and two legs to suitably walk, the two diverse spiritualities were the two wings of my flying towards God...

There would be much more to say, and it will come along in the following pages.

The huge company of people who deserve these words of gratitude are nothing but the presence of Divine Providence all along my life, from Montcuq, France, where I was born and grew with most of my 9 siblings until I was five, then Montauban, where I had the chance to go to the Catholic school of the Sacred Heart, then Rome (Italy), and the Vatican City, when I met Chiara and we started together the new adventure which, later, brought us in America...

Let us see how it came out.

A first warning had already come.

I must refer how in Rome I had clearly the sensation of being prepared to leave the excellent position I had in the Vatican. Deeply inside, I knew I was ready. Such a feeling was so strong that for a while I thought that I was in the process of dying.

Not being sure about how to handle that strange awareness I went to visit my confessor, Fr. Joseph de Finance, at the Gregorian University. De Finance was 91 years old at that time and was well known for his simplicity and sageness. He gave a different interpretation of my feeling. "In spiritual life", he said, "When people feel that they are going to die and they are ready for it, it often means a great adjustment is in progress in their life." He insisted; "You're not going to die. More likely a great change is coming forth and a new life will soon start for you".

I got surprised.

In the same period, however, consulting with Giuseppe Zanghì, a Focolare philosopher, the answer of de Finance was confirmed.

Both were right. Few months later our whole family was leaving Europe for the New Continent. Our journey had begun.

Nonetheless a big notice is necessary to make here. This book should be considered almost as an historical narration, because everyone coming from Europe today would have a totally diverse surprising discovery.

What we found in this continent provided us a surprising surrounding which would be barely the same today from those coming from Europe, because in the meanwhile, the whole European country changed a lot.

Tableau # 3
Calling Out

LEAVING ROME WAS A SUDDEN EVENT FOR MY FAMILY.

It was the unavoidable result of things coming together at once.

At times, our logic can gather several answers, yet, there is always one we must choose. Amongst many options, pieces were added together, one by one, leading to a single logical direction... We had to go.

Actually, it is a clear sign from Divine Providence, when suddenly your whole life become insufferable, and many plans to improve it are soon shown to be not doable. The plans then, which you try to elaborate in order to make a good change, are found impracticable, while, at the same time, a tiny issue of happenstance becomes the deciding factor. With us this time it was someone asking for a favor, which would actually lead us elsewhere. All great doors are locked down. And a small track, which doesn't show great perspectives, becomes, soon, the only one way. And it is practicable.

I was involved, in Rome, in several businesses and got a few liabilities. I was, at the same time, President of the French school at Trinity of the Mount, President of the Cultural Circle depending on the French Embassy, Civil Servant in Vatican Curia, with the title of Vice General secretary of the Holy Childhood Society. Finally, I also was philosophy professor both at Regina Mundi and at the Greg, which is the nickname of the pontifical Gregorian University, which has its seat in Rome but depends on the Vatican City state.

In my courses of logic, I usually offer this riddle to my philosophy students: "When do six plus six equal seven?" At first the students are lost and this is a good start to provide some insights of logic.

Then, asking this question again, I usually add that there is a trick.

The riddle demonstrates the difference between a regular demonstration, the so-called syllogism, and a demagoguery fake, which is a sophism. A syllogism is a grounded reasonable demonstration, while the sophism plays with words as Greek politicians often did, and some public personalities still exhibit nowadays. Here lies the challenge, and I will repeat my question again: "How do six and six make seven?"

Some offered a response saying that Mr. and Mrs. Six got a baby to whom they gave the name "seven" — Which is not a very good answer. It is still, however, an attempt to solve the riddle.

Other students would present that six businessmen of a company have a meeting with six interlocutors of another firm and are able to conclude the meeting at seven. It is not better, as an answer, but it clearly indicates what demagoguery is.

After some pondering and random guessing, some of my students would answer that "SIX + SIX" is spelled out in seven characters or symbols... "Right enough!' I would tell them.

However, my riddle had an acceptable solution in my mind. In my family we are six Italians and six French: My wife, Chiara, is only Italian, born in Tuscany near the Mediterranean Sea, and the five kids, born in Italy are Italians, too. Myself, I am only French, born of Gascony. Sometimes, jokingly, we used to tell friends how the worst of French characters —a Gascon—paired with the worst of Italian characters —a Tuscan— form the strongest marriage, from which we had five kids. My kids are — from oldest to youngest — Marie-Claire, Marie-Therese, Michel (which is a French name for a boy), Marta and Marco. All five are both French from their father, and Italian from their mother, and they hold both the Gascon and Tuscan characters in them. Therefore, the family is made by six Italians and six French, for a total of seven people. Thus, six and six make seven.

Sometime in our house, we have more firecrackers amongst us than at Fourth of July Celebration. But this is the way we are and this is how we've learned to communicate. Often the greatest bonds come from the most intense oppositions. Our feuds don't form an open war, as many neighbors might believe. It is just our regular Mediterranean family behavior of talking.

This has always been true, even when living in an old stone-faced apartment building in Rome. The building did not have an elevator, but since our apartment was only on the third floor, we didn't mind climbing the stairway steps of stone, leading upward through cavern-like corridors. Our apartment was just big enough for the seven of us. The two boys shared one large room, and each of the three girls had their own. What Americans call the "living room" had high ceilings, but the kitchen was just large enough for daily cooking, with an old dented stove and a gas oven that sometimes scared the children, as they said.

In February of 1995, as a layman, I was at the top of Vatican positions, which I could only have dreamed of, before moving from Rome with my wife. In the Vatican, I had a great office with vast walls, located in the building of Propaganda, which was used for running and organizing a good number of ministry missionaries. My office was lined with tall shelves filled with wide, leather-bound books, and I sat at a beautiful desk made of cherry wood, with a crystal top surface. As I was working on some documents at my computer, a good friend of mind came through the door.

Renée was a Bishop working in the Secretary of State, under John Pope Paul II, and he came to visit me one morning to compliment me on my success throughout my career at the Vatican.

"You are among the top three persons in the Vatican, who should be selected for a diplomatic position," he told me. "Your curriculum is amazing. In your previous position at the Dicastery of Eastern Churches you created the office of Roaco, which coordinates help for eastern communities and raises today a budget of over four hundred million dollars a year."

"Additionally, you are an excellent philosophy professor in two Vatican universities, President of the French school under the French embassy near the Vatican in Rome, and President of the Circle of the French Community in Rome. What might be your plans for the future?"

Without hesitation, I answered him, "I will probably leave soon."

"You want to leave!?" His tone was that of shock, and he took a step back to settle himself.

"It doesn't matter much what I want. I feel inside that I am done here."

My answer stunned him. His eyes widened a bit and he was at a loss for words. He did not reply much else. Whatever he had come to tell me, or perhaps offer me, had met a roadblock upon my response to his praise. We did not have much else to say between us.

After he left, I stayed in my office to think a little longer. Sitting in my chair and looking around my office I thought of how quickly I had climbed the ladder of the Vatican's Hierarchy. When 25 years before I applied for the job in the Vatican an excellent priest, co-founder of the Focolare Movement, don Pasquale Foresi, gave me a suggestion, which guided all my behaviors along these years: "Working in Vatican you must behave in a specific way... So, never try to understand the reasons why they ask you to do this or that, just do it the best you can." This was actually the key of my successful endeavor in Roman Curia.

Then, many past situations came to my mind as a fast movie. There was actually one, in which Foresi's words acted dramatically opportune. At a Roaco meeting in the building of Eastern Churches, in January 1972, A.E.D. - *Aide à l'Eglise en Détresse*, also known as "Church in Need" — a society promoting rehabilitation projects beyond the iron curtain and the poorest areas of the world was absent and the other members had been very censorious against it.

I thought that many of these words of criticism were not justified and decided to ignore them in my report to Vatican superiors, who were present at the symposium. It was then a surprise that no one of my superiors blamed me for that omission.

So, it encouraged me to do more for A.E.D. I decided, later, to pay them a visit at their national office in Via Vittorio Emmanuele, just beyond the bridge at the top of Via della Conciliazione, just a few hundred yards from the Vatican building, seat of the Eastern Churches. where my office was. I could have walked there. It was less than a mile away.

I asked Archbishop Mario Brini, the Secretary of the "Dicastero", permission to go there. When he heard about my intentions of leaving for a visit oustside, Head Office Msgr. Emilio Gilardone, my direct superior, was furious and decided on stopping me; but Bp. Brini

interrupted him, "Let him go. There is nothing to lose. Just consider that he will be absent from office the time to get a coffee at the bar as you usually do every day." The eggs were broken, so I left the plaza.

I walked towards A.E.D. national headquarters and I explained to them the situation. Then I submitted the 11 projects that needed financial support. They immediately agreed to endorse 10 of them. When I was back at the Eastern Churches I entered directly into the Secretary Office.

Msgr. Brini was in a meeting and I was going to leave for not interrupting, when he stopped me believing, as an obvious option, that much of my visit had been useless: "You did not get anything with A.E.D. Did you?" I replied timidly, "Well, actually they decided to endorse ten projects." He jumped to his feet, showing a great surprise and asking again, "Did they?" I said, "Yes, Your Excellency, they did endorse ten." He immediately uttered an order, "Alain, report it immediately in writing to the Cardinal Prefect and do not forget to refer that I am the one who sent you there." I had no hesitation to agree and said: "I will do that, Your Excellency."

A few minutes later, I was at my typewriter. There was no computer available at that time. My hands were poised and ready to run for the formal statement, when Msgr. Gilardone entered my office in a fury: "I want to remind you that His Excellency Brini asked you to stress in your report that he is the one who sent you there." I was surprised by his insistence and I said, "I know that, Monsignor." And Msgr. Gilardone added, "But do not miss to write down to the Cardinal that I am the one who suggested you to go there." I was even more surprised, but I said: "I will do that, Monsignor." I'm still laughing in my heart about that story, but I had no difficulty to give them the credit of that embassy. It was the price to pay for a moment of peace in Vatican business.

I believed in those days that the suggestion of Fr. Foresi was the key for properly behave in Roman Curia. It took me a long time to understand that such a suggestion is valid not only for Vatican affairs, but for every job situation, every social endeavor, every good function in society. Every responsibility must be taken in a way that supports the whole business. In everything we do, we must agree to

our superior's demands and then do our best, following our own conscience. It is an excellent exercise for the mind and the soul, a growing training in human relationship.

I continued to reflect for a while about the brilliant career I ran up inside of the Roman society, and a curious situation came to my mind. In fact, years earlier I had played a game with friends as I walked the streets of Rome. At the time I was just engaged to Chiara, and we were walking through Rome downtown visiting places. The city was somehow new to us: many buildings raised our attention.

At one point we found ourselves walking in Piazza della Pilotta, with its ornate bridges, that is flanked by the monumental church of Santi Apostoli. We looked up at the great building there, which belonged to the Gregorian Pontifical University. In front of its gate — a huge gate — I asked my friends, "What is this?"

"Oh! this is the Greg. It is a Pontifical University."

"One day, I will be a professor there," I told them.

They all laughed.

We continued walking and we passed by the church of Saint Andrew of the Bushes, and we went past another huge gate. I asked again, "What is this building?"

"Oh, this is a Vatican building. It's the ministry of the missions."

And I said, "One day, here, I will be an executive." All my friends laughed again.

We continued our walk and arrived at Piazza di Spagna, in front of the Spanish stairs. I asked, "What is that building over there, near to the church?"

"Oh, this is the Trinity of the Mount, and the whole building belongs to the French embassy near the Vatican."

"Ah! One day, I will be an authority over there."

My friends started to laugh less: they were wondering then how much I was kidding or serious in my announcements. For I was smiling, but convincing.

Our walk continued until we arrived in front of the Quirinal, which is the plaza of the Italian president. I was about to say some-

thing, when Chiara stopped me.

"Alain, that's enough. You cannot continue this way."

Therefore, I said nothing, and we continued our walk. Curiously, coming back in thoughts to my office, I was considering on how I had accomplished every promise I made along our walking through Rome that night. From professor of philosophy at the Greg and at the Regina Mundi—which is affiliated to the Greg—to my position of vice general secretary of missionary society at the Plaza of Propaganda, and on to the edifice of Trinity of the Mount, where I became both President of the Francophone Society and President of the French School... the game I had played that night on my walk, crossing through Rome City, had been fully fulfilled. For a moment I wondered what would have happened if Chiara had not stopped me in front of the Quirinal... Who knows?

Yet still, some feeling told me that, all this business was just a training, for a future mission, which I was meant to accomplish.

Except, I did not know, at that time, what would be happening in the future.

I looked around my office and reflected on how I had built this place in a few years. In a short span of time, I had organized as new the ten-room business, in a department helping children across a hundred-and-fifty nations in the whole world. As my job developed, I had helped coordinating missionaries for protecting the rights and the welfare of poor children everywhere. My thoughts settled down the office rooms, which I had personally designed and formed using furniture I moved from Paris: bookshelves, desks, filing cabinets, armoires, archive structures... I also had helped create a filing system to keep everything organized and usable.

All along I had helped to set up the area so we could make the best use of the space available. On this purpose I had helped recruit the right people to fulfill the mission. Our employees had come from the four continents, and now, together in Rome, they had been working for almost ten years, under the guidance of my direct superior, Msgr. Henri Bodet, from Angers, France, who wanted me at his side. I accomplished all these amazing achievements under his directions. Most of the credit for such good deeds was due to our good relationship.

I also had grown a deep relationship with all of these good workers, who had devoted their passion and love to help the needy in the world. And now, I felt in my heart, that it was time to leave. A year earlier, a new department director had been assigned. His name was Julio, a squatty Columbian man, with deep olive skin and a heavy chin. He had a twitchy behavior, suspicious eyes, and a shifty mind Which, often, had trouble focusing on one task. At times, I pretended to slip up his name, and called him Julius, as in Caesar, because he had come into our department expecting to be crowned as an emperor.

He had no experience with the Vatican before coming here. I tried to help him to settle into his position. My spontaneous availability made him suspicious. He kept his distance from me, thinking I might try to sabotage him. Soon I had come to know him, as a man too small for such a big job. He was excellent at creating chaos out of the meticulous filing system we'd held together over the years. Sometimes he would ask one employee to fetch a document or study a situation, and later on, her turned to the wrong employee, asking why he/she had not reported it to him yet.

One day he came into the office embarrassed because he needed to leave for India and did not have his diplomatic passport, which was needed for the business travel. I offered to help him, but he refused.

"I can do it on my own," he said.

"If you wish to do it on your own, you may, Julio. But I fear you won't be leaving by tomorrow, then."

"And you're so much better, Alain!?" He looked at me with his eyes showing suspicion and much pride.

"Not a question of being better, Director. It's just the question of being familiar with the Vatican system for acquiring the passport. I would be glad to do it." He remained silent, which means agreement in diplomatic behaviors. Without expecting further, I left the building aiming towards the Secretary of State department inside of Vatican walls.

In fact, I was glad to get for him the diplomatic document. Everyone in the office was looking forward to his leaving. Everything was running so much better during his absence. And by the end of business hours, he had his passport to leave for India. When I gave him the passport, I stressed and showed that the seal and signatures had been made, with the same date. The trouble was that he never forgave me for having accomplished something he had not been able to do on his own.

With a man like this, being now in charge of the business, that I had contributed to built, I thought that, perhaps, if I would leave he would become a calmer man. He always looked at me as someone who stood in his way, therefore leaving could have been a true favor to him. I then reasoned that, maybe, he would be able to work better on his own, without our butting heads constantly over every project. At the same time, it was also clear, that I could not remain in Rome with five kids. I no longer saw a future for us here. The traffic amidst the narrow streets was terrible, and I could never drive the kids to school and make it to work on time in the morning. Every day Julio reminded me eventually of how many minutes I was late.

For a while I resorted to the bicycle, strapping little Michel to the handlebar and the smaller twins, Marta and Marco, in the back. Marco would ride on my shoulders in a carriage back-pack, and Marta would sit on a make-shift chair behind me. We would knife through the traffic more quickly this way, but I saw no way we could do this forever. Already Marco was getting even heavier than his older brother, Michel.

That very day, when I told Renée that I would be leaving, I found a letter home mailed from La Roche College in Pittsburgh. The letter invited me to take a position of visiting professor for a year. They had received a scholarship from a Texan foundation that would fund my travel expenses and teaching. "I am only fifty years old," I thought to myself, and "I can still learn English and pursue a new life with my family." It would be worth a try.

In the three months following the letter I put things in motion so I could pursue this new future. Within a week I went to the American embassy in Rome to ask for visas for our family, so that we could leave for the United States. I also made arrangements to find a house to rent in Pittsburgh. The same day I called a local airline to see what would be the earliest tickets for Pittsburgh, Pennsylvania, at the lowest cost. One way!

Once I got confirmation for the tickets for the whole family, I called my wife.

"Chiara, it's been a while now, that you've asked me to take you to the United States. Finally, I have the tickets."

"How wonderful!" she said. "When are we leaving?"

"In three days."

"But… [short silence] Are we going there on vacation?"

"No." I told her. "We go to stay."

P.S.

I must express, here, a huge gratitude towards my wife, Chiara, who supported me in every decision I took. It seems that she was confident that, when I made a choice, it was the result of a mature decision, taken after pondered reflection, looking at our common good.

The same I should comment on the children, who never complained, all along, in such a great and unexpected endeavor. Marie-Claire, however, was not so happy to leave Rome, as it will be explained later.

I insist: in front of my determination, Chiara and the kids were willingly addressing the adventure. No doubt, of the presence of the Divine Providence acting on everyone and all of us, including me, in such circumstances.

Due to my engagement in the Vatican, many aspects of such a reflection are too delicate to be shared with anyone. As usual such a business needs more a proper behavior, and no discourse.

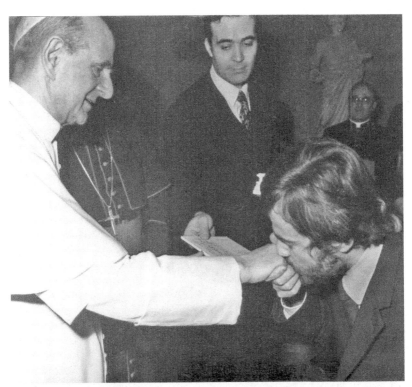

Tableau # 4
Close Encounters

IN THE GOSPEL, JESUS SAYS THAT WHEN WE DIE, WE BECOME LIKE ANGELS (Luke 20:36).

For now, we are communicating with the dead, in the same manner that we talk with the angels.

All we need is a simple act of intelligence and will, and especially a great and pure heart. The same heart which is said: "Those with a pure heart will see God" There is no need for the sound of our voice to speak, nor any specific ritual. Just thinking of our guardian angel keeps us in contact with him, and the whole company of them, under the watch of Our Lady.

It is in the same way that I have been in touch with Adrian Monmayou all along, especially after his death. We were connected in thought, in love, and in memory. I was in touch with him while living in Rome. I was still in acquaintance with him, years later, while moving with my family to Pittsburgh. I had many times the feeling of his watching over me. It has been in moments of prayer or in times of fear. I could sense time to time his watching gaze. Because of this relationship, it's no wonder that one day he decided to make himself more explicit, as he did through Brendan in Texas.

I do remember my first meeting with Adrian Monmayou, back in the 1950s. I was barely five years old, living in a large house in the Gascony border together with my siblings and our parents. Adrian, a farmer, lived a few hours away. Once he invited our family over, to share a meal with him and Maria, his wife. At the time I only had five brothers and sisters, but my father decided to bring only me and two of my sisters along, because he understood well, about the chaos, we would cause, the three of us, being much less than the whole six of us. Later the family enlarged with the other two who will be born.

33

Actually, I did not take into account the two siblings that were already dead in those days, Benoît and Marie-Thérèse.

All five of us, including my small, yet vibrant, mother, crunched ourselves into a little old car called the Rosalie. The automobile was much smaller than even a miniature Bug, but often times we had fit as many as eleven people inside, considering that traffic in the country side was free as we wanted it to be. I sat in the back seat with my sisters, pressing my hands to the glass, and watched the countryside slip past as we drove.

My father was a middle-sized man with great charisma. He had a high brow, and often his eyes held a gentle type of peace within them, brimming with the kind of patience and care that are vital when raising eight kids. With his knees bent against the Rosalie's dashboard, he spoke to us of his friend, whom we would meet soon, but I did not pay attention. I figured it was a conversation meant for my sisters and mother. I was too little and fussy to worry about descriptions of old friends living as farmers at Lunel.

With calm eyes, I watched the beautiful countryside. The roads were narrow, passing through vast fields of corn and grain. Farm houses lay scattered among the hills with cows and goats grazing the land. The main road led us to a smaller one dipping into the valley. Rocks and dirt crunched beneath the bald tires. This tiny road led to even a smaller strip, which climbed up a hill. The Rosalie growled and fussed, pointing us toward the sky. More and more grain fields stretched below the hills, like sheets of golden wheat, each stem touching hands with one another beneath the brilliant sun.

This must have been at the end of July when the stems of the plants were already high and the ears of the corns mature, just a few weeks before harvest. A blue sky roamed over the hills with gentle clouds gliding in motion, hiding and revealing the sun in their passing. From the breeze coming in through the cracked window I could smell the fragrance of fruit trees and the agricultural country. This is to say nothing of the typical smell of manure, which was often as present in our countryside.

The final stretch of our car trip felt very long to me. The trail was narrow and bumpy and so my father had no choice but to drive slowly. Adrian's farm was the very last in a long row of old constructions, distant from one another. His fields were the richest in the whole area. I could smell his wheat above all else — even above the very manure that helped it grow. It was the smell of the soul of bread, a common food at the dinner table. A meal was never complete without a glass of wine, a tray of cheeses, and freshly-baked loaf of bread.

The first to welcome us to the farm was Adrian's dog, who barked ferociously. The black dog had sharp, steady ears and a snout that seemed ready to bite. He circled our little car as we drove slowly into the grass. The dog followed us as my father parked the car behind a cluster of trees.

"Do not worry. He won't bite," said my father from the wheel.

We stepped out of the car, and the dog's barking continued. I was surprised not to see anyone calling the dog back, but this is how it was in our countryside. In our parts, the farmers often allowed their guests to come all the way to their door's entrance before calling off the dog, which would trot and bark around us in circles. This was the way of welcoming guests.

In front of the little house stood a water well, which was thought to be of great privilege and wealth at the time, especially for a house up in the hills. The entrance to the house was in the side. We walked around, passing between a small stable and even smaller shed to reach the doorway.

The house stood in the shadows of trees. Through the open entryway I saw two silhouetted figures. One was tall and broad shouldered. The other one was much smaller and tidy. The taller figure finally called off the dog, and called us to sit down at a few chairs just outside of the house.

Out from the shadows of the house stepped Adrian Monmayou

with his wife Maria. Adrian was a tall man with a slight hunch due to his work in the fields. He wore a wool sweater over a brown checkered shirt and long, long blue pants. His face was plain accented by calm eyes, but he had a gruff mustache over his heavy lips. He wore a felt hat with a stubby bill over his head. He and his wife greeted my parents. They cheered one another in conversation. I paid little attention to their talk. I knew nothing about the tall figure, even as my father introduced me to Adrian. Except, I was caught by a surprising welcome — and I'm still impressed today — by his careful gaze. It was as if he were investigating me, or trying to read inside my very own heart.

We sat there at the table and our conversations began as we waited for the meal to be ready. Maria, the smaller figure of the two, served us a few refreshments, which in this French countryside meant wine. Even my sisters and I drank a small glass of it. This was an area which produced and consumed a good wealth of wine. Few were the people who ate grapes.

"We don't take wine by pills," was often said of vineyards and grapes, "We just drink it."

When I had a headache, even as a child, my parents used to give me half a glass of wine to soothe it away. When I had a stomach ache, they gave me wine to calm it down. When I had fever, they gave me *vin brulé*, which was a kind of warm soup of wine, which brought you to a big sweat that kicked away the fever. I remember uncle Gontran, my mother's brother, who used to put wine even in my broth. I hated that, but this was the culture I grew up in.

So were our refreshments under the shadows of trees.

I don't remember much about our meal. Maria probably served a bread and onion soup with roasted duck, which was a common Sunday meal for farmers in the area. What I do remember was how Adrian sat in his armchair, napping, later that afternoon. He had rocked back against the wall, with his face rested on his shoulder, his dog heeled at his side. He breathed with his chest rising and falling, soaking in the fresh air through his sleep. Moving slowly, I approached him close on the tips of my toes, feeling curious by his figure. He flinched awake at a draft of air sweeping past, and his eyes widened.

"Oh, Marie-Jean," he said to me, thinking I was my younger brother.

To say the truth, the friendship of Adrian to Marie-Jean had a strong impact in my brother's life. It produced some kind of familiarity that my brother got and developed with the whole of creation and at first with the animals of the farm.

I got surprised that he knew members of my family, while I did not even know him at all.

My thoughts were interrupted. Adrian's eyes fixed something upon my left shoulder for a long moment in a bit of amazement. I said nothing, standing there quietly, in the shadows, watching him in his deep gaze. In that quiet moment, his eyes remained on my shoulder, and I looked to see if perhaps a bee had settled there, but there was nothing. I brushed off some crumbs of bread from my shirt, but still I could not figure out what he was looking at.

"I'm not Marie-Jean, I'm Alain," I said to him, hoping his eyes would lift to my face.

He remained silent for a while, but continued to look as if something were standing beside me or hovering over me. I tried again to draw him out of his daze.

"Hello. Hi. This is Alain," I said to him. "I'm a son of Raymond."

Then, out of courtesy I think, Adrian came out of his daydream and began talking to me, except that he spoke in Occitan dialect, which was the original language of Gascony, with similar roots as Spanish, Catalan, and Italian. He used idioms I did not know. Often, the people of each valley — even within a small region — had their own vernacular of Occitan. Even from one valley to another, the language gaps could be wide. This is why we often spoke modern French amongst strangers as a common language. In the town of Lunel people did not speak the same Occitan as that of Montauban. The only dialect I knew was that of Rocamadour, where my mother was from, which my uncles and cousins were familiar with. But it came out later to me, as I will say afterward.

I had to stop him once more.

"Adrian, I speak only French. I do not understand what you say.

Please, talk to me in French, too," I said.

He insisted, "Are you Alain or Marie-Jean?"

"No, this is Alain. Marie-Jean didn't come today," I told him.

I tried to talk to him a little bit, but very soon it seemed he had gone back to his day dreams. I had to wait until my father came to have Adrian present in mind again. But they spoke together on topics I was not familiar with and which seemed of a different matter. Yet, even though we didn't carry an animated conversation with one another, I still felt impressed by Adrian who seemed to be of high intelligence and great knowledge.

At one point, I referred to him the reputation he had in the country, for holding a secret device to get the best corn cultivation of the area. He smiled. So, I asked him how come his grain fields were so beautiful and bright.

"Do you irrigate your land more often than your neighbors?" I asked. "Do you use more hay? More manure?"

"Only prayer while I work the fields," he said, and he smiled.

"What prayer do you use? I asked.

"I did not talk about a prayer, but about prayer" he said quasi enigmatically.

"What's the difference?" I inquired. Actually, I was getting his views, but I just wanted to be sure.

"Prayer does not consist in words and formulas," he said, "You may say many liturgical prayers and never pray."

"Liturgical?"

"Church prayers" he precisely indicated... "There are beautiful. But it is only when your mind and your heart are involved with God, that what you say is a prayer"

"How can that be so?" I insisted.

"Ask your father. He knows it well. He wrote a booklet on it, which I like. When you are full of the desire to be a saint, to do well, or to be in touch with God, then everything you say and everything you do is prayer."

38

"When with my sisters we wash the dishes and say the rosary, do we pray?"

"Only if your mind and your heart are full of the desire to know and love God" He specified. "Saying the rosary with your parents is beautiful. It is a prayer only when you say it out of love" Adrian said.

"I heard people, last Sunday, in the parking lot, in front of the church, saying that it is useless to say the rosary, because it is monotonous and we do not always think about what we say" I added.

"Do you think your mother is displeased if you say and reiterate to say that you love her?" He asked in reply.

"Well, I do not say it to her very often"

"That's a shame. Tell it her often, in many ways, for example saying that you like the food she prepared."

"Oh, that I say everyday"

"The rosary is the same: we congratulate our Lady on her deeds, and ask for help now and forever. It is a talk among lovers"

I was not sure about what I got, I tried anyway: "I see, being cool to God is true prayer."

During the last interacting words of the conversation, Adrian looked distant again. He did not reply anymore. I think he was in agreement.

It could be surprising that at only five years old, I might have such a deep conversation. For long I thought that I probably made a mistake in my recall about my age on that day. Fortunately, many years later, I had similar conversations with Michel, when he was five, and I understood that five can be the start of the age of reason for a child.

I was impressed. Even my parents behaved in front of him showing great respect. My father nodded often at his friend's words, and held a patient smile whenever Adrian paused to think between sentences. It was as if my father and mother allowed Adrian all the time he wanted. It was as if even the sun kept calm, and did not persist through the shadows, while this sage farmer spoke and thought.

After a while, Adrian decided to take me and my parents out, going to some woods, just a few miles away. My sisters stayed with

Maria, the wife, and we rode in our little car the size of a shoe box. The woods he showed us were known as Espis Woods. There, Adrian talked about Our Lady, the angels, the end of times, and about a few children who had, on occasion, come there to pray to Jesus and Our Lady. Finally, he referred to a recent trip he made to Rome, with one of them. Once more, I did not involve myself into the conversation because I felt it was mostly between Adrian and my parents. Instead, I decided to take a walk through the woods by myself.

A few days later, late in the morning, my dad and my mom drove me again to Espis Woods. The way they talked about that place was as if we were taking a pilgrimage to a shrine. It was almost in the same way they would talk of Lourdes, which was a cavern we used to visit two or three times a year, located a hundred miles from home, or to the shrine of Rocamadour, which is a medieval site of prayer, near to Meyronne, where my mother was born. Even in Meyronne there is a shrine, in a grotto on the cliff. They call it "*La Dame au Rocher*," (Our Lady of the Rock). As a result, I was not surprised to be brought with my parents to a place to pray.

Many are familiar with Lourdes. Nonetheless the first time I spoke to my children about it, I had to explain that Lourdes was a place where we went to pray to Our Lady, where a statue of Madonna was held inside a small grotto. The grotto of Lourdes was where Our Lady appeared to a young girl named Bernadette, to let her know she was full of grace. The Lourdes apparitions had happened in 1858, as a heavenly validation to the *Dogma of the Immaculate Conception*, promulgated soon later by Pope Pius IX. The very reason why Our Lady appeared was to confirm that the Dogma was true, while its promulgation may have gathered doubts in the hearts of the Catholic Church at the time. After the first one, several Lourdes apparitions happened, as an affirmation of grace. The grotto of Lourdes has since become the destination of prayer, for many Catholics coming from Europe and the whole world.

Similar insight could be said about Catherine Labouré at rue du Bac, in Paris, or to Maximin and Mélanie with the Lady at La Salette, which anticipated the events of Lourdes.

Witnessing my parents speaking of Espis Woods, with similar reference, caught my attention, even as a young boy. Much like they used to say, "We go to the Grotto" they were now saying "We go to the Woods."

As soon as we arrived there, my father led me to different places upon the hill. They were places where my parents had stopped by, while they were talking with Adrian the week before. Each spot in those woods held a very specific meaning and provoked a typical conversation among them. At a certain moment we stopped before a large tree. It stood higher than the rest, and its trunk had stood out even from a distance. My father talked for a long while and insisted that I should look at that tree. He insisted that I look again. He even asked about what I would see...

"Seeing what?" I asked.

"What do you see here?"

"I see a tree."

"But on the tree, do you see something else?"

"Well, I see the bark."

"But don't you see a crucifix here? The nativity? Saint Joseph?" He pointed to where the two large branches split from the trunk, forming something like a fork in the road.

"No, I don't. Where are they?"

My father looked very irritated and disturbed. His usually calm brow filled with heavy lines. He began yelling at me, persisting again and again that I should see those things. He persisted that they were there. He became so angry that I knew he might hit me, feeling insulted by my lack of seeing. My mother stopped him.

"Come on, Raymond. Do not insist," she said to him. "It's clear enough he doesn't see it. Why pester him?"

"What is it that I cannot see?" I asked. "I can see everything". And I insisted: "I'm not blind... I can see everything which is here."

"No, you don't," said my father.

Much later on, I realized what had happened. In those woods Monmayou had explained to my parents that almost all the children of the neighborhood had been able to see the presence of Our Lady,

41

of Saint Joseph, of the Saints, the figures of Jesus and of the angels. It seemed that the entire Heavens spoke to the children in that place. My father had been disappointed that the Heavens had decided not to speak to me. It was there, but it could not be a witness. I was probably the first child brought in this wood-shrine, who could not observe with his eyes the Heavens' presence.

And that was my good luck.

I was lucky for not being able to notice anything from above at the time, when almost all my friends were seers at Espis Woods. This luck helped me understand that it is not necessary to see with our physical eyes to believe, and that many things can be perceived and understood with love, hope, faith and sincerity. Even when we do not see spiritual proximity with our own physical eyes, we may know from their effects that they exist. From its fruits we recognize a tree. Similarly, from their effects we discern spiritual entities and understand what they are.

It is clear to me, today, that a similar ignorance, on my side, was the gift I received in that place of Moissac. I became a companion of seers without having to see myself. Many pressures and sufferings were spared to me because I did not see. For years, the Diocese of Montauban, on behalf of the Catholic Church, screened and observed those seers meticulously, sometimes using very little leniency. Those who saw were questioned continuously by Church authorities. The trial proceeded for years. Many seers gave up. Some became even ridiculed by other people because of it. A few remained faithful to what they witnessed and remained silent afterward as they had been asked to be by a priest or the bishop in charge.

Was I spared those trials because I had another mission to accomplish?

Was that in connection with the mission that Monmayou entrusted me?

Tableau # 5
Departure

"THE LORD SAID TO ABRAHAM, 'GO FORTH FROM THE LAND OF YOUR KINSFOLK AND FROM YOUR FATHER'S HOUSE, TO A LAND THAT I WILL SHOW YOU.'" (Gen 12:1)

Every migrant is a follower of Abraham. As we travel and journey with our family, we reproduce his experience of following the track of Providence. We trust in the Lord to show us the way, and we cannot expect this to be easy. Every departure is a dramatic change. It is nonetheless a gain, too. In April of 2007, Pope Benedict XVI recalled how migrants are a gift for the countries into which they enter, and how, all things considered, the migration of people provides for the growing process of globalization.

So, our family became migrants in July 1995.

After my visit to the American Embassy in Rome and my phone call with Chiara, we had only a few days left to pack before departure. Those days would be full of motion and preparation, and broken by little sleep in between. From packing our belongings to setting arrangements with a rental house in Pittsburgh, there was so much to do that even if I had wanted to plan everything properly it would have taken at least a week to do so. Fortunately for us, intricate connections that have the name of Providential paths made all the planning. Since then, my motto became: "Every idea is a responsibility." My mind was already full of responsibilities just to prepare for the flight, that I had little room to think of much else. I simply followed and obeyed every thought as soon as it came to my mind, hoping that God would equip us with the resources to match our responsibilities.

Every event is a new occurrence, but it never happens at random. Every new fact has roots. It was the same for our moving out towards the New Continent. Even if the decision to leave was taken almost suddenly, many circumstances had made us ready for it. The previous year I had been traveling with my two sons to visit a friend living in a hermitage in West Virginia. It was during our stay there, that matured the decision to find a place more adapted to our family...

On the last day of our trip in the U.S., we entered a hot dog store in Oakland, Pittsburgh, not far from the well-known Cathedral of Learning. It is there that we crossed paths with Giuseppe, who was the owner of a moving company. I did not know in those days that I would need his help, within the following year. Actually, Giuseppe's moving company came to our home, near Piazza Navona, Rome, and packed a large amount of our belongings and furniture. They were able to box over ten thousand of my books, which made half of my library collection ready to go. When they came home, it was a surprise to be told that Giuseppe had died and his son Andy was in charge of the business. Before he died, Giuseppe, asked his son to take care of our moving to the U.S.

While packing, I thought about Pittsburgh, the vast, dynamic city that I visited the previous year with our two boys, Marco and Michel. It was the place we were supposed to see again in a few days. I thought of all our belongings crossing the oceans, jumping from Rome, the city of Peter, towards Pittsburgh, the burgh of Pitt. We had antique furniture handed down my family line in France, and expensive desks and bookshelves given to my wife from her own grandparents. There were silverware and dishes, sofas and bedroom sets, furniture... How much of this would get broken or damaged on the way?

The moving company suggested shipping everything from Naples harbor. This worried Chiara and me. To be respectful of Naples people, called Partenopeans, I'll just say that they are very famous for their street smarts and quick-handed in taking care of their own affairs. I was not sure that Naples was a good option at that time, but I had to decide quickly. In the end, it turned out to have been the best choice after all. Nothing was lost or broken once the container arrived in Pittsburgh.

The moving company worked quickly and efficiently. In two days the forty-foot transport container had been packed and ready to go. The new company's owner, Andy, was a trustworthy man and handled our move with every ounce of attention. As I already said, before dying, Andy's father — the person we met in Pittsburgh with the kids — said to him, "You should have care for Alain's family if they decide to move to the States." Andy followed the request as it was his father's last will.

Andy's father, Giuseppe, was another touch of Providence's blessing upon our family. When the boys and I met him during our visit to Pittsburgh the previous year, we were chewing down hot dogs and thick hamburgers at a busy little shop called "The O" near the University of Pittsburgh campus. Each of the two boys had their own burger but argued over who had the bigger one. We sat at a tiny booth in the corner with a Vietnamese nun, Sister Cecile, who was showing us around town. The boys paused their arguing as we took a moment to pray.

We bowed our heads, elbows against the table and hands joined in prayer, and we recited "Our Father" in Italian before our food. Just then an older man wearing a checkered shirt, and long slacks, came to our table and spoke to us in Italian.

"Father," he said to me, "What a blessing to hear my own tongue here."

He thought I was a priest because he'd noticed Sister Cecile in her gray robe. The boys resumed their arguing, now deciding on whose burger had more cheese and who had the better fries. This man who came to our table was Giuseppe, and he had come to America for a surgery on his liver, which had gone bad in his late years. He joined us for our meal and as we talked I soon was told about his business, a moving company. It was Giuseppe, who before dying, made Andy promise to take care of us in our move, if that had become our decision.

As I write these lines, I realize now how deeply God's providence was taking care of us along our travel. Until now that I am putting down these facts, I never even realized how perfectly the pieces fit together. The commitment of Giuseppe explains why, when I called Andy, his company worked so quickly to help us out. They packaged and care for every item as if it were their own belonging. Italian business was not well known for deeds that paid close attention to the details or took great care in the affairs of other people.

During our packing, Chiara looked through our clothes and linen to decide what we should carry with us to the airport. As a family of seven we had enough clothing and linen to satisfy a small nation. She took great care in washing it all before our departure, but we did not own yet the type of luggage we needed to carry it all.

The air company allowed two suitcases for each traveler plus one carry-on for the flight. Therefore, I drove into downtown looking for large enough luggage that could help us bring all our personals. I got lucky, and found exactly fourteen, coffin-sized rubber cases with wheels and handles. For our carry-on, I found exactly seven red back-packs, the last ones remaining on the shelf. My children know me well for my fascination with backpacks, suitcases and bags — especially the kind with many pockets — so I praised God when I found bags of such great quality.

When I returned home, Chiara was almost finished with washing the sheets. She was stuffing, unloading, and reloading everything into our small and rumbling washing machine. Unfortunately, we had no dryer. These were uncommon in Italy in those days for a middle-class family. In fact, they were reserved only for the wealthy. The majority of the population simply hung their sheets on ropes outside their windows. Yet, even though it was July—a very warm, Mediterranean month for Italy—few of the linen had dried in time before our departure.

We packed all of it inside large plastic bags, wrapped with perfumed soap bars to prevent them from becoming musty and moldy during the trip. Chiara and I barely slept in those days. We were just packing, and packing.

And packing.

In the morning of July 19, 1995 we were finally ready to go. Two friends of ours, Luigino and Franco, offered to drive us to the airport. We had already rented a large van for the purpose. But we crammed it with all of our luggage, leaving no empty seats besides the driver and front passenger. Fourteen large rubber coffins filled a lot of volume, and cars have always been small in Europe — even the biggest vans were just a squeeze compared to a regular American car.

We were touched by the kindness of Luigino and Franco, who had insisted on driving us. Before that day, I thought that the van would have been more than sufficient, but it was not. Their presence, then, was undoubtedly providential. It made us reach the Leonardo Da Vinci Airport in their support and friendship, which was a great encouragement for this new adventure. Their friendship never stopped comforting us throughout the years. We have always kept in touch. We still appreciate their nearness even to this day...

On our drive to the airport, I sat in the front seat, next to my good friend, Luigino. The children were sleeping in the back, a needed rest for my wandering mind.

"Almost forgot, Alain," Luigino said to me, cutting left and right through lanes—the Italian way of driving.

"Yes?" I said.

"Congratulations."

"What for?" There were many things he might have been congratulating me for, but I did not know which one he was thinking of in particular.

"Today is your birthday. !"

"So it is."

"It is wonderful to spend it all together with your family. It is a true party. And you celebrate it in so many places at once!" He knew our schedule. Our flight would leave Rome for Amsterdam. From Amsterdam we would fly to Detroit. And from Detroit we would reach Pittsburgh. This was the only flight program that our travel agency could find one way in order our entire family could travel together on such a short notice, in this most busy time of the year. "Especially during summer, since affordable prices were hard to come by" Luigino commented with some surprise accented in his voice.

"That's true," I told him. "It has never happened before that I could celebrate my birthday in such a gorgeous way."

At the airport, Franco grabbed every cart in sight. Luigino helped unload the van, with the rubber luggage stacked to the max. There is no way we could have checked in and caught our flight without their help. At that time, our oldest daughter, Marie-Claire, was fourteen, and she was the only one big enough to help carry the load. The rest of our kids were too young and small. In those days Marie-Thérèse was eleven, Michel, ten, and the youngest twins were nine. Somehow, we managed. Every face turned to look at us as we moved through the airport in one long file. Each of the children had their matching, red backpack strapped to their shoulders, leading the way as Franco, Luigino and I pushed three carts stacked with the purple, rubber caskets.

Finally we said our goodbyes, checked in our luggage, passed through security, and boarded our first plane, leaving Italy behind us.

Landing in Amsterdam we met with a few problems. The customs officers became very suspicious because of such a huge load of luggage, and took Chiara and me aside to question our purpose of passing by Amsterdam.

"Why do you carry so much luggages?" the customs officer asked us, immediately. He was a tall, solid man, dressed in a snug, dark uniform. He was clean shaven and pale faced. His eyes held firm with a careful but serious regard. "Why pass through this airport? What business do you have through here?"

"I did not realize this was such a delicate airport," I said, hoping to reveal a respectful tone.

"Delicate? Do you call us delicate here?"

"No, I only mean that your airport is taking us very seriously."

They were surrounding with care. The one who asked questions was not discourteous or brash, but his face held worry and his tone was suspicious.

"Why Amsterdam?" he asked again.

"It is just a city to us. It could have been any other one." I tried my best to keep a calm tone. Chiara remained silent for the most part, answering only when the questions were directed at her.

"Yes, any other city... But it is not another city... You came through Amsterdam. I ask you again, why here?"

All I could repeat was what I had told him from the beginning, "It was our travel agency, which arranged our itinerary. Our travel agency made the planning. They set our flights. They planned the trip this way. I'm not sure. They're Dutch."

"Who's Dutch?"

"The agency."

"That may explain some things," he said, which seemed to reveal the mood. They held us a while longer, until I explained to him for the third time that we had departed from Rome and our final estination was Pittsburgh. Amsterdam and Detroit which were only passageways for us.

I'm not sure if, in the end, he believed us or not, but after a while longer, they let us go and we were able to catch the flight. On the airplane, my wife and I slept for the first time in days. The flight was over ten hours long, and I treasured every moment of it in my sleep.

Once we landed in Detroit, more problems met us, as we entered the States for the first time as a family.

None of us knew English, and the words spoken over the announcement systems sounded like shouting and mere noises to us. The airport was busy and at every junction we stopped to ensure we did not lose one of the kids. As we passed through the security in-country, we had trouble answering questions and communicating with the officers. They stopped us and had pulled our luggage back for check-up before we could travel to Pittsburgh. We couldn't understand why for a while, but then we realized we had to check them in once more.

As we loaded them onto the belt the customs officer lifted his nose and started sniffing.

"What is that smell?" he said in English?

"I'm sorry?"

"That smell, what is that smell."

I looked to my wife and she looked to me. The kids fussed around behind us and were playing, offering no help. I needed any kind of suggestion, I could get, in order to communicate with the custom officer. I called Marie-Claire, the eldest kid, hoping that she could be of some help with the English.

"That smell," the officer said again, pointing to the rubber cases.

49

"What do you have in there? What is that odor? Scanners detected strange smells!"

Marie-Claire looked blankly at us. "I think he smells a funny odor," Claire told us.

The customs officer detected the soaps fragrance, which Chiara had packed inside every rubber coffin with the moist linen.

"You have roses packed in there? Roses? Apples? Bushels?"

"No! There is only odor. We used soap," We told him.

"No, not you. Not your smell. The luggage. What smell is that? Do you have flowers in there? You can't carry flowers."

"Yes, flavor soap. We used them to avoid moisture and rotten stink. We put soaps in there." We tried to say.

"Okay sir. I understand you use soap. But in the luggage. What do you have in the luggage?"

"I tell you the odor..." My poor English was a handicap and I was unable to formulate a full sentence that made sense for him.

"What?" he said.

"The odor. I tell you."

"Then what is it?"

"What?" I said, meeting the border line of a rotten communication.

"What is the odor?"

I looked to my daughter. She shrugs. My wife looked to me. Then she tried to explain to the officer with gestures how she wrapped our linen in soap. She explained what she can with broken up words.

"Our sheet," Chiara tells him. "We fold sheets in soap for smell."

"You what?"

"Sheets!" she insists. "We filled the sheets with soap to avoid moisture." Our improper pronunciation and lack of vocabulary was not helpful at all...

"Your sh--? I don't understand..."

"Yes, the sheet. We throw all in luggage. We use soap for smell because our sheets are wet."

This seemed to baffle the officer even more. He had us open each of the big cases and checked, piece by piece, all of our contents. My wife would show them each of the soap bars, but they continued digging through the linen to see if the soap hadn't been used to cover the smell of hidden flowers or plants. It took a few hours to go through. When we had finally gone through every piece of our luggage, we became confused in trying to find our flight.

We eventually lost the connection to Pittsburgh. The gate on our boarding tickets was no longer valid because we had missed the flight. Fortunately, we understood that some other connection could be found As the officers saw us in our distress, they helped us and loaded our luggage onto a motorcar and drove us right up to a new gate. The children giggled and laughed as we cut through the airport corridor and people shuffled aside.

When they dropped us off at the gate, I looked for my wallet for some American bills to give them a tip. To my surprise, they refused. I was touched by their gesture. They provided all that service not for money but simply to help our family reach a plane to Pittsburgh. This was our first taste of American culture, made with great courtesy and human sensibility....

The last portion of air travel was our trip from Detroit to Pittsburgh. It looked very fast, but we were exhausted. After landing at Pittsburgh, we found all our bags on the baggage claim belt. Looking around, I rented the largest van available, but, once again, we found it not large enough to fit all of us and our load. Then, we would have to drive out of Pennsylvania toward the border of West Virginia and stay there near the Catholic church of Littleton, in a house that a friend of a friend made available for us, because the house we had rented in Pittsburgh was not ready yet.

Fortunately, our good friend Sister Cecile was at the airport with her own van. Together we drove out towards West Virginia. Near Littleton Fr. Patrick owned a cabin in the wildness. It was a hermitage, which actually was his hermitage. Nearby, he had built a church, and a house, large enough to offer a small center of prayer, meditation and solitude amidst the hills and woods.

I was so tired that I could barely grip the wheel, and found myself obliged to stop at every rest area or side of the road to buy a coke from every vending machine in sight. From what I remember, I guzzled more coke for those ninety miles than the van drank gas.

When we arrived at Littleton, near Hundred, West Virginia, just out of the south-west corner of Pennsylvania, the parish priest who was taking care of the house let us stay there, while he moved to another parish house in the next township. Sister Cecile continued towards her cell under the chapel built on the hermitage. We went to sleep with little trouble.

We had come to America.

Tableau # 5
Synderesis

EVERYONE IS A SEER. BUT EVERYONE WATCHES WITH HIS/ HER OWN BEHAVIOR AND ORIGINAL CHARACTER. This was the teaching I received from Fr. Joseph de Finance, while we were talking about revelation, when I was visiting him at the Gregorian.

In everything we do we must always follow our conscience. Following Scholastic tradition, Thomas Aquinas says that at the top of the conscience, there is a special place called Synderesis, that never fails. It means that, at every moment of personal life, everybody is able to understand the truth. This was also the old teaching of Socrates, who claimed that his business was to open everyone to the awareness of the truth hidden inside: "know yourself!"

According to the scholastics, synderesis is the gate through which, as long as we want to, we meet the truth at every moment of our life. Aquinas also indicated that "This is also the gate through which, continuously, God speaks to us." For this reason, we must never make any compromises with our conscience.

Adrian Monmayou explained very well this particular connection of every human being with God. The few times we had conversation together, I did not fully understand his teaching. His knowledge, however, became clearer and clearer over time. Today I'm surely better able to understand, and explain, what it is that he tried to help me to learn.

Adrian did not simply teach me to comply with the voice of my conscience. After Mom and Dad, Adrian trained me to be attentive to the value of life, to what is beautiful, just, insightful, good, true…. Doing so, the whole world becomes a field of recovery. Such an endeavor makes us more awake, and helps us to better become who we really am. It let us move toward a call. It moves us to pursue the appeal of improvement, which never ceases to make us grow.

Later, reading Maritain, I suddenly understood some of the words of Adrian. In his work entitled *Creative Action in Art and Poetry*, Jacques Maritain explains what the unconscious truly is. He confirmed the subconscious of Sigmund Freud, which is an unconscious of limitations and handicap coming from below, to which, he added on the top of our conscious, a large panorama coming from above, which is an unconscious of enlightenment, of freedom and betterment, which Maritain gave the name of surconscious.

It is the unconscious of value, which makes me free and calls me towards happiness. For Maritain the unconscious includes subconscious and surconscious. It was to that surconscious that Adrian had the expertise of constantly putting us in the presence of. It was always a presence of betterment.

He never said that the subconscious of Sigmund Freud was erroneous. He clearly asserts that such a subconscious is incomplete... He insisted to say that when Freud explains the subconscious, he affirms that our conscious is just the tip of an iceberg, the top of a pyramidal structure... the bottom of which disappears inside of the subconscious.

I remember how at the Sacred Heart Major Seminary, a few of my colleagues were convinced that Freud made a mistake... because it was obvious that a human conscience does not depends only on obscure and restricted foundations. How would it be possible to emerge from there if the foundations are solely restraining. It was necessary that there exist some call from above to make it complete.

In the above reference, Maritain indicates that Freud did not commit any mistake, he was merely incomplete. The lines of the pyramidal structure do not stop, in its upper part, at the level of the conscious, or, if you want, where the conscience emerges. Not at all, the lines continue to grow and to move upwards in the luminous calls from above.

To represent the whole picture on the blackboard, it would be sufficient to mark on the board a cross of St Andrew. Where the two sides meet, the conscious is indicated by a circle around the point of intersection, above, in the large virtual opening towards the ceiling, grow, what he calls the luminous unconscious, or, if you want, the surconscious, while below, we have the subconscious of Freud. Together, subconscious and surconscious, compose the whole unconscious.

Similar attention to what I deeply am makes me more sensible to that voice and more capable of discerning that invitation to improvement, which comes, precisely, from above.

Some years ago, pope Francis recalled to the chief redactor of the Italian paper *Republica* that ignoring the command of our conscience is like somebody who stops training his body and lets his muscles atrophy. Listening to our conscience signal increases our capability to hear and understand it. Ignoring it provokes a sin, even for non-believers.

It is true to say that everyone is a seer: Through conscience everyone hears and sees the truth that God is. This is what theologians call the eyes of our soul. Moving our family to the States was following one of these calls that we could hardly refuse. In spite of the many difficulties, we would have to face, and against the many around us who did not understand our endeavor, we wanted to remain consistent with the invitation from above to do so. It required us to overcome more than just some small inconvenience. Sometimes the difficulties showed, even more evidently, the purpose of our endeavor.

The difficulty with our rental house, which was not ready for us when we arrived, was just a signal of the more trouble awaiting us. La Roche College, which had called us out, offering me a teaching position — for which we got our temporary visas — was our first mix up. The position was no longer available, when the whole family arrived in Pittsburgh.

After settling down in Littleton, West Virginia, my first trip to Pittsburgh was to visit La Roche College and have confirmed my engagement there, with the Philosophy Department. Unfortunately, when I entered the human resources office, I was told that Vice-President Matthews, who had offered me the job, months ago, had just left for Chicago. Now there was no longer an offer on the table.

When Chiara found out, she asked me, "Alain, what are we supposed to do? We already left our jobs in Rome. You resigned from the Vatican, and I did the same from my employment as a teacher in public schools. We also sent an entire container to America, filled with our belongings. And now, here we are, without a job?"

She expressed fully what the situation was. But, at the same time, she was calling me to action.

"Well," I said. "We can probably get something, at least temporarily. Let me try it."

I went over to the president's office of the college, Msgr. William Kerr, who, surprisingly, agreed to see me right away, with no appointment. Kerr was a robust man in his fifties who spoke with hand gestures and good tone in his voice. He was a perfect communicator. And this was vert helpful for us, since we did not understand English very well, yet, at the time. Entering his office, I explained the situation. I'm not so sure how I was able to communicate. My English was, in fact, so chopped up, so bad, that I struggled to detail what we were facing right now, as a family, just arrived from Europe.

Somehow, we were able to grasp one another's thoughts and beliefs, and I still praise him today for the act of faith he took on my behalf. I was aware of the fact that, while we were here, everything might be possible, as far as our finding a way to stay.

On that ground, we would manage later, eventual future developments.

After a few minutes of conversation, Msgr. Kerr agreed to my proposal, and gave me the job for a year. While I agreed to the one-year term, I also asked him to update my working visa so that we could stay the whole year. He agreed to supply the paperwork. An important step was settled.

Now there were still other matters that we had to accomplish. Driving back to West Virginia, that evening, I knew that I could not, afford to keep the rental car. any longer So, we would have to find a car, to begin with. Then, passing through the township of Hundred, I lost directions. That's when I found a car salesman who had exactly what we needed. It was a Ford Country Squire.

I immediately alerted the family.

When our kids saw that big car – it was, actually, bigger than even the minivan we drove in Rome, they all shouted for Chiara and me to buy it. Never, in our lives, had we seen a car that big. It truly was a regular size American car. Such a car would never have moved through Via dell'Orso, which was the street we lived on in Rome. Once, a limousine tried to drive through the street, and got stuck in the corner of our road, then, for hours, it blocked all traffic. And this one was even bigger than that Italian limousine...

The salesman sold us the large Ford wagon, with three seats in the front, four seats in the middle, and another four seats in the back, which could flip up from the luggage area. My kids learned to call it the "woody-wagon", because of its wooden exterior panels. They were enthusiastic for such a large vehicle, which was perfect for a large family like us.

If I had not met across the dealer, so providentially, that night, it would have been only the car of our dreams... We picked this car, over some other opportunity, especially the Chevy, in the lot, because the Ford was larger. Also, the seat belts worked and it looked more comfortable with a smaller price.

With time, this proved to have been a first-class car. After all, Arnold Schwarzenegger used it as a getaway in his second *Terminator* film. To our family then, it was a typical American car. With an electric dash and headlights that turned on their own when entering a dark tunnel or getting dark in the evening. Also, when driving at night, it would automatically flash  its lights when crossing a driver with their high beams turned on. Our family traveled as royalties.

Whenever we drove our Ford, the engine was powerful and it could haul all seven of us, plus our luggage without a strain. We soon noticed that, driving in the States, was much more pleasant than driving European streets and roads. First of all, with an automatic transmission, I could keep one hand on the wheel at all times, and reach back for one of the kids, if they became too rowdy. Ah what a joy: a

57

car that gives control back to the father!

I did, however, have to familiarize myself with the new road signs and driving regulations. In Europe, all of the signs simply had a symbol without writing, but now almost every sign had some words written on it. All you had to do was to read American language, with which we were not yet too familiar.

I remember the many times I drove back and forth between Pittsburgh and West Virginia and I would see signs that read "speed limit" with a number beneath. What was this word "speed"? "Speed." I wrote it down in my notebook to check it later. It wasn't until I looked up the word in the dictionary that I realized I would have to drive much slower.

I was in a bit of a shock that, in a country with roads so large and straight, drivers were allowed to go so slow. For the first time I realized that there was a different style of driving in America. While in Europe driving was an act of surviving amongst vehicles, people and obstacles, here, I understood that you could drive slowly without being harassed or insulted...

The Angels must have been with us because the day I discovered that some speed limit existed here, was the first time I would pass by a police car parked on the side of the road. The funny thing is that I would first cross a state trooper, and I thought that now I could resume my European speed. But I did do not do so.

Minutes later I passed by a federal trooper as well. Truly, my guardian angel was guiding me along, because on my first days of driving, I sped so much that the police would have taken away my European license, and probably our car, too.

I suddenly realized, on Highway 79, that American culture was a culture of peace and relaxation. We drive slowly, with peace, and without having to be aggressive against other drivers. It really was a new experience. In Italy, at the time when we left Europe, I could not drive under the speed limit without having immediately a driver behind me, honking at me, to let him through. Yes, we had entered a new land, living under diverse cultural parameters.

Soon, I paid more attention to the road, to eventual other signs. Actually, some other road signs were new to me as well. A Stop Sign, for example, had a diverse meaning on this side of the ocean. In Italy and in France, the Stop sign appears only on roads considered less trafficked, with no right to go until the other road is free of cars... When coming to such a Stop Sign in Europe, I would have to let all other cars pass by before being able to go. I never have seen, before, an intersection with multiple stops. It would have been an enigma.

This happened in Pittsburgh: just driving towards the place of our future home in McCandless, I entered through Duncan Avenue into the five-way-stop intersection of Duncan Manor and I had no idea of what to do. I moved near to the stop sign and I waited, expecting all the other cars to pass by first. Then, when a gentleman finally waved me to go ahead, I realized: "Wow. Finally, we've come to a place of civilization!"

I will never stress this strong enough. Never before, had I seen a driver make gestures that expressed anything other than... well, let's call it, general disgruntlement. Another good surprise was to see how the red lights are adapted to the traffic. In Rome, when there are few cars on the crossing street we would "burn the red"—meaning run through the red light. Before coming to Italy, I was living in Gascony, where road signs make the rules. This is why, on the occasion of one of my first stays in Rome, when, one night, I stopped at a red light, a car crashed against me from behind. The man had gotten out, and started yelling, saying that the light was just a guideline. "The red light means nothing", and I was roughly invited to keep my eyes on the traffic, and not on the traffic signs. Here it was a totally different figure of what I was familiar with...

In Italy, and especially in Rome, when you're sitting at a red light and you see that the cross lights turn yellow, that's good enough for you to burn the red. In America this is much less of a habit. So, it was such a relief to be able to drive just by following the rules without having to interpreting the traffic signs and change your interpretation from moment to moment, from neighborhood to neighborhood, and from town to town. In America they use to write on the signs the directions of what you are supposed to do. What a relief!

While driving back and forth between West Virginia and Pittsburgh every other day, the rest of the family experienced their first impact on the local culture. The small town of Littleton, in West Virginia, offered us a very warm welcome with its tight nit population and close faces. There was not a day when someone didn't come with a meal, equipment for the kitchen or blankets for our deprived beds. Some of our linen, they knew, had gone musty from the travel. We felt their warmth and generosity, often not knowing how to properly respond.

Sister Cecile organized a camp, with around twenty children, from the area, in order to help our kids, familiarize with them. She was impressed to see how Marta, Marco, Michel and Marie were able to communicate without knowing a word of English. None of the local children, of course, knew any Italian. The additional purpose of the camp was to prepare and practice singing the chants of the coming Sunday liturgy. There was a small chapel, propped beyond a creek, where the kids would have their chance to sing.

To make the chances equal for everyone, Sister Cecile made all of the songs in Latin. She didn't realize that even for our Italian children, American Latin (read Latin with American accent) was still a foreign language. But what impressed us the most, during Sunday mass, was hearing our kids singing in Latin, with the perfect American pronunciation. That was an effective work of enculturation. We were never able to thank Sister Cecile enough for ushering our children into their first friendship with American kids.

Marie Claire, our oldest, refused to go to that camp.

She told me, "I will never speak English in all my life. I refuse to learn American, ever."

At this point I had to make a hard decision, difficult for me, but even tougher for her.

I made an arrangement with Derek, dean of the Education department at Duquesne University, and president of Vincentian School, in Northern Pittsburgh, who organized a three-week course of preparation for the new academic year. He offered to take Marie Claire into the campus, for a full English immersion. Here is why, the following day, while I was back in Littleton, I told Marie-Claire in the morning,

"Have you ever seen Pittsburgh?"

"No, I have not," she said.

"Would you like to come with me?"

"Oh, I'd like to."

Then I told her to bring her bag, because we might have to stay a few days. She did. Then we drove to Pittsburgh, and during the one and half hour drive we spoke of simple things, about the weather, the traffic, the beauty of this country… We drove directly to Duquesne. When we got out of the car, I told Claire to grab her bag, and while we were in the middle of the campus, I told her, "Now you stay here for three weeks. I don't care if you want to speak English or not. But if you want to eat, it would be better you learn some idioms. See you in three weeks."

And I left.

She looked at me with amazement, glaze filling her eyes. She couldn't believe I would just drop her off. She began screaming and shouting, telling me that she despised me.

"I hate you Daddy. I hate you."

"I love you, Claire."

I couldn't say anything more, but I simply hoped in my heart that she would soon understand that this harsh decision was the best effort I could at an act of love.

Driving back to Littleton that day, I prayed that Claire would take this well. And while I was praying, I noticed how many churches stood tall in this country alongside of the road. And for the first time I realize that in Littleton, which has a small population of less than 120 people, they have four churches, each one of a different denomination. In Italy for any village with less than five thousand people, it would be hard to find more than one church. This is when I understood that, here in the North-America continent, atheism was a scarce option amongst so many beautiful churches and congregations.

The following day when I called Derek to see how Claire was doing, he told me that she had started to socialize well, and that they even made a special meal for her in the cafeteria. Because she refused to eat, and because most of their meals had meat, they thought she was a vegetarian. So, they ordered special items just for her. Taken by surprise, she decided to accepted such a wonderful deed of courtesy. And soon she developed the perfect American speaking that she still has now.

This is a true story, consisting of true events and true people. Even the names have not been changed. I wanted to make the reader more comfortable, and free to appreciate, and check the work of God amongst people. Willingly, the story avoids making judgments about anyone according to the words of Saint Francis de Sales, "When a slap starts, it is the will of man. When it is received, it is the will of God." This indicates clearly of how, through the human deeds, God's Providence is in charge and leads all events. For it is exactly what it happened to our family.

Jacques Maritain used to say that a story is not something that we are supposed to explain but it is the gathering of facts that we must contemplate and let them teach us. Besides, inside of the whole story there is a kind of direct line of understanding which supports all events. It is the underground efficient work of Providence who leads everything for the good. It is our business to follow the signs and understand the meaning.

A new environment involved a kind of conversion. It goes beyond our own agreement: a different context produces diverse behaviors. While we were barely able to gather as a family in Rome, here, in this side of the ocean, we became truly a family.

Meanwhile, our life had already started on this side of the Atlantic waters. It was then that I understood the discernment we were able to make in order to pursue our endeavor.

Tableau #7

Adrian Monmayou

DRIVING IN PITTSBURGH, IN 1995, YOU OFTEN GET LOST. Usually, I had a map to help me, as today people are finding their way with what they call the "G.P.S." – a necessary device for someone trying to exit my home office, if one should dare to enter, and then want to find a way out, in the midst of the utterly confusing clutter of papers, documents, letters, books, and belongings. The first weeks we came there, a city map was impossible to find. When I finally got one, the cover showed an impressive ad: "We've performed an impossible task: we've made the design of the labyrinth. We made the eighth wonder of the world! Here is the Pittsburgh map!"

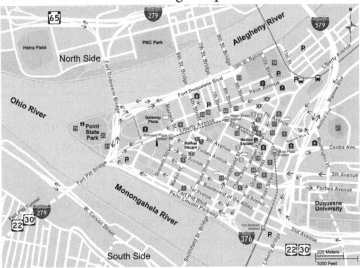

It was surely difficult, at that time, to make a map of Pittsburgh. It was even harder reading it. Pittsburgh competes with San Francisco for the number of hills. It also competes with Venice and St. Petersburg for the number of Bridges. Because of so many bridges, the map would show roads intertwining or merging, when *de facto*, they are going above or underneath one another. The map remains diffi-

63

cult to interpret. Some streets which cross on the map do not actually meet. Often, the long way on the paper reveals to be the short way in town… Thus, just to be able to read and understand the map, you would already have to become familiar with the city, achieving the purpose of the map itself.

The very same thing is true about Adrian Monmayou. Speaking of Monmayou with the purpose of creating a map of his character and persona, and making him familiar to those who don't already know him is only a first step. There is an element to the man that intertwines him, and while you may think of him one way, he reveals in fact to be of another. It is not just because he's a Gascon, which already corresponds to such a rich character, but also for his connection with abodes above and beyond. Such connection with the afterlife makes the difference and explains the gap between the "map" we read and the facts. It is necessary to make a closer encounter with Adrian, in order to make the map effective, otherwise big misunderstandings would happen such as had happened already to me with the map of Pittsburgh: yes, a direct contact becomes necessary. It is desirable and possible. Adrian was surely not aware of the fact that he was a mystic. He was easily talking about fields, harvest and vineyard and we soon realized that he was just explaining the events of the end times. For him, however, it was just talking about yesterday, today, and tomorrow. Everything was just present to his mind.

Adrian's exuberant character involves many outcomes. Besides, Monmayou is alive in the people who met him, as he is still alive in my own life. Looking at the great decisions I make in my life, sometime even for simple behaviors, brings me back to that enigmatic personage. Adrian's spiritual enlightenment marked my soul as cattle are marked by firebrand. Monmayou is also involved with our family's move to America. There is obviously the dramatic fact that the one who moves forward carries behind his old stories, but even more he moves to be consistent with a call, which always is a call for betterment. Such betterment includes important issues. Adrian brought us into them. The connection emerges from specific circumstances.

After the death of my father, when I spoke of Monmayou with friends or family members who knew him closely, an unexpected difficulty arose. Every single one held a different memory of him. It was impressive to see how every single one held a different understanding of who the man was. It is somehow understandable that every rich personality leaves diverse tracks of his or her proper life. Two painters provide diverse perspectives on a single countryside. And both can be true even when they seem contradictory. To know the facts requires getting the diverse perspectives beyond the kaleidoscopic scenery. Concerning Monmayou the facts are more obscure. Even my own siblings have a diverse judgment, which involved Adrian, his wife Maria, the events of the woods of Espis, near Moissac, and the numerous witnesses of these events.

Fortunately, there is a common friend, whom I also was introduced by my father... When I met Fr. Emmanuel de Floris, he was a Benedictine monk in the monastery of En Calcat, near Dourgne, in Occitany, near the Black Mountain. I suspect that my father, Raymond, was the one who put Monmayou in contact with Emmanuel, during the year 1947. That friendship between Adrian and Emmanuel became a fertile source of wisdom for my parents, for all my siblings, for me, and later for my family in Rome. It was actually Adrian and Emmanuel who spiritually prepared my parents, my siblings and me to meet the Focolare Movement, which reshaped my whole life.

When Adrian Monmayou died, on Sept. 21, 19XX, nobody but close friends knew it.

Nobody else was aware of the event, because all Adrian's friends were still under the restrictions of the Catholic Church's local authorities, who ordered the whole community to be silent about him, about the events at Moissac, about the shrine at Espis, about the many conversions, pilgrimages, devotions, healing, foreigners and visitors which surrounded the events at Espis. That is why his departure happened without any notice.

Later, after my Dad, Raymond, had died, there was found in his personal notes important data about Adrian, which raised our curiosity. I was living in Rome at that time, but when I was told about these notes, the whole story came back to my mind. My mind, however, was somehow confused, and I needed to check many details. Unfortunately, it was too late to get more information from Raymond, my father. We referred then to my mom, Marthe, who was extremely shy on the matter. Her discretion was due to her desire to be consistent with the interdiction of the bishops of Montauban, first of all Cardinal Clément-Emile Roques, who had been called for consultation, Msgr. Pierre-Marie Théas, who was the bishop of Montauban from 1940-1947 at the time of the events (before moving to Lourdes), and his successors: Louis-Marie-Joseph de Courrège d'Ustou (1947-1970), Roger Joseph Tort (1970-1975), and Jacques Marie Sébastien de Saint-Blanquat (1975-1995), who required and confirmed the order requiring dad to be silence on the subject.

Marthe, my mother, just told us that Raymond, my father, was ordered not to speak about the whole matter, unless he would have been explicitly questioned on the issue. At first, she spoke as if only Raymond would have been able to provide answers. Soon we discovered that Marthe, our Mom, knew everything. But she died too soon to allow us to gather more pieces of information. Then, in addition to the good acquaintance of Mom and Dad, there was also an excellent friend of Adrian, who would have been able to provide the news we were looking for. I refer precisely to the Benedictine monk Fr. Emmanuel de Floris.

I knew Fr. Emmanuel long ago, when I was a child and he was a Benedictine monk of En Calcat Monastery. As far as I can remember, our family would travel to the Benedictine Monastery of En Calcat,

near Dourgne and Castres every few months or so. This not only since I was little, but it was a sort of family behavior even before, I believe, due to the friendship with my Father and the great esteem of my mother for a man of God.  My parents passed on that cheerful respect to every one of us, siblings and siblings-in-law. En Calcat, Dourgne, was distant a little more than an hour's drive from Montauban. My father would drive our little car, packed with most, if not all, of our family. The monastery offered our family a destination to spend time together, sharing, playing, rejoicing, and praying... It was there, that we would meet Father Emmanuel, dressed in black and grey woolen Benedictine robes.

I realized later that Fr. Emmanuel de Floris has been a friend of my parents since the days they were in touch with Adrian Monmayou, which means since I met Adrian as a little boy. Soon, Fr. Emmanuel became my spiritual director, mostly while I was struggling as a teenager with questions of faith, then especially years later during the days of my activity as a civil servant in the Vatican, and while I started building a family with Chiara, my wife. Emmanuel was a man of extreme gentleness. He knew how to joke with every person, and had a different way to put everyone in touch with God. When he spoke, even when I was a little boy, my ears were attuned to Father Emmanuel's words.

These two diverse poles of attraction, Monmayou and Emmanuel look contradictory. They are not. They show the concern of my parents to get spiritual directions and prayerful intimacy with the Lord. Most of the insights they got from Adrian were later explained to them by the Benedict monk of En Calcat.

By the time I was fifteen years old, I would spend entire days with Father Emmanuel in the monastery because I felt very conflicted over a few questions concerning the world, human life, Providence, and the Church. I would ask him question after question, unsure of my belief in God, and repeatedly Emmanuel would tell me that the answers to my questions about God would not be found in the contents of theology, nor even in studies, but in Jesus' life. Yet, despite this answer, I insisted that he give me a theological response that actually never came.

Soon thereafter I lost contact with Emmanuel and turned to atheism and existentialism as my philosophical crutches. Once I reverted back to the Catholic faith, I sought out Father Emmanuel for advice. By that time, he was no longer living in the Abbey of En Calcat, but had retreated to the Provence high mountains as a hermit. It was near the Alps mountains. For a long time, we had exchanged words and he answered my questions through letters, always coming back. But one day, when I went to visit him amidst the mountains, we had a chance to talk further of Monmayou.

After my Mother died, referring to Fr. Emmanuel became even more dramatically relevant. At that time Fr. Emmanuel had become a hermit in the Alpine mountains, between Grenoble and Digne, at Montmorin, near Rozans, which belongs to the diocese of Gap. It was not easy to reach his hermitage; and the first time I decided to pay him a visit with my family, driving from Rome, I got totally lost in the woods of Montmorin. Especially after the pass of La Tournelle, getting out of the thick fog, I knew that we really were in a godforsaken spot. It was then that I saw an old road sign "Montmorin", which suddenly indicated that we had found the place. To tell the truth, it was just when I had become sure that I was lost, that I found his hermitage.

Fr. Emmanuel was an authoritative, man from the noble de Floris family, having intimate connection with many civil European authorities. During our encounters, our conversation showed that he knew firsthand the intricacy of politic leaders of many countries, from Atlantic Ocean up to Ural Plateaus. Being a hermit, had made even easier, his eventual contacts, with current Presidents and Army Generals of the whole continent, and over, who used to come and visiting him, with a shopper, without the embarrassing eyes of journalists or authorities. He had good contacts with the local police, which[1] was closing all roads around for the time these significant visitors needed to consult him…

It was under his direction that all my kids made their first communion there, in the hermitage of Montmorin. This was the connection. And this was also the way to develop my relationship with Adrian Monmayou. Now, as a first presentation on Adrian, I will refer to the story that I was told by Fr. Emmanuel. It is through this contemplative and judicious hermit, that I got insights, which made me able to offer the deeper understanding on the mysterious figure of Adrian.

According to the words of Fr. Emmanuel, Monmayou was a bit of a character in the township of Lunel. He became famous amongst the people for his aggression against the church, God, and for the blasphemies he used to shout at his oxen when plowing the land, to make them push faster. He became a sort of leader, among the local population, while contending against the township's parish. The people of Lunel used to call him Mister Mayor as a title.

But as I already said, among the persons I spoke to about Monmayou, everyone remembers him differently. No one in the neighborhood remembers calling him *"Monsieur le Maire"* (Mister Mayor), not even the people of Lunel. There is not even a trace of such a thing in the administrative building of Lafrançaise, which holds the municipality archives. Yet,, Father Emmanuel, from whom this story comes, was very clear that it was so. He insisted again and again that this was part of Monmayou's character, individually and socially. These were the bridges that formed his map, intertwined and crossing. It was a wondrous man in this world, indeed, to deserve such a title.

For one thing, parish priests and church goers often avoided passing through Monmayou's land. If ever they saw him passing by in his own carriage and mules, they would veer away into another road just to avoid his gaze and insults.

One of Monmayou's favorite nicknames for the priests was "Thieves" or "Burglars" for the offerings they took from the people during Mass. He often called them hypocrites or liars when he saw them in the streets. He also referred to most of the local Christians with nicknames familiar to his own livestock. But these were some of the kinder insults he would shout. Some of his more colorful vulgarities were better known amongst the people, but it won't be proper to repeat them here. Monmayou, who often came up with witty blasphemies against his mules when visiting his fields, loved to repeat them against the members of the Church.

Without intention, Monmayou had become a leader amongst local groups, who opposed the Catholic community. Often, they called him "Freemason", in reference to the brotherhood who organized against Christianity. This, however, may have been a bit of a stretch as title, according to Father Emmanuel. All being considered, Adrian Monmayou was an honest man, a hard worker, who thought the Church was just an excuse for false men to take advantage of villagers' money.

In his own way, Adrian was also a righteous man. As a child his own family had suffered injustices by the hand of the church. Since then, he had grown up, with the thought in mind, that anyone who believed in God was a person of hypocrisy. He viewed the Catholic Church as a community which acted with the excuse of the Lord as a way of achieving self-serving means.

It was a Thursday in June, when the local parish was about to celebrate the feast of Corpus Christi. This is a celebration that happens in the Catholic Church eleven days after Pentecost. On that occasion, the people praise both the body and blood of Christ. The celebration is also known as "*Corpus Domini*", the Body of the Lord. There was a type of parade, which moved through the streets, with an altar boy

leading in front, with a large cross in his hands, followed by two more altar boys, each one carrying a tall candle, leading the way for villagers, a few parish priests, and finally the town's elder priest holding a chalice, with the Eucharist or a monstrance, cupped in his hands. During the parade the people would sing litanies of the saints and the sacred heart, some hymns, and the *Ave Maria* of the rosary.

This parade usually took place in the evening when the people had finished with their work in the fields, but there was still light in the sky. This may have been around five in the evening. The parish priest would wait in front of the church, ready with the altar boys and his assistants, so that the people would group, and once so they would all leave together in their cortège, moving towards the countryside to circle around the village. The lead crucifix was a heavy cross cast in silver; and oftentimes during these parades, the altar boy, who was usually eleven or twelve years old, could not make it far before passing it on.

Their walk advanced for about three hundred meters, as the boy began to sway and dip from the weight in the boy's arms. The boy huffed and struggled to keep it steady. He would not be able to hold it up much longer. The villagers asked themselves who would be next to carry the cross, as it was often passed on to one of them. The other two altar boys were younger and smaller than the lead boy, and they had their own candles to carry.

Finally, the boy was going to fall.

Suddenly from a nearby bush a voice came that shouted,

"No! No! Definitely not!"

In addition to the doddering, the boy holding the crucifix panicked at the sound of the voice, and stopped. And so did the people behind him. The whole procession stopped, witnessing a bizarre situation.

"I don't want to! I will not do it!" shouted the voice again.

Out from the bushes jumped a huge, bizarre man who ran towards the altar boy and snatched the crucifix from the lead boy's arms and stood at the front of the parade, shoulders fixed and broad. This was Adrian Monmayou.

The young altar boy, turned toward the parish priest, eyes questioning, asking what to do. The priest simply gestured the boy to continue, to stand next to Monmayou while the man took lead in their procession. Amongst the villagers, who watched Monmayou take the lead, whispers spread back and back of what just happened. Many of them believed that the procession would end there because some day earlier rumors had spread that Monmayou, had been arguing against the procession passing through his land. There was a moment of dismay amongst the congregation. Everyone was ready for the worst. A few of the youths readied themselves to fight, just to allow the parade to go on. Fists might have to be an option.

At the surprise of the people, Monmayou knelt before the Eucharist, which was held in the parish priest's hands and asked for permission to lead the procession. The minister didn't know what to think. Then, seeing that many of the villagers, behind him were ready to fight, he gave Monmayou the lead just to keep the peace. So Monmayou directed the parade across his land. It was the first time in years, that the Corpus Christi had passed through those fields. Never had the country side of Lunel echoed with religious chants so powerful. The parishioners sang with vivid lungs, many in shock and adoration. A murmur rose beneath the notes of those hymns. A question wedged itself behind those chanting voices.

"Who was that?"

"It was Monmayou!"

"That's impossible!"

"Are you sure that it was him?"

"Adrian would never do so, I know him. It must have been someone else."

"Had Monmayou converted?"

Tableau # 8
Conversion

IT IS TRUE. ADRIAN MONMAYOU DID CONVERT.

Yes, very few remember Monmayou as the mayor of Lunel. In contrast, there is not even one who does not remember his dramatic conversion. When I started to ask about it, in the area, everyone had a personal story to recall. A kind of encyclopedic book could be made with such a large amount of testimonies. On such a fact, all those who knew directly or indirectly Adrian Monmayou agreed unanimously.

Except, it hadn't been an easy thing at all for Adrian to renounce his animosity towards Christianity and distinguish the difference between the few Christians who had caused his family to suffer and those who are the followers of Christ, the perfect, who died on the Cross to dissolve all of our very own imperfections, break the seal of the closure to the heavens, and open wide the gates of paradise. This was a change that surpassed Adrian's own strength. It never would have happened without a strong pushing, or, better, a dramatic pulling, from above.

In fact, this is exactly what had just happened:

During a burning, hot Saturday, in that month of June, Adrien was coming back to his farm and decided to inspect his wheat crop stored in his corn loft. This had been left over from the previous season, and Adrian wanted to see if this was still in good condition and how much room was left for the new harvest. As he opened the door to the granary, he realized there was no need to flick on the light. The entire place was lit brightly, but he couldn't recognize this small structure as his own granary. The grain had been replaced with some kind of huge picture window.

Through this window, Monmayou saw the hill of Moissac, where the Espis Woods resided. He recognized vaguely the place, only because it was one of the neighboring hills, but this was not a place visible from his own land. For a long moment, his head began spinning, and he wondered to himself, "What is happening?"

He saw Espis Woods as if it stood before him. As if those very trees encircled his land. And amongst those woods came out a luminous figure, which stood in the room beside him. It was a beautiful young woman approximately sixteen years old. She began to speak to him.

"Thursday you will take the cross and guide the procession of my son across your land," she told him.

At the time, Adrian couldn't understand. What cross? What procession? Who was this woman? But as soon as he glanced at her face, he understood and rebelled.

"It's not possible," he said.

"Do not be troubled," responded the young woman.

"You will go on and you'll do so. My son will give you the strength. He has listened to your grumbling prayers. For every insult you shouted at the face of a Christian was like a calling for help, for every suffering you've endured. He has seen the honesty in your heart, and places great plans upon your shoulders."

Just as she had appeared from the darkened woods, the young woman disappeared. And even the window vanished. Only then did Adrien realize he had been on his knees, amongst the bunches of wheat. He remained there for a long while, meditating. This encounter had left him with a great sense of peace. On his heart, the acrid layers of burdened soil had softened. Except, he had no idea of how he would carry out this order. He never spoke with the local minister in his life except to insult him, and he understood that if he were to jump amongst the crowd, they would not welcome him.

He had spent too much time already and expended too much energy in insulting the Church. It was Saturday evening, still deep into the darkened night, and there laid before him only five days before he would find a solution. He remained still a while longer to think this through.

From the outside he heard his wife Maria's voice calling him.

"Adrian! Adrian! Where are you?"

Finally, she opened the door to the corn loft, screaming,

"Adrian where have you been? I've been looking for you for two hours!"

When she saw him on his knees, she thought he had suffered a heart attack.

"Monmayou, what has happened to you? Are you feeling sick?"

Slowly, Adrian came to his feet, as if taking a flight from a dream.

"I feel well," he said simply.

They were simple words, but they radiated such a sense of peace, and calm, that Maria became shocked by the sound of those words. She didn't dare ask, but she understood the basic need, behind those words. Adrian was well. This is as much as she understood. And she understood, as well, that something had happened, which she

75

did not know. But she was confident, that he would tell her about it, since they had never kept any secrets between one another.

Simply she said, "Come. Soup is ready, and it's getting cold. I was looking for you for supper... I couldn't find you..."

Without a word, he followed her. They moved towards the kitchen and, in silence, they sat before their table. Maria poured the soup into their bowls, watching her husband, studying his calm demeanor, trying to read his unruffled brow. Truly something must have happened, because he seemed more erect. Sturdier. His presence at the table seemed to empty everything else surrounding them. Almost as if he himself was lighting the room.

Then, just before spooning their soups, something happened that left Maria without words, neither on her lips, nor on her mind.

Adrian moved his hand towards his spoon; but before doing so, he made the sign of the cross, and then began eating.

Maria remained stunned and watched him without moving. Her jaw dropped slightly. It was Adrian who brought her back to reality.

"Look, if you don't begin eating, the soup will get cold. You are the one who likes it hot," he said.

Even the dog, which enjoyed keeping them company under the table while they ate, remained silent. Yes, even this dog understood that a message had passed between the couple in their midlife, as if a deep, festering wound had begun to heal. Maria finally spooned her soup, keeping her eyes fixed on her husband. He was erect, and looked youthful, vibrant, alive more than ever. This man before her, although entering his forties, reminded Maria of the young man she had fallen in love with before he had entered the service. It was a young, sturdy man who vibrated with life and assurance. She recognized him as if he were an apparition from the past.

These are the facts we know about his conversion. They are the shell of what really occurred. Actually, yes, something really happened between the young Lady and Adrian. And it will be revealed successively piece by piece, but probably never totally. All the people around, however, witnessed the evident outcomes of the event. Because of its effects on Adrian's behavior, the conversion was confirmed. All things considered, his conversion may be compared to many others. Every conversion is a dramatic and unexpected miracle.

When somebody is touched by the divine, his or her life is changed. As soon as someone is enlightened from above, a transfiguration is in effect. Everyone converts after meeting someone from above. This is true for each one of us, even for conversions which are not so apparent. To tell the truth, every conversion is sensational, but it is not always immediately visible from outside. Besides, we all convert, because we met in someone the presence and the call of the absolute. Notwithstanding, some spectacular conversions still exist. Charles de Foucauld entered the confessional of a Parisian church, and was staggered. Ernest Psichary, in the Sahara desert, saw a few Muslims in prayer, and was touched by the divine. Louis Massignon had a dream in Bagdad which changed his life. Paul Claudel entered a church at Christmas and turned out to be a believer. André Frossard witnessed the same: he entered a church and returned Catholic. When someone, during his conference in Paris, confronted him that if he had entered a Mosque, he would have become a Muslim believer, he replied "In a Mosque, in a Temple, in a Synagogue, or a Church if we enter and convert it is because we meet somebody from above. The building has nothing to do with it. In fact, so many times I entered an airport, and when I departed, I never was a plane!" He also added, "I entered so many times a train station and, when leaving, I was nether a wagon, nor a locomotive."

Actually, every conversion is provoked by an unexpectedly strong meeting with the transcendent. People may pronounce prayers all day long, and never meet the Lord, because they actually never are in touch with him. We only meet the Lord when we turn our mind and our heart towards him, thirsty and hungry for God in his goodness, whenever it is, wherever we are, and whatever we do... It is never what we do, or what we say, that makes the meeting. When people really pray, other people, too, get the benefits of it. There was some visitor, in Lourdes, who converted from seeing the way Bernadette was standing before the Grotto. Her behavior astonished him and he converted. The same can be said about the disciples of every saint. It was impossible for them to be near their company and not be transformed. Today, our conversion may be provoked by reading the biography of Bernard de Clairvaux, Francis of Assisi, Vincent de Paul, or meeting one of their followers, or just to come across some holy person. When we are in the presence of the Lord, he changes our life forever. It may happen even right now, while reading these notes, or in so many different ways.

Personally, the German philosopher Friedrich Nietzsche had a strong impact on my own conversion: he expressed so well my need for eternity. Also, Nietzsche denounced in the philosophy of the hammer, the many places where God is not: God cannot be found in any church, when the so-called believers disregard his presence; he is not in the Ministers, unless they are acting as another Jesus. Some of his terrible accusations fired me up: "You should look more saved in order that I may believe in your Savior." "You should bring better good news, if you want me to believe in the Good News of the Gospel."

Nietzsche understood that God is near to us but requires our capacity to look at him, to convert. Meeting the Lord requires the capacity to take a way, which is not a simple road; it is a step of transcendence. When I read Nietzsche works, during a summer in Rocca di Papa, near Rome in Italy, I was fascinated: in one month, I read the whole 5000 pages of his works, and commentators... all those, which I could find in the library. His cry of "God is not here, God is not there, we are the ones who made God absent in our lives..." sounded to me like the cry of somebody who enters a room looking for his wallet: "Oh! My wallet is not here. Oh! It is not there either. Oh! I lost my wallet, maybe it was stolen!" Nietzsche would be not denouncing so strongly the absence of God, in our society, if he had not been so greatly looking for him! His cry is proportionate to his disappointment! He was dramatically deceived by those who claim that they know God. Here is why Nietzsche says that we Christian have been betraying our faith, hope and charity. Here is how God was killed in our present society.

Such a cry from Nietzsche woke up my sense of... I don't know what, but something inside of me was moved. I was nineteen when, as a Sorbonne student, Friedrich W. Nietzsche provoked me and induced me to decide and make my life an answer to his cry. Since then, I wanted to make every behavior of mine, to be an evidence of the presence of God among us. It was not just my business. It only was the concern to let God speak in my life. The thirst for God was so urgent in Friedrich Nietzsche that he provoked me and made me meet God! I even remember the moment when such an event happened. I can say where, how, who and what provoked such a dramatic change in my life. Yes, doing so I finally met Adrian in his new life. This would be another long story and for now it would add nothing to the great improvement that Monmayou, after the event of the barn, produced in many souls around him, during his life.

Every conversion is typical and similar to the one of Monmayou. What we may discover, in Monmayou's conversion, is the way the Lord speaks to us, either directly or through one who would act on his behalf, Angels, Saints, or more usually a brother, a neighbor, a visitor. Christian communities are right to stress the unique presence of the Lord, which shows above all possible intermediaries — as it is said in Matthew 18:20.

While I was a civil servant in the Vatican, my mother visited me once and had a chance to meet the pope, John-Paul II, who took her hand for a while inside of his hands. And she received his blessing. After my mother had greeted through her hand the pope, she blessed her hand because of him. She never, however, confused her hand with the pope. It is the same with those who introduce us to the Lord. We never confuse the messenger with the one who sent them. We do not confuse the door with the room it gives access to. Nonetheless we praise the door for doing so. Yes, we are pleased, when a saint, an angel, or a visitor is introducing us to the Lord. We must not focus all our attention on the gift and forget the giver. Here was the lesson of Nietzsche, and this is the teaching of Adrian, too. No angel, no saint, not even Mary may cast a shadow on our meeting with the Lord. It is important to stress that, before moving further.

The process works the same along every step of conversion… What is supernatural makes sense to the natural and transfigures it. How many times have we prayed in the cellar where Monmayou spoke with the heavenly visitor? No, it was not the cellar that we worshipped, but praying there, helped Monmayou to relate to us what really happened, something that he was not even fully aware of, due to the fact that everything happened in a way that even Adrian himself does not understand fully. What happened during the two hours Our Lady was visible for Adrian? The many times we visited the place to commemorate the event, did not disclosed fully the secret of such an event.

There is some evidence, however, which provides interesting pieces of information. Everyone, who met Adrian afterwards was gifted with a boost of hope, friendliness, and trust… in many different ways, according to the circumstances and who knows what else.

I would like to manifest here how, when God, or whoever on His behalf, meets us, our life is dramatically changed and from then on, everything and everybody around is involved by our transfiguration. Everyone who is reached by God irradiates his own enlightenment.

Let's me talk about some examples. I'll take an easy one, concerning my younger brother, Marie-Jean.

When Marie-Jean was seven years old, Monmayou presented him with a little turtle dove. (My brother believed it was a male dove. It was actually a hen.) That gift was the start of a brilliant adventure and even of a specific human career.

First of all, the she-dove escaped the dovecote. Fortunately, she did not fly very far away. She settled down upon the almond tree in our back yard. It was there that Marie-Jean asked me to catch her, for he was afraid he might hurt his pet. Even worse, he was afraid to lose her animal friendliness, if he was the one who captured and caged her.

That dove accompanied him everywhere, every time he was in the garden or in the yard of our house in Montauban. Mom, in fact, had forbidden him to have the dove with him inside the house. This probably was the reason the dove left the cote — she was looking for him.

Since he was seven, Marie-Jean was another Saint Francis of Assisi: at all times the dove sat on his shoulder and used to eat from his hands. Besides, this bird's friendship was contagious… for after influencing the dovecote it affected the hen house. Master cock and mother hen started behaving like the dove, never leaving him alone when he was walking in the yard.

Most of our neighbors and friends were wondering where this Marie-Jean gift of talking to animals was coming from. The truth was that Adrian cherished Marie-Jean and Adrian's natural intimacy with heaven had somehow influenced Marie-Jean and made him familiar with part of creation.

This kind of gift comes from above and when you act in accord with some of these gifts, they look so natural! This friendship has been a characteristic of Marie-Jean throughout his life. It also has been provided with a special flexibility and gentleness with everybody. Similar behavior is far above the average person.

Other examples of the consistency of his improvement could be found in Adrian's behaviors after the day of his conversion. No blasphemy, no anger, even not an insult to anyone could be heard from him. That was very unusual indeed! For his neighbors, that kind of behavior was astounding. It was a dramatic transformation. Then, the whole metamorphosis exploded during the *Corpus Domini* parade, and became the event of the month.

O VIRGIN, EVER FAITHFUL PRAY FOR US.
*Make to flow from thy soul those benefits
which we expect of thy goodness.*

Tableau # 9
A Long Week

THE MEETING IN THE GRANGE, ON SATURDAY AFTERNOON, LEFT ADRIAN WITH A GREAT SENSE OF PEACE. He showed a quieter behavior all day long, and more serenity of mind than the usual. Nonetheless deep in his soul a struggle was raging, which curiously had no apparent externalization. It was, indeed, well present inside: "How would I comply with the young lady's task?" - "What can I do about the *Corpus Domini* procession?" "How shall I handle the duty she asked me to perform?"

Notwithstanding, it's worth noting the fact that he never asked himself why such a task was given to him. Such a consideration was not his business, not even worthy of his attention. He had concern enough, with what he was asked to perform. He only was focuses on the manner to manage, in order to deal with what he had been asked for. And it was supposed to be done only few days ahead.

⁣— SUNDAY ⁣—

Just as any other day in the country, Adrian woke early at five in the morning. He cleaned up the kitchen quickly, rinsing dishes and wiping off the table, then moved to the cowshed to tend to his livestock. He began milking the cows and brought them to the fields, before finally returning to his kitchen for breakfast. By then it was around seven and had been calm and rising for an hour now. Adrian grabbed a loaf of bread and sliced a few pieces and ate a breakfast of bread and ham, joined with a glass of red wine and a mug of warmed coffee. Adrian was not a man of many words. Nonetheless, today he notably was a silent man. He couldn't prevent to have his mind focused and reflected over the prior day's sight and of all that had been asked of him.

Maria, who couldn't bring herself to ask any questions, took steps around the quiet man, pacing in her own silence. Just to engage him in conversation, she made some top-hand try and asked him, "This week the chickens have laid more eggs than usual. If you like I'll make you some for breakfast."

He nodded, saying nothing, and she began working the kitchen stove. She grabbed a few pieces of wood and stacked them under the old-fashioned stove, which was a slab of cast iron heated by flame. She opened and moved through the different little metal compartments and swivel doors that helped control the stove temperature. She made more noise than her usual quiet demeanor just to give the room some sound. As she worked, she tried to make more conversation.

"Where will you go working today?" she asked, hiding her eagerness to ask any more.

"I will work the vineyard."

"Would you mind if I joined you today? I'll help with cleaning the weeds."

"Yes. Gladly."

Except both of them knew that the vineyard was just an excuse for speaking more of what lay on his heart. Even though it was Sunday, every day was a working day on Monmayou's land. The day of the Lord never existed on his farm. Except today, around eleven, as the church bells rang to call back the parishioners for mass, Adrian rose from amongst the wines and hanging grapes and stood in silence. Maria came to his side, and remained standing in silence.

In some way, while working from one wine plant to the next, Monmayou told his wife of what he had seen inside the grain loft. He spoke with broken phrases, trying to recount the brightness and the face of the young woman. Trying to describe what could not have happened but did. Maria listened without comment. She listened without judgment, her face placid and welcoming to all of his words.

MONDAY

When Adrian woke this morning, his mind was still unraveling the serenity with which the young woman in the grain loft had left him.. Except, there was uncertainty that grew on his mind as well. Thursday seemed to be coming closer already, and he did not know, if he would be able to jump into the Procession of Corpus Christi, as asked. Meanwhile, he decided to take a walk through the countryside towards the parish and reflect.

Before leaving, he asked his brother-in-law, Paul, to care for the animals. Paul looked at him with surprise, because he knew how much Adrian enjoyed taking care of his chores personally. He understood that there must have been a very important reason for Adrian to change his daily routine. In Gascony, people are curious to know each other's intimacies, but are also respectful of them, so Paul decided not to ask directly. Nonetheless, such a request was so unusual that Paul knew he could not resist asking.

"Is there a market fair today? Are you going into town to sell?"

Adrian replied, "No, the fair is tomorrow. Today I have some important business to take care of."

Paul understood that he would not receive any more information from Adrian, but perhaps, after caring for his animals, he might learn more while sharing breakfast with Maria, his own sister. She might be more willing to explain things.

Adrian left, walking, which surprised Paul even further, because the quiet man had not left his house on his horse and carriage. Adrian walked alongside the fields, cutting a path through the fields instead of on the roads. He had never crossed the camps before that day, for he had never dared to tread upon his own or somebody else's sprouting crops. The air whistled to him as Adrian kept his head low, thinking and not thinking at the same time. What was there to think of? What choices could he really make? If this was God's will, sending the young woman to him as a messenger, what use could his own distress serve him now?

His feet finally brought him before the town's parish church. This was an old, gothic structure with the stones faded by the sun and brittle from the years of wind. No. Not an old church, but an aged one.

Perhaps still young in the face of time. It must have been beautiful once, this church, when first erected in the twelfth century. The countryside daylight brightened by the minute, and the church's stained-glass windows matched the day's rising warmth.

Adrian stood there, and then took a knee to grasp a handful of dirt, testing the soil. It was hardened here, stiff and brittle. No. Those were not the right words to describe this land. This soil was not meant for cultivating grain or wheat. This soil right here was meant for cultivating and supporting a church. He wiped the grittiness off from his hands, feeling the resilience of this land upon his palms.

This quiet man with screaming and insults inside his heart released himself in the wind. He expected those insults to leave his lips, thrown against the church as stones. He expected himself to call this structure a beast poised to devour the people money. He expected himself to call it a gothic monster, built and supported by minions of the cloth. But as he opened his lips to speak, all he could release was a silent moan, a frail attempt form a prayer.

"Lord..." he thought, but did not know where to go from there. He tried to think of the last time his mind settled on a prayer. He must have been a boy, at least thirty-some-years younger than his current self. Yet, he knew that prayer was what he needed now. It tumbled about inside himself, this prayer, not knowing what shape to give it, what words to use, in which direction to send it. Send it towards the heavens? Send it towards the church? Send it down at his feet, onto this very land before him?

"If God is who He claims to be, He will hear it no matter which direction you send it," Adrian thought to himself. He half-expected this thought would serve as a type of mocking towards God, displaying a challenge or a demand for Him. On the contrary, it filled him with reassurance. This thought was no mocking. It was a reassurance that Adrian could not go wrong in his prayers.

The words came, first in thought and then in broken whispers. His uttering moved then louder into parching words. Adrian spoke. God heard. God listened.

No great response followed. No raging winds or clapping thunderstorm. No trees fell down. No churches crumbled. No heaven shook. No patch of land quaked. Adrian's prayer had been meant for calm. With this calm the Lord answered him.

"But how, Lord, am I to complete this task? How am I to carry your cross?"

Adrian saw the bushes, which were not aflame, but he knew that God was pointing to them.

Suddenly a small, yellow nightingale chirped from a nearby branch, rousing Adrian from his thoughts. He understood then, it was time to return home before the villagers might notice his presence before the church. On his walk back home, his thoughts were no more peaceful than before. He still wondered now if he would have the courage to go through with his calling.

Meanwhile, Maria was sharing breakfast with her brother Paul.

"Adrian said not to wait for him for breakfast," she told him.

Paul could not resist his own curiosity, so he asked immediately: "Does it happen often for Adrian to take early walks in the morning before breakfast?"

"No. Never. This is the first time."

Paul understood that Maria would not tell him more. Even though she was his own sister, there would always be sentimental secrets kept in a marriage. Paul understood well the Gascon idiom, "Between husband and wife, never place a strife."

TUESDAY

During the day's market fair, Adrian felt uneasy inside himself. Something had changed within him. For the first time at the market, Adrian saw the local merchants as simply community vendors. He no longer saw the faces of the other merchants as people whom he was competing with. They weren't rivals trying to outsell him, as he had always seen them before. Adrian's reputation at the market, however, was already well known. All the villagers knew how hard he came down on haggling prices. They knew well his expressions and his calculating eyes. Every sale with Adrian had always taken place after long back-and-forth discussion and lots of persistence on each side. But one thing had always been sure, that once a price was agreed upon, Adrian shook hands firmly and stood just as firmly on his promise.

Amongst his stock, Adrian sold cows and heifer, and usually when an interested merchant would come to him for purchasing, Adrian would always begin with his prices set impossibly high. Only after an aggressive bargaining would he lower the prices, and only if the buyer used his words carefully and showed promise in his offer. Except this Tuesday, Adrian showed no aggressiveness. He showed no hardened distrust for onlookers of his stock.

A merchant, knowing Adrian and his style of sales well, came to him this morning to buy a heifer and asked him how much he wanted. The merchant's nickname was "Maquignon"— as in "the mask-maker"— because of his craft in masking a malnourished and sick livestock and selling it as if purebred and healthy. When Maquignon asked Adrian for the price of this one heifer, Adrian responded a simple quote, much lower than expected. This surprised Maquignon, and roused him with distrust.

"What illness do your beasts have today," asked Maquignon, "that you would sell them for so low a price, without a fight?"

"No, friend. You're a merchant and companion of long standing, and I simply want to make a price right for both you and me."

Maquignon did not believe his words, so he inspected the heifer with much more detail and attention than the usual. He found it in perfect heath and good strength. Still, he expected either a joke or a cunning trick, so he went around the market asking for more information on Adrian's new demeanor. One of the farmers passed on the inquiry to a man tending land nearby Adrian's own, asking how Adrian and his livestock was doing of lately.

"I'm not so sure. I saw him little this past week, working more in the vineyard than in the fields," answered Adrian's neighbor.

"Yesterday I saw him on his oxcart," said the neighbor's wife. "But there was something strange. One thing surprised me. He spoke to his oxen without blasphemy. It seemed strange to me."

Maquignon, listening into the conversation, knew well Adrian's cussing and blasphemy while tilling the land. He too remained surprised by this little detail, but he was not able to find any more information about the livestock itself. So, he returned to Adrian.

"How much did you say you wanted for your stock," he asked.

Adrian told him the price again, which was a high beginning price but nowhere near the impossible amount he would normally have asked for. Maquignon decided to test the man right then, and responded with an offer even lower than the usual, asking to buy both the cow and heifer this time.

Adrian replied, "At the Montauban market you would be able to resell each one for twice that price. If I accepted your offer, I would not be able to present my face here any longer. Everyone would laugh at my presence. And you know well this is not a right price. So, you make me a decent offer, and I will give them to you. I do not want to cheat you, but I also do not want to encourage you to cheat me."

Maquignon had never heard Adrian speak this way in his life. Where were the insults? Where were the fists shaking in the air, condemning him as a thief, rather than warning him from becoming one? Even more surprising than Adrian's own words, it was his tone of voice that stunned the mask maker. Adrian spoke for the first time as an actual friend.

Maquignon answered, "No, it is you who sells. You know the market well. You may set the price."

Adrian made an offer, lower than his starting price. Maquignon's eyes widened, and remained stupefied as if a tree limb had fallen on his head. The price matched perfectly the amount he would have been able to buy them for, knowing he would be able to recover twice the price in some other market. He did not dare believe his ears, however, and hesitated.

Thus, Adrian responded, "What have you? Did lightning strike you? What is your answer, friend?"

"For me the offer is splendid, but…" he cannot finish the phrase. He doesn't dare tell Adrian that he had never met an offer so good with such little effort.

"There are no buts. If this price pleases you, here is my hand,"

89

Adrian said, offering him his palm that would seal the sale. Money switched hands, and the two men shook. Maquignon left with gusts of happiness lifting from his figure. But even Adrian is just as happy, who knew he had earned the money he deserved and done so quickly. Now he can buy the few things he needs at the market and return home early, where he can take care of the choices pressing his mind.

WEDNESDAY

On this day, on the eve of Corpus Christi, for Adrian feels as if it were Holy Wednesday, the day on which Judas accepted a purse of silver coins to betray Jesus. For Adrian this is perhaps the longest day of his life, filled with worry and indecision. He understands that his response to the invitation of the young girl — whether he decides to jump into the parade or not — will change the course of his life from here on out. Whether the course be good or evil, he would have to decide by tomorrow. Yet, more than taking a decision, Adrian would have to take action.

In a hidden pocket within his soul, a slight suggestion rises. The beauty and love of that young woman invites him to follow suit with action. Perhaps heroic, but simple. The thought of pleasing the young woman revives the serenity inside him. Except this very action still needs to be taken.

"Will I have courage enough?"…

What Adrian was not aware of yet was that such an impossible task he was to accomplish was actually nothing in comparison to the other endeavors with which he was soon to be entrusted.

THURSDAY
Corpus Domini

We read, a few pages earlier, that Adrian had the courage to perform the mandate he was entrusted with by Our Lady, and how he handled his task. We saw how he overcame every personal human resistance and finally decided to show up at the head of the parade and carry the cross to lead the religious march of Corpus Christi through his own land.

Such a behavior amazed the local population and compromised definitively Adrian, making a break with his previous conduct, and showing a new concern and fidelity to a higher authority.

Such an endeavor is connected with other events that had already started in the woods, upon the hill of Espis, near Moissac.

Amazingly, Adrian's story is also present history, as if his mystical experience had made him present at any moment of time with a huge impact of hope, trust, and charity that shines on us too.

Because Adrian showed fidelity in this first assignment, he will soon receive a new one, which will be even more demanding. He does not know it, while he is walking back home, crossing the fields by their borders, with the heart in peace, and the soul dwelling the sweet presence of the Holy Spirit...

Today Adrian is happy: he just complied what the Lady asked of him. This deed of courage has compromised for ever his reputation as the leader of every disobedience to the Church. But such a behavior liberated him. His lungs are breathing as if they never were truly able to get air before.

Arriving at the farm, Adrian decides to pay a visit to the granary right away and thank the young lady for having been able to comply with her commitment.

Adrian is not surprised, when entering the barn, that the young lady is already there, as if she was waiting for him: "My Son is happy today... You paid him the homage that he deserves... The whole township witnessed it!"

Adrian is speechless... he is the one who would like to say thanks, but no word utters from his mouth. The lady however, is still there, and looking at her is a delight. He would like to stay there forever.

The lady continues to talk: "There is still one thing that makes you sad, my son".

Adrian raises his attention... He is wondering if something went wrong during his efforts at the parade. The expression of deep sadness on the face of the lady brings more concern than just for a small misbehavior. He keeps himself listening...

"There were so many graces that were supposed to be disclosed today, and so few were given because people don't dare to ask for what they need. Surprisingly they even ignore that the Lord is ready and anxious to provide what they are supposed to ask for... He is ready to give to the extent they want it, as long as they ask for it..."

Adrian is not sure to understand what he is being told... He never knew that the Lord is so respectful to human people that he does not interfere in their life if they don't ask him to. The voice of the young lady continues to resound in his mind:

"There are so many graces ready to be distributed..."

Adrian understands that an overflowing stream of love is ready to pour upon earth. His heart is filled with gratitude for such magnanimity, and he would like to cry over the hills how great, personal, and immense is God's Love. But who would listen to the skeptic he was up to a few days ago? Who would listen to him, when they don't even trust the Lord:

"Too few are asking."

Yes, in reply to the humble offer of the Lord to support our needs, people are required to be humble to and ask for their needs. We are supposed to humble ourselves before the Lord pleading for help. It is necessary that people ask for the needs they have, in order to receive the help they want, which actually is what the Lord is anxious to give. In Adrian's mind, the situation is reversed – when we pray for help, it is not a prayer of demand, for our demand is actually the answer to the Lord who put us in the situation for us to ask what he prepared to provide. Every demand to the Lord is an answer to the need in which the Lord put us in order to start an intimate relationship with us. A game has started, which is poorly seen on earth. The Lord likes to play and to give. People, however, don't know that the eagerness of God to help us is so much stronger than our mere desire to receive.

Oh! Lord! What humility your love shows to us!

How immense your Love is!

Tableau # 10
O Pittsburgh!

THIS SECTION WAS PREVIOUSLY ENTITLED "O AMERICA!"

Soon, it became evident that such a title would be improper.

I realized, in fact, that it would be a great mistake to speak generically about America, while referring to the United States, only 25 of which I had visited.

Besides, I know some of them just because I drove through, while traveling from Pittsburgh to another destination, like Corpus Christi, Texas, Chicago, Illinois, or Chertsey, Quebec. It would then be an exaggeration to claim that I am familiar with them. *De facto*, my acquaintance with some locals is limited to the brief impressions I got in passing. Second of all, there are many differences from one place to another… and there is probably not a place that could be considered as representative of a whole area. The United States is almost a whole world unto itself, which is inserted between Mexico and Canada.

Yes, it is impossible from the experience of one place only, to properly speak about the whole territory, which is bordered by Canada to the North and Mexico to the South. Notwithstanding, a few places we visited and became familiar with are extremely significant. Among the many locations we visited in the vast area limited by these two borders, most have common characteristics. This is actually something we discovered during our stay on this side of the Atlantic Ocean.

As previously explained, we entered the country in three steps, landing first in Detroit, Michigan, where we passed through customs, then flying to Pittsburgh, and finally driving to Littleton, West Virginia, near Hundred, while waiting for the house we rented in McCandless, Pittsburgh, to become available.

I like to insist: unrepeatable situations may be found here and there. Along the way, typical settings were found sometimes. Local characteristics are due to earth's features, countryside, population, housing, trade, economy. I recall some unique scenery in West Virginia, in Northern Kentucky, or south-east Missouri. Also, traffic reflects the rare specificity of place and time. I heard once: "If you see a car, and within a minute you see another car: that means there's a lot of traffic!" I agree that a similar definition fits nowhere but in Montana.

There are also local characteristics which look unequaled elsewhere and are nonetheless common to almost the whole country – like the weather, which is continentally changing. In Chicago, Detroit, Nashville I was told the same thing: "Here there is a local saying: if you don't like the weather, wait for an hour or so and it will be different!" This is true in Pittsburgh, too. It is not unusual, during winter to get within the same day bright sunlight, smooth wind, gentle rain, and snow... and get a temperature move from 20 to 70 degrees (Fahrenheit) within 24 hours. Probably, what many places have in common, is continuous change, which then invades all areas of human activities.

Visiting New York, I was told that "An occasional week-end visitor is ready to write a book about the city. When he stays for a month or so, visitor's reflections can be included in a simple article. If the visitor stays longer, it could happen that, he or she, has nothing to say any more." It may be true for us, as Europeans, such as we were, when we visited and arrived in Pittsburgh. Nonetheless, entering the States as a family developed more changes in our life than in a single visitor's behavior, and the process to settle down had been longer. It is not even finished yet. After fifteen years of U.S. residence, the country still surprises us. This is surely an additional reason for us to so much enjoy living here. Within ranges, being in the States is an actual kaleidoscopic experience. This country trains you to be prepared for many occurrences, but you barely can predict what they will be.

The welcoming manner that supported our arrival in Pittsburgh surpassed our highest expectations. The gentleness of the people, who witnessed our entrance into the American society of Pittsburgh, relieved the struggle that emerged with our transfer. Moving from Europe to America was, in fact, a risky leap of faith.

Many novelties surrounded our landing on this side of the sea. It was not only the language, the food, and the weather. It would be not easy to share the surprises we got in many issues and circumstances. Actually, it looked at first almost totally peculiar. It took us a few weeks to settle down and find references to deal with. For the first two weeks, our family was hosted in Littleton, West Virginia, waiting August 1st, in order to be able to move into our new home in Pittsburgh. During a fortnight, I drove back and forth between Pittsburgh and Littleton, West Virginia, located near Hundred just a few miles from the southwestern border of Pennsylvania.

During the first two week, the 70 miles I used to drive every day, back and forth, between Littleton and Pittsburgh, offered me breathing times for reflection. It would be impossible to describe the bereavement of these first weeks. At the beginning, we were almost lost in the country, and we had no words to express it properly to our new American friends. And supposing we would have been able to express to a neighbor some of the many questions we had, our English was too poor, anyway, to correctly get their eventual answers. Yes, we were almost alone in a foreign country which, luckily for us, was extremely welcoming.

Our provisional aberration found differences that we could identify along our way toward our establishment. I'll try to provide some glimpses of our first steps, especially in Pittsburgh and thereabouts.

The amazing game of Divine Providence continued to challenge and stupefy us on this side of the sea as it had previously on the other side. One of the immediate needs of our five-kid family was to get a car.

I like to repeat the circumstances which made us purchase a car. In fact I already said earlier, how, within our first week in the States, we purchased in Hundred, West Virginia, a Ford Country Squire, similar to the one used by Schwarzenegger in Terminator movie. I'm not sure if any one of us had occasion to ever see a car of such large dimensions. Our previous van In Rome was a Bedford Rascal, three of which could fit in the Ford station wagon. When they saw it, our children liked it right away. They were amazed by its many features: its three broad sitting places at the front seat, its four places at the rear bench and still four other seats accessible by the back door, which may open as a regular door or as a pick-up hatch.

Additionally, the on-board computer commanded many mechanisms such as the ignition of the headlights at nightfall, automatic high and low beam adjustments, speed setting with cruise control (a very important feature here), and alerts for the best time to stop... It was an old but beautiful vehicle, which gave us the immediate feeling of a comfortable living in such a large nation. The children could finally bring their friends along for the ride.

On August first, the day when we were finally able to enter our home in Pittsburgh, the container (45 foot long), which had left Rome in mid-June (out of an act of faith we had already moved part of our belongings, without yet knowing if we were going to join them on this side of the sea), poured furniture, tables, clothing, tableware and about 5.000 books, half of my personal library. I could accommodate all these books in the main room of the basement, using improvised shelving. The room became my home office.

The house was large enough to allow every child to get a personal bedroom and take care of it. All rooms were beautifully furnished. Each one was provided with table, chair, bed, cupboard and cabinet. Everything that arrived from Rome filled the lounge and several other rooms. Friends of West Virginia gave us whatever was needed to completely furnish the bedrooms of Marie-Thérèse and Marta. Each child was so pleased to have for the first time his or her own bedroom. The new home was delightful to everyone. Yes, by coming to this country we were getting a better place to stay.

Pittsburgh is renowned for its schools and universities. The population is young. The dramatic transformation, made in the 1950s, started a process of continuous updating. It is also one of those rare American cities in which Roman Catholic population reaches almost 50% of inhabitants. Large department stores offer meeting places that the youths love to walk around and are breathing areas. There is a large choice of malls near home. Urban configuration makes one live really in countryside while being in town, since each house is surrounded by trees, flowers and gardens and green space that no fences interrupt. Commercial centers, however, together with schools and offices are there, invisible but very close, very well inserted in the natural context.

Being home in the evening, we were able to savor the really magnificent colored sunsets, along with the beautiful groves of trees. It is a spectacle that changes with the seasons and which transform completely the landscape: in winters the absence of leaves allowing a view the lights of the distant buildings, while during summer, the abundance of trees make everything quiet, serene, and relaxed, as in the country, while still being within the city limits.

Additionally, people have here a weekly routine, quite different from what we were accustomed to in Rome. All the people in this country work intensely on week days, they then get rest on weekends. Again, opposite what we were accustomed to in Rome, during the week-end all stores are open. There are food stores, like Giant Eagle and Wall Mart (or HEB in Texas) that remain open 24 hours a day. So, Saturdays and Sundays, we enjoyed being there together as a family. It offered a very welcome change from Rome, where we so rarely had occasion to spend time together.

Yes, coming here helped us to be a family again.

Somehow, it happened to us contrary what we were told. Instead of losing our family life, we finally found it on this side of the seas. Yes, on this side of the ocean we started to live together with an intimacy we never had before experienced. On the other side of the ocean, we were cautioned by our Europeans neighbors o expect cold business-like relationships, the exact opposite of what we encountered. American customs made the seven of us a true family. And while we seven could barely meet together in Rome, where we were surviving through a sort of continuous nightmare, here we finally got the time to live.

Can you believe that? Yes, it truly happened.

Another happy surprise – and not the least – that we got in this nation was the school bus service. Those yellow vehicles, coming in the morning to pick up the kids and drive them to school, were making our life so much easier than the heavy commitment we had in Rome. And they were bringing the kids back home in the afternoon, too. What a pleasant surprise!

In contrast to conditions of life in Rome, where it was so difficult to bring our kids to school before going to work every day and still arrive at the office on time, the U.S. way of life made us forget such struggles. What a liberating relief!

Such an evident difficulty is probably one of the reasons why Italian families rarely include more than two children. How many times, in fact, our Roman neighbors asked me or my wife "what sect do you belong to?" For it was not reasonable in their eyes to have more than two kids in a family. It was even worse than that: many couples in Rome have no children at all, and this is considered there an obviously normal manner of living a marriage. Having one child is considered a very generous concession, two is a heroic endeavor; beyond this point any more would be seen as a sign of craziness or irresponsibility… or fruit of some strange fanaticism…

Chiara and I had five kids and were very happy. People around could not understand it. Someone asked once if we were part of some Vatican experiment, or if we were getting special remunerations for it. There was no fanaticism, no experiment, no sectarianism, we were simply Christian, faithful to God's will. Nonetheless, it was very difficult there to perform every-day chores.

Being here in the U.S., since August 1995, I started teaching philosophy at La Roche College, just a couple of miles from home. Checking the acquaintance of students, every fortnight I was happily surprised to see how well they proceeded in study advancement. I was delighted to see the learning capacity of students on this side of the seas: metaphysical teaching was not at all difficult to grasp for those youths who never had a course of philosophy before. This was actually one of my rather pleasant amazements. Students showed excellent capacity of speculative learning. All things considered, yes, living here was even more enjoyable than it was before we entered the country.

Notwithstanding, the new vice-president had a different option for the department of humanities. She told me, during the following December, that La Roche was not intending to renew my contract for the coming fall. I had to find something else for the next academic year. This was not advantageous surprise! And I had no alternative solution, for I was not at all sure of being able to find some new job. I was even sure that, in Europe, I would have no possibility to getting one. But, again, the new continent and its unexpected surprises, did not leave Divine Providence unprepared.

The Lord is always calling for a betterment...

Tableau # 11
Student Revolution

TEACHING AT LAROCHE WAS AN AMAZING EXPERIENCE. I was supposed to teach Philosophy in English while I knew almost nothing about the language. I did my best to prepare my lessons with an abridged *Webster's Dictionary* by my side, which I gave the nickname of "Portable." This was a joke, because it was still a volume the size of a cinder block with four thousand pages between its binding. I called it portable only because I always had it by my side, and I drove around with it, in my car everywhere. Except the fact that, this good dictionary was not enough to learn English. To be sure in preparing a good lecture, I used to write out an outline for each class. I decided to prepare them as handouts to give out to the students so they could follow along with my broken English. Then, I needed to submit the notes to somebody who could help correct them in proper American.

This is how I met Larry.

Larry was a History teacher at the college. He moved to Pittsburgh from Montana, and was looking around to get some friends. I invited him to dinner at our place on a Monday; and, at the end of the dinner, I handed him a few notes so that he could help me correct them.

The dinner was pleasant. Larry told us how he was originally from Baltimore, and had been teaching History in Montana, for a few years, and then took the position at LaRoche so he could be nearer the East Coast. He had only his mother and a sister in Baltimore, which he pronounced "Balmore." As we talked more about one another's pasts, he learned that I had been a civil servant at the Vatican, and he immediately called himself a faithful Catholic. This was the first occasion for Larry to have dinner inside a household with a family, and for myself it was an opportunity to have a close friendship with an American, who could answer some of the many questions we had on the language and the culture on this side of the ocean.

101

Our first meeting working together on my English was terrible. Larry could barely understand what I had written down as a guideline for the students. I had to reformulate my thoughts four or five times because my way of speaking was so entrenched in the French way of thought. Even as I spoke, my words often mismatched my intentions or my meaning. I needed to rephrase myself several times so that Larry could gather a sense of what I was saying. For the first time in my life I realized that my typical French way of thinking didn't translate well into the American language.

So that night there was a very long conversation about philosophy, and it took a very long time for us to finally agree on sentences in English that I could assign to the students. My own speech was almost incomprehensible, and his suggestions were mostly in disagreement with the thought I wanted to express. Somehow every sentence in my notes was a battlefield. And we were both arguing with passion, which proved to be the dramatic display of a meeting between two different cultures. American wisdom with Sorbonne philosophy.

The fruit of such a dynamic meeting, to say the least, has been amazingly good. In fact, at the end of each class I taught, I handed the students a quiz for them to bring to the following lecture. It was a pass/fail test, and while the students believed it was a reflection of their understanding of the philosophy information, in actuality, this was the only way I could see if the students could understand my words.

After the second day of class, when I read the student quizzes, I had a shock. The first two quizzes I read were horrible, and I was ready to accept that I was completely incapable of teaching. However, the following quizzes became different; and as the classes went on, the student responses became better and better. I finally was beginning to gain a grasp of English — thanks to Larry.

I also had another concern. During each class, I wanted to have a short conversation with my students to allow them to ask some questions. But my ability to understand American was so bad that, instead of trying to understand the entire sentence, I would focus on just one of the words spoken, and I would try to answer based on that single word. After every question that I had answered, I used to give a wide-range general answer, in hope to hit on the question originally asked.

Two things surprised me the most about the students at LaRoche. First of all, there was their flexibility towards my horrible Gascon accent, and secondly their open mind to philosophy. Teaching philosophy in college classes in Italy or France was much more difficult because the students had already studied it, in high school, and they would come into class with a slew of biases and prejudices, making it difficult to overcome and accept a diverse perspective. At LaRoche College, like seemingly everywhere in North America, most students begin Philosophy in college, so I found their minds to be "tabula rasa", like a blank sheet of paper, ready to gather a new body of information. This allows the teacher to provide much more room to insert insight and pieces of wisdom, making the students even more willing to learn.

There was also a third point that surprised me, however. Students also had the capacity to think metaphysically which left me nothing to envy of those students I had taught in Europe. This proved that even American students had the ability to speculate with a Philosophical mindset, unlike the prejudice held in Europe, where their minds were only capable of doing so.

Throughout the semester, Larry would come to our place on Mondays, for dinner and, afterward, we would hold our philosophic meeting, while he corrected my notes for the students. These meetings became an improving experience of sharing in philosophy and in spirituality. The quality of my English was improving as well. Very soon it appeared that philosophy served as a tool that helped students improve speculatively, psychologically, and spiritually. Philosophy, as I often taught, is a school of life.

Once, Larry asked me, "Aren't you afraid of addressing a group of students in such a new cultural neighborhood?"

I replied, "It surely cannot be worse than May '68."

"What was May '68?" he asked.

"Did you ever hear about the Student Revolution?"

"Oh, you mean the riots in universities and colleges in places like California and Detroit?"

"Something like that," I said. "It was a cultural shock that changed completely the configuration of Sorbonne studies. In those days the students had a slogan. "Keep your dreams, and change the world."

I told him about the time I was a young student at the Sorbonne in the middle of the riots that changed the Sorbonne institution completely, during the time of the General de Gaulle government. My mind drifted back to those days. I remembered the motto, which was hailed by students and written all over the walls of Sorbonne University. "Make your dreams a reality." This was a time when students believed they could change the whole world. They were convinced that they could make everything possible and transform all projects in plausible and tangible endeavors. Their dreams would be actualized, they believed.

The influence of Mao Tzey-Tung's words [today we prefer to say "Mao Zedong] gathered in a small red booklet, clutched and wrinkled with reading by almost every student hand. Even the students,

who were the true promoters of these chaotic riots, were surprised to see, how easily, the entire city of Paris and few others towns in the country, had completely shut down. As the heart of France, Paris also paralyzed the economic, governmental, and structural functions of the neighboring boroughs. The chaos the students instigated was inconceivable. For an entire week the French President General de Gaulle disappeared, and some believed he had fled from the country to hide in Germany.

104

The metropolitan railways had come to a standstill. Store fronts and shopping areas had shut down. Workers went on strike. The student movement influenced even workers who had nothing to do with education or university life. A whole nation had succumbed to crisis.

Starting as a cultural movement it ended up as a chaotic semi-revolution. On the side of the students, it was already a revolution in act. All institutional authority had disappeared from the buildings of the Sorbonne, and every activity was handled by the students. It's still unclear today what the scope of the riot had been. Change, as vague and glamorous as were the notions that word held, was the main scope. The students wanted to change the structure of power and the obsolete studies carried by passé professors. Yet, many of these students were not sons and daughters of countryside villagers. These were young men and women who belonged to the bourgeoisie society. They were men and women called to fill the future wealth and economic comfort. As a result, it is tough to say that their revolution was fueled by some social class struggle. Perhaps each student had his or her own dream meant for reality, and instead together they all created a destructive movement none of them could possibly have dreamed.

Actually, it was then that I started to understand what a revolution really is: the attempt of an emerging class in the society to rise and get more power. Sometimes they pretend that revolution should be the rebellion of the poor against the rich. It is, actually, a totally diverse picture: it is always an attempt of an emerging class to erase the privileges of the ruling class, which had already lost riches and power. It works always in that manner. And those days were an expression of such a change in the whole cultural context.

Almost every day a few hundred students would meet in the amphitheater of the Sorbonne and made decisions dealing with the university government and the city's structure. This great assembly of students thought of itself as sovereign, and when a decision was made, groups of students would leave their seats and carry out orders, that would close specific stores or occupy strategic locations in the school or in the city. These groups called themselves the Committees of Deed, and wore a red scarf around their left arm. No one dared stop them, not even the police.

During the days, but even more so at night, students would attack police officers and built barricades surrounding the university and strategic streets. They would strip the streets of cobblestones and threw them against policemen, whenever a fight would break out. Any person who represented institutional authority met also the blow of a hard and heavy stone.

The only stores that remained open in the city were coffee houses and restaurants. It was stunning to see the terraces of these dining places filled with people, all smiling and laughing because there was no work or business to worry about. The students believed they had transformed the face of the city. Instead of carrying the long metropolitan mugs, the people smiled.

The general assemblies that took place in the large amphitheater began every day around ten o'clock a.m., and at times would go on, with little interruptions, until two of the following morning. Here was the time, when I understood what direct democracy looked like. It was a social framework, where the very people were the ones who made decisions. These assemblies took up issues on which professors needed fired, for the less… Which curricula and college courses should be scrapped, and which others should be taught anew in the whole University.

The students reveled in what they considered a great accomplishment. They decided on building structures, and how to divide ownership of the university campus. Often, in fact almost always, these important decisions were made at two in the morning, when most of the assembly had dissipated and gone to sleep and only the most radical had remained in the amphitheater, heads still full of dreams. On the days following these grand decisions, a mural scroll was kept updated, informing of the student body of the new changes. The assembly truly believed they were in charge. They were convinced they had initiated a turning point in history. They even believed that every aspect of the society was now in their grasp and under their own control. Direct democracy was now instilled into their living reality.

It was astonishing to see how out of these assemblies were reminiscent of the general assemblies which took place after the French Revolution of 1789, a time when the people of France fought to abolish the monarchy. Except the difference was that back in 1789 it was the representatives of the people who had been elected to the assembly, making the decisions. Thus, they had created an indirect democracy, in which the representatives made laws in the name of the people. Here, during the days of May '68, it was the body of selected students, who directly made laws for themselves. Many truly believed they had restored in those days the structures of direct democracy. They were sure that a new historic era had begun.

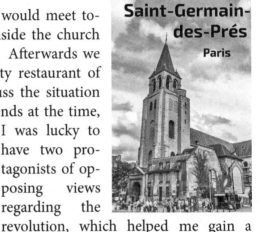

Saint-Germain-des-Prés

Paris

With a few friends, we would meet together at the noon Mass inside the church of Saint Germain-des-Près. Afterwards we would dine at the university restaurant of Mabillon, in order to discuss the situation around us. Among my friends at the time,  I was lucky to have two protagonists of opposing views regarding the revolution, which helped me gain a wider perspective. One of the two was Hughes Emmanuel le Barbier de Blignère, an interesting guy, of noble descent, whose views leaned to the far right. My other friend was Alain Desaint, stood in the far left. Together, all three of us decided we would try to influence the assembly at its next meetings. This became a fruitful experience, which proved both interesting and entertaining.

We had it all planned out. During the day's assembly, Hughes would begin a speech tailored to his right-wing mentality. The general student population knew Hughes for his stance, but today he would tip the scale even further. He presented himself before the assembly speaking of control and domination. He spoke of a new generation of professors and teachers who would in this new structure of university life occupy positions of total dominion over their educational material. These professors, who would be elected by the assembly, would reserve the right to expel any student who disagreed with their teachings. They would even reserve the right to punish future students opposing the hard and defined structure this assembly had worked so hard to recreate. Hughes' tone held firm, unsmiling and dominant. The people saw how serious his intentions were.

"The doors should be locked during teaching, so no future generation of young thinkers can damage what we will create," he would say, and his suggestions would become even more and more extreme. There would be curfews. There would be fines to students who brought a damaged book to lectures. There would be public beatings to those who failed to conform…

The assemble became more and more agitated with each of his repressive suggestions.

"You fool!" shouted my other friend Alain Desaint in the middle of Hughes's discourse. "The control should be with the students. If we are working toward anything it is with the power of the students", he said.

At this, the members of the assembly calmed down again. Finally, some rationality was emerging. Some cheered for support. But then, my good friend Desaint took up a strident and fanatical tone:

"It is the student who should control the class and beat the teacher for suppressing him with old and trite lessons. Any student, on any day, should have the power to expel any boring or passé professor. The power is with the students."

His speech went on for a few minutes longer, proposing that if locks should be placed anywhere inside the university, it should be to imprison professors at night, so they would not be able to rebel against the students. It should be the student body, who would lead education and decide what should be taught. It should be the student body who hailed control and beat any professor publicly who failed to assign interesting texts as lectures. Every student should be promoted and passed regardless of professor influence. They should decide when exams should be taken, and each student should retain the right to decide what vote he deserves.

This is when I rose and spoke my own part. At this point, Desaint's harangue was taking such a ridiculous turn that I knew it was time for me to interject. I spoke to the assembly advocating balance.

"If no challenge arises in the studies, how do we ensure a valuable education for the student body? How do we ensure a progress within the learning of society? True, the professors cannot have all the control, but neither should the students. I propose a balance."

"Let's vote on our decision!" shouted a random voice amongst the crowd. Even this voice belonged to another friend. We had planned it all before hand. Hughes would begin with is far-right approached, then Alain would counter-balance it with his own leftist suggestions, and I would strike with balance. Immediately, then, a fourth friend would call for a vote so that no more discussion would follow.

We did this, three or four times more, at different meetings. Always my own suggestions became accepted by a huge majority, knowing that the only other two offerings were far too insane. Within this dynamic political endeavor, my friends and I began to test how true were the words of Aristotle, later repeated by Descartes, "There has never been any stupid idea that hasn't had a philosopher to promote it."

As I was telling all this to Larry at my household in Pittsburgh, my American friend interrupted me.

"But in a situation so contentious, who gave you the light, more so the strength, to go on?"

"Monmayou was with me," I told him.

"What does that mean? What's Monmayou?"

I explained to him briefly who Monmayou was and told him that this farmer had influenced me so deeply as a young boy that all of his teachings remained alive in my heart even as I grew. I could still hear Adrian's voice saying, "Be simple." - "Don't let yourself become influenced by big words coming out of large mouths." - "Do not answer that question…" - "Hurry up; hold that vote still."

At the time of the student assemblies, any vote could be stopped by a "point of order," which was essentially any stance with new information that could help redirect the opinion and votes of the student body. Monmayou was like a voice of conscience inside of me, guiding me through duress and with calm conviction. He spoke in my moments of tension. Above all, however, I always held in my heart a key phrase which he spoke often, "It's important to always have faith. Never despair. He who perseveres will be saved."

Larry interrupted me once more. "Alain, now it's very late. I should head to bed, but could we continue our conversation tomorrow at the cafeteria?"

"I will be more than pleased to do so," I told him.

I took the notes that Larry helped me correct, and I wished him a good night.

Tableau # 12
At the Cafeteria

I WAS EATING LUNCH AT LA ROCHE COLLEGE (La Roche University, today) when Larry joined me at the cafeteria. Immediately he reminded me of the conversation we held the previous night.

"Tell me more about the student revolution at the Sorbonne," he said.

"Well, I told you about the Deed Committees, which were provocation teams intended to break the gears of the society."

I tried to explain to him with gestures, how each of these Committees was much like a crowbar, meant to insert and dig into a groove and crack open the door so that the student revolution could penetrate and take over every aspect of the society.

Larry listened attentively, gathering and understanding what he could from what I tried to explain.

I went on with the story.

An interesting aspect of those days is the fact that there were a strong percentage of Catholics present among the students at the time, and they made their voices in opposition heard loudly against the forceful chaos present there. Because of this chaos many new activities and decisions arose almost spontaneously or out of improvisation thanks to the lack of structure in the throngs of students. Each student responded to these improvisations in his own way.

One morning, for example, I found out that some students were stealing books from the Sorbonne Library.

Immediately, I together with a few friends of mine who used to meet for noon Mass at St. Germain des Près, went to the front entrance of the library, grabbed a table and some chairs and sat in front of the entrance with red banner around our shoulders to display our authority as members of a Deed Committee.

From that desk we searched every student who passed our way to see if they had stolen any books, taking back anything that looked like it might have been stolen.

At a certain moment, a small group of students came out of the library wearing that same red banner around their arms.

One of my friends, Philippe, whispered in my ear upon seeing them, "They belong to a Committee, we should let them through."

"No," I told him. "We're here to examine any suspicious acts. We will search them too."

From the group, a tall student who seemed in charge held a leather bag by his side, and I waved him over to the table, asking him to open it. In fact, inside the bag we found a few hardbound volumes.

"No book can pass through this point," I told him. "I apologize but I must take these back."

Amongst the books in his bag, I also saw a small booklet that seemed like an antique.

"Look, this one booklet is my own," he told me.

I opened the book and saw that it was stamped with the library's label.

"Is your name Sorbonne Library?" I asked him, pointing to the red inked stamp.

The student remained in silence, searching for half-words, not knowing what to say.

"I apologize," I told him. "But I should do my work here and ask for that book back from you."

He handed it over, and I returned his leather back to him.

"You've got quite some courage," Philippe said to me.

"How so?" I asked him.

"There were seven of them, and only three of us."

"Yes, sure, but they didn't know that. We're sitting here, and for all they know there could be a whole bunch of other members of our Deed Committee waiting for our orders to intervene," I said with an assured smile. It was so in fact.

Nearby where we sat, there was a room named Center of Information, where several telephones were stored. Here somebody had placed a microphone, from which you could speak into speakers,  which broadcast in the large Sorbonne courtyard, where a great number of students congregated and socialized. Knowing this, an idea came to mind. If we took over that Center of Information, we could have great influence over the whole revolutionary movement.

I met the next day with the usually group at the Mabillon restaurant. There were typically between twenty and thirty of us who met. It was the same group that attended Mass previously at St. Germain. At the restaurant we planned a way of taking over the information center, knowing that once we did, we would have to keep surveillance, twenty-four hours a day.

During our discussion, we decided we would find a way of influencing the students, in a manner to prevent them from coming up against the police. We wanted to try and establish some peace and order.

We would send out scouts into the city with motorcycles to see spot where the police were congregating from day to day. Each scout would then report back to us with the information, and we would use that knowledge to misdirect those hot-headed students, who went looking for battle with the police. Using the information center, we would broadcast the wrong police location, and avoid confrontation.

The next day a few of us went back to the inspection table in front of the library, and from there moved into the information center where only two students were stationed.

"We're here to relieve you," I told the two.

"Finally! It has been ten hours since I've been here. I couldn't take it anymore," one of them responded.

From that location we were able to gather material and informa-

113

tion about different student activities and police locations, and for a few good days we were able to influence and calm the revolution endeavor.

Much of the information that flowed in and out of the Sorbonne was in our hands. From there we filtered out messages, passing through only those that helped cool the waters.

One of the student leaders, Jacques Sauvageot, came to the information center with two body guards, whom we called "gorillas" because their bodies were so thick...

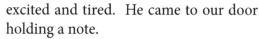

Sauvageot was a thinner character with dark hair, with eyes both excited and tired. He came to our door holding a note.

"May I broadcast something?" he asked.

I tried to gesture him to hand me the note, and said, "We could take care of that if you like."

"That's quite all right. I would like to do it."

The two gorillas stared at me and Philippe, knowing that either one of them could overtake the both of us.

"Please, make yourselves at home," I gestured them in.

I pointed Sauvageot to the microphone, and the wiry student sat at the chair both exhausted and energized by his purpose. He clicked on the microphone and broadcasted the location of different police activities, and immediately Philippe and I tensed-up, knowing that this might destroy everything we were trying to accomplish here.

As Sauvageot continued, he urged the students for peace, telling them to stay away from those very locations where the police would be. I understood then his intentions were genuine but that he would cause exactly the opposite. Every hot-headed student group would move exactly where Sauvageot was asking them to stay away from.

I reached over for the microphone and clicked the switch off.

"What is this?" he asked, and rose. He was much taller than Philippe and I, but thinner in frame. The gorillas stepped forward.

"You cannot be broadcasting that information."

"And why not? The two of you have been broadcasting police locations all week."

"You don't understand," I told him. "You're compromising everything."

"Compromising?" the one gorilla asked, tilting his neck and bringing his brow into a scowl.

"Is this how you speak to your leader?" the second gorilla said, grabbing for my red band wrapped around my arm.

"Leader or not," I said, shaking the gorilla's grasp off me, "Here we don't need imbeciles."

The words shocked the three of them. Philippe tensed up by my side, but he followed my lead and held his jaw tight and stood firm. The two gorillas watched us, disbelieving, jumping their eyes back and forth from Philippe and me.

Sauvageot placed his hands on the shoulders of both his bodyguards. There must have been authority that they sensed in our eyes. Perhaps our looks convinced them that our authority had come from a higher leadership rank in the student body.

Whatever was the case, they could have easily handled us physically without problem. But it must have been the tone in my voice that made them rethink it, because Sauvageot simply stepped back and turned away, murmuring some apology on his way out. The gorillas followed, and Philippe and I stood there in disbelief.

A few mornings later another member of our group, Jean-Paul, called me at home and told me how in the middle of the night Sauvageot had come with five times the number of gorillas, by his side and kicked out the few members of our group who had been assigned the night shift at the information center.

"What do we do now?" Jean-Paul said; his voice was sullen.

I understood then that the most important thing was to cheer him up, the best I could.

"Don't worry. There is still much for us to do."

Just in that moment the voice and teachings of Monmayou returned to me: "There is nothing that happens to us unless it is allowed by God". And one more sentence came to me, spoken by Saint Augustine, which reassured me, "Whatever wrong may happen to us, God allows it for a greater good."

I tried to explain these words to Jean-Paul, in hope to lift his spirits. I also added a phrase by Saint Vincent de Paul, which I had just read. "All the wickedness that others may bring upon us, God will use it to save us."

I told him, then, that I just heard that the movement called Pax Christi had just composed a message of peace meant for the student body and did not know how to broadcast it or deliver it to them. I told Paul to get in touch with the movement and have them send him fliers so that we could distribute them around the campus.

That way, instead of sending out messages from above and through the central speakers, we could infiltrate peace within the very body of the students. We did not realize, however, that doing so would require much more courage, because this meant distributing a Catholic message, amongst a vast mass of Marxists, Maoist, and Trotskyites, who would disagree with such an endeavor.

An hour later, he called me back saying that Pax Christi had the pamphlets ready for distribution, but couldn't find anybody willing to risk handing them out. We discussed how many students we could group together, knowing we would need at least fifty people to reach the entire campus and the city. They would have to go in pairs, covering over twenty-five regions to reach the whole city of Paris.

"Why in pairs?" asked Jean Paul.

"Because some places would be dangerous to go alone. One can hand the pamphlet while the other takes the watch."

We contacted the students we would need and all met together at Saint Germain des Pres church to catch Mass at noon. Later on, to clarify our strategy we gathered for lunch as usual at Mabillon.

When we first met at noon at the Latin Quarter, we saw that the news had spread of our plans, and even more students had shown up to take part of it.

The staff, from the local newspaper of *La Croix*, wanted to help us distribute the pamphlets, and took this as an opportunity to redistribute their own print, which had run low on favoritism ever since the student movement had been matched with extreme left wave newspapers and journals.

As a Catholic newsprint, *La Croix* saw that this would be an opportunity to help reestablish balance in information.

Also joining us was the group of Lycée Rodin, which was one of the most prominent and largest high schools in Paris tailored to the studies of philosophy.

Père Sinoir, the minister of the Catholic center at Lycée Rodin, put at our disposal their printing press, with which we could print a continuous flow of fliers, newsletters, and pamphlets, to counteract the extreme leftist publications of the days.

The most dangerous of our resources was to sell and market the catholic paper, *La Croix*. For that, we would travel in groups of four. One would sell the copies of the paper, while the other three would pull security or stand by in case of trouble, ready to call for help. It was inside the Sorbonne itself, where we had to be most careful, since this was the very center, where the revolution got pushed every day.

I was walking into the courtyard of the Sorbonne, shouting: *"La Croix! La Croix"*. Naturally, there, nobody wanted to purchase any issue of the paper.

Just near to me, I saw a young student selling *L'Humanité*, which was one of the more prominent communist publications. He himself shouted for sales, *"L'Huma! L'Huma!"*

It is then that an idea came to my mind, while I was watching students come and go with ease purchasing copies of *"L'Huma"* issues.

I went up to the young sales boy and said, "Want to switch?" And I handed him a copy of La Croix. With surprise and a bit of unease, he took my journal but folded it away, hiding it immediately into his pocket.

On the other hand, I took a copy of the communist issue and put it in my external vest pocket where the title of the communist paper was largely visible to anyone.

To anybody watching me, I looked like a *L'Humanité* reader, who just happened to be selling something else. It worked.

Once the students saw me with the other print in my pocket, other students started coming to me: "Ah, let's see this garbage," a student said, eyeing out the Catholic journals. It made it easier now for them to pretend to dislike the journal while being able to purchase it.

"Yes, of course. We should always be aware of other imbecilities, if we want to fight them," I replied. With this, more and more students came by and began reading our print.

The more copies I sold, the closer I got to the gate, and I signaled to the other three, who were waiting by, to show them that the coast was clear. They came in and, while I sold *La Croix*, they went around to the readers and handed them pamphlets and fliers, with information explaining the Catholic position on the student movement.

The pamphlets spoke of order and peace, and showed a refreshing compassion and sympathy towards the students, who had begun the movement out of anger and frustration and yearnings for power.

Most of the students in the area were surprised. They knew little of how to react, considering that the whole area was so immersed in the communist mentality. This area, which we had gauged to be very dangerous, actually turned out to favor our movement. It was because we had taken a step of courage in entering such a dangerous situation, that more and more students greeted us, mostly out of curiosity, instead of violence.

After just ten minutes of hurried print sales, and handing out fliers, we scurried away with sweat on our back, knowing that likely, we had just risked our lives, to pass out some ink on paper.

The rest of the day we passed out the pamphlets through the streets and targeted key areas, which needed influence.

Then by the street we came across a priest, whom we recognized as Cardinal Marty. He had just been nominated the bishop of Paris. He was a small man, with a jovial face, and short cropped hair. He wore the Roman collar, which made it clear to us that he was a priest. This, too, took an act of courage because any group of students would

have gladly beaten a priest, just for being there.

"Who are you fellas?" Marty asked when he saw us with the printed media hanging by our side from a satchel.

"We're the "*Amis des sans amis*", Father, Pierre said. His way of labelling Marty, as Father, showed his poor familiarity with clerical context which never misses to call a cardinal "Your Eminence." Card. Marty was pleased with this unusual familiar tone. The "Friends of those without friends," is the name that our group took as its own identity", I told him.

"What does that mean?" he asked with curiosity.

"Peace, serenity, and faith. All of those things are supposed to be disclosed with charity. We're the voice of all of those things amidst the chaos of the student revolution." we said.

"But where do you come from?"

"We're tied to the spirit of the Focolare Movement," someone answered.

The Focolare was new at that time, but already well known among the Catholic hierarchy of the time, as a Catholic wave of spirituality and a movement organized and lead by an Italian lady named Chiara Lubich. Originally based out of Rome, the movement was now spreading and encouraging youths to regain peace and friendliness in the city of Paris.

"What brave men," he said with surprise and happiness. "What daring courage. This is just what I've been praying to influence, and yet you've already taken action. This gives me encouragement to see young Catholics so involved and dedicated in opposing the chaos here around us."

It came to me, then, to utter some of the inspiring words that Monmayou had instilled in me from a younger time. I spoke to the priest of these emotions erupting. "Always believe in the love that God bestows upon us. There's no need for surprise there." I added how we are supposed to do always what we feel is right, then allow God to work our actions through his providence. I spoke with clarity and certainty. And I finished with one thought, familiar to my father, that seemed to help the priest reflect:

"When you're carrying the cross, it is the cross that carries you."

Among those days, many of us had gone through the experience of evangelizing the students around. While doing so, we felt that such a similar endeavor was very close to what earlier Christians had accomplished amidst the pagan people.

One of us, for example, Imré, who was from polish descent, had spent the night in one of the Sorbonne halls and, in the morning came face to face with students of a Deed Committee, who were some of the more revolutionary ones, and strong headed.

The leader of the group came in, walking tall, and stood before the people in the room, asking: "Here we are all atheists, are we not?"

Immediately, Imré stood up, with calmness in his bones, he spoke, "Not me. I'm Catholic."

And right away, two more stood up, and calmly repeated Imre's words.

"Me too. I'm Catholic."

"I'm as well."

With just those few, who had stood up for their Faith, the whole committee walked away without another word. The leader had wanted to organize an attack on a local church, but thought twice of it, for being at the sight of members of faith. Later on, Imré called me, on the phone, and told me that he didn't know, where to stay any longer because he was afraid of being outnumbered by nonbelievers.

Then, I picked him up, with a car borrowed from a friend, to bring him over to a safer lodging.

We met in a more tranquil part of the city, where there was little worry of student movement. Except that, when I went there, I saw a Police truck, with a huddle of officers watching us. I didn't realize, then, that they were waiting by, to see if we were meeting to organize some kind of attack. At the moment I just thought they were there to usher us, through that section of the city, and to simply provide a watch on the area.

Later that night I made phone calls to some of the key leaders of our group to find new strategies for selling the newspaper and hand out fliers.

During our phone conversation there emerged the fact that the student assigned to go and pick up the newspaper distributor, had been stranded without gas. We couldn't pick up the papers anywhere else.

Suddenly while I was on the line with one of the leaders, stationed at the Sorbonne, we heard a voice saying,

"Here, National Security of the French Police, Listening table number two, Information Desk number two, we have gas for your transportation."

"Who is this? What information desk?"

"We're the police. We've been tapping your phone."

"Tapping our phone? For what?"

"Do you want the gasoline or not?"

"Sure, of course. Yes, of course. We want it"

He told us, then, where we could go and grab the fuel for transportation.

The next day we picked up the gasoline, and we realized, very soon, how the police had been afraid we were organizing something against the government, and had been tapping our conversations and activities, as they do with many others groups.

When they realized that we were working to promote peace, friendliness and eventually reestablish order, they had come to our side to provide support.

From this, an anonymous relationship began between our own committee and the police, which started informing us of future involvements and organizations that were taking place.

Sometimes they informed us, of eventual police raids so that we could usher students away from rallies or actions of violence. For a week longer we sold the papers until finally our courage seemed to no longer entice curiosity but anger.

It was the kind of anger we had expected from the beginning, so we were scarcely surprised by it. Students handing out fliers were beaten and humiliated in the more centralized parts of the university, and we knew that once again we would have to switch to new strategies to make influence and shape cohesion.

By this time the police had been running out of patience. They could, no longer resort to Billie clubs when riots broke out. Students were still throwing cobble stones and found inventive ways of injuring or even killing service members.

The army could do little without using force. Their strategies had

to turn to more aggressive means. They no longer held back from shooting aggressive or dangerous students at riots. Somehow, instead of creating more chaos and violence, this actually seemed to stifle the student effort.

Some results were showing in opposing the movement. Exasperation had begun to creep into the minds and bodies and efforts of even the more revolutionary leaders. In good number they persisted, but even their progress, many felt, needed a moment to breathe and break away from the revolution, which had become their life.

They needed a moment to refresh and recharge. They needed a vacation.

Originally, the student movement that began on May 11 of 1968 had forced the government to shut off fuel supplies in Paris to immobilize the students and even the whole city.

This, in a sense, had worked, because nobody had been able to leave the city, but it had also formed a chaotic centralization.

The good thing was that, overall, the riots had been confined to Paris, but now the government strategy was completely revised.

French President, General de Gaulle, used the student exasperation as an opportunity for an impressive military strategy. De Gaulle knew that Pentecost weekend in June would present a perfect timing for it.

Every year, the time of Pentecost, offers what people use to call "a long bridge" – which means a "long week-end", providing additional days of vacation. Then, it would be a three-day weekend, and the students would have done anything to just get away for a little breathing rest out of town.

Suddenly, on the previous Friday, just before Pentecost Sunday, the President restored distribution of fuel in all of the gas stations in the capital area. Naturally, at the time, the strategy was kept secret.

Additionally, many in the city believed that the body of students was responsible to the block of the supply of gas. And under the suggestion of the government, the news encouraged such belief. But the whole endeavor was, actually, according to the whole design of the government. And the heads of the students knew there were not responsible for blocking gas provision.

Notwithstanding, the key leaders of the student movement believed that, finally, the Government had given up on fighting with fire and had decided to appease their wishes. The gasoline came looking as an offering for peace or a first step to a series of agreements and negotiations.

Immediately, with much hurry and little delay, every student who owned a car filled up his tank. Every student who didn't have a car hopped a ride with a friend. They were sick of the city and the graf-fiti-blighted walls upon which they had manifested their power. Vacation lay a road-trip away. In just one day the city became deserted

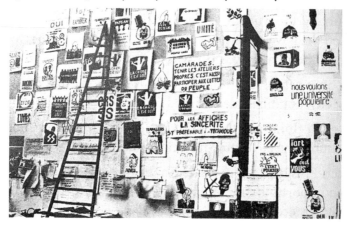

of students, with little organization or thought to reflect on the consequences.

The whole populace spread to the countryside, breathing in their success and celebrating the break they had earnestly deserved. Ah, yes. A little fresh air would do them good.

Except the fact that… the one who returned that Monday, which was still part of the three-day Pentecost celebration, found out that the government had already moved in swiftly.

In absence of the students in town, Police and Army units had taken over the Sorbonne, occupying key posts, information centers and centers of student debate like cinemas and theatres. Police stations had been re-manned to the max. Enforcements had come from outside the city to take back the whole agglomeration of Paris, the whole city which they had been forced, already, to lose in a matter of such a few violent weeks.

In such a typical executive manner, the government took back the whole city!

Coming back from the three-days-vacation the students could not find any place to meet again. The "Student Revolution" was over.

Then, almost immediately, the Government divided the Sorbonne into fourteen different colleges.

Within months, the authority re-established a working and functional education program, even more strict and governing than the one prior. If the students wanted to continue their studies, they now had to submit to a system composed of even more control than what they had worked so democratically to destroy. As a result, however, professors and faculty organizations decided to recreate and reconstruct education programs that were modernized for the time. The teachings became contemporary and advanced. If nothing else, the students had at least gained this…

I stopped talking for a while and reflected.

Larry asked, "What did you learn from these events?"

"A lot," I said, but continued to reflect.

"For example?"

"The most obvious would be that surviving this chaos, I was made able to address many other difficult situations. Teaching at LaRoche in a language that I don't know yet, is not a big deal. I just need to learn the language. But there is much more."

"What do you mean?"

"Well, these events of May '68 in Paris, raised a lot of questions in my mind as in the minds of many. Somehow, I connected these city struggles with the end times, which Monmayou told me about. There would be riots everywhere and even the Earth would be troubled by earthquakes, change of season, and alterations of average temperature.

But such disorderly situations happened only in a few cities in the world. So this was probably not the announcement of the end times, but only fore-facts of future larger disorders.

"God never does anything without preparing us, and I took these chaotic situations as a prelude of what will happen very soon everywhere. Almost like the cramps of a pregnant mother announce delivery."

"Do you really believe it will happen?"

I remained silent, and Larry matching silence was an echo of my own.

May 1968 by Joan Miro

Tableau # 13
American Language

IN SEPTEMBER, AUTUMN ARRIVED IN PITTSBURGH, and we had the grass, the front yard, garage access, all edges and paths of the house, and every corner where our eyes could turn, yes everything was covered with leaves, acorns, branches... It was like a carpet which provided natural protection to plants and animals before winter comes.

We had to sweep away the whole mass of leaves several times a week, if not daily, from the driveways. Confronting that amount of foliage on the ground, Chiara made a joke. She said, with a laugh in her voice: "I understand, now, why, in American, the same word "fall" is used to say the process of "falling" and to indicate the season of "autumn". It made sense.

The children delighted in playing with this unexpected manna: collecting the thrown pieces for feeding the fire in the fireplace, but also to fill colored bags on which they painted mock figures and manufactured scaring forms to decorate and illuminate the surroundings of the house with frights in prevision of the end of October, when on the eve of All Saints' Day, people celebrate here the night of the ghosts with Halloween. On that occasion the children wore costumes as they used to do in Rome for Carnival. At nightfall, they walked in the neighborhood, from house to house, playing a comedy and receiving candies in return.

At first, I found it curious, and even strange, but it is not as incongruous that it seems, after all!

There is more. It is impressive to see how, every quarter of the year, a new celebration is in progress, announced in the yards, the stores, the offices and even the classrooms at school and the university — It seems that, this country is a permanent festival, helping people to celebrate Christmas, Ash Wednesday, Saint Patrick's Day, Easter, local parishes or townships during the summer, and finally Thanksgiving... These festivities alternate with national celebrations, which are integral part of this convivial society. Undoubtedly, similar series of events display the characteristic youth of this country, and show the dynamism of this civilization.

These games, in the yard and at school, involved our children, too. Michel contributed particularly with his excellent capacity of painting and drafting. He is gifted. He was good to the point that in September, several comrades, and even teachers, were asking him for so many drawings, that he was forced to work at night to cover the orders. To restore his serenity, I was obliged to prohibit him from drawing for 15 days as a means to calm him down.

In the morning of November first, the snow surprised us, covering the whole house and the surroundings, transforming the whole neighborhood and the city. It was followed then by cold temperature. As well as the summer was hot, reaching easily above 95 degrees, the winters was rigorous, reaching 20 below. There is, therefore, some physical activity to provide, in the morning, all through the long winter, to make usable the driveways and prepare the car to start. It is necessary sometimes to warm the engine with a heater... One day I failed to make the necessary preparations and in trying to start the frozen engine, I broke the belt... It was a lesson to remember.

Snow, ice and cold is fortunately not an every day experience. The snow, however, was so abundant at the start of the following January that it took a couple of hours or so, actually twice the same day, to clear the driveways before being able to get out and then get in the car. It was our good luck, that day, having Franco Riccardi and his son Marco visiting us from Rome, and while we were beginning to get tired of that exercise, they were happy to help shovel the snow with us. It was a new experience for them.

Not to mention storms and sudden changes in temperature which, with the snow or rain, caused damages all around: a few mornings in winter it happened that TV channel 12 advised us to stay home, announcing the closure of schools and offices. It was a real surprise for us. It is something that never happened to us while living in Rome. Again, the changes of weather were fast, and within hours the days took on a totally different character.

That day our children dreamed about having the family transfer to Texas.

Around us, a large part of the population is of Italian origin, especially from the Abruzzi, from Calabria or Sicily. Many know a few words of the dialect of origin, but they actually are more comfortable to speak plain English. Even if what they call English is surely not British, as we use to call it "English" in Europe. The language of this country is a different idiom that I would prefer to call "American". Italian presence around explains why the stores stock so many Italian products: wine, pasta, food, clothing... even oil and sauce. This is astonishing because the French products are less available. I would easily have thought the opposite, considering the nearness of Quebec. As a result of this Italian atmosphere and field of behavior, language, habit, and food we could live in harmony with our original Roman traditions.

At Christmas children dreamed of eating some "prosciutto", our typical home ham. For them "home ham was "Parma's ham". I did not know, however, how to say it in plain American: and I visited unsuccessfully of few stores looking for it. Finally, in an Italian store in Bloomfield area, after a long explanation with the attendant, speaking half-English and mid-Italian, I made myself understood and the seller exclaimed: "Ah! But you want Prosciutto of Parma'" and we have been wonderfully served. It must be said that American is very different from French. It does not fear to get different words from diverse vernaculars, so American picks up its vocabulary where it finds it useful. This also is a characteristic of the country.

In those days at La Roche, Larry, the American colleague told me a joke:

"What do you call somebody who speaks three languages?" He

asked me.

"Trilingual, I believe," I guessed.

He asked again:

"What do you call someone who speaks only two languages?"

"If my first answer was correct, this one is easy: bilingual," I replied.

"And what do you call somebody who speaks one language only?" He finally asked.

I remained silent, understanding it was a joke...

After a moment's pause to increase the effect of his humor, he said: "It is an American!" And he laughed loudly.

I remained silent again. Even if I was happily surprised by the American capacity of laughing at themselves, I disagreed with him and I said it right away.

"It is not so, for learning American obliged me to study five diverse languages at once!"

"How is that?" He replied with a blink of surprise in his eyes.

"American is different with any other languages I had occasion to become familiar with, French, Italian, Spanish, Portuguese, German, Greek, even Arabic..." I insisted.

"How is it possible?" He asked again...

"In all these languages, when you get vocabulary and grammar you get everything and you're good to speak. It is not the same in American."

"Why?"

"First of all, getting the vocabulary obliges you to learn three series of insights: spelling, phonetics, and meaning which are not so tightly connected together as in another tongue?"

"What's the difference of American with other languages?" He insisted, asking again.

"In Italian spelling and phonics go together. It is the same in Latin and Greek. When you have the spelling, you know the phonics and vice versa. Here is why Italian is so easy to learn: it takes two weeks for an Italian child at school to learn how to write and read, it is not the same in English.

Oppositely to American language, Spanish and Portuguese have an easier connection between spelling and phonetics. German resembles, too, with a few exceptions. In French, when you have the spelling you know the phonics, but it is not totally reversible: this is why dictations are part of the process of language learning, in every French school. Nonetheless the rules of reading and speaking are tightly connected with the spelling or words "orthograph", as they call it, over there. On the contrary, in American speech, spelling, phonics, and meaning have more sophisticated relationships, and every word has its own connections.

"I never was aware of that," my colleague Larry said. For a while he looked at me with suspicion: he was not sure if I was not making fun of him.

But I was not.

"This is the reason why the pronunciation is so important in American language. English pronunciation and syllable stress is much more relevant than in other languages. I dare to think that American is the language that you can more easily read on the lips. Reading a speaker's lips is more difficult in French, where the reference to written words is the main credential… or even in Italian in which reading and spelling are almost the same speech: you'll barely find an Italian asking to another about the spelling of his name, spelling follows phonics and vice versa, sounds fit the spelling perfectly, whatever words you utter.

"It is a totally different figure in American language. The words have a kind of body, which is the skeleton (spelling), and doesn't tell anything about the skin (phonetics) and both do not indicate its behaviors (syntax), and the people it goes with [prepositions), then it can even be included in some unusual grouping (idioms).

All these figures need to be learned and remembered separately. Yes, learning American means learning five languages at once!

"And I said nothing about the meaning of words which is tricky, too."

"How is that?" he asked.

"Well. 65% of American words come from Latin through French, but each word had its own historical process, for example, "reading" means "*lecture*" in French. But "lecture" in American is translated by "*conférence*" in French. And the American "conference" refers to "*congrès*" in French. Then, the American "congress" is the equivalent of the French "*parlement*"... The same words, with the same spelling in American and in French, have in American a meaning that is different of the equivalent French words, which they come from.

When French people study American or when American people study French, they are used to call these words false friends... because they look familiar but they ultimately are tricky.

"Sometime English and French play ping pong with the words.

"What do you mean by ping pong game? Larry asked again.

He was not at all bored by my detailed language explanations.

"Take for example a French word like *tonnelle*, which means "pergola" in English. It was spelled and used differently in England as "tunnel", then as "tunnel" it came back in France, with the same spelling and meaning that in English it refers to.

Historically, the Channel was a continuous area of a lot of comings and goings for trade. Language words followed the trades.

"There is more to say. This kind of meaning displacement of American words is typical in this country... American culture used to pick up words from foreign languages to express specific issues giving to the words not the original meaning, but a similar one. It happens to refer to the 'Prime Minister' with 'Premier', which simply means 'First' in French. It is like the Italian word '*capisce*?', which is used to ask to someone if he/she does agree on what it was said, and which, originally, only means "do you understand?", and it is said differently in Italian when we speak with one or two, familiar or unfamiliar interlocutors."

"Interesting," he insisted. "But you said that American language includes a five series of learning. I understand what you mean for the first two, spelling and phonetics, which sometimes is perplexing us, too, and I can accept what you said on the meaning, but can you tell

132

me more about the other two?"

I stopped a moment for the time to reflect on the manner of choosing my words: "There is first grammar and Idioms," I said.

"How is that?" He asked again.

"Grammar is elementary in English, less sophisticated than in every other language grammar, but in many cases, idioms replace grammar."

"What do you mean by that?"

"Well, consider the usage of the prepositions for example. It does not go with the meaning as in the other languages I am familiar with, nor is it replaced by declination cases like in Latin, Greek, German, and Croatian... In English most prepositions go with the verb, the noun or the adjective as part of them, for example: you say. "I belong to", but "I depend on", or "to be able to", and "to be capable of"... and so on. Each expression requires a diverse preposition. You know that because you grew up as an American. However, coming from another culture, with familiarity with another language, while entering the U.S. country I have to learn all of it and even not all dictionaries provide the information I need, to speak properly.

When I came in and started teaching at La Roche College I always had, with me, what I dare to call "my portable dictionary", which is the unabridged *Webster's Third New International Dictionary*, a book of almost 3,000 pages, that I was carrying always along in a special case. I always had it with me everywhere. The only difficulty to deal with was not to confound British English with American English, which was another barrier to overcome.

I continued to explain to Larry: "This aspect of the idioms is probably the trickiest configuration of country language. Also consider how a preposition is part of the verb and produces a totally different signification like "I am off", "I am in", or "I am through", or else "I am out". Obviously it is easy for you, while it is new for me!

"Then many colloquialisms replace regular words. I like to quote here just a few, which show that the meaning of the sentence has nothing to do with the usual meaning of words. See for example sentences similar to:

- "Blowing one's own trumpet" to indicate an excess of pride;

- "Going off the deep end" to express a sudden wrath;

- "Giving someone the brush off" for be rid of somebody;

- "Having got a close shave" for saying to be safe by the skin of the teeth;

- "Treading water" to tell being in trouble;

…to name a few."

"Similar colloquialisms exist also in French and Italian as exceptional expressions but, in American, idioms are integral part of the vernacular".

After a moment of silence, I concluded, "For what I know, American is the only language, which to speak it properly you need to learn five different idioms that include spelling, phonic, meaning, syntax and idioms…"

The colleague argued again: "Every language has meaning connected to words. How the meaning would be different in American?"

"Well, it is the way, English was born. It started as a poor French speaking, barely spoken by Normans when they moved to England in 1100, after the victory of Hastings, and used to speak French in their castles and Saxon outside and they continued to do so up to 1476, when for the first time at the Chamber there was a talk made, which was not in French…

"Here is why American got that curious and unique case when animals have a different name as they are alive and as they are dead. In plain English, many animals get a Saxon name when they are alive, while their names are French when they are dead. Actually, Normans used to speak French inside a castle and Saxon outside. As a result, they used to speak French around a dinner table. During meals inside of castles, they used to say Beef (from *boeuf* in French) what they named Cow (Saxon) on the field, and *Mouton* (French) what was named Sheep (Saxon) outside, and Pork (from the French *porc*) what they used to call Pig (Saxon) in the farm-yard, and Venison [for the French *venaison*] what they used to know as Deer (Saxon) in the woods.

"I discovered a similar curiosity while I was teaching metaphysics, because it allowed me interesting developments. In Ontology, speaking about animals, a substance is a living animal, when it is dead, it can be cut in many pieces without changing its new entity of being not a substance any more... but mere accidents of a previous substance.

"Here is why, even the meaning needs a specific learning in American...

"Coming in the country obliged us not to simply learn one language, which would be American, but five diverse categories of signs, which together articulate the American language... I was amazed, actually, to see how the children got it so fast and spontaneously. I'm also wondering how such a sophisticated way of speech is so universally successful... American speech enters every country and every other vernacular all over the earth."

"Additionally, - I said again - there are other forms of speech that an American is familiar with..."

"And what that would be? Larry inquired with surprise, believing that everything had been said on the issue, already.

"When you drive a car you're dealing with road signs, which constitute another plain language"

"Ho, that's true!" He commented.

"Today," I continued, "phone messages, and internet communications require another language, too!"

"I see" he concluded...

"So, it would be improper for that reason, too, to say that an American is monolingual!"

I was pleased to consider how coming in this country helped me to understand aspects of human behaviors and communications I never paid attention to before.

For a moment we were silent together in the cafeteria of La Roche.

Tableau # 14
Native Americans

I'M AFRAID THAT WHEN SOME AMERICANS WILL READ THESE REFLECTIONS on civilization in this side of the ocean, they will find everything evident, and maybe boring. Nonetheless, for us Europeans, entering the country in 1995, most of its cultural specificities were surprisingly unfamiliar.

Notwithstanding, it would be difficult for me, not to stress all these aspects, which, at first, looked so unusual, and appear, even for us now, so appropriate.

Native Americans, which Europeans call improperly Indians, and Red-Skins — which are received here as an insult, similar to that of "negroes" provide [sic] - have somatic traits easily identifiable. They also have specific rights due to their origin. They have the right to circulate freely, without a passport, between the countries of North America: Mexico, United States and Canada. They are officially recognized as the first inhabitants of the whole territory and, therefore, they do not need any document providing identification to live home. This feature would be not easily thinkable outside of the Northern America continent.

Actually, the native American are not the typical American any more. The whole characteristics of the U.S. today, shows the astonishing fact that today Americans come from every part of the world and, while living here, became a totally new entity. This country changes deeply everyone.

Among the original values: American flag is an "icon" which is always seriously taken. It is the summary of the values of the nation. It symbolizes the common engagement of different people, with different credos, in the same God. It calls for hard work to safeguard and promote "democracy", which is a combination of individual freedom, independence, accountability, and general concern for the common good. An official ceremony at a school, a university, or an administration, starts with all attendants standing, facing the American flag, and chanting the national anthem. In contrast to many European patterns, every US celebration begins with a general prayer [called invocation] and concludes with a blessing, headed by a minister, who can be religious, priest, pastor, or rabbi. After our arrival, the twins, who were in elementary school, told me: "You know, dad, when in the morning before class all sing before the flag 'America, America', in our heart we add 'France and Italy'". These worshipful behaviors in official celebrations show attitudes in total contrast with many European assemblies, in which emerge atheistic and secular patterns.

Landing in Pittsburgh International Airport, in July 1995, I sought a map of the city. To say the truth, it was not easy to find. Not at all. Decades of changes in the city made the map an unbelievable endeavor. After a few days, I finally found a Rand McNally who professed proudly: "Here is the Ninth wonder of the World: we have achieved the impossible! It is the first street map of Pittsburgh. Here is the map of the labyrinth!" The changes however are still in progress in Pittsburgh, and that map is already a historical piece of colorful paper.

In the 1900s Pittsburgh was the undisputed international capital of steel, with a wide working population. And the city was also deemed as the most polluted of the world. A white collar was required to change shirt at least three times per day to stay presentable. Inhabitants never saw the sun. The sky was obstructed by the fumes, which

obliged the lights of the city to remain lit 24 hours. This global role became a disability in the redeployment of the production of steel in the world, which happened in the middle of the century. In front of such challenge, Pittsburgh city government used this handicap as a cause of development: the city performed a spectacular conversion, which became a pilot action in North America.

The turning Point occurred in the fifties. Pittsburgh witnessed the most radical transformation which may exist in the world. In a few years the city was completely rebuilt: she became an international capital of electronic activities, glass production, medical care, computer management, banking, and residential homes. Entire neighborhoods were rebuilt. Roads got redefined. The old industrial plants became malls, museums, or leisure centers. An industrial Swiss director confessed to me: "A similar processing is not possible out of United States. It was sufficient that city government and some industrials agreed to the project and the conversion began… It was then executed without delay. This kind of cohesion, necessary for an endeavor of such magnitude, would be scarcely conceivable in Europe".

The urban change was rapid, effective, and enormous. Many thought the endeavor desperate and impossible. The course of action was brilliant and successful. Steel production was abandoned in favor of industrial and commercial activities, national and international conferences, services, banks. Today the city is famous to be one of the safest on the continent. The three rivers Monon-

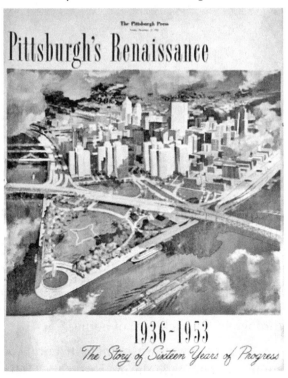

Pittsburgh's Renaissance

1936-1953

The Story of Sixteen Years of Progress

gahela, Allegheny and Ohio, deemed as a cesspool unhealthy and unproductive, is today a basin of crystal-clear waters and it is even frequented again by fish. It is an ecological model. Delinquency, formerly dominant, has been so well blurs, that since 1980 the city is considered amongst the first ten cities safest and most pleasant to live, in the whole nation.

Around the built-up area, nearly every family has its particular home, a dwelling on three floors, basement included, with garden, except in some neighborhood like Shaler, where erected by people of Dutch extraction, homes can be up to five floors, but are in the narrow, caught between other similar constructions, leaving most of the yards in the back. This kind of homes explains how outside of large buildings of the center the city extended. Since the township of Washington in the south until New Castle, in the north, there are 75 miles to go! And since Coraopolis, near the airport to the west, up to the Benedictine abbey of Latrobe in the extreme east of the city it is

at not so shorter distance. Paris, which certainly is a more populated city, is much less extended!

When a councilor of Washington Papal embassy, Antonio, came to visit us, shortly after our arrival, his first reaction was to ask: "but where is the city?" The answer left him speechless: "But you see it already, it is here!" he thought he was still in the countryside, because in 80% of the city you live in the magnificent site of an exuberant flora and fauna! Not be surprised then, when you see a doe passing through in the back yard of home.

Near its downtown point, Pittsburgh offers some architectonic configuration, made during the years 1960's, which anticipated the urban configuration of many European cities, like the 5th *arrondissement* in Paris, where square, roads, and building are integral parts of a same urban project. If you climb Mount Washington on the western side, you may admire the marvelous constructions of downtown area, bonded by the two rivers, Monongahela and Allegheny.

It would be improper to believe that Native Americans have nothing to do with such mutation. I don't know if similar transformation can be noticed elsewhere. In the same manner that it is impossible for a teacher to write on a blackboard if the lumber is not uniform, solid, and clear, such multiple change was made possible from a great culture of welcoming, of great silence, hospitality and magnanimity, all of which are included by Aristotle among the virtues necessary for people to develop and grow... It would to easy to ignore the background that made it possible for this country to become one of the best business, activity, culture, resources and management in the world... We cannot write a letter unless we have a clean good paper...

De facto, the whole Pittsburgh agglomeration develops from the mouth of the three rivers and grows accordingly. The point of the three rivers was occupied by the French soldiers of the general Duquesne, in 1745, who moved in from Quebec, following the Allegheny river, which flows from north-east, and they stopped at the crossing with Monongahela, which comes from South-east. Where the two rivers meet marks the birth of Ohio, which will throw 1600 km further in the Mississippi river. The word "Ohio" comes from its Indian name, which means "beautiful river." The whole countryside forms, in fact, a splendid scenery.

When the French Government abandoned Duquesne to its own fate, it had no other issue than leaving the place in favor of British general Forbes troops in November 1758. General Forbes named the place after the British Prime Minister William Pitt. and replaced Fort Duquesne with Fort Pitt. The surrounding land became the cradle of a new population gathering. The flow of German immigrants of the XIX century provided the name of "village of Pitt," Borough of Pitt, Pitt's borough => Pittsburgh. Then, a referendum of the State of Pennsylvania in 1827, decided, against all expectations, that the official language would not be German, but English, as it was spoken in the country.

Since then, all peoples who settled, by successive waves, in the urban agglomeration, speak the American language. Then another etymology of the name was "invented" on British sources this time: 'the fort (Scottish "burgh") of Pitt. Pitt City developed with the assistance of several European national communities, each settled in its own neighborhood: Italy central of Abruzzi in Bloomfield, the Poles at North-Side, Slovens and Croats to West-View, the Dutch to Millvale, the Austrians to Sharpsburg, not to mention the African Americans along Fifth Avenue, and Asian, especially Chinese and Korean, who congregate around McCandless. Each national community belongs to a proper neighborhood, which offers a common administrative.

After the end of Independence War, in 1783, a few French engineers led amazing improvements in US territory, including the cities of New York and Washington. I am probably the first astonished observer to see that: what the French made in this country, they never were able to achieve in France. The organization of streets and roads according to a geometric plan was never accomplished in the old continent. The configuration of the whole national territory and many cities was a pattern of grids like checkerboards served by roads and streets identified by their horizontal and vertical vectors, named accordingly, and numbered progressively from south to North, from West to East. The number of a road tells you where in the space between Mexico and Canada you are moving. Such a configuration makes it so much easier for an inexperienced visitor to identify the place and find his way.

I found many American travelers who were highly surprised not to find such an organization of good roads in the old continent. On the other side of the ocean, previous cultures did not manage to do so.

There are Americans, who never visited Pittsburgh and think the city has nothing special to offer. They believe it is not worth a detour. Actually, if you visited Pittsburgh before 2004, you would not recognize it today. The whole agglomeration increased fast, and everyone feels the difference! Pittsburgh is also one of the best American cities for job density. In our days Pittsburgh shows more job offers than many other places. Among my friends, whoever made some application recently got an immediate interview and finally got a job.

This was also my own experience. During the summer 2010, I became 65 years old. I made a job application and found a new job engagement that I intend to keep during the ten years to come... On these same days, many European cities witnessed strikes and manifestations of people protesting to refusing laws, which moved the official retirement age from 60 to 62, like in France, while a large amount of people suffer the lack of a job. The States show a completely diverse figure. Unemployment reaches the average of 12% in some European areas. The States have unemployment, too, but it seems that in this side of the sea people are more concerned with regular activities than eager to protest against governments using unemployment as an excuse.

To say the truth, there is also in Europe a general feeling of exasperation against authority and a social discontent expressed in a common and continuous belligerence, which does not appear so dramatically on this side of the seas. The reason may be due to the fact that European governments are the arbitrators of social and work issues, while in this nation people are supposed to refer to local authorities and use more common sense which, actually, is good sense.

The gathering of students ready to break everything on their way in the streets of Athens, Madrid, Paris, Toulouse, Lyon, Rome, Milan, and Turin, struck me. I would find it difficult to see similar gatherings in the States. They usually happen for the Marathon in New York or the Pro-Life protesters in Washington... which are annual commitments. It would not be so doable to gather all the students of Chicago, Detroit, Saint Louis, San Francisco, Boston or New York as it happens so easily in Europe due to a series of fact, among them emerge that university charges are too expensive in the States to allow students to compromise so easily their annual studies. When you are supposed to pay a fee of US $ 20-50 thousands a year just as a study fee, in addition to lodging and food: an insufficient grade in some field would make a student lose bank support and could not pursue studies. It seems that European students do not know similar contingencies, and on days of protest can only be something of a fun time without consequences to their studies. Additionally, American students have a job to cover personal expenses while most European students are still on parents' dependence. Demonstrating on European streets is a way of affirming some independence. In the States similar behavior would only be a sign of immaturity.

Major and rapid changes seem to be a habit of the agglomeration. Pgh (if you like shortening the name of Pittsburgh) is today a great center of social and economic activity, dramatically expanding. This is not the result of the circumstances but the fruit of a decision wished and conquered by its inhabitants along history, anticipating time to time eventual challenges. Rapid conversions of the past made it a present model of an urban project, in architecture as well as in ecology, culture and business. Since 1980s Pgh is among the first cities in the world for surgery and medical care. Its health quality and configuration also make it an important military place.

Universities also are an integral part of city striking growth. They concur to bring in the city students from all US states and from outside countries.

I do not dare to say that after I became so "Italian" as many of my siblings accused me of being when I lived in Rome, I begun here to become too much American. It could be so, and if it true, it cannot hurt me, for a true American never loses the proper roots. As a result, in case I have changed into a true American, I also remained a true Gascon! Of course, the experience I described is not only for the people and the cities I did encounter, for it is still in progress. America is immense! And I wish to say more.

Personal experience allowed us to discover the originality and integrity of what I dare to call "American Culture". I never could imagine that such a topic would someday emerge in my mind and become a true delight: discovering what makes this nation so appealing.

De facto, when I landed in Pittsburgh with my family, I used to think like many of my French or Italian compatriots. To say it in a few words, I simply believed that there is no such thing as "American Culture" and it would be just useless talking about it. I would eventually agree that a similar issue would likely be simple residue of external imports. Here comes appropriate to myself the amazing sentence of Aristotle: "There is not such a stupid idea that had not some good thinker to promote it." Yes, it is common overseas to consider that American culture does not exist. They eventually think that "It cannot exist." A similar consideration is deeply established in European hearts and heads, even when they say the opposite for distraction or courtesy. It also happens that some, who claim that such a thing does exist, still believe that, in any way, it is not comparable to "European culture". And so on…

Living in the States provided us the evidence that such a fact actually exists. I was wrong at first. Proverbial American simplicity led me astray. It took me time to realize that many nations, from all over the world, including European countries and not merely them… It took me time to see that the whole world, which is effectively represented in Pittsburgh recognizes a common identity under one flag with an original endeavor, which includes permanent friendliness, eagerness for hard work, acknowledgment of the excellence of others, admiration of good endeavors, desire and ambition to succeed, continuous optimism while fighting together with the hardship of weather and land, all of that being expression of the magnificent setbacks of absolute confidence in God. Notwithstanding, all of this is naturally organized in a way that shows to be simple, loyal, and honest.

Of course, there will be always someone to show that something is missing in American culture. Yes, something is missing. It is that which every new settler is going to introduce. American culture proceeds according to a continuous progress. Valéry used to say that every culture offers much more to everyone than what everyone would be able to provide to it. This was our experience, too. We surely received in this country much more than everything we were able to provide in return. It is a positive endeavor that started here for our family. Actually, what we found here rebuilt our family, which is more united now than it was at the time we left Rome. All being considered, it was a good endeavor to come. Yes, it was a wise decision, to make such a dramatic change.

Other topics surprised us, which are shared here and there along the pages. The whole context of daily behaviors in the US is based on a pattern which is unusual for foreigners. US society has its own specificity. It is not at all the European copy that many would like to expect, or dare to say.

Surely these considerations are the ones we made with the background we came from, and our recollection of Europe goes back to our arrival in Pittsburgh in 1995. Many things have changed since on both sides of the sea.

At the time we arrived here, all these aspects, that are now well understood, were full of surprises for us.

While living in America, we returned, a few times, visiting our homeland. And we were also surprised to find that over there, in the Europeans countries, many changes are ongoing.

As a result, I must say that, today, many of our observations, which were consistent at our arrival, in 1995, appear somehow obsolete to a new eventual current reader. Obviously, every new visitor or newcomer raises other perspectives and, at the same time, brings additional values, resources and contribution of improvement. It is the task of every newcomer to do so.

After twenty years of residence in the States, we are now part of the nation. Michel, our first son, also spent one year in Iraq and gives his share, as an American soldier, to the betterment of the nation.

If reading these remarks, you believe that some circumstances are inadequate, you probably got to the point where you understand better where we came from. In any case, while you're reading these notes, if I neglected to refer about something, do not hesitate to complete it by yourself. While doing so, you make the reading a dynamic endeavor with the book. Having an interactive reading is a first step towards the true way to address every work... Until a work is practically applied to life, reading it is not good enough.

In other words, these observations are not mere considerations... I wish they may help to understand the best of our civilization today to improve it, leaving what does not deserve our attention and keeping the rest. I hope that such considerations may help to receive the additional forces to come with new settlers and help a process of snow ball which would make things for the best.

All these notices, even the most interesting considerations on our tangible experience in this side of the seas are a pale painting in comparison of the colorful facts which stand behind. These observations, in fact, reflect the deeper reality that we all belong to. It is the multifarious and wonderful presence of a new civilization.

It is not easy to say so, but I'll try nonetheless to explain.

Every place is unique and provides nonetheless universal insights. Tangible considerations reflect a deeper quality of facts, which stands behind. Such a matter belongs to the same mystery of the whole world. It looks difficult to explain. It is, however, evident: every single being is an original expression of the whole world. And the variety of places and situations reflects the deeper diversity of their supernatural origin.

Yes, nobody may decide in place of anyone else. Everyone's relationship with the world and other people is unique, irreplaceable, and personal. At the same time, and even better, such a relationship with the surroundings is the direct outcome of the original connection every individual entertains with our Maker. Each one on earth is an unequaled expression of the absolute. As well as there are not two identical leaves in the whole world, every human person is the uttering of a single word that the Lord says once and forever.

As an outcome, everyone is both expression of God's love on his or her person and at the same time a point of articulation of God's love towards those in North America to understand it. And I have the feeling, that actually, this is the teaching that Native-Americans are providing today, through the generations of new Americans coming into the country, which they never cease to be the owners. It is, actually, more than a teaching, it is the same configuration of what we become, while living here.

Vice versa, spiritual entities are unique, too. Spiritual world is more sophisticated than the physical one. It involves more events, colors, situations, it shows greater diversity. Our relationship with the supernatural is various and personal, too. Our relationships take shape according to the person we deal with. We stay related to our relatives in afterlife in a specific way, which is different with each one. Even with the same person, the association does not develop in the same way according to situations and time. Again, it does not work the same while we have business with a particular saint or with another one.

Every Angel is unique, too. Even guardian Angels are special and not duplicated. Besides, there are several choirs among the Angels.

147

Each category of Angels is engaged in a specific task. Individually they have a specific commitment, too. An Archangel, for example, has not on earth the same function as another. Examples are given in the Bible: Gabriel spoke to Mary as the prophet of the Lord, Raphael healed Tobit as divine health. Michael leads the fight of angels against evil as God's fighters. Rael lost his beauty as God's splendor and became only Lucifer, the light provider. His "vocation" was to bring God's light, and he continues to bring light, but now he brings a dual light. His own existence is the living evidence that each one of them was free to serve as God's messenger or go away in their personal darkness. Even in doing bad a creature continues to show God's love.

Besides, having a connection with heaven is never a mere consideration, observation, or cogitation. Every time we think on someone over there, or we want to, we actually meet a spiritual presence. As immediate outcome something happens on earth accordingly. Pope Paul VI used to quote Elizabeth of the Trinity who said: "Every time someone looks up, the whole world rises up." To say the truth, every spiritual thought is not mere thought; it is a deed, too. The same can be said about our own relationship with the Persons of the Most Holy Trinity. Our relationship with each one is consistent, original, and true. Are we aware of the person we speak with when we pray? Is it the Son? Is it the Father? Is it the Spirit?

While traveling in France or Italy I was used to see Eucharistic Jesus under every church tower and entertain him along my trip. During the summer, I was joining my family at the beach in Tuscany, which is something like 200 miles from our home in Rome, driving on week-ends to strike the distance. Along the way, I was used to dealing with Jesus at every church tower. A similar behavior developed a great intimacy with the Son. It produced every time a rich dwelling of the Son in my life and made every driving trip a spiritual experience.

It does not work that way in the States. Under every church tower I cannot find every time a tabernacle with Eucharistic Jesus. Only Catholic churches provide such presence. Besides, there are not as many church towers visible from the highway here in the States. Oppositely, there is more room for plants, animals, and countryside along the way. Traveling by car in the States puts the driver more in contact with the whole of nature. Suddenly, a new enlightenment popped up

148

inside of my mind and of my heart: this country offers more opportunity to get a relationship with the Father. United States invited us to enter in a deeper relationship with the maker of the whole world, of which every plant, every animal is an externalization. This also was our experience while staying in the States.

Besides, driving in the States, distances are longer than in Italy or France. Driving from Pittsburgh to Texas, for example, when I go visiting my daughter in San Antonio or my hermit friends in Rancho Maria, Hebbronville, near Laredo, would be in Europe like driving from Paris or Rome all the way to Moscow. So, my prayer along the way gets a totally different configuration! The result of that intimacy with the Father makes a totally diverse mystical experience. At my arrival at Rancho Maria, near Hebbronville, Texas, I am filled with a great presence of God, dwelling in my soul, but this time it is the presence of the Father.

To say it shortly: in the footsteps of Adrian Monmayou, I learned that everyone would meet the Father in the whole of creation, meet the Son in everyone we encounter, and grow all along in the presence of the Holy Spirit. This precise spiritual experience was recalled to me, later, when I encountered the Focolare movement. Every true spiritual experience provides a specific original configuration.

What I said previously about meeting people in Pittsburgh and other places is even more strongly true among the spiritual entities, which are reflected by the physical world.

I was also taught by Adrian that everything has a specific function on earth because everything is out of love and has a unique connection with its Creator. Because of it, it will never be stressed enough how everyone is a gift to each one else and all the others, including the whole of creation, are personal gifts to each one. It is mysterious, but true. It is the same mystery of love.

Adrian's teaching prepared me well to find, understand and appreciate, years later, the spirituality of Chiara Lubich and the Focolare, which became soon my spiritual breathing. Adrian and Chiara were successively my spiritual tutors, complementing amazingly each other. The experience of the Focolare increased the awareness of Adrian's teaching and made our insertion in the States even more stimulating.

According to similar insights, each country shows a diverse personality and provides with its own people diverse characteristics... As well as every person we are associated with has a distinctive character and performs a unique vocation, every township, every community, every country does the same. Staying on this side of the ocean we discovered that the nation shows an exclusive entity, too. And America was now the cradle of our family.

While I am writing this tableau, I receive a letter from Marielle G. who is recounting the difficulties she has to go through while moving back to her native city, Lyon, France, after the few decades she spent in Rome, working for some Vatican entities. "I never thought that moving back home could have been so dramatic..." she says.

Among other reflections, my reply includes the following:

I experienced myself the feeling of being a foreigner in my native country the first times I travelled back to Paris, France, from the U.S.... and it was the same, months ago, in Rome, Italy, which was the country where Chiara and I married and our family grew up.

If I was supposed to move back to my previous country, either in France or in Italy, it would be very difficult for me to re-acclimate over there... for my heart and my mind are now accustomed to a larger space and less sophisticated laws, which allow us to work. For what I understand, contrary to what happens in Europe, it is sufficient to start a new activity, or open a new business to create work in the States.

Obviously, such flexibility produces outcomes and consequences... the whole society continuously changes. Since we entered the continent, we saw how a few years were sufficient to transform entire U.S. areas... Today Pittsburgh provides many more job offerings than people can apply for... A similar situation is the reason why the city is involved as a fast growing process... People are moving here from everywhere of the States and of the world... Part of the city was totally rebuilt during the last five years, and the surrounding hills, showing a wild country only some years ago are now malls, residences, offices. If you knew Pittsburgh five years ago you would not even recognize today its three-river fronts.

Think about some department store which, within two months, became a clinic, or a movie theater, which was transformed into a large parking lot, and further on a previous parking lot is now a food store... not referring, then, to the many businesses which closed and the many other which were built there, banks, auto-repairs, department stores, headquarters, offices... The entire city neighborhoods were transformed with the speed of a fairy-tale.

With my European eyes, I say wow!

When we moved back from Texas, during the summer of 2004, the whole agglomeration population counted around 1 million 750 thousand inhabitants. It grew up to 2.5 million today, in 2011, and it is still increasing. We were living then in the country; we live now in a new downtown. There was no need to move: it was the city which changed configuration around us... It is in a totally diverse city that we live in now. A few hills, covered then by woods, show now buildings, offices, banks, malls... Mounts and combs disappeared to become large hills supporting extended malls... Some large avenue, built to provide speed access between outside and the center of the city got new names from every day drivers who gave for example to "McKnight road" the nickname of "Nightmare Rd" because what was built as a speed road, ten years ago, is now a kind of slow promenade between malls. The size of the road did not change (or was even enlarged here and there), but car traffic did change. It is not a rush avenue any more.

'Try to consider for a moment the difficulties known by Mary, Jesus and Joseph when they moved back from Egypt to Nazareth... and, may be, you will understand our feeling when we moved to this country. They, too, knew the precariousness of immigrants... I'll pray that all of them may help you and us in the many ways they know, while our days are too short to address the most urgent needs.

Your short letter reminded me how the beginning of our sojourn in the new continent had been difficult... In moments where we felt lost and with too much to do, I found refuge in the present moment... confiding the past to His divine mercy and the future to His providence, addressing only, moment by moment, the emergency popping up in the mind... forgetting all the rest... You'll see good results soon.

151

In addition to the dramatic change that involves our process of moving from another continent, there is also the fact that the places we live in follows a proper process of change, too. I also must say that since we entered the States we had to move where the opportunity was the best for us. What we did may seem impossible to someone else. Reality bits fiction at times. Actually, we moved from one house to another, no less than 12 times in the States, including the moment we entered the country in 1995.

Driving back from Corpus Christi, Texas, which covers a distance similar to the one which brings you from Paris to Moscow, we had the incredible luck — understand the good care of Divine Providence — to find the house we had before and that our Real Estate Agent was unable to sell during our absence... So we got a place to stay when we moved back here, in Pittsburgh, during the summer 2004.

It would be useless to tell the number of furniture, clothes, belongings, books, notes, documents that were lost while moving from a house to another. There was a great advantage though: every time armoires and attics became lighter, but above all we got more unattached to things, our hearts became freer and we had a wonderful opportunity to start anew.

These words were only my way to tell you, Marielle, that we somehow understand your trouble. We pray with you the Lord in order you and us may understand what heaven want us to do.

But above all, trust the Divine Providence who closed doors for you in Rome to oblige you to move back to your native town, where Providence is expecting you for a mission that you cannot see yet. Notwithstanding there is no doubt that she is waiting for you and will help you in many ways. I would say the same for us. Providence brought us to a new continent, and the reason which brought us here, the need to become a family again, Focolare activity, friendship with the hermits of the Eucharist, assistance to the seers of Toronto are probably not the main reasons of our moving overseas. Each would suffice however to move into the continent. Sometimes we are the last ones to understand the evident task we're fully involved by God's Providence...

In one word, moving to this country made us typical Americans, for those who are not native Americans came here from diverse other country of the world.

It is almost funny of realizing that coming from outside makes us typical Americans. And here we are.

If someone had told us a similar change of identity, we had barely believed it.

Nonetheless, beyond the facts and our specific endeavor, every human story followed a definite pattern, for nothing happens at random, every endeavor has roots, the connections and outcomes that are difficult to see in the opacity of this world, but are clearly understandable under the perspective of our Heavenly Father.

Chiara Lubich used the example of a tree. Its foliage is proportionate to the roots. Also, the whole process is a combination of days and nights, cold and warm, rain and sun, winter and summer... She recalled the words of St. Teresa of Avila, that "joy and pain must remain the secret of our intimacy with the lord. Joy shows the care of the Lord, acting out of love on us, while pain manifests our way of returning our love to him. Both should remain the secret of our intimacy with the Lord, but the light that such intimacy provides is spontaneously disclosed". So is the tree, which receives water, sun rays, food, put down hidden roots and provides shadow, regenerates air, and show colors, but finally grows.

Our own lives are part of a divine history. The game of pain and joy is the frame of our growing process, and of our increasing relationship with everybody and with the whole world...

Tableau # 15
Cultural Shock

PITTSBURGH ALSO COUNTS A LARGE POPULATION of German and central Europe roots, who speak only English today. The city also benefits of an important Jewish community, very active and influential, living in Shadyside and other neighborhoods. You can see large synagogues all over the city, from South-Strabane to McCandless. There is also an important Muslim community with prominent mosques in Oakland and around.

Christian denominations communities are many all around. If you are curious to know the many cultural and national communities which compose Pittsburgh population it would area be sufficient to pay a visit to the 52-floor-tower, called Cathedral of Learning, in Oakland, which is the headquarters of Pittsburg University. You can have there a tour at the second and third floor of the national classrooms which recall the different populations that made up the city.

Overall, I would like to stress the spiritual maturity involved with sacrifices, engagements, breaking, commitments promoted by our installation in the new context: New activities also promote renunciation, development, reflection, and fervor towards new bonds. Teaching philosophy, speaking American, daily chores, administrative procedures, children's needs, homework, required us to work hard in this new cultural neighborhood and begun to change us before we became aware of it.

The many daily adjustments produced a true conversion in all of us toward the country culture we had entered. Physical accommodations involved spiritual improvement. All the new involvement contributed to the human quality and spiritual health of our family. It was for us almost like a fish changing water to live. We never could imagine before leaving Europe, how a parish community is demanding. It does not require just a visit to church on Sunday. In the States, a parish is a living community, a local business, a specific forum of education. It was not the same in Rome when we left. Every community involves a lot of participation. But also city neighborhoods have their identity, adopted by local people. We found ourselves involved in links and bounds that we were not familiar with before. I believe that such involvements are the key of a strong society. What they call individualism in the European places we were familiar with, does not exist here, we found something else that people use to call democracy.

Amazingly, on this side of the ocean, our family was built more genuinely than before. All involved changes have surely produced the necessity to work together, and it helped, but the cultural configuration of the place was the main cause of such impressive improvement. Obviously, a concatenation of causes was involved... Nonetheless, it was ultimately the fact that we were living in the States that made the seven of us a family again.

We finally were able to behave here as a family, while we weren't able to do it previously in Rome any more. Here we finally could eat together, walk together, have fun together, and pray. If that would be the fruit of "democracy" as they say, democracy is welcome. Maybe it is not sufficient yet. But it is in any case better than what we experienced before in Europe. For a while our future was uncertain. In spite of it, the whole life configuration on this side of the seas made our family life more intense, serene, and significantly enriched.

The Catholic families which we encountered around us manifested a surprising simplicity in prayer, which we were not accustomed to. Meeting with them is warm, even today. The Sunday following our arrival in Littleton, West Virginia, the whole congregation welcomed us with a warm applause at the beginning of the Mass and, at the end, they sang "Happy birthday" for my fifty years. I am still totally moved by such an enthusiastic welcome.

I discovered how common it is here, after Sunday Mass, for the whole congregation to be invited to get a coffee or a picnic offered by a parishioner. Parish population helped us greatly since we arrived, covering most of our needs, while we had not yet any job. They taught us the meaning of hospitality. They provided sheets, saucepans, towels, linen, blankets, and regularly came for news and to be sure we were OK! I will never thank well enough the parish priest, Fr. Hegg, and the parishioners of Littleton for what they did for us. I discover with them the true meaning of human values like conviviality, generosity, amiability, friendliness, and solidarity. Because of their warmth and welcome we began to be part of the nation.

In this country, people show a considerable amount of energy. They have an incomparable capacity to work. Each week students have tests in the classroom, and a mass of homework, and they like it. And homework needs to be graded, too. It is a kind of intense activity I was ignorant of before I came on the continent. Both high schools and universities are organized here after a model which looks like the one adopted in France for "*Grandes Ecoles*", which are specialized schools reserved for talented selected students. Here the method applies for all, without discrimination. Similar academic activity would suffice to exhaust most European people of my knowledge.

Additionally, students work besides their academic commitments to meet their personal needs. At a high school meeting of parents where Marie-Claire is studying, the director insisted that the parents not allow their children to work in town for more than 15 hours per week! This was the most unbelievable statement I ever heard before in Rome when no school student is allowed to take any work... Chiara and I understood then we had entered a totally different country. It was almost like being on another planet. How school students of this country could get energy to address job activities in addition to their school commitments? It was for me an unbelievable story, but it was real. Where do they get time and force to address a job? Marie-Claire inserted perfectly in that neighborhood and besides her academic activities she offered to make translations from Spanish into Italian using our home computer.

We made another unexpected discovery about American culture: the sense of parsimony. Before entering the county, we thought along with every person living in Europe that U.S.A. is the typical country of consumerism and of the throw-it-away! Is it not the country where it was invented the products called use-and-discharge-it? At the university, when I asked my secretary for an envelope to respond to a President's letter, I heard that for internal correspondence people are supposed to reuse the same envelopes. I thought it was a joke. Eh!

Well! It was not. It was standard behavior.

Here people throw away almost nothing. Later, to illuminate the campus, at Christmas, Duquesne used regular light bulbs placed in plastic bottles of milk, which had been consumed in the cafeteria. Can you believe that? And the result was fine! Even in the family, now, we are accustomed to do it. Most of the time, we throw away in the whole week less trash than the equivalent of what, before, we were throwing away, each day in Rome.

No, this America is not the society of consumerism, Europe is! Now we understand why the waste management workers come in the neighborhood to pick up the trash bins only once a week, and it is more than enough! We don't throw away most of the food boxes, for they are reused in the freezer, or in some storage area. Then, when, finally, an American throws something away, he recycles.

When the winter came, we needed to buy warm clothing for the children. A school director, middle class person, gave us the address of stores selling used clothing or of second choice where she used to go. That practice was another cause of amazement. We never did such a thing in Rome and surely we would never had the courage to tell it to someone else! Those stores like Goodwill, Saint-Vincent, Gabriel's or Draft helped us consistently. And those stores are not like small boutiques, but may compete by their size to some department stores. At the end of every season, if you have home objects or clothes which are no longer useful, you're not throwing away anything. People give to some endowment company like Veterans, Saint-Vincent, or parish containers or they put a sign on the street "Free", which means "Take, it is for you", or "garage sale" or "yard sale" and visitors may have pieces of furniture, stationery, grocery, and clothing for a few bucks... It works in both directions.

During our first year in Pittsburgh, we got a bicycle for Marta for $5, and Chiara was happy to find a tea table for $3. In front of similar behaviors, many European costumes look to us now as excessive consumerism. I remember the quip of a friend visiting us in Rome who said: "You know, the America of consumerism many talk about is not overseas, it is found in Europe, now'. He was right.

Americans are generous with their peers and other people. They would consider it inappropriate and strange not to help the poor and the needy. There is not a week that you are not offered the opportunity to help: it could be over the phone, at school, at the store, or even in office. Sometimes you are asked to sponsors a parish festival, some elderly residence, local donations, police and firemen associations, ambulances, medical research, and blood bank. I even saw at the university a lady who made cookies and sold them there for her own needs.

Most of the time, charities improve the living conditions of some in your own neighborhood. This is an charitable commitment that usually Europeans leave to the care of public administrations. Here it is believed to belong to private initiatives not to the state, not even to the federal government. Even universities or offices organize similar activities among students, teachers and employees. This practice still belongs to what they call "democracy." It is a typical local practice that surely deserves deeper reflection.

Another big surprise came from the field of religious activities. It differs a lot of what we were led to believe by French or Italian mass media. We met communities with living faith, as a complement of the blossoming of human dimensions. In Canada also, I met the same quality of ardent fervor of faith and prayer. As an example, shortly after our arrival, Marie-Claire went to an overnight at one of her comrade homes. She told us that her girlfriend was used, before going to bed, to kneel down at her bed for her evening prayers. She was surprised by a similar candor.

And her friend was surprised too when she knew it was not a usual practice in Europe. And her friend was nothing but a regular believer... There is no need to say that in church every week day morning there are between 30-50 people for 7 o'clock Mass. It is the same for the Mass at 8 a.m. and 9 a.m., and for noon Mass people in attendance are easily 100. I could verify the same level of attendance on week days in Pittsburgh, Boston, New York, Washington D.C. and Detroit.

On Sunday the churches are crowded. If you come late, you can barely find a place to park in the parking lot, next to the Church, and even a place to seat inside. Concerning the kneelers, they are more comfortable on this side of the ocean. And each church is accordingly equipped and better maintained!

Religious meetings show therefore here a particular nature: in addition to their convivial character, typically American, they also include the interfaith aspect, and even something else, difficult to define... Even among friends do not hesitate to pray before or after the meal, or when someone submits to you a particular intention; even over the telephone, it is not uncommon to pray together right away. If it is a priest who speaks over the phone, it happens that he gives you his blessing before hanging up.

North America is also an international surrounding. I thought before that Europe was international. After knowing how North America is, I changed my mind. People also read with an interest that I did not suspect the news from Rome and the Vatican. They appreciate the teaching given by the Holy Father. I found English editions of *Osservatore Romano*, the Vatican newspaper, in university libraries, and sometimes in the back of churches.

An interesting reflection would be needed on the school system. Many schools and universities are private. They do not depend on the State, neither for their accreditation, nor for their finance. It is an amazing structure, which at the same time provides quality and freedom. The accreditation procedure goes through partner institutions and does not pass under a national approval. Even if university centers follow the requirements fixed for state universities, they belong to a form of cooperation among peers. This also implies the sponsorship of religious communities and the involvement of local manufacturers and businessmen. They offer an education structure which is both independent, efficient, and adapted to the work market.

A similar educational system should be considered as a model to solve the many problems existing in Europe among similar institutions. It would be barely thinkable that students would like to strike or publicly rebel against rules that do not concern them. In Europe, the fact that every government is supposed to rule all business contracts and arrangements show the inadequacy of European society to address present situations.

Concerning religious issues, it must be stressed the importance given, by priests and parishioners, to piety practices often considered marginal in the European countries that we left. In addition to daily Mass, daily rosary, weekly way of the cross, there are numbers of other devotions, like scapular, novenas, Saints and Angels devotions, special restorative Mass attendance on first Fridays and Saturdays of the month, the 3 o'clock rosary to the Divine Mercy of St. Faustina, without forgetting the prayer groups Padre Pio. Often a meeting between friends ends with a rosary together! I am surprised. I was accustomed to more human feebleness and less courage to show faith in Rome. Private revelations also play their role. There are many pieces of information on the subject at the back of churches, merely considered for what they are, without prejudice and outside of excess in favorable or unfavorable comments. It is heartening.

A striking feature of the States is the fact that we found here a society where atheism is very discreet, or even non-existent! It's a contrasting figure with every European country where non-confessional labels are the pattern or every public endeavor. Excluding intellectual or university circles, atheism appears in this country as a foreign option, if not strange. It appears for what it really is: a biased option, a fruit of prejudices. On the opposite, the approach of faith is considered an integral part of any human approach. If the philosophy wanted to exclude, one would think that we want handicapping of the thought. Christian values dominate. In Littleton, West Virginia, which hosts no more than 150 inhabitants, there are three churches, including the Catholic Assumption church, the Methodist, and the Church of God... I shared with amazement my discovery of a country of believers with the Catholic parish priest who with surprising ingenuity told me, "if Christ wants to gather his Church, perhaps the United States will be used to start with, because faith is alive and the different communities coexist peacefully." Such a peaceful cohabitation is not due to an ecumenical option, as in Europe, but by the need to overcome together concrete emergencies and working together at society improvement. Hard weather makes better people. Convergence of needs coagulates good intentions.

Then, inter-religious neighborly relationships showed many diverse behaviors at variance with European habits.

Among many issues, it was surprising to detect that at a crossing there is not the traffic rule that gives priority to the driver who shows up on your right. That elementary rule of driving which regulates the traffic all over European countries does not exist in the States. Here what counts are not the signs but the people you come across. I wondered later if the absence of such a rule is what causes the atmosphere of friendship and cordiality that makes the traffic more fluent on this side of the ocean…

Driving back and forth everyday between West Virginia and Pennsylvania we found road signs we were familiar with, but some did not mean the same commands… Here in the States, a stop sign, for example, almost never appears alone at a crossing.. It is often placed on each of the four roads which make the intersection. So it is clear that another rule is involved when we know that in Europe a similar symbol indicates that the cars running upon the other way or ways have priority… Seeing the four stop signals together at a same crossing makes us understand that driving in the States is another endeavor. The first time I got "trapped" at a five- road intersection in northern Pittsburgh with a similar mark on each road, I got lost and truly did not know what to do, until one of the other drivers told me that it was my turn to go… I got surprised… My first thought was to consider that I had landed in a civilized country… I never met in Rome or in Paris another vehicle driver who invited me to pass. If they communicate you a wish it is to invite you to stay aside and let them go.

As a European driver, on the turnpike or the highway, I had to drive even more carefully, when the exit and the entrance of a car may proceed either on the right or on the left side of the way, which would never happen in Europe and would be considered an anomaly. Such varieties on the traffic pattern oblige actually the drivers to have more control and keep them more awake than in the monotonous European standards. When your attention is so continuously required, it makes the roads safer and prevents accidents. Besides, the lanes are not tediously the same as in Europe. They are standard, too, but in a diverse manner. First of all, North American roads are larger than the European ones and never change size.

Moreover, staying on a lane on this side of the seas does not keep you on the same position in the traffic as a European lane does. Supposing you drive in one State's highway on the right lane you may soon find yourself exiting on the left of the traffic if you keep that lane all along. If you want to stay on the right lane you must carefully change lane every time it is needed, for the lanes continuously change status. In Europe they usually don't. This tedious standard actually makes European highways less secure. The continuous changes in the lane pattern keep State drivers better awake and more caring of the traffic.

Beware again on the motorway, to turn left, as in Texas for example, you must cross the earth-full central, following a maneuver which is never allowed in Europe... It surprises Americans who visit Europe and do not understand that it is forbidden to cross this directional islet: they are surprised that this action is banned while there is no indication at all on the intersection to forbid so... Here is another case of misinterpretation for Americans driving in Europe... Here in the States prohibitions are written on intersections that are not supposed to be known by a general agreement. A general agreement on all roads does not exist in this side of the seas.

This European "oxymoron" is not the only one for American people. Europe has standard rules on its territory and don't care to recall them on the road. In the States, the rules adjust according to the place and the time of the day. Each intersection has its own rules which are clearly indicated to drivers and adjust electronically according to day time or week day in connection to the traffic. What is not prohibited is permitted, like for instance turning right at crossroads when you get red light, or turn left at red light, too, when you cross a one way street which streams toward your left. Identically, you may park backwards (while inwards is standard), or take exclusive expressways when two or more persons are in the vehicle... Most interpretations of road signs are implicit in Europe, while explicitly conveyed in the States.

Another characteristic of US marking: intersections are announced only once... and if you miss your crossing and ask for your path to a traffic policeman you risk a fine for distraction at the wheel and non-respect of panels, quite simply! Americans who visit Europe have the feeling sometimes that road administration assumes the motorists are people who are not very awake... to say the least. Yes, "why so many panels for the same information?" Then policemen over there are ready to provide additional information, too. In this side of the sea, a policeman is not supposed to be a road and tourist informer.

Also, in Europe, for what we remember from France and Italy, cross lights follow a standard schedule which is independent of the actual traffic... This is why it happens that you get a red light while no one is driving on the other road and no one is supposed to go through. A similar anomaly often induces European drivers to disregard the signal of red light for some places at some hours of the day, which can easily become usual to the point to provoke great car accidents sometimes. On this side of the sea, when a cross light shows red, there is some reason for a similar occurrence. Drivers know it and more easily respect it.

European traffic lights are placed at the front of crossings. It is there that cars must stop. It is a totally different figure in the States. Here traffic lights are placed after the intersection. Such a procedure requires placing the lights only once and drivers can see them at all time. To say it more evidently, when in the US if you stop the way you do in Europe, you have already crossed the intersection. And if the light was red you made an infraction. At every American crossroad you must stop before the intersection, look at the traffic and follow light and other directions.

Curiously, a similar behavior rules human relationships, too. People are supposed to arrive at meetings before schedule rather than on or after schedule. I'll be more explicit with an example. At a gathering in West Virginia with Sister Hue for a stroll with the children, the appointment was fixed at eight a.m. and, contradicting our Roman habits of arriving in the following fifteen minutes, we decided to anticipate the meeting time and we were very proud to arrive punctually at eight o'clock...

Being there at the precise meeting time meant for us that we were in early. It was even better than the usual fifteen minutes of Roman flexibility. Notwithstanding, we were unexpectedly almost insulted by the Sister who put it bluntly uttering: "You are late!" and supporting her words with a wounding look. We remained open-mouthed. Then we understood that for an appointment in this country, if you do not arrive early, you are considered in arrears. The French saying: "Before meeting time it is not accurate, after time it is late, on time is only punctual" has no worth in this side of the ocean. In this part of the US being punctual means to arrive earlier than what Europe requires.

For Europeans like us who almost never left Europe, unless for few days of vacation, it was surprising to live inside a neighborhood which shows diverse criteria of behavior and judgment. We came here believing that North America was a kind of extension of Europe. With amazement, we must admit that it was not. Everything is not only different, but it is even based on a diverse pattern. It's like American language: pattern and meaning are unique.

The day after our arrival in our new house in Pittsburgh, for example, I wanted to throw away our garbage as I was used to do in Rome every morning. Surprisingly I was not able to find any garbage bag on the side of the road. I checked a few hundred yards along the street... There was nowhere any garbage bag... I did not know what to think... "*Would it be possible that people do not throw away garbage in this side of the sea? What do they do with their left over?*" In spite of any reasonable supposition the evidence was there: with no doubt, this morning no garbage was left on the road side. I checked the situation during the following mornings... and my surprise increased... I wish I could ask my neighbors about that. First of all I wanted to be sure of not asking some strange question if those people had a totally different method of dealing with left overs, and second of all, and that was definitive, even asking I would barely understand their answer... So I decided to wait and see. I did not know yet that a similar behavior was a typical American one. I got my first lesson of pragmatism.

About the garbage there was no need to have it picked up every day as it happens in many Europeans countries... Here once a week is more than enough in almost everywhere in the States. When it happens that we talk in Europe about the consumerism society, we mentally refer to North America. It is actually more appropriate to define as such the European society than the people of the New Continent.

Difference in garbage management is only one indication. Besides, it is prudent not to leave around any garbage bins or bags during the week because the raccoons would open them and spread the contents in search for food. They are of an apparent great ingenuity.

One evening we saw them, from the large bay window of the veranda of our home. It was a whole family, standing on the grass, and looking at us through the large bay windows of the veranda. My first thought was that one of the children had made a joke, putting stuffed puppets out of the window to amuse me. Opening the door next to the yard, I saw they were not at all puppets but real animals. I got bent out of shape trying to give them food that evening. Since then, they came each evening to look at the menu of their evening meal. It had been very difficult for us to get rid of them. Even the dog was not enough and we had to protect him from them. They are adorable to see, but appalling to attend.

Their presence in town, in home backyards is due to the specific manner of inhabitants not to put fences around their properties. So animals run freely all through, from one house to another. There is a woods behind the house, on the flank of a hill. It gives us the feeling of living in the country while being in town. Because of the undulations of the ground, each house is necessarily at the foot, the flank, or at the top of a hill. The unevenness of the land, together with free territory to go increases the housing of wild animals around.

Here, we meet a large fauna near the house: rabbits, squirrels, chipmunks, marmots, opossums, raccoons, deer, sometimes even large wild cats (maybe bobcats?) or black bears (I saw them two or three times around the house), as well as a large number of birds, from the wild ducks with magnificent colors up to the red cardinals. The fact that the properties have no closure is more ecological and promotes the movement of animals and their profusion, even in the city. I am surprised that some protocols, such as that of Kyoto, have not faced the question of dwelling divisions which is one of the major reasons of animal extinction in Europe.

Discoveries were daily. After a few months in Pittsburgh, the amazements were far to be finished yet, they accumulated again. We were almost like in the *Iceman* movie with John Lone when the prehistoric iceman woke up inside of our modern scientific culture, which he was not at all familiar with… All the same, many endeavors were new for us and because we were lacking in the local language communications were poor.

Fortunately, here and there, we could find people who were able to speak Italian or French and help us along our steps of acclimation, while we were still in the process of getting the language. Anyway, even if we had been able to speak English when we landed in the States it would have been necessary to adjust.

United State language is definite. An American is not, and wants to be not a British. British language is misleading. The words may be the same, but they express a soil, a human context which is so diverse! You may speak English and understand American words, or phrases, without understanding anything of what is said. Being too confident in English language may lead you off the track. In England, a thunderstorm, or a storm, is simply "rain" in the States. vice versa, an American storm would be a catastrophe in England, it would correspond to what they call tempest, hurricane, tornado, and anyway a cataclysm. Significant is the fact that most American universities require that foreign students take a language test. Such a requirement includes the British. It is one of their first steps of enculturation.

Original also is the hierarchy of assessments. Beyond common ground of activities, differences show up that shape behaviors not everywhere the same. The configuration of criteria of excellence is therefore not completely homogeneous within the nation, but there are singular constants. Differences are clearly defined, from one neighborhood to another inside of a same city, as it happens among Europeans at the border between countries like France, Germany, and Italy. In the US different nations shape every neighborhood. Different people work together and pattern the society. A new notion of community is born:

The name of such a community is conviviality. It is the capacity to work and live together belonging to diverse national roots. When the distinctness is an Internal feature this variety is typical of American culture. The assortment evidences the presence of parallel zones of cultural expressions, who roam the nation. The cultural birth of people — African, Asian, or European — becomes here the characteristic of a category of persons, which is uniformly spread out from one ocean to the other, on the whole American territory. As an example, African Americans have the same speaking accent at Pittsburgh, Los Angeles, Washington, Detroit and New York, and everyone recognizes them easily on the phone. Oppositely, the Caucasians, which means European people, speak with a totally different speech pattern, recognizable all over the country. This is a typical American feature. It is not the same in Europe. In France, you do not distinguish over the phone people who are originating in the Caribbean islands or in Africa. Some of them are taxi driver in Paris and have the typical Parisian way of speech. In the US, every ethnic group has its proper pronunciation. The white Italians have the same inflections everywhere on the territory. The same can be said for the Poles, the Czechs, etc.

If before coming here we had been told about this conviviality we probably would not have believed it. We had to come here and see to understand that we had entered a completely new civilization.

"Latinos", are obviously present in Pittsburgh. I was surprised to find out that "Latinos" has nothing to do with the Romans and their language, but indicate the citizens of Latin America who are now throughout the USA and whose language, Spanish, became the second language on the continent of North America. They represent a significant minority. In Pittsburgh, they live mainly the collective buildings of Green Tree. It should be mentioned that for the inhabitants of this side of the ocean, America form two continents and the world counts seven continents (with Australia), instead of the five continents we were used to count while living in Europe.

In October 2009, in Pittsburgh downtown, at the "Meeting of the 20 most developed countries" president Obama presented Pittsburgh as a prominent city of the continent, which should serve as an example to many, including Detroit that must tackle a difficult economic challenge… He did the praise of Pittsburgh and not only because of its sports teams of American football (Steelers), ice hockey (Penguins), baseball (Pirates) and basketball (Panthers) which are world famous. He spoke of his works of avant-garde architecture, stadiums, and bridges which are important works of art. The city is in competition with San Francisco for the number of hills, with Venice and St. Petersburg for the number of bridges, with Miami for the number of retirees who selected the borough of Pitt to enjoy their last days. And president Obama praised particularly its economic success, which ex-

168

plains its exponential growth and the rapid increase in traffic despite of enlargement of access routes and of crossing highways through the city, and many other devices, such as expressways, reserved to "vehicles of high human density " (i.e. those which have two occupants or more) and which are of a single direction toward downtown in the morning and become one way to periphery in the afternoon.

As most American cities, Pittsburgh city has very few areas adapted to pedestrians. A similar configuration is surprising for Europeans. Usually those who live in downtown are the wealthiest people in Europe and those who live in suburbs are considered "series (B) citizens", which means "lower class citizens". The opposite is true on this side of the ocean. Living in downtown offers apartments which show not to be as wealthy and comfortable as the houses scattered in the surrounding areas, and the suburb townships; they are single family houses of two or three floors with yards, often neighbored by a run or woods... On this side of the sea, wealthy people live in the suburbs, and the in areas nearer to downtown live low class inhabitants. Some large areas, however, like Shadyside or Squirrel Hills are like suburbs islands inside of the central large agglomeration... Compared to Europe, American urbanism has surely a diverse connotation in the States.

A difficult note must be added at the end of the tableau...

Beyond the facts and our specific endeavor, every human story followed a definite pattern. Ultimately, nothing happens at random, every endeavor has roots, connections and outcomes that are difficult to see in the opacity of this world, but are clearly understandable under the perspective of our Heavenly Father.

Chiara Lubich used the example of a tree. Its foliage is proportionate to the roots. Also, the whole process is a combination of days and nights, cold and warm, rain and sun, winter and summer... She recalled the words of St. Teresa of Avila, that

> *joy and pain must remain the secret of our intimacy with the lord. Joy shows the care of the Lord, acting out of love for us, while pain manifests our way of returning our love to him. Both should remain the secret of our intimacy with the Lord, but the light that such*

intimacy provides is spontaneously disclosed. So is the tree, which receives water, sun rays, food, puts down hidden roots and provides shadow, regenerates air, and shows colors, but finally grows. Our own lives are part of a divine history.

The game of pain and joy is the frame of our growing process, and of our increasing relationship with everybody and with the whole world...

I already referred how in Rome I had clearly the sensation of being prepared to leave the excellent position I had in the Vatican. Deeply inside, I knew I was ready. Such a feeling was so strong that for a while I thought that I was in the process of dying. Not being sure about how to handle that strange awareness I went to visit my confessor, Fr. Joseph de Finance, at the Gregorian University. De Finance was 91 years old at that time and was well known for his simplicity and sageness. He gave a different interpretation of my feeling. "In spiritual life", he said, "When people feel that they are going to die and they are ready for it, it often means a great adjustment is in progress in their life." He insisted; "You're not going to die. More likely a great change is coming forth and a new life will soon start for you". I got surprised. During the same period, however, consulting with Giuseppe Zanghì, a Focolare philosopher, the answer was confirmed.

Both were right. A few months later our whole family was leaving Europe for the New Continent. Our journey had begun in a totally new neighborhood. Yes, the feeling was right, we are dead, already, from our previous life. The cultural shock is not just a surprising new life, it is a totally diverse living, almost like moving to another planet.

Nonetheless a big notice is necessary here to make. This book should be considered almost as a historical narration, because everyone coming from Europe today, would have a total diverse surprising discovery.

What we found in this continent provided us a surprising environment which would be barely the same today from those coming from Europe, because in the meanwhile, the whole European country has changed a lot.

Tableau # 16
Mister "C"

EVERYTHING HAPPENED QUICKLY. A character of Pittsburgh intruded in our life. John Connelly, a rich industrialist, who wanted to

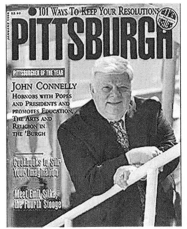

establish contacts in Europe, decided to meet me. He called me one morning offering to see me downtown for lunch at the Sheraton Hotel, which he owned. I refused.

My answer surprised him deeply and excited his desire to see me. My refusal made him more enthusiastic about me: I was the first in years who refused to meet him, while he was almost harassed by numbers of requests by people wishing to meet him and seeking for some favor... I saw later, with amazement, how entire tables of his home, and desks, at his company offices, were covered by letters and notes of those asking for some help. They were calls from all parts of the nation. John, or Mister "C", as his collaborators used to call him in office and beyond, had a few secretaries working for him on these mail inquiries, at the seat of his business, in Noblestown Road, Pittsburgh, where he was running 14 companies.

It was the first time in his life that someone refused an invitation to his share. He could not endure it. He called again later. I reminded him that one of the reasons why I left Rome was to be able to live together with my family, away from Embassy parties, Vatican social gathering, or parish entertainments. I explained to him that it was not my intention to start social relationships, that could prevent me from enjoying family life. I was not supposed to be part of associations or exclusive clubs again, even if he belonged, I was sure, to a group of very good people, leading interesting businesses.

As a reply, he invited me and my wife to dinner at the Sheraton hotel in two days.

"But we'll go nowhere without our children" I replied.

"Bring them, too" he said.

"There are five" I added.

"I know" was his comment.

"They are young, too" I insisted.

"I know " he said again.

At this point there was not much to argue. I told him over the phone: "Please hold on a minute, I want to ask my wife what she has to say..." Talking with Chiara, we could not find a reason not to agree... and I told to Mister "C" we accepted his invitation.

On January 6, we had then an excellent dinner, all together, at the Sheraton, with Mister John Connelly and his daughter, Audree. The whole restaurant room was almost empty because of a snow storm all around the city. During the meal John Connelly asked us if we liked the States. Receiving our enthusiastic answer, he asked if we would like to stay here. We immediately agreed, explaining, however, that we had no prospect of business in Pittsburgh after the coming summer. As a result, he offered me a position of adviser in one of his business companies, in addition to a teaching position at Duquesne university, which he knew was in need of a philosophy teacher. He was going to provide the money that was needed for the position.

Here is how, during our dinner at the Sheraton with Mister "C" our future in the States was settled.

Then as "*Cacio sui maccheroni*" (cheese on the top of spaghetti) as we used to say in Italy, the meal ended up with another gift. Before leaving the room, he called the Chef: "What are you supposed to do with so much left over from your kitchen, today?"

"Well" the man said, "You know better than I that I have no use for it"

John continued: "Do you see this man?"

"I see him" the Chef said.

"He has a large family," John added.

"I can see that," the chef confirmed.

John insisted: "He also has a large car"

The chef shook his head: "It's good to know".

And John concluded with: "Please fill his car with everything you can from today's meal!"

Looking at the number of boxes that were in process to be carried out to our car, Chiara looked at me with some concern, "How would we put all these blessed goods?"

I put her at peace: "We actually have in the basement another large fridge that works. "John, who was observing us, assented with a large smile, which made his bright face even larger than usual. We all were very happy. And we got food for a whole month… And it was, actually, excellent food.

A few weeks later, La Roche College announced to me the termination of the contract for the end of the academic year. John Connelly, who was used to support Duquesne University, offered us the opportunity to continue our journey in the States. Now, it would depend on me to deserve his trust.

Duquesne was founded in 1878, by The Holy Spirit fathers. It was classified among the country universities as "very competitive", with a student enrolment of almost hundred foreign countries. Duquesne is also the place where the Charismatic movement was born in the world, before choosing to settle down in Ohio, at Franciscan University of Steubenville.

To tell the truth, when I had the opportunity, later, to visit Steubenville, I loved the site and the spiritual atmosphere of its campus. I even had a deep moment of prayer in the *"Porziuncola"*, where, 24 hours a day, students adore Eucharistic Jesus. I admired the place,

with the small adjacent cemetery, which hosts the body of aborted babies. I found there a conscious experience of the Gospel, and I had the strange feeling that the Lord wanted me to come there and teach, so inside of the chapel I asked the Lord for the grace of teaching there someday. I was not surprised, afterwards, to find in the campus a walk along the *Via Crucis*, and points of meditation, on the main stages of Franciscan way. Worthy of notice is the campus church, so crowded during the three daily masses that students leave their bags out of the doors to make more room inside.

Soon many new contacts emerged and kept me busy. I loved the exceptional site of the University of Notre Dame du Lac in Indiana, just south of Michigan Lake (7 hours driving from home). Answering the invitation of the Ukrainian community, I also used to go from time to time to Toronto, Canada (6 hours), passing by the fantastic scenery of Niagara Falls (4 hours), the Focolare community of New York (9 hours) or in the Marian Pilot City of "Luminosa", near Poughkeepsie, New York (8 hours), not forgetting Rancho Maria, Hebbronville, Texas (Driving for 3 days – Pittsburgh-Hebbronville having the same distance that Paris-Moscow), or a prayer group I met in Monterrey, Mexico (it takes a day by bus from the ranch), and Catholic Solitude in Littleton, West Virginia, (2 hours) where the appointments were weekly, for a while.

These new contacts required a lot of driving. During the first year of our journey in the States, our car covered near to 40,000 miles (around 60,000 km to say it in European manner). To say the truth, I love the way the Americans drive: it is generally peaceful, quiet, regular, sure. Apart from the expressways in the outskirts of very large cities such as New York, Chicago, or Washington, I have rarely seen drivers speeding. Using the large motorways is relaxing. For the first time, I'm taking the endeavor of driving in this country as a living experience. In Europe I used to consider driving as a lapse of time between business matter, or as a gap between things to do... Here it is a completely different dynamic.

Driving is an opportunity to think, to enjoy the road, to admire the landscapes, to reflect on a meeting before or after it. It never was that way in Italy or France before. Over there, driving is like a fight, which does not provide you any moment to think peacefully. Besides, a European car is a tool. Here in the States, a car is a second home. It is a place to eat, to phone (from a phone booth, without leaving the wheel — before the diffusion of cellular phones), to bank, to shop, even in a drive-in of some pharmacy. Many people in the U.S. have a second pair of shoes, and sport clothes in their car, to change before engaging in some new kind of activity.

While we were living in Rome, I used to go home to change cloths. Here the car is the first place to resort to. When I visit the Focolare center in Washington, D.C., almost every month, I very much appreciate, how comfortable it is to drive for five hours... and be perfectly efficient when I get there, for the meeting. Driving in this country is not a commitment, it is a rest. In fact, I am so pleased to drive here, thanks to the regularity of the traffic, the capability to program the journey with precision: knowing clearly the time needed on the road from town to town.

In this country, a car is an extension of home, and the other drivers look like neighbors. Relationship between drivers develops accordingly. For the first time in my life vehicle traffic is not a battlefield, but a living neighborhood. Other drivers are fellow companions rather than competitors, of even hostile rivals in the attempt to go through. The contrast is striking. While driving in Italy, when a motor vehicle gives you signals, whatever it is, it claims priority of passage. On the roads of the new continent, I got surprised of traveling between civilized people, who give also signals to tell you to pass, as it happened to us so many times.

Meanwhile, Mister "C" kept me busy with his business.

Most generous as he was, John Connelly showed also to be greatly demanding to those working for him. I could verify it when one day he came with his Cadillac to pick me up at my place, to bring me, immediately, to his private plane in Pittsburgh. We flew, then, up to New York, where we embarked directly — i.e. without going through any check point — in first class to an intercontinental plane, flying towards Rome, Italy.

In four days, in Rome, we had to do such an amount of business that, for the first time in my life, I understood what "work" actually means. I'm not even sure if I could sleep more than eight hours in all these days. That was really intense business. And the comfort I was offered did not replace the rest I would need. Nonetheless, such a comfort surely helped. He asked me to make many phone calls in Italian for him, to getting appointments, then attend several important meetings…

He was even, for a few months, thinking of involving me definitively in some of his activities.

I always said "NO" to his offers.

My anxiety over teaching philosophy was too much present in my heart to make me accept, as a definitive endeavor, any other endeavor. All through these days, I was more than ever anxious to teach, and to teach philosophy. It seemed to me a non-sense starting to do mostly business. I could accept to do so, for a while, and help Mister-"C" the best I could.

And I have the feeling that in many occasions I made him happy.

Over all he made us all happy to have come in this country.

Tableau # 17
Duquesne University

Mister "C" kept his words. The following August, I started teaching at Duquesne.

It was a *tour de force* teaching in a language that I only began to speak the previous year, just after landing in the country.

Sometimes epic misunderstandings happened, but the students showed positive attitudes towards foreigners, and got accustomed to the most un-graspable accents: many teachers are Latino, Chinese, Japanese, Russian... A French-Gascon, as I am, did not surprise them.

What I did not know was, that Mister "C" asked Duquesne to keep me under near observation, and report regularly to him, for making him aware of the quality of my teaching. He wanted to be sure that I was good enough for what he promised to Duquesne University.

Duquesne University, was actually, pleased to hire me.

They put me in a class in front across the corridor, in front of the secretariat, and left the door open. In that manner whoever was in there could follow my teaching. It was not unusual to hear their comments.

At that time, my English was too poor to get their comments, but good enough to understand I was concerned by their opinions and these remarks seemed very favorable. I even had the feeling that their observations were willingly made about me and they wanted me to know.

In any case, I was too much concerned to running the class to find the time to offer too much attention to these observers, that even the students could notice. Nonetheless, I do remember the kindness of the students who were helping me in many ways, raising sometimes questions, just for the purpose to made me aware of the right pronunciation of some words which were said by me with too much of the

French accent, and even sometimes, with the full French pronunciation. Such a cooperation from, the students, did surprise me greatly.

It is useless to recall that, even at Duquesne, I continue to carry with me, what I called, my "portable dictionary", which was an unabridged, large size, *Websters' Third New International Dictionary*, of almost 3000 pages, inside of a tote, so that I could consult it at any time, anywhere. There was, notwithstanding, the only inconvenience that, sometimes, that dictionary was not enough to avoid my confusing American language, with some typical British expressions.

Nonetheless, I had the chance soon, and almost every time I was teaching, looking for the students to easily correct my mistake.

I was deeply surprised, however, when John Connelly called me, in September, to tell me that my teaching was good, not only understandable, but also consistent and original.

Wow! This man does not leave his deeds to chance. He wanted the assurance that his gift was appreciated, both by me, and above all by Duquesne university.

Meanwhile the position of teaching at Duquesne had become beneficial for the whole family. Yes, we became able to continue living in this country and improving our whole life here. And, amazingly, we never have been such a good family before entering this country.

On the side of the children, they inserted and studied efficiently at school.

Marie-Claire studied so well in her first year at Saint Vincent School, that North Allegheny High School offered her to skip one year ahead of class for graduation: she made together in one year the last two academic years of study.

At Carson Middle School, Marie-Thérèse was well appreciated by her comrades and teachers: she received the special prize of the school for the student who made the greatest learning enhancement in a single school year.

Michel attended the same middle school.

Marco and Marta had the chance to go, half a mile from home, to Peebles elementary school.

All of them receiving everywhere a warm welcome.

They made many friends, and never get a chance to be bored.

Additionally, they also had homework to address every day, after they return home. We were told, in Europe, that American schools were not too much demanding. We were told wrong, at least considering the schools of our sector. North-Allegheny, where the schools got several times the Blue Ribbons from the White House due to the education quality they provide.

And they intend to keep deserving such an excellent reputation.

Chiara soon got offers for teaching Italian, Latin and for providing some tutoring.

Notwithstanding, before we received the Green Card, she was not allowed to do so. This is why she had to refuse any business opportunity, in order not to compromise our process of insertion into the States. For the first five years, I was the only one who had a working visa. Nonetheless, this limitation was finally an advantage for all: it made her more concerned with the whole family issues and needs… and her industrious endeavor, in similar businesses, was determinant for the children study, and the comfort of us all.

All being considered, taking into account all issues, during our process of adaptation, disadvantages and newness since the beginning, the balance was positive. We were pleased to be here, busy with our new challenges, addressing everything with serenity and quietness. We knew that nothing was decided yet for our future, and we remained each day attentive to the eventual invitations that Providence might provide through the circumstances.

In one word we were happy. We unwillingly activated the words of Gascony wisdom: "Happy people are those who are too busy to be aware of it."

We wouldn't have experienced such serenity in the middle of our daily concerns if we had been missing that consistent friendship with Fr. Patrick, founder and hermit of the Brothers of the Eucharist, whom we previously met in France. He is the one who invited us to join him in the country. His American background provided us the double advantage of providing us explanations for our many demands and supporting us not only spiritually, but also giving on occasion his help as concrete aids..

To say the truth, it was Fr. Emmanuel de Floris, the Hermit of Montmorin, who was also, through my father, a good friend of Adrian Monmayou, who urged Chiara and me to stay near to Fr. Patrick Meaney. He probably knew how both Fr Patrick and us could be helpful to one another.

That solid friendship with Fr. Patrick, has been the background, which always encouraged our endeavor, supported by the welcoming behavior of Pittsburgh inhabitants, rich of their typical American conviviality, and, time to time, by occasional friends, like the parish priest and the parishioners of Littleton, West Virginia, who hosted us the first two weeks in the country, and provided then furniture and appliances for our home in Pittsburgh.

Many other friends followed. It would be impossible not to quote here the continuous friendship with our roots in Rome, with Chiara Lubich, who wanted to greet all of us before we left Italy, and Don Pasquale Foresi, who wanted to celebrate the Eucharist, which we all attended, as a blessing for our endeavor, on this side of the ocean. and with the members of the Focolare. They all were present all the time in our daily life.

Obviously, we must refer, here, to Fr. Emmanuel de Floris, who previously was a Benedict monk in the Abbey of En Calcat, and later became a hermit in Montmorin, on the Alpes Mountains, where my father used to meet him, as he did previously at En Calcat... .

Fr. Emmanuel, had been encouraged by my Father, to receive, in his solitude, the visit of Adrian Mionmayou.

It is in the chapel of his hermitage, that each one of our children got their First Communion. We were used to going there almost every three months, leaving Rome after work in the evening, and driving the whole night, arriving in Montmorin the following morning. We usually stayed there, each time, for a few days.

Every time, I met Fr. Emmanuel, at the hermitage, it was a wonderful moment of friendship, of enlightening, but also of updating. A reciprocal updating. It was for Fr. Emmanuel the occasion to verify the notices he had of the Vatican Curia, and for me, to know many topics concerning the social and political situation in the whole world.

It was through the same people of the township of Montmorin that I got the surprising notice. Actually, I was told by them how Father Emmanuel was so well informed concerning the whole situation in so many places throughout the world.

They informed me how it happened that some afternoons they were ordered by the local police to bring home their flocks earlier that day, for they could not get out of the village in the evening, when the whole area would have been surrendered by special security forces.

They explained to me that, in those evenings, a chopper would land in the field of the solitary dwelling in some area near the new monastery or the chapel, and someone would come out to converse and seek advice from Fr. Emmanuel.

It was usually, most of the time, some authority, belonging to some European government, who needed insights in his own business. This is why Fr. Emmanuel was so well updated on the social and political situation in France, Italy, Germany, and even Russian... And, surely much more than what I can really say.

I was impressed to see how accurate were his pieces of information. It was something that I could barely get from the news. When some authority had started to meet him in such a manner, many others followed, from other areas of the world. And every time, the personage coming with the chopper was so well comforted in his concerns that, soon, the news spread out.

Fr. Emmanuel is the one, who strongly encouraged, Chiara and me, to stay in touch with Fr. Patrick Meaney. He probably knew that Fr. Patrick would leave Montmorin, and return to his ranch in Texas, and such a friendship would have been a reciprocal blessing.

De facto, at the onset of our new residence in the country, we used, every month, to spend a weekend in the hermitage of the Brothers of the Eucharist in Littleton, West Virginia.

The children enjoyed playing in the surrounding woods, where they easily met deer, marmots, raccoons and an unlimited quantity of wild birds: pheasants, turkeys, peacocks, redbreast, and the astonishing hummingbirds.

More than once, one of the children met, nose to nose, with a she deer, or its small offspring, to say nothing about the squirrels, of all sizes and colors, which abound everywhere in this country.

The place offers, to visitors, solitude, peace, recollection, meditation, following the manner of the old *"lauras"* of the Middle-East… It is both a place of retirement and of spiritual training, rich of human and spiritual education, an irreplaceable meeting of Christian life.

Meanwhile, at Duquesne I continued to learn English while teaching philosophy.

I was compelled to understand philosophy in a new manner, because of the context of the new language. It was really a discovery. And I am grateful to Duquesne for giving me such a wonderful opportunity, to move deeper in metaphysics, and in introduction to philosophy.

Tableau # 18
A Trip to Montauban

SIX MONTHS OF OUR PITTSBURGH SOJOURN HAD PASSED when I was asked to meet Bishop Roman Danylak, in Toronto, Canada.

Bishop Danylak was living in Italy, during the last years, while we were also living there. The first time that, actually, I was suggested to meet him, it happened at the south of Rome, when I visited Emilio and Claudia Pisani, who held him in great esteem.

They invited me to reach him. It was the first occasion for me that I heard his name. Emilio and Claudia are the editors of Maria Valtorta writings on Jesus' life, elaborated as an extensive version of an additional Gospel.

Then Thiara and Mirta, from Monterrey, Mexico, wanted to reach Josyp Terelya, and asked me to get in touch with him. Josyp was a Ukrainian, who, because of his faith, spent 24 years in Soviet Concentration Camps.

While Josyp was still a child, his parents, too busy to take care of him directly, because of their commitment with the soviet party, asked one uncle of him to take him home and make his education. Since then, Josyp Terelya became a believer. His belief was a spot of shame for his parents, who were two KGB officers. They even did not know that the uncle was Catholic.

When they took Josyp back, at the age of 16, they discovered, with horror, that in the meanwhile he had become a Catholic believer... Here is why they asked the police to put him in prison. They were convinced that, because it was just young, it was a childish infatuation, which they could easily make him freed off. They thought that Prison could have been a good training for his future career, would have offered an excellent experience of reflection and had surely induced him to change his mind.

It did not happen as predicted. Josyp's belief did not weaken. They decided, therefore, to abandon him there... They even asked the guards to kill him. Surprisingly, when the other prisoners understood what was going on, they prevented such an endeavor to succeed. They threaten to destroy the building if someone had insisted to torture Josyp. As a result, in spite of several attempts to kill him, operated in full agreement with his parents, Josyp survived in prison.

Thiara and Mirta wanted to communicate with Josyp. I had no idea how to reach Josyp at that time. I was told that he lived in Toronto. Here is why I decided to contact Bishop Roman who was Ukrainian, as well.

I drove to Toronto with Chiara. The traffic in Toronto looked confusing to us. It was not easy to find the place we were directed to, but we did. We finally stopped in Franklin Avenue. The appointment was at the bishop's house, in front of the Ukrainian Cathedral. We were walking on the side way, near that house, when Chiara noticed a beggar at the door of a house. She got surprised. She asked me "What a beggar is supposed to do at the door of a private home?"

I could not tell why, but at that very moment, I knew that the man at the door was not a beggar, and I replied: "The man you look at is the bishop. He's expecting us!" Chiara's comment was eloquent: "It's impossible. It cannot be!".

To say the truth, when you are fresh from Rome, as we were in those days, it's difficult to imagine a bishop dressed in beggar's cloths, with spots and holes, as occasional decorations. Nonetheless, I was right: the man at the door was the bishop.

The Bishop had no clue about me. He did not know, who I was, when I called him over the phone, a few days before, asking for a meeting in Toronto. Knowing however, during the phone call, that I was a previous civil servant at the Vatican, Bishop Roman decided to test my manners. He couldn't be even so sure that I was not a spy entrusted to refer about some of his diocese's endeavors. People, like him, who have tight connection with the behaviors of eastern European territories, under the soviet regime, have always reasons to be suspicious. When he realized that his game was over and saw me laughing at his joke, he totally changed his mind about me and Chiara. We became friends at once.

Then, when I told him that I was looking for Josyp Terelya he understood better the reasons of my coming in Toronto, and he said that he was his spiritual director and he would manage for us a meeting with him.

A good relationship had already started between us and we spoke freely about several issues. During the conversation Bishop Roman spoke about seers, living in Toronto, who came from Kibeho, Rwanda. They had been forced to emigrate from Kibeho, Rwanda, into Burundi, and later up to Canada.

One of these seers, Ernest, had interesting issues to tell. I offered to help the bishop for his work of discernment on Ernest and, in order to introduce my expertise on the field, I told him about my previous familiarity with seers, when I was a child in France.

Bishop Roman knew, actually, about Gilles Bouhours and his private audience to the Pope in May 1950, but he did not know that the one who brought Gilles inside of the Vatican to meet the Pope was Adrian Monmayou.

It was in that occasion and in the following meetings that Bishop Roman suggested that I gather additional pieces of information on Espis. Here is why I had to organize a trip to Montauban, where is the seat of the headquarters of the Catholic diocese, which Espis depends on.

Obviously, I could not make the trip officially under such a purpose. Another acceptable reason to go was easy to find. It was a long time since my Mom had had the opportunity to spend a few days in her home, which is, precisely, in Montauban. So, I offered my siblings to have care of her, there, during the following Holy Week.

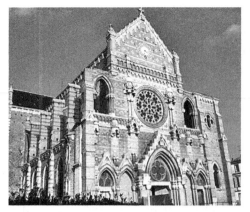

My mother was so happy to have the opportunity to pray, during the Holy Week, in Saint-Jean-Villenouvelle, which is the church where she used to go, every morning, to attend Mass, together with my father, when he was still alive. It happened even better than planned: as soon as my mother knew that I was expected to visit France she immediately asked to see me.

Everything, then, was organized accordingly. And along with the trip over there, I asked to meet with the current bishop. Unfortunately, Msgr. Bernard Houssé, Bishop of Montauban, asked his secretary to tell me that he was not available to talk about Espis.

Later, as soon as I was back to Pittsburgh, I wrote down a report of my journey, a copy of which I sent to a few authorities, including him, the Catholic authority in Montauban, who subsequently acknowledged it.

There follows in the Tableau 20 the translation of that official report. It is the original text. I only made the amendments necessary to make it understandable in the article.

Some issues stress topics which have been already shared in previous tableaus. It includes however important news concerning the events of Moissac, to indicate otherwise, which were the events of the Espis woods.

But before presenting the full report of the journey, please allow me to furnish you with a few pages of interesting background information about the town of Moissac along with a brief account of the "Apparitions of Espis", which miraculous events are source and center of all that follows in this book.

Tableau #19
Moissac

MOISSAC IS A SMALL MEDIEVAL TOWN, LOCATED IN THE NORTHWESTERN AREA OF MONTAUBAN. Its inhabitants live by agriculture, breeding animals, corn, grain, and above all on the vine. The white grapes are reserved more for the table than to make wine. The famous "Chasselas" grapes are known for the regions. It's also a place for escape and vacationing where river houses face the gentle-moving Tarn.

The town is a tourist center. Visitors stop at Moissac to see its medieval structures such as the Gothic churches built in the 12th Century. Even more famous, is the Cluniac Abbey of Saint-Pierre. Throughout the centuries this monastery became a major pilgrimage church appreciated for its Romanesque structure.

According to a local tradition, in 507 A.D. the Frankish King Clovis founded a priory, which is an important church with a community of priests who gathered and prayed together to evangelize the local regions. A century later, the priory was transformed into an Abbey by Saint Didier, bishop of Cahors. The surviving of the monastery was difficult because of raids by the Moors and Norsemen, which allowed the structure to evolve into a fort until, during the 11th and 12th Centuries, the monastery of Moissac became affiliated to the Burgundy abbey of Cluny. It received the name of Saint-Pierre and became an outstanding masterpiece of Roman and Religious art.

Upon the outside walls and entrance gate of the church, the designs depict and retell the history of the monastery and its involvement with the community that eventually grew around it. Because

of the articulate and story-telling designs, this artwork served as a kind of teaching panels for the people, who wanted to relive or retell the course of their surrounding history. Even the cloister inside the monastery was artfully manifested, which was a square-shaped courtyard with a walkway built around. The member priests and monks of Saint-Pierre, would meditate and pray while walking through this square hallway and relive the church's rich history with each passing step.

Much like today, and for many years now, the rosary serves Catholics as a piece of prayer which helps relive the mysteries, miracles and life of Christ, these columns surrounding the cloister served as an opportunity to meditate and reflect on the courses and motions happening within the history of the Saint-Pierre church.

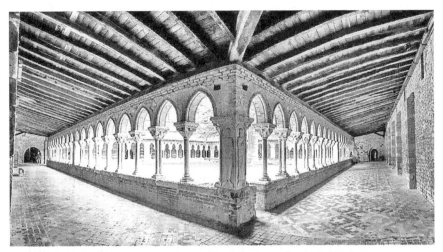

In the year 1201, roughly three miles northeast of Moissac, on top of a hill named Espis, the local monks built a small church dedicated to Our Lady of the Pines. This was a time of great evangelization, an epoch when Saint Dominic and Saint Anthony had been preaching in this area of France. Saint Anthony was sent to evangelize Gascony by Saint Francis of Assisi in person.

It was on the side of the hill, covered by woods, where extraordinary events began around 1946 and 1947. At the time, a local newspaper published an article untitled, *The Apparitions of Espis*, which recounted some facts and unexplainable happenings that took place in those woods.

Here are some of those moving events:

Thursday, 22 August 1946

Today was the second time that the church celebrated the feast of the immaculate heart of Mary. Around five in the evening, two children, Nadine (9 years old) and Claudine (5 years old), took a flock of geese for a walk out of the house. They were walking on the grass that stretched the length of the Espis woods when suddenly they became surrounded by a great light. From forty feet away they saw, just to the left of the wood line, a stunning woman. The vision paralyzed them, but the woman said to them,

"Come. Do not be afraid."

The young woman was very attractive in appearance, but the two girls took flight and ran away. As they ran, the young woman sent them a kiss. They run all the way home where they tell their mother what they had just seen. They tell her that the woman was dressed in black, her gown was decorated in daisies without the yellow center, of which half the petals were white while the other half were of many colors. She wore on her head a diadem made of brilliant pearls, much like that of a queen.

The mother of the two girls decided she would go back to the woods with her daughters, but the girls refused. The following day, toward the end of the day, the girls finally agree to descend from the hill with their mother. With them, came also their friend Marcelle, 11 years old, whose parents work for their mom as farmers and live upon the hill across the woods.

The mother didn't see anything, but she noticed how all three girls were watching something spectacular. They would later tell her that they saw the same lady fifteen feet into the woods. They would later call the spot where they saw the woman "the altar" because she appeared on top of the short steps built because of an embankment digging into the terrain. This time the young woman was wearing a white gown with a celesta belt and a small crown with white roses. On her left wrist hung a rosary of which the white beads became brilliant. The crucifix and the small chain holding together the rosary formed a yellow light even brighter than the beads. The woman seemed poised in prayer with her hands touching flatly at her breast, wearing a smile.

190

Her eyes watched the sky, but, every once in a while, her eyes would gaze on the children with kindness. This tableau lasted only a few minutes.

The same thing happened the following day. The woman never spoke, but simply smiled at the three children.

Sunday, 25 August 1946

That morning, Marcelle saw the Lady at around 8:30. She was wearing a light blue dress. The encounter lasted only three minutes. That night, Madame B., who lived on the side of the village church, went into the woods with five of her daughters: Suzanne [14], Jacqueline [12], Odette [10], Jeanne [8], and Carmen [6]. The Lady is seen by all six of them, including the mother. They all saw her, dressed in white with a crown of roses on her head.

Jacqueline took courage and asked, "Who are you?"

"I am the Immaculate Conception."

"And what do you want?"

"Prayers."

Then the children saw written in the sky, *"I am the Immaculate Conception."*

Since that day, Jacqueline would see Our Lady almost every day in the woods, at home, or at the Jeanne-d'Arc boarding school of Moissac.

She continued receiving the visit of Our Lady until the end of the following month of February.

Most of the time, the Lady was dressed in white with a matching white or Celeste veil, holding a rose by her feet. In two or three occasions, Jacqueline also saw her dressed in black.

When in black, the Lady looked sad. The other times she always appeared praying, every once in a while, watching the young girl, smiling.

Her younger sister, Odette, also attended the same boarding school and saw the Madonna. The two young children were always filled with a great joy around the Lady, and prayed often.

Wednesday, 28 August 1946

The news of the extraordinary events had been, then, spreading all throughout the township of Moissac, similar to a trail of gunpowder catching flame. The people began flooding to the woods. Some came to pray, many others out of curiosity.

Thursday, 29 August 1946

Around a hundred-and-twenty people went to the woods.

Amongst them, there was a school teacher who brought with him a few students, to show them that any manifestation from above was impossible. "The supernatural doesn't exist, and these things are just illusions or matters of suggestions", he said.

He had not finished talking, when one of his students, the young Pechberty fell in ecstasy.

He was unable to speak, his eyes fixed on something that provoked admiration on his face, filling him with a joy without expression. To his schoolmates, he looked illuminated and glowing.

He stood just above the steps in the woods, and descended slowly toward the rest of the group without leaving that happiness behind, following the appearance that overtook him. He alone was able to see it.

Then the vision stopped on the lowest step. The boy stopped and turned to face up into the woods, remaining in ecstasy.

After a moment he turned to the people and said, "The Madonna wants you all to come to your knees."

The group obeyed immediately and the boy recited the rosary as the crowd responded to the prayers.

A little while later he stopped and said, "The Madonna says to rise. It seems that she doesn't want you to become tired." And he continued reciting the rosary.

Some of the schoolmates, out of curiosity, came closer to the boy, but Pechberty told them to stop.

"Hold steady. Can't you see you're about to run into her?"

When the rosary was finished, a few people asked him to address the Lady with a few of their questions.

So he asked for them, "Will you make a miracle?"

"Yes, a miracle will come."

"What do you want?"

"I want your souls."

"Will you make yourself seen to the adults?"

"Many of them are not suitable."

Then the child asked the Lady to heal one of his companions, André, who had not come to the woods with them. André had been paralyzed for over six years, with a broken spine, after falling from the Moissac watermill.

The Madonna told them to ask the boy to come and see her. Then, she would be pleased to heal him.

Friday, 30 August 1946

The crowd who came to the woods had grown even larger. Over two thousand people visited Espis Woods at once by now. The main road is filled with stopped cars, with so a intense traffic that the Mayor of Moissac had to send the region's national guards to help direct the flow of incoming cars.

The immense crowd stood in the great field, stretching between the woods and the road D957. There, the people awaited the promised miracle, but did not pray. Overall, the people remained quiet and respectful in their waiting, not noisy and not complaining.

Amongst this large crowd, a smaller group of about a hundred huddled, just before the wood line, watching the three steps.

Just then, one of the girls saw the Madonna, and a great voice spread through the people saying that the paralyzed André refused to come to the woods, therefore the miracle would not come.

Just then the young Pechberty had entered the woods, from the upper region of the woods, and ran down with his eyes fixed on something that dragged him closer to the three steps.

And even though he ran fast and didn't watch his footing, his steps never failed him as he crossed the rippling folds of the woods with vines sticking out and loose dirt and ditches in the ground. Around ten of his schoolmates tried to follow behind but struggled, keeping their own eyes on their footing.

Once he came to the lowest step, Pechberty fell to his knees and shouted, "The Madonna asks for your prayers."

Pechberty had come late to the woods because his mother didn't want to accompany him because of the heavy criticism, which accused the boy of inventing the whole charade.

Finally, the mother decided to come with him, and this is why they had come from the upper left section of the woods.

Amongst the children who could see the Lady, Marcelle asked the Madonna what Huguette needed to do to regain her sight. Two years prior, when she was twelve years old, Huguette had become blind from a hunting accident.

"All she needs is prayer," responded the Lady.

That same night, a young girl of nine-and-a-half, Paulette, who lived eight kilometers away, in La Madeleine, decided to come to the woods after dinner with her cousins.

When she came to the steps, she saw the Madonna. Maria was dressed in white, and her crown was even brighter than usual. The Lady's hands were hidden by her veil as she smiled.

Around fifty people or so were still standing in the grass field by then, and as soon as they realized that the young girl could see the Lady, they surrounded her to direct questions to her.

Until eleven o'clock that night, the Lady would disappear and reappear at each question.

At each coming she wore a different gown, white, rose, black, golden… often with a bright halo, and other times with a crown, but always in the same place.

As this went on, Paulette asked, "Are you going to make a miracle?"

"Yes, but you will not see it, because you will be sick at home."

Around eleven that night it was time to return home, and the cousins struggled to drag little Paulette home, even as the Madonna accompanied her for a brief section of their way home.

The Espis booklet contains 5 more pages of narration of events, which I find useless to reproduce here. They do not bring anything new, or very different and would be useless to be reproduced without specific comments. It will be eventually interesting to provide them in due time… with appropriate comments.

It is necessary, now, to insist on the fact that the message given to Gilles Bouhours was provided by Our Lady during the events which characterized the apparitions in Espis woods of Moissac during those years.

Some commentators affirm that in the same manner that Our Lady confirmed, in 1958, in Lourdes, the dogma of the Immaculate Conception, She confirmed, in 1948, in Moissac, the dogma of the Assumption.

Other similarities characterized the apparitions of Our Lady, in Lourdes and in Moissac.

The father of Gilles, told me, that a few priests, including their parish priest, encouraged separating Gilles from the other visionaries of Espis Wood, in the same manner that the ecclesiastic authorities separated in Lourdes Bernadette Soubirous from the other children, who claimed to see Our Lady in the Grotto of Lourdes. It was said that there were around 40 in Lourdes, while in Moissac they were less than 20. Such efforts to hide that information were successful.

Also, several booklets have been published on Gilles Bouhours, and almost all tend to ignore the role of Adrian Monmayou for the visit of the child to Pope Pius XII. His parents, actually, wanted to organize that visit by themselves, disregarding the request of Our Lady to put Adrien Monmayou in charge of that endeavor.

Gilles was entrusted by Our Lady, to bring a specific message to the Holy Father. Gilles travelled twice to Rome, with such a purpose.

Obviously, for the first trip, Gilles went to Rome with his parents and failed to get an audience, which would allow him to talk directly to the pope.

Sometimes, the few accounts on Gilles omit to relate that for the second trip, Gilles was taken to Rome by Adrian Monmayou.

When the parents Bouhours brought their child to Rome, in December 1949, and made public the purpose of their journey in Italy, all the local papers reported the visit of the child to the pope. In fact, they arranged for Gilles and his parents to be part of a public audience to the pope. His parents were happy, then, and were convinced they had accomplish what they believed was the purpose of their travels. They were sure that everything was done. Unfortunately, while traveling back to France, Gilles told them: "We have to come back to Rome and see the pope again, for I was not able to tell him the message of Our Lady". Such a statement left them speechless, and they finally allowed Adrien Monmayou to take care of the new endeavor.

Worthy of notice is the mission of Gilles to the Pope. The manner in which they entered the Vatican was somehow unusual. Msgr. Martin told me that Adrien and Gilles went to the bronze portal, at the end of the colonnade, on the right side of St. Peter square. Something happened then, which surprised all those who witnessed the event.

Yes, for the second time, when Gilles traveled to Rome, it was Adrian Monmayou who led him to the Vatican. Among the booklets referring to Gilles, several disregard the fact that Our Lady did ask for Adrien Monmayou to lead Gilles to Rome from the first travel, his parents, however, decided to disregard the suggestion of Our Lady, and wanted to travel in person, with the result that we know.

Besides, Gilles' travel to Rome is only one of the endeavors which characterized Espis events. To explains such a statement, it would be sufficient to refer to the processions, and other celebrations regularly organized in Espis woods, with all people around led by Gilles. Numerous are the witnesses, who were part of it.

Later, unfortunately, when Montauban bishops, Msgr. Théas and Msgr. de Courrège, for fear of letting some deviation from the true devotion get started, provided a warning which opposed any manifestation in support of the Espis events, the whole situation changed. And many of the persons near to Gilles, including his parents, tried to separate the whole life of Gilles from the events of Espis, even if it was properly in Espis that Our Lady called Gilles to come from Arcachon Bay, and spoke to him. They tried, in this manner, to provide Gilles with more favorable conditions that would allow the ecclesiastical authorities to deal more freely with his business with the Pope. They wanted to make easier the investigations into his endeavor. I dare to think that human "prudence" will never twist the Divine Providence.

The attempt exerted by Gilles' parents, together with ecclesiastic authorities, to separate Gilles endeavor from the experience of all the visionaries of Espis, contributed partially to make Gilles personality more acceptable in the view of the institutional Church. Nonetheless, it is more than probable that such a procedure did not allow access to the full teaching of the Moissac events.

Human prudence is always a poor endeavor in front of the work of Divine Providence… Nonetheless, even a wrong endeavor, if it is so, continue to serve the will of God… Almost in the manner that Augustine spoke about the original sin as a *"felix culpa"*… an "Happy Mistake" which induced, later, to the word becoming flesh… Because nothing is strong enough to oppose the work of the Lord… inside of creation, even if it will never interfere in a manner to alter the proper relationship between human freedom and the grace of God.

Maybe, the events of Moissac teach us how heaven is near to us on earth, and we must persevere and never give up to work and walk in the grace of God, like Elijah did for forty days and forty nights up to the mount of Horeb, which was the place where God was expecting him... We must do the same, knowing that all the heaven surrounds us all the time...

Then, from such an endeavor, Our Lady will lead us where we are supposed to go... as She did with Gilles... Let the Lord work inside of our lives. Nothing may oppose the Divine Providence, including the game between our freedom and the work of Divine grace...

Then let us work according our own call from above... and, with the grace of God, let us do it without giving up.

Among the few excellent messages that Petit Gilles left in my

heart, pop up the words he told me at Moissac, on 17 August 1953, while we were visiting him after a trip in the Pyrenées: "Two days ago, on Assumption Day, Jesus and his Mother were sad because people did not ask for the many graces they were ready and willing to provide..." Even today, these words resound strong in my heart. They continuously enhance my spiritual endeavor, and push me to ask for hope and trust, especially when news look bad.

Other events followed... Many others... There are too many to report here.

Events happened for years, with almost every day frequency, in that place of Espis woods, especially between 1946-1950. Most of the time a full encyclopedia wouldn't be sufficient to gather fully what happened in a single day. Fortunately, we receive and get much more than we are able to fully understand. As Jacques Maritain suggested: "We understand first with the heart… we may explain later through the head". This is why St Francis of Assisi suggested: "Preach through your endeavor first… then, when some words are needed, you may also speak…"

Saturday, 15 August 1987

On April 15, and on August 6, in the lapse of four months, Raymond, my father, and Joseph, my brother, died. My brother had been buried just a few days before. My mother and I wanted to go to some shrine of Our Lady to pray. Lourdes was too far away for her. She could not endure a drive that, back and forth, would have taken the whole day. We decided then to go to Espis. Back and forth was doable in a few hours on the same afternoon.

A long time had passed since our previous visit, there. Consequently, it was a surprise for us to find the shrine of Espis protected by a fence and closed with a gate. The gate was locked. I really wanted to enter the shrine, and my mother, too…

I asked her: "Mom, give me the key"

"I don't have the key!" she said.

I insisted: "Please, give me the key to your place". She did but, afterwards, she was stunned, and couldn't stop repeating: "… But… this is the key of <u>my</u> place" - "But… this is the key of <u>my</u> place"…

Meanwhile, her key opened the gate of the shrine, and we could enter, driving the car. Then, we prayed inside in a few places. We prayed in the Chapel, on the top of the hill, then at some altars in the woods, where some tracks were left, and we finally got some water from the source…

We drove home afterwards, happy of having got some intimacy with Our Lady….

When we arrived home, in the evening, I asked her, "Where do you want me to store the water bottles coming from the shrine of Espis?"

Her answer breathed sageness: "Put Espis bottles together with the water we received from Lourdes. It is the same water!"

For Mom the many places where Our Lady and His Son, Jesus, come to speak on earth have no difference. They are places to meet God, as well as every Church and Shrine. People have no need to raise a crusade for any of place of private revelation, as they call them: if the Lord is not heard somewhere it will speak elsewhere. It is that simple. Besides, for those who go to church, there is no need to other sources of information from above. These private shrines, however, are places where the Lord shows that Church is dependable, congruous, suitable, and consistent. Yes, Church teaching does not provide chimeras.

This is also the teaching of Fr. René Laurentin about the many places where Mary comes today to recall the Gospel teaching. Mary and Jesus are the same everywhere, and there is no need to make distinctions, neither between those place of private revelation [as he himself call them] nor between those private place and the Church. They eventually complete each other, not about the doctrine, but about the pedagogy of the Lord. What people do not accept by the main door, the Church, they often notice better from the window, the private messages. The picture, however, is the same.

All things considered, it would only be confusing to oppose what comes from the same source. All together Espis messages complete our catechism, they help to better understand matters of charity, hope, faith, and the Kingdom.

"Put them together, it is the same water."

Her answer was comforting.

Tableau # 20
Reporting on the Trip to Montauban

Here now is the journal I promised you in Tableau 18:

A Journey in France

I'm back from my travels in France.

My leaving was in answer to the call from my Mom who said that she wanted to see me before she died.

To say the truth, this same journey was also properly arranged and directed by Divine Providence.

Mom expressed seriously her great desire to see me. She spoke over the phone, from her hospital room in Rouen. When she knew that I left Pittsburgh, she felt better and she considered the possibility to join me in Paris, and then, even to move down to Gascony by train together, towards her place in Montauban. And so, we did.

Wednesday 1 April

When I landed in Paris, at the airport Charles de Gaulle, I felt I was a foreigner in that country which is my native land… Paris is the city where I lived during my studies in Sorbonne. Fortunately, Prof. Dr. Geneviève Contesso invited me to visit her place, where she has the talent to make everyone comfortable and feeling at home. Every Wednesday, and it was Wednesday. She used to received home a few friends for a gathering.

I did enjoy that little "Academy" there, which is a sharing of opinions and ideas towards a common reflection and better understanding. Without even being aware of it, many of the youths, who are used to attend such meetings, are spiritually regenerated, and deeply enriched there. Similar gatherings have produced, in the past, great philosophy schools. I met good friends that evening, which I would be glad to talk about some other time…

Similar meetings recalled to me the Cercle of Meudon, organized by Jacques and Raissa Maritain, while they were leading weekly meetings in their home in Meudon in the neighborhood west of Paris, after they came back from Germany, and before they moved to the U.S. together with Vera the sister of Raissa.

Thursday 2 April

I could renew the good tradition of making a pilgrimage to Rue du Bac, walking through Paris streets, my bag on the shoulder and my American cup, full of coffee, in my hands. Later on, I was before the altar of Our Lady, to whom I had so many things to recount. I also had to thank her for my earthly adventure, including the members of my family. All friends were present in the conversation. I put everything that I know and everything that I did not know in the meeting. I prayed for those who are in need and for those who have already left to move up to heaven.

I had also a special prayer for those that I was going to meet, and for the situations which would occur during my traveling… and the people I would encounter.

Leaving Rue du Bac, I was expected by Claire and Franklin at the Archives of History Sounds. Their museum keeps the sound testimonies of many events of universal history. We discussed together about common friends, like father Thomas Philippe, O.P., which was, until he died, the animator of "Faith and Light", the movement started by Jean Vanier, also known as "The Ark".

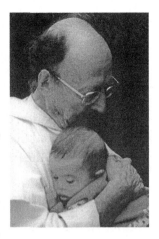

He was the elder brother of father Marie-Dominique Philippe, O.P., founder of the Brothers and Sisters of Saint-Jean. We intensely talked about father Patrick Meaney, who started in Texas and in West Virginia the Lauras of Catholic Solitude. We also referred to Joe Terelya, the Ukrainian leader that I met in Toronto, who suffered for his faith in the prisons of a communist regime and was miraculously saved there by a direct intervention of Our Lady, and who, since then, has been responding to her invitation to work towards the renewal of the Church.

Friday 3 April

My brother Jean-Marc picked me up and together we visited several members of the Focolare Movement in a few places they stay in Paris. It was the opportunity to meet again some of them I was familiar with before.

Saturday 4 April

Mom reached us. Our sister Marie-Bénédicte and Alain, her husband, who live in Rouen, brought her to us. On Palms eve, during the celebration, we faced a case of conscience: one of Jean-Marc's children expressed the desire to make immediately during Mass her first Communion. Knowing that the joy of Jesus to enter a heart is even greater than the desire which he himself inspires inside of those who desire to receive him and checking on the spot that Carole had the adequate preparation, we could agree that her request would be granted.

Sunday 5 April

On Palms Day, Mom and I took the TGV [High Speed Train] at Montparnasse station. The trip was excellent. It was especially an opportunity to engage with Mom. Even if we did not talk that much, through one another, the communication was great. She was happy. I could see it. In Montauban, then, I had the joy of seeing again the house which was our family home since I was five. I wanted to revisit, one by one, each room. I especially spent time in the oratory, where, until they lived there, Papa used, once or twice a month, to spend the whole night in prayer. I also get some rest in the grotto, which he built in the back yard inside of the garden where he loved to get moments of rest and meditation during the day. There still was the statue of Our Lady, which he had been pleased to put there. The whole time I spent in the house and the garden were days of nostalgic recollection.

Monday 6 April

A letter reached the house with the mail. It was from a Canadian bishop. He was requesting my help to collect information regarding the apparitions which occurred in Espis woods, near Moissac, from 1946-1950. He was asking to me, to document the story of supernatural events, supported by conversions, witnesses, eventual miracles like extraordinary healings, such as the one of my sister Marie-Bé, or that of Marthe Rigal. He was asking for everything I could gather concerning the celestial phenomena observed and the eventual messages given by Our Lady.

The bishop knew that in the days of these events, I met the seers personally. Similar to what happened in Lourdes in 1858, almost 40 children claimed to benefit from celestial occurrences; but just as in Lourdes, only Bernadette was bearer of a mystical mission, in Moissac only three children, Paulette M., Robert A., Gilles Bouhours, and an adult, Adrian Monmayou, had been strongly endowed.

I knew them all, because I was used to visiting the Moissac area, and particularly the Espis woods with Raymond my father. Even if I was only five years old at the time, many people and situations abide in my mind forever. I was too young, however, to remember all. Nonetheless, some facts marked me profoundly, and I still remember them. Among those incidents, the deeds of the farmer, Adrian Monmayou, mayor of the neighboring village of Lunel, who emerges with his astounding conversion, which was detailed in Tableau 8.

All the other seers were children. These events have gradually been forgotten by all of us, especially because we were forbidden to talk about them at home after 1950. It was because of an order by the bishop of Montauban. When my father died, on 15 April 1987, my brother Joseph came in our home, and tried to organize the large amount of documents, files and other pieces of information filling the house of Dad: the home desks, bookcases, and furniture. While doing so, he regained references to the Moissac events. When he asked me about it, everything returned to my mind so clearly.

Joseph and I asked Mom why Papa never spoke of the Moissac events inside of our family after 1950, when actually we moved from Montcuq (located 10 miles at the north of Moissac, but belonging to the diocese of Cahors) to Montauban. She answered in plain French: "The Montauban bishop, Msgr. de Courrège, forbade him to ever speak about Moissac. He was allowed, however, to eventually answer questions, should he ever be asked about it".

When she said that, both Joseph and I had like a blow to the head and we understood in a flash the immense suffering which tortured Papa for years and to which we were witnesses, even if we could not understand the cause. The inquiry on Moissac thus became the main reason for my sojourn in Montauban.

The bishop's letter referred particularly to the child Gilles Bouhours, to whom the Blessed Virgin requested, "go and say to the Vicar of Christ on earth, that I never died, and went up to heaven with my soul and with my body".

The child then asked to his parents, "Who is the Vicar of Christ" and "Where does he live?"

He asked again insistently.

"It is the Pope in Rome", he was told.

"Then we must go to Rome!" — and he urged his parents to make the trip.

After the public audience of 15 Dec 1949, while his parents thought they had satisfied his request, on the path of returning in train to France, Gilles said: "We must return to Rome, soon. There were too many people around, and I was not able to tell the Pope what was needed".

His parents were shocked. They suddenly became ashamed of not having performed Our Lady's explicit request that Gilles should be brought to the Pope by another person. And they were not ready then, to repeat the journey.

A few months later, the second trip was made. This time, complying with Our Lady's request. **It was Monmayou, who made the journey with Gilles.**

"Gilles had 5½ years when he got by a phone call, please, the path to the pope inside the Vatican", said to me Mgr Martin of the French Seminary in Rome. "Gilles got a private audience, on 1 May 1950, during which he put forward the message directly to Pius XII. It was Msgr. Montini in person, the future Paul VI, who took care of him in the Vatican." Later Gilles talked about this "small Monsignor, who asked me to be recalled to Marie in my prayers."

The message of Gilles consisted solely in the assertion of the dogma of Our Lady's Assumption, which Pope Pius XII promulgated a few months later, on the 1st of November 1950. Many Italian newspapers reported then the visit of the child, unusual messenger of Our Lady, to the Pope. They also published his photo at the Bronze Vatican gate.

I was invited, thus, to collect material on Moissac. I refer in my notes to Moissac because the town is better identifiable on the map that the small woods of Espis, on the edge of the departmental road 957, where these events started. I also like to think that these events are associated with the splendid mediaeval cloister and abbatial Church, Saint-Pierre de Moissac, which, along history, witnessed many deeds of charity, asceticism, and holiness.

Tuesday 7 April

In the morning, attending mass I met across with Msgr. Jean Vernette, Diocesan vicar, which reminded me that a month after the proclamation of Assumption Dogma, the former Montauban bishop, Msgr. de Courrège, officially uttered the statement that "at the end of the month of August 1946 began to occur in Espis and in places nearby, around Moissac, extraordinary facts" which "have hardly discontinued until now."

Nonetheless, he stated that the movement which begun with these events "does not present any mark of divine inspiration." He then, consequently, uttered: "Therefore similar occurrences have no supernatural origin". This judgment, I hope, will be reviewed, some day.

Not being sure of how to start my inquiry, I decided to put everything in the hands of Divine Providence: I put myself in prayer, and I simply drag Bishop's letter, inside of the photo album, that I carried with me everywhere I was supposed to go in order to show to parents and friends and tell them about our life in U.S.A. Since that day, I met a lot of people, among personal and family friends, who were visiting our home, to say hello to me and my mother.

Since then, there developed far and wide, almost spontaneously, a movement of information. The question of Moissac started to become popular. The news was spread by words of mouth, and a few people showed up willing to see me. Robert A., one of the first seers, who was eight years old at the time, made me understand, beyond his own words, or in between if you wish, how deep he had been wounded by the sort of persecutions which followed the apparitions. He remained however calmly submitted to the ecclesiastic authorities who requested him not to say a word about the Moissac events.

Here is why he was happily surprised to learn that, in Mexico, the U.S.A. or even in Canada, there were people showing interest to Moissac events and was pleased to hear that the Virgin Mary manifests personally, in other sanctuaries today, the same teachings that she provided in Moissac. His surprise escalated in learning that other seers are familiar with the wood of Espis, through the locutions of Our Lady.

Wednesday 8 April

Many friends showed up, like Alain and Madeleine, Yvette et René R., Henriette and Raymond B., Henriette and Antoine B. Our family house was living again a full movement of people in and out. Thérèse C. that I was so pleased to greet again, after years without any communication, brought me a series of articles, collected at the time by Jean-Louis, his brother, in the local newspapers. I also gathered here and there pieces of information and documents.

But the greatest surprise was the visit of Simone and Rémy G., a family who had inherited material on Adrian left by Maria Monmayou and by my Dad. They received such a precious quantity of documents, with the invitation to release it, in due time, to the designated person. They did not know really what that would mean. When reading the letter of the bishop, the previous morning, they decided that the time had come to release their valuable files and documents. Providence works in unexpected and wonderful ways!

In these circumstances, they told me that, a few days before his death, Papa placed these files in sealed containers, hidden successively in a large commercial bag of flour that was buried in a well on the property of Georges Campagne. Today, this land accommodates the supermarket Leclerc. Before he died, Georges, in turn, remembered it and entrusted this treasure to a new location. Here then is the detour which these documents took in order to finally get into my hands. How great you are, my God! How sovereign is Your Providence!

Skimming these files, I saw clearly how the messages given at Moissac, constitute a magnificent fresco of history of the Church and a preparation for coming of the times of renewal.

They are a kind of living catechism, an updated Gospel. They recall, somehow, the stained glass windows of great cathedrals, which are beautifully designed illustrations to teach sacred truths in proportion to what we already know and are capable of understanding. The more we look at them, the more they teach us.

Moissac is a similar device. It is a small Encyclopaedia on the history of salvation. With, additionally, a huge breath of kindness, love and hope, because it announces the "marvels of God on the whole Earth". Jesus warns that it will be always present to those who seek him.

Moissac invites us to experience hope for the return of the most beautiful event that ever happened, the return of the one who was born for all, for each one and for the whole earth: "I will help you to revive, and your spiritual birth will give birth to a new earth, and to a New Heaven (…) Sing the Gloria, because it is announcing my return" (AB#116).

Thursday 9 April

In the morning of Holy Thursday I visited Espis woods, in honor of the main teaching given to Espis pilgrims, which concerns the Eucharist. I made a few pictures which, later, showed the presence of many Eucharistic particles everywhere in the woods that I could not see while I was there.

Later I joined my sister Jacqueline at a Café, in the central square of Montcuq. From there, Jacqueline and I made a short trip to Our Lady of Rocamadour and to Meyronne, the native town of our mother, where we saw our warm and enthusiastic cousins, who welcomed us with a magnificent meal. They had even organized a pilgrimage to Our Lady of the Rock, in the cliff grotto, where my mother was baptized. Traveling with Jacqueline was also an occasion to reflect together on Moissac.

Moissac invites to trust God, to actuate an active participation with the grand designs of Providence, by conversion of heart, prayer, penance, apostolic zeal and ardent adoration of the Eucharist. The renewal of heaven and earth will produce a "permanent state of kindness, of serenity and beauty that we cannot even imagine" (ibid.).

In Moissac, Jesus clears already any of our doubts: "Do you think that it is impossible for me?" In *Redemptoris Missio* (SO 2,84), the

Holy Father announced a new spring in the Church. Espis says the same, and talks about the struggling which will precede that glorious event, almost like pain prepares a mother for a new delivery.

It invites us to overcome any kind of evil and, from now on, to live the redeeming mystery. Be already a new creature in Eucharist Jesus (Gal. 6:15). At that time believers thought that the transformation of the world was imminent.

They were not wrong since the "Earth already suffers the pain of childbirth" (Rom. 8:19-22). Regarding the moment of the event? At Moissac Jesus said that, "in his Divine Providence, God extends the time of his mercy, because he wants to save all people."

The way by which I became the recipient of this supply of wisdom struck me: God prepared these specific circumstances long ago. It suddenly became obvious that my entire life had been mapped out by Providence: the experience in my family when I was 5 years old at Moissac, successive meetings at 7 and 8 years old with Gilles, my decision at 8 years old to enter a minor seminary in Montauban, religious identity crisis at 14, conversion with the Focolare at 18, philosophy training in Sorbonne at 23-25, then a 25 years of professional experience in the Vatican Curia, during 14 years of which I was Professor of Philosophy at the Gregorian University and 7 years of teaching at Regina Mundi, responsibilities in teams of Our Lady like Equipes Notre Dame, the Focolare, the Circle of Trinity of the Mount, then our family maturation in Rome... and finally our departure for United States.

All these events get a new meaning today as an integral part of a Mission in favor of Church renewal. Actually, this is what it is about, due to the fact that we entered this country with the purpose of helping the Church renewal, with the Catholic Solitudes and the Focolare communities. Finally, there also was my appointment in a Canadian diocese as member of a commission of discernment on visionaries... But let us go back to Moissac. <XXX>

Friday 10 April

The Holy Week was marked by the intimacy and intensity of interior dialog with the Lord. In addition to multiple meetings with friends, the Holy Week was also marked by the gladness of seeing siblings that I had not occasion to meet yet: Christiane, Annie, and

Marie-Jean, as well as nephews and grand-nephews, like Marc and Joel with their spouses. It was fantastic. I am glad of each of these moments. And I was especially grateful to Mom for the trip that instigated so many blessed events.

On Good Friday, she was tired, but serene. During the celebration of the Holy Cross, we were placed at the edge of a bench, just in case we had to return home because of Mom's fatigue. I was moved by Mom's kindness when she said: "I hope I don't die this evening, because I do not want to embarrass you".

Saturday 11 April

So much gladness concentrated in so few days! It was a masterpiece of human and spiritual experience. Easter Sunday was particularly pleasant. It was the perfect liturgical time to reflect on the redeeming mystery of death and life. Most Christians ignore that affliction, distress, and adversity, when endured with offering love, are pregnant of resurrection.

Among Espis pilgrims, many express today a life of faith and of prayer which is the outcome of their conversion at Moissac during the period of apparitions. Someone noted that those who are now responsible for Espis shrine live adjacent the institutional Church. During the conversation, however, a psychologist stressed that a beaten child does not often acquire an irreproachable conduct. In Rome, I was told by a bishop that in Moissac the local Church neglected its basic obligation to pastoral care of the pilgrims: as the sky confirmed in Lourdes the dogma of Immaculate Conception, the sky encouraged at Moissac the dogma of Assumption.

Being bishop in a place where there emerge signs from above is certainly a serious responsibility before the universal Church. Obviously the Vatican respects the decision of a local bishop in such a matter, unless there is evidence that contradicts him. I do not dare to criticize the bishops of Montauban, in particular, Msgr. Théas and Msgr. de Courrège, who had to make important decisions at the time of the apparitions. Some pilgrims to the Espis shrine said that the bishops committed serious faults against the truth and produced many sufferings all around.

Whatever were their deeds, it is our duty to pray for them in order to ensure that they would eventually in heaven help their successors to complete the work of God, and if necessary, to repair whatever evil that may have been committed. Without doubt, many other bishops in their place would have done even worse. In the Gospel, Jesus invites us not to judge anyone, and that is what we have to do: not judging anyone. In every circumstance benevolence must resolve our heart. We are commanded to never miss a chance to love and to show great respect toward all other people's deeds. Ultimately, whatever is done, the mysterious action of Divine Providence will lead everything for the good of those who love God. Providence will get the best fruits from the worst situations. Nobody has the right to judge, but we all have the duty to love and we have to do so with the required discernment.

This prudent behavior, however, does not allow us to ignore the facts. Among Moissac pilgrims, several claimed that Montauban bishops denied evidence and stifled a movement of fervent piety, which spontaneously emerged. They refused to provide pastoral assistance to seers, who in the eyes of Msgr. Théas were only guilty for not belonging to Lourdes and for promoting a movement of piety which was not organized by the diocese itself. According to observers, similar intolerance was a serious mistake and showed that there was no respect for facts that would have disturbed diocesan habits even when coming from God. Members of the diocesan committee did not hesitate to say that in Montauban the bishops willingly ignored pieces of evidence that were released to them, not to mention the testimony of piety which is still alive today. It would be a crime if they willingly disregarded signs of God's love. They were afraid of addressing some irrational facts, but they intended to organize a more rational diocesan life which soon produced a decrease of faith in the whole diocese; and because their peers from other dioceses supported their decisions, even at Lourdes, the consequences were terrible in the whole nation.

Caution would suggest paying more attention to eventual deeds from above in favor of common people, especially poor and small people. A Roman observer considered that these clergymen repeated the attitude of the Sanhedrin during the time of Christ. They were afraid of losing their authority and preferred committing injustice. The same observer said that they have been more severe in respect to the community of Espis than the Sanhedrin was in respect to the Apostolic community, because they decided to kill the movement at birth instead of leaving to Divine Providence and time the care of proving its authenticity. The rejection of Moissac apparitions was also followed by a terrible failure of pastoral activity in the diocese. Espis condemnation is surely not the cause of a similar disaster. Nonetheless the lack of the clergy's concern towards Christian people is surely involved. There is, however, the fact that afterwards, precipitately, faithful participation of weekday and Sunday liturgy has dramatically decreased in the diocese and many Montauban parishes today do not even provide weekday Masses any more. It was actually one of the difficulties I had to overcome every day during my sojourn, trying to find a Mass in town.

I am wondering if it is true that the institutional Church failed to fulfill at Moissac an important appointment with Divine Providence. Was there an abuse of authority over the consciences, using the blackmail of excommunication for imposing silence on visionaries and witnesses? A few ecclesiastics I met in Rome agreed with the assertion that Montauban diocesan authorities got blindsided by Moissac events. Everything went so fast that they were afraid the situation could go out of control. Similar considerations were reported to me in Rome by Mgr Marcel Martin, who followed the case closely. Some of the witnesses of Espis had already forgotten the facts when I met them in Montauban. With prudent words they shared their personal struggle to solve the contrast between the invitation of Espis to be faithful to the Church and the disposition of the bishops to ignore it. It was even the opinion of one distinguished bishop of Montauban, I had the honor of knowing. Mgr. Martin told me that he was preparing to revive the case of Espis when he was transferred. I believe that everything must be placed in the mercy of God and all these events must invite us to greater love and greater humility. In his letters to his fellow priests during the small "Sling" revolution, St. Vincent de Paul, invited them to trust the Lord, stressing that "God uses every situation for our own good." To the superior of one Congregation's house, which was occupied by soldiers, he even wrote: "Don't worry, even if somebody made plans to destroy you, nothing will happen without God's permission, and even the most sophisticated tactics, which would have been elaborated to ruin you, God will use them to save you." Whatever people do, they are too weak to stop God's kingdom and prevent God from using them according to his designs. This also works for our own shortcomings and of those in authority. These reflections express wisdom, and bring great comfort.

Many see the authoritarian structure of the Church, the ecclesiastical hierarchy composed of priests, bishops and cardinals, as responsible for the loss of faith, the decrease of religious practice and the lack of vocations within the people of God. They say that career care and power concern keep them away from promoting a cradle of love and renovation of the family of Christ. It would be unjust to generalize such accusations, and it is even more important to consider that Providence always works, using human weakness to make changes apt to increase the Mystical Body of Christ who is the Church. The details of such adventure will be soon recognizable, unless Providence wants her action to remain silent for a while, almost as it happened in the Middle-Ages, which took its name from the conviction that nothing good had been produced during its time, while the opposite was in progress. Human wisdom improved and acted with silence and discretion. Later the Middle Ages were discovered as being one of the richest eras in human history.

Notwithstanding, the weakness of the institutional Church today and the lack of vocations have consequently promoted a better involvement of lay people in Church life. There is also the rediscovery by ecclesial movements of the charisms, which characterized the first Christian community in Jerusalem. Previously, Church authorities used to stress only the role (and the charism) of Peter, the coordinator of the Apostles, as if the only function of the hierarchy was to promote, transmit and manage Church power. Many other charisms were often overlooked, for example, the charism of Apostle John, a charism of love, evangelization and prophecy, which is also essential for the progress and the life of the Church. Many disregarded the charism of Apostle Paul, to bring the good news to other brothers and shake Church old structures to open it to the world that changes. Little is known about the charism of James, the brother of our Lord, responsible for preaching the Good News among the Jews, our elder brothers. There was also the charism of Matthew to preach among

214

Hindus and outside the people of the book (Christian, Jews, and Muslims). Undoubtedly there is also the one of Jude on intimacy with Jesus by the continual prayer, which Eastern Churches retained and implemented. Each Apostle has a specific role in Church life and edification, a specific role to play, which constitutes a pole priority action of the Church in complementary relation to the other eleven. And above all, there is Mary, the Mother of all apostolic charisms. Mary, actually, was present among them at Pentecost when they received those gifts. It is not surprising that ecclesial movements are particularly attached to Mary's presence.

These charisms are wonderfully expressed in more than 70 ecclesial movements, which emerged after WW2 from inside the people of God. I was blessed to meet directly some of them: the Focolare, the New Catechumens, the Ark, Faith and Light, a few Charismatic Movements, and Communion and liberation... On 30 May 1998, on Pentecost eve, Pope John Paul II wanted to meet them. The answer was unexpectedly enthusiastic. Ecclesial movements filled the place. Roman commentators stressed how that meeting gathered the largest crowd which ever showed up in Vatican square. Yes, a crowd of 500.000 people filled St Peter square, extending into Viale della Conciliazione, and all the other streets around from the Tiber River up to the Vatican basilica. Such a crowd paralyzed the traffic in a large part of the city. It was an event which marked a historic reconciliation between the institutional Church and the people of God. That same day, the Pope spoke about the need of both charisms in the whole Church, stressing how Peter's charism needs the living presence of Our Lady. He indicated so to the whole Church a new direction to go, inviting all Church authorities to welcome similar movements everywhere on earth, in their parishes.

That day it was not only an historical event for the Church in Rome but also for the whole world. JP2 was officially stressing how inside of the people of God the Holy Spirit was in process of renovating the Church. The following day, a large article from the *Roman Observer*, the Vatican paper was significant: referring to that meeting it offered the title, *The Wonderful Day that the Lord Made*.

Many testimonies which were provided in St. Peter's square before the Pope that evening stressed the lessons given in Moissac. I think,

for example, of the role of the poor and the little ones for the promotion of the Kingdom. At Espis Our Lady implored us to be grateful to those who suffer: they are "children martyrs offered to God for the forgiveness of sins in the world, for the conversion of those who mock God and are cause of so much sorrow (...) you are the martyrs of the New Times".

And also: "Through you all, Jesus speaks to the World. Thanks to you love remains alive in the world, and will save it from misfortune". It seemed to me I heard an echo of it at Saint Peter's square in the testimony of Jean Vanier, saying that "Jesus speaks to the world through the smaller ones, those who are excluded from society" stressing that "when we believe we give to the poor, it is actually the poor who teach us and introduce us into the Paradise of God". <XXX>

During Holy Week I encountered in Montauban friends who edified me by their perseverance within suffering. I do not report names here to respect the secret of their intimacy with the Lord. Before the Easter celebration on Saturday evening, I had a phone conversation with Gabriel Bouhours, Gilles' father, who stressed the Lord's blessing on his whole family and friends through Gilles, who was involved with the Espis events. He also stressed how Gilles was familiar with Eucharistic Jesus. We prayed together over the phone.

Sunday 12 April

On Sunday afternoon, everyone had left. I was alone in this large three-story house. Suddenly I saw the emptiness of the house and felt it inside of my heart. I understood then how many graces surrounded me and how the sojourn was in the hands of Divine Providence. Fortunately, I had a few visits: Marie-Jean and his family passed by twice, first in the evening and again during the night. Christian Mallet came, too. He made a detour to the house while he was just returning from his travels to Portugal and Lourdes. These visits helped me to assemble pieces of the mosaic and conclude well my stay in Montauban.

Monday 13 April

On Easter Monday I did not know how I could take with me the impressive mass of documents which I had received during my visit to Marthe, my mother, in Montauban. It was impossible to get to the train station with it: I had no car anymore and a taxi refused to take

me. Fortunately, two friends, Simone and Rémy, came to see me again in the morning and Jacquie showed up too.

It was a glad surprise to have a brunch with them at home. Without their help I could not have taken the train in the afternoon. These visits allowed me to leave Montauban under the best auspices. When later on I saw the pictures, which they took on the platform, before I boarded the train, I remained impressed to see how much luggage I had: stacked one atop the other, the boxes surpassed my height.

Here the words fail me to say the joy that invaded me during the entire journey back to the States, first by train from Montauban to Paris, then by plane from Paris to Pittsburgh.

Leaving Montauban I used the 6-hour trip to pray and write letters. At the arrival of the TGV in Paris, Jean-Marc was waiting for me on the platform, right in front of my car. I understood that Jacquie provided by phone the information to Jean-Marc as soon as the train left Montauban... It was such a pleasant surprise.

In their home, Jean-Marc and Catherine welcomed me in admirable ways. My nephew, Charlie, kindly offered me his bed for the night and his sister, Carole, made me the present of a splendid man-made red rose. It is the only brand of flowers that we are allowed to import into the U.S.A. The rose summarized the many gifts I had been granted during my journey in France. I told her that her Rose disclosed happiness. I also saw the flower as a symbol of the presence of Mary throughout the entire trip. Actually, does not Christian liturgy in Latin and Eastern rites address Mary as "Mystical Rose "? Yes indeed!

Monday evening, I was obviously concerned with the luggage to carry on the plane the following day and did pray repeatedly to the Lord how much I really needed his help. I weighed my package with Jean-Marc. It greatly exceeded the standards of acceptance of 70 pounds: one pack was around 110 lb, the other of 90 lb. And I was not even sure that I was allowed to put more than one bag on the plane.

God loves it when people who are in need turn to him for help. When we trust him, the Lord enjoys helping and he provides even more than what we ask for. He likes those who rely on him. All saints encourage people to seek God's assistance and beg with confidence.

But I was not sure about what to demand. The situation was con-

fusing in my soul. I did not know what to do... when suddenly the light came on inside: I had just to redo my suitcases and alleviate them at best, sacrificing especially what my heart would be attached to. Because aid was supposed to come from above, the heart first needed to be free and light. And our Lord was asking me to show that I really made the whole journey for him and not for some other enjoyable business, even fully legitimate. It was his journey, not mine.

Tuesday 14 April

Therefore, at the first light of dawn, I began to fill Charlie's room with any kind of superfluous belongings: toiletries, shoes care necessaries, portable pharmacy, six boxes of conserve of goose, several books, notebooks and new folders, working notes, and other stuff... including some records concerning Espis events copies of which I was sure I could get elsewhere.

When the whole process of repacking was over, the two bags weighed around 80 lb, which was still far above acceptance standards. I therefore needed to keep the heart tied to the Lord in order to remain at the high level required by the situation.

My heart was actually, beating forte in my chest. Jean-Marc could see that emotion of mine when, because of it, I forgot at the post office counter the money I had just withdrawn. Fortunately, from the high speakers of the airport, the clerk called me back, while I was getting the airline check in. With Jean-Marc we laughed together on such a distraction of mine... Yes, all my attention was above, in a way I wasn't accustomed to yet. But when we arrived at the luggage registration, the lady took the bags without saying a word about the overload which appeared to the meter... Carole's Rose continued to boost my blessings.

I wish to conclude the section with a few words on the departure of my Mom for heaven, which happened the following year. She was one of many witnesses of Espis, but one of the few who never forgot these events. She never ceased not only to comply with Moissac messages but she also never disobeyed Church authorities about it.

It was not easy to understand how she could do so gently, pleasing Our Lady with good deeds, and accepting the words of Montauban bishops and priests against it, demanding everyone to ignore Espis events, to never go there any more for public worship, and never speak about it. She did so. And because public pilgrimages were organized on the 13th every month, she used to visit privately the shrine the following day, on the 14th, or some other day later.

During our sojourn in Montauban I asked her once: "How do you see the contradiction of Our Lady urging devotion to Jesus in the Eucharist and on the other hand Church authorities forbidding everyone to hear her voice?"

Her answer was clear and simple: "We must comply with both"

"How it can be?" I asked again.

"Our Lady knows everything. She esteems priests and Church authorities, too. Respecting them we please her."

Her few words were an important teaching: God never demands us impossible things to do. Besides, as Jesus said, a kingdom cannot be divided or it would destroy itself. When they come from above, private locutions or apparitions would never go against the Church, which witnesses God's presence, but they support Church betterment. Private apparition shrines are not supposed to replace regular churches but they eventually support them. It was the lack of confidence in the Lord that showed contradictions where there were no contradictions.

This gap was sufficient then to break harmony and pull people through a lack of confidence in the Church and finally give up: when brothers fight inside of the Church it, develops disinterest int he Church itself. Nonetheless, Augustine's words remain true and bring great hope: "There is no wrongness that God wouldn't allow if it were not allowing a better good."

The better good is still to come. We cannot predict it but we must prepare for it. Moissac was a warning from above in favor of greater Eucharistic life and more authentic experience of the Gospel. It fails only on short range for those who didn't trust it. Our Lord needed to die on the Cross to bring us life with his resurrection... We, too, must accept to die from personal and private beliefs to be born in the larger

219

garden of the Church... The Church, however, is not merely the actual Catholic Church. Here is how divisions serve the better good: they actually prepare us to dissolve bigger divisions inside of the whole of mankind, beginning with our own family and the whole Church. On Holy Thursday, John reported after dinner the Prayer of Jesus to Our Father: "That they may be one..." [John 17:21]. Such a prayer, intended to gather all in one unique brotherhood inside of God, our Father, concerns not only institutional Churches and congregations, but all Jesus believers, and eventually the whole mankind that we, the believers, are entrusted to reveal the Good News of the Gospel to. The whole panorama is far better than the best prospective individual people may have. Whether we know it or not, it will happen soon. It seems to me that the next twenty years will go through the most dramatic changes in history of mankind. And it will be huge fun.

All of that, obviously, will never happen in contradiction of the Gospel, which means that the cross and suffering remain the way to resurrection, otherwise said in American words: "No pain, no gain". They seem words, they are facts. Bernard de Clairvaux used to stress enthusiastically how "suffering is pregnant with resurrection". Here is why it can be difficult to understand how my mother was able to comply peacefully with both, Espis and the Church, while, actually, for her, it was the same voice, speaking with diverse accents. It is easy, however, to understand that she made it through great struggles and suffering. Fortunately "we know that all things work together for good to them that love God" (Rom 8:28).

When many had forgotten Moissac, Marthe Montazel, my mother, did not. Mom was one of those who witnessed several Moissac events identified by many as true miracles. Among these I must mention the healing of some pilgrims, who were without hope from a medical perspective, including my own sister, Marie-Bé, and Colette Rigal, a family friend. Details on the issue would eventually make these pages too voluminous. Among famous miracles, there was the one in the sky... on 2 March 1947, when Gilles's family had recently moved from Bordeaux to Moissac. [XXX]

Mom was the main source of information for me on Espis, not only because of what she witnessed, but above all for her wisdom. With her departure to heaven disappeared the important source of acquaintance I used to refer to. It was eventually the last living source I was still able to consult. It is appropriate, then, to give her the homage due to her great help on the story of Monmayou.

Her "*Natus Est*", her leaving earth on Wed. 20 October 1999, was the actual conclusion of my previous journey to Montauban. Mom was a wise countrywoman, levelheaded and shrewd, from whom I loved to learn. Even during my worse days of identity crisis, when I was between 14 to 19 years old, when I would have not the courage to meet my father, I was still pleased to visit home, from time to time, and talk to my mother. I did not realized in those days that the difficult relationship with my father was reciprocal: he was afraid of my replies back, and how I could argue against his beliefs. I did not know that and I was unfair: my father gave me the opportunity to make studies that he never was given the chance to enjoy, and I was using the knowledge I got because of his care against his own convictions, which where the whole meaning of his life. Meanwhile, Mom was able to tell me her true opinion without hurting me. It was a gift she had with all of us in the family.

One day I came back home after I had another terrible discussion with my father. I was trying to draw her on my side, stressing how I was right and how Dad was wrong. She did not fall into the trap. She only said: "Alain, he is your father!" Those simple words, "He is your father", still strongly resound in my heart. With this simple reply she directed my mind to essential values: being right or wrong was less important than respecting my parents, and she was right.

It was after a trip from Detroit to Chicago that upon my arrival I was given the news of her departure for heaven. The following day, being back in Detroit, I wrote this email to Bruno Venturini in Grotaferrata, Roma, Italy, whom I was used to be in touch and entertain a continuous spiritual sharing. I wrote him how I experienced her departure.

It's almost impossible writing something about my Mom's good departure to heaven and not talking with her, too, while putting down these reflections onto paper. I wish these notes reflect more than simple memories. I hope the reader will get from these pages the prudence and wisdom my Mom used to spread around with those who met her. Please God that she could speak, too, in these pages.

Here is the message I sent, dated Thursday 21 October 1999.

Dear Bruno, I'm back from Chicago where I spent the night at the Focolare center and get some news about the movement irradiation all over the world and its continuing growing in Gospel experience. Above all it was the opportunity of enjoying the agape atmosphere at the place. In a few days Bill will visit you in Rome and will tell you how deep were the moments of unity we spent together. The visit offered me also the occasion to begin reading the book As Rainbow, which shows how people blossom developing through the Cross in all human dimensions. Reading it was true gladness.

"Yesterday, while I arrived there, Bill invited me to call home. I did. Over the phone Chiara told me that, Marthe, my mother had left this earth a little earlier, at Grenoble, France. It was the consequence of falling down in the house of my sister Christiane, trying to get the phone. She was left alone and she hurt badly her leg and broke her hip. After that happened, I spoke with my siblings in France. She died in hospital in Grenoble. Saturday morning her body will be brought to her home, in Montauban, Gascony, where relatives and friends are expecting her. Then the funeral will be celebrated in Saint-Jean-Villenouvelle parish, where she was used for years to attend morning Mass, every day, together with my father... Her remains will be buried in Villefranche-de-Rouergue, 60 miles away to the northeast, where the whole family has its tomb.

"Mom was ready to go. Since my father died, followed three months later by Joseph, my brother, she was even expecting to go. Maybe we, her children, were not. so ready to understand it after all. She was longing to reach my father over there. Because of her unhealthy conditions she was given by the bishop permission to keep Eucharist Jesus in her room. The permission was renewed by every bishop of the places where she had moved: not being able to live alone any more she was moving from a place to a place staying time by time with one of her children. Similar changes, from house to house, were producing a continuous struggle for her: as soon as she finally adapted to a place the time had come to move to another place and start to adapt again to the new situation... She ultimately

would prefer to stay in her home in Montauban, but no one, among us, the siblings,, was able to leave his own place and stay there with her permanently. Even the perspective of a turn over did not work. We would like to do so, but it was not affordable: all siblings were living too far away, with job and family commitments. It was surely easier to have Mom moving from a sibling home to another. Notwithstanding, being obliged to successively leaving homes, where she finally had just become pleased to stay, were increasingly pushing her spiritual availability to leave earth.

At this point comes to my mind the great commitment that my parents entertained with the Focolare, which was the greatest pledge of their life.

Focolare community in Montauban area developed because of my parents. My Father looked the most enthusiastic and active organizer, but he never would have been able to do anything, and he even would not dare to, without the strong supportive behavior of my Mom. We understood better that effective relationship between both of them after my Dad departure in April 1987. Everything started because of a visit that my Father made to a Focolare center, during the summer 1958, while he was in Paris attending a conference. There he met Gino Bonadimani,, who impressed him strongly by his peaceful and deep commitment with the Gospel. So my father invited Gino to pay us back a visit home, in Montauban.

Not having any answer he repeated the invitation. So in November 1958 Renata Borlone and Nuzzomaria Grimaldi came to Montauban and stationed for two weeks in our house, meeting the people who was used to visit my parents at home. From these almost daily and numerous encounters a great ferment of "Ideal life" was born in town, which induced later the Focolare movement to monitoring so intense activity from the nearest city, Toulouse, which is second to Bordeaux in Gascony. Toulouse was only thirty miles away from Montauban, driving south.

After Benedict monks had left Tlemcen, Algeria, Fr. Emmanuel, from En Calcat Abbey, France, who was a near friend of my parents, was seeking some association or community to handle the buildings and property of the previous Tlemcen monastery. When she heard about that concern, Mom was suggested to making Tle-mcen a center for the Focolare movement. Here is how, during the years 1960s, the Focolare started activity in Algeria, at the borders with Sahara desert.

Both, Raymond, my father, and Marthe Montazel, my mom, became the first married Focolarini in France... Their commitment with the Focolare increased dramatically after they organized the journey of several families from Montauban, in Gascony, to attend in Fribourg, Switzerland, the summer Focolare gathering, known as Mariapolis, during the summer 1960. Their impressive activity for promoting a living community in Montauban area induced the Focolare movement to move to Toulouse the men center they had in Grenoble.

The great hospitality and charitable endeavors of my parents to-wards the Focolare induced Maras, who was in those days the lead-er of the community in France, to believe that they were gifted with large financial resources, which actually they were not. Here is why Maras decided to entrust my father with the news periodic Nouvelle Cité of the movement in Paris. But the project did not go through for the effective lack of financial availability of our family. Maras asked my father to leave his job in Montauban and move to Paris, to work for the Focolare paper. But Maras was offering no compensation in return for such commitment.

In those days, the needs of the family were still high, due to the fact that some of my siblings had still the age of attending school, while the three eldest sisters were already married. The request of Maras was urging. My parents believed it was part of their commit-ment with the Focolare to agree with it. After few days and nights of prayer and a long sharing together, weighing the pros and the cons, our parents went to the only one affordable proposal to the family: the three eldest girls would have take care of the three young-est boys, Marie-Jean, Joseph and Jean-Marc, who were supposed to move from home and go live with them. Our Father was supposed to move to Paris, alone first, starting the job, and, as soon as an apart-ment would have been found, my Mom would join him in Paris, together with Marie-Bé, our youngest sister. Then our family house in Montauban would have been sold in order to support their needs.

I was not directly involved in the dramatic decision, because I was living in Loppiano, near Florence, Italy, at the Focolare center of formation for new members of the Focolare. I was independent, already. I was, however, indirectly involved, due to the fact that my parents believed, either it was true or not, that refusing Maras' proposal would somehow jeopardize my "vocation".

Fortunately, the Lord did not allow that their generosity could damage the whole family. Mom and Dad called for a family meeting at home, in Montauban, and presented the project. As usual, Raymond, my father, was talking for both. Marthe was silent, but supportive. At first Raymond explained the request of Maras, the details of the situation, and tried to convince the family to agree with the project of generously agreeing to the difficult endeavor... stressing the opportunity of serving the Church through the Focolare, accepting Maras' request in spite of the restrictive perspectives.

The family meeting thrilled. My eldest three daughters, Jacqueline, Annie and Christiane did not accept to see our family falling apart and they supported the unconscious concern of our Mom and Dad to see the family destroyed by such dramatic division. In spite of several attempts from my father to convince the whole family, the project was rejected.

Before this denial, Maras refused to see and talk to my parents any more, and he asked the Focolare leaders in France to behave the same. Nonetheless, both mom and dad continued to support and be generous with the Focolare in many ways. My parents suffered very much the situation. It happens, sometimes, that the Lord allows his followers to suffer because of those they love the most...

My parents' generosity was not a fake. My parents always enthusiastically supported my conversion to the ideal of the Focolare and my commitment with the Work of Mary, which is the official name of the Focolare movement. I was totally involved in Focolare matters at that time. In those days I was living in Loppiano, near Florence, Italy, fighting for conversion and taking a pledge with the new experience of the Gospel as proposed by the Focolare. Even if they did not know my exact situation, Mom and Dad asked my brothers and sisters not to say a word to me on the struggle that the family was going through in order not to disrupt my eventual agreement with the Focolare... And my brothers and sisters had been consistent with the request of Marthe and Raymond to be silent with me on the difficulties endured because of the Focolare. I heard about these events and the volte-face of the movement towards them long time after it happened.

At the moment the Focolare ignored the struggle of my family and my parents, together with my siblings, were unable to explain the real situation to the Focolare. This was the result of a lack of a clear communication. Sometimes the Lord allow people to suffer the distance of being rejected by those they serve and love the much. Such miscommunication happens every day in daily life. My parents were good friends of Padre Pio who had been deceived by some expert of the Vatican who made some inaccurate report on him to the Secretary of State: as a result, the Vatican did not understand the real situation of the monk. It is by God's permission that Providence allows similar situations, which ultimately put to the test those which the Lord wants to improve the holiness. It is a case when human imperfection serves supernatural grace.

Miscommunications happen more often than it should. Nonetheless it happens.

Despite the fact that for a mutual misunderstanding, Raymond and Marthe experienced the event of being alone, for they were excluded from the Focolare, they continued to promoting the movement in Montauban area and to helping maintain there a living "Ideal" community. From Montauban area, many Focolare members, volunteers and supporters showed up. There are permanent members of the Focolare, the so-called Focolarini, like Patrice Pagès and Nicole Calmejanne, who are still engaged in the movement today. Many other members showed as well like Cecile and Alain Pradeau, Gaston Jonquière, André Gleize, Robert Dubéros, Denise and Henri Bonjour, Madeleine and Alain Bonjour, Yvette and Renée Roques, Simone and Rémy Gabens, Henriette and Raymond Berthomet, Marie and Georges Campagne, Mimi and Christian Mallet, and many others who remained faithful to the ideal of the Gospel as promoted by the Focolare.

As an example, my Dad used to organize a monthly meeting that used to gather regularly from 50 to 100 people. For a while, Fr. Abel Salesse, parish priest at St. Jean Villenouvelle, made the church available for the meetings. These meetings were transformed for a time as a monthly prayer to Our Lady, and were always hold on the first Saturdays of the month. These meetings continued even after my Dad died. They were organized then by René Roques.

In addition to the trip to Fribourg, my parents were also pleased to organized similar journeys for Focolare meetings in Toulouse, Paris, summer Mariapolis in Saint-Laurent-sur-Sèvres, near Angers, or even in Grottaferrata, near Rome, Italy. All meetings there, in Villa Maria Assunta, remained a spiritual corner stone to all those who attended. At that time my parents became tight friends of Danilo and Annamaria Zanzucci who were in touch with married Focolare all over the world.

Few days ago I could speak with my mother over the phone while she already was in hospital. She was facing great suffering, but she was at peace, as she always used to be. I asked her to pray for my students who had in those days a midterm exam... Some of them were taking their written examination in class three days ago,, just after that conversation over the phone. Mom was still asking news about the Focolare movement all over the world in addition to our family news here in America. She amazingly remembered all and showed love for everyone. She and I were very close. She was ready to leave. For some months her sight had decreased and it was very feeble, therefore the rosary had become her favorite prayer. In addition to the feeling of great solitude she was going through, she was enduring a high level of physical suffering, due to a cancer of the intestine. Because of it she dramatically lost weigh. Only in the last two weeks she had lost 5 pounds. Her weigh went down to barely 90 pounds. Then she fell, breaking her hip, and the accident was decisive in speeding up her departure to heaven.

I am happy for her, because she reached in heaven my father, my brother Joseph, my sister Marie-Thérèse and also Nuzzo-Maria and Renata, who remained forever some of their best freinds.

I'll be unable to attend Mom's funeral in Montauban. My visa precariousness may not allow me to reenter the country. I would need a specific permission to go and come back. Besides a similar absence from the States during the process of getting the Green Card may jeopardize its success. Going there would oblige me to make too many deeds in a few days. On the other side I see that my sisters and brothers are following all things very well. So there is no reason to be concerned and I'll be there spiritually.

While I drove from Detroit to Chicago yesterday, I halted to a rest area on the highway with the desire to call her over the phone. It was near to two o'clock here, so it was eight o'clock of the evening over there. It was a good time to call and talk to her after dinner and before she started sleeping for the night... Then while the phone was ringing, I suddenly was afraid of waking her up from an eventual precarious sleep and I hung up.

I knew later from my brother that this was approximately the time of Mom's departure to heaven. I am pleased to have had a loving thought precisely at the moment she left us and joined our relatives over there. That moment of loving intimacy keeps my heart warm. I am grateful to God for it.

Returning to the seminary today I found a great solidarity from all:, administrative, superiors, colleagues, and students. Various priests among them will say Mass tomorrow morning for her. Also in Pittsburgh, where I'll drive tomorrow after class, some priests will say mass for her Saturday morning at 8, which will be likely the time of her funeral in Montauban.

Her departure produced great serenity in my heart. For the love that Mom always showed to the Focolare, it seemed to me a good sign that she was offering her last breathing at the time I was going to get a first sight to the Focolare in Chicago.

While I am writing these lines, I receive a call from my wife, Chiara, who tells me to have received a very affectionate and warm fax message from Don Pasquale Foresi. He sent it as soon as he heard the news of my mother's death. Please, tell him how much I appreciated it.

I remain near to him and to you with Jesus and Mary.

Alain

Tableau # 21

Back to Pittsburgh

BETWEEN PLANES IN CINCINNATI, THERE WAS THE CUSTOMS INSPECTION TO GO THROUGH. In my prayer, I had totally forgotten the US Agriculture Department, which prohibits the importation of any food product, in particular the pâté which I had been given at Meyronne for Chiara. Of course, the scanner did detect it. But I went through without difficulty. My only explanation is that I was so serene that the customs officer told me to put back everything in my bags and pushed a button, which moved the baggage and me away on the conveyor belt.

He actually was in perfect compliance with his duty, and the people before and after me learned it at their expense. Somehow his move was a surprise for those who surrounded us, including his colleague. But it went so fast that I only became aware of it after I had been sent away, while as a stubborn Gascon, I was trying to reorganize my bags orderly. The situation was funny. A word of my Dad popped into my mind: "The Good Lord provided a hundredfold!". It was like a joke in which Mary, represented by Carole's "Mystical Rose", was continuing to protect me with her providential shield.

After the customs inspection and before taking the next plane, I called Chiara over the phone and then Mr. Connelly's office. I was not even home yet but I was already back in sync with the intense American work pace.. Four hours later, I landed in Pittsburgh, tired but so happy because of the journey.

Wednesday 14 April

Today is my father's *Natus Est*. He died during the night following April 14. What a happy coincidence! I was back home at the conclusion of a trip which he continuously was recalled and, I assume, he was present with his care.

Business was waiting for me at 9 a.m. at the University. I was already launched into action even before I had time to catch my breath. I was pleased to be back and be urged to undertake the many activities in which I was involved: the university, Connelly company, the parish, Catholic Solitudes, and the Diocese of Toronto, Canada. We certainly run a life which is not monotonous. Yes, our existence in the USA is much happier and even more intense than it was in Rome, but with something more: **peace**.

The following weekend we were in Baltimore (a 5 hour drive) for a family of the Focolare. From there we drove to Washington D.C. to visit Chiara's cousin, Sara, and see her newborn baby.

During our overnight in Washington, D.C., I got the flue... I was in terrible shape. But it probably was the least that could happen to me, as a European not yet well accustomed with American intensely moving on. Nonetheless, 5 days later, I drove to Toronto. It is during this trip that my car meter exceeded the threshold of 165.000 miles, which means that since our arrival in the U.S.A., 34 months ago, I put more than 75.000 miles on the road! Back from Canada, I drove to Catholic Solitudes, Littleton, West Virginia. Then I visited the doctor in Pittsburgh: I had bronchitis, which I cured the way Americans do, that is to say, carrying out all chores according to the usual business.

There is a word to say about our new housing. On Easter Monday, with Simone and Rémy G., we started a novena to Our Lady of Espis. Well! There is an interesting occurrence to notice. The evening of novena 9th day, 22 April, at 10 p.m., Chiara and I signed the agreement to the purchase of the house. To tell the truth, we could no longer live in our first Pittsburgh house: the rental fee had become too high and over all it was no longer fitting our needs. But a solution looked impossible to find. I knew that it was necessary to move, ignoring however how to do so. Everything happened quickly: a friend provided us his professional expertise. He contacted a broker who found our position comfortable enough to guarantee a loan. The bank put the only condition for us: to get a three years visa. That condition looked insurmountable at first. It contradicted the fact that up till then our visas were renewed yearly. Additionally we had just presented our application for visa renewal, which usually took a few months to go through. It seemed at first that we were out of luck for the purchasing the house. Curiously, new Congressional dispositions canceled our visa category and the Immigration Department decided to give us the visas for the most available extension: three years, and the visas were granted immediately. They were just released in those days. Near to our home a house became available. It was perfect as far as location and number of rooms for our family. We made an offer. It was accepted. And everything went through. Yes! It was a miracle! There are a few adjustments easy to make. The house is magnificently located, with a run in the backyard and woods over the stream. It is a true gift from heaven, rich of space, quietness and intimacy. It is an excellent fruit of my journey.

End of April

I brought home my precious load of documents. When the Canadian bishop saw a similar harvesting of good news, he immediately asked me to include it in the archives of the Search Center for the Fefense of the Church. Fatima, Medjugorje, Kibeho fully confirm Moissac. These messages are coherent and complete one another. A Mexican seer disclosed some explanation about Our Lady of Espis:

> *Soon, from Espis, as well as from all the locations where my mother uses to speak to the most humble members of God's people, will emerge the triumph and the renewal of the whole Church. Make yourselves ready. It's going to occur soon. I already knock at the door.*

That is, in four lines, the five pages of information that I received on the subject.

It would be imprudent to disregard the quantity of messages of the kind that are given today. Our Blessed Virgin who recently cried in Civitavecchia, near Rome, is a spark among many other… In every shrine people are healed, convert, and meet in prayer. According to Fr. René Laurentin the number of these events is congruous. At Notre Dame University, Indiana, Fr. Ed O'Connor stressed how these interventions from above exceeded in number during the 20th century all previous private visions and revelations including all those which happened since the Ascension of the Savior. These are facts to consider.

On Pentecost 1998 in Saint-Peter square, Rome, those who follow these events from above met and reconciled with those more involved in the institutional Church. They need one another. They all are part of the same mystery which leads history of salvation.

Now, in addition to the usual activities to have care of, there is the business concerning the amount of notes, testimonies, photos, records, handwritten or printed note about the events of Moissac… It is an enormous job to manage. I willingly undertake it, slowly but surely, leaving to the one who brought Gilles to the pope, Monmayou, the care of continuing to spread the message of Moissac. This written work is my part in the process which serves the blossoming of the Church and the Glory of God. If there is more to say I'll keep you informed. I pray the Lord guide our steps and let us grow in his Love, his Truth and his Hope.

Yes, come back soon, Lord Jesus!

Tableau #22
Green Card

LEAVING DUQUESNE WAS A RISK. I had no other job to turn to. Nonetheless I was not comfortable to remain there and be the cause of a fight between the philosophy department, and President John E. Murray.

In those days, the philosophy department favored atheism, existentialism and phenomenology while President Murray, was pleased with my teaching as a believer, which was more consistent with the charism of the Fathers of the Holy Ghost, who were the founders of the institution. Additionally, the president made the commitment to help me get the Green Card. I was teaching in return.

I knew that philosophy is open to all human characteristics, including Christian topics. Human configuration comprehends transcendence and values. Among these values, the one of charity emerges, which identifies the whole Christian endeavor. It looked contradictory to me that, in the name of charity, I was going to promote a fight that would bring no real improvement in the department... I reflected on the situation for not long, maybe a day or so, maybe hours, but the Gospel suggestion "Before engaging in war, consider your strength and compare it to the might of your opponent..." and it was clear that I would have been alone against the majority of the professors in the department. Those who would favor my side wouldn't publicly hazard any word against them and thus risk jeopardizing their own careers. In private, however, I received good words of solidarity, which were much appreciated.

All things considered, I was not comfortable to continue teaching in a hostile environment, where eventually my own words would have been twisted. No one in the philosophy department would openly support my commitment. Even Roland M., who was indicated to me as a Christian, told me: "Here in America your way of teaching is not acceptable in a philosophy department. Your course contents are not supposed to include your experience of faith." I was astonished.

My reply was immediate: "I totally disagree with a similar perspective. Philosophy is one. Even if the whole country had a diverse opinion, that did not make them right, philosophy as such should include Christian values to be universal and to properly remain true philosophy. Every other endeavor can be a study of the history of wisdom or of the main philosophers, but it is not philosophy yet." I said it almost automatically, being surprised that Roland would disagree with me. "I don't understand," I concluded, "how a Catholic university would foster such a pagan endeavor!"

I was shocked that a known Catholic professor like him withdrew from his faith in his teaching, and even justified his behavior as a correct attitude. It seemed strange to me that entering the classroom at Duquesne, a professor was supposed to "leave outside the door his coat, his hat, and his umbrella and also his faith…" That was my way of repeating the famous words recalled by Maritain about the conflict between science and faith during to the 19th century.

The same words were also quoted by Jean Guiton and Teilhard de Chardin… I surely could not agree to reduce my teaching to mere knowledge, or worse to pseudo-scientific knowledge, which would fit with a pagan perspective. All that seemed to me a betrayal of everything I did since I reverted, at 19 years of age, to the Catholic faith. Without including the whole of human perspectives, which comprehend spiritual topics and values, philosophy becomes merely a science of partial knowledge, but it is surely not philosophy. Deprived of Christian excellence, that expertise has nothing to do with wisdom and barely anything to do with true knowledge.

Nonetheless, Roland insisted "It doesn't work that way in this country!" It was his indisputable conclusion. His words sounded on me like a blow with a club. It was his last and final argument. My mistake was to believe it was true. Today I think that with good intentions, maybe, he was trying to mitigate my behaviors in order to manage some compromise. My mistake was to believe that he truly believed what he said. I did not know at that time, that he willingly provided me wrong information. So, I trusted his statement and felt it was useless to continue fighting a lost battle… Providence sometimes, uses your own mistakes, and lead you where she wants you to move, and where she is, actually, expecting you.

When I told Mr. Michael Weber, the Academic Vice-President, of my decision to leave Duquesne, he tried to stop me: "Duquesne made an arrangement. You were supposed to teach here and get the Green Card…"

"I know that", I replied, "but unfortunately there is a disagreement between the orientation of Dr. Eleanor Holveck, the head of philosophy department, and my commitment of teaching an open minded philosophy… Ultimately, I want not to force President Murray into an uncomfortable conflict… that, I was told, is hopeless"

Vice-President Weber remained silent… respecting my decision. I left the room without further words.

Leaving Duquesne that day I had no idea where to turn or what my options were. I was obliged to seriously consider the eventuality of packing again and moving the whole family back to Italy or France. It was not a pleasant prospect. I was too deeply hurt inside to make a new attempt of teaching in the States. My thought was: "if this is an American behavior, I can barely teach philosophy in this country." A few days were needed to reflect, meditate and pray before deciding what to do.

Incredible circumstances allowed us, however, to get through the ordeal and ultimately remain in the country. I looked for a new place to pray, a place where I supposed I would not meet anyone I knew. I wanted to stay alone for a while with the Lord. Visiting Saint Teresa parish, where we had never gone to Mass before, I also found a new confessor. I did it on purpose, in order to get confession with a priest who was not likely to know or recognize me. The confessor did listen to me; then he asked a few questions. Including how I was doing. The questions embarrassed me. The priest in the confessional that day was Fr. David Poecking. I was pleased on that day and during the following weeks to talk with a confessor whom I never knew before. I also planned to never meet him out of the church box. By prudence, I did the confessions through the grill, avoiding to use the face to face room and create any new friendship.

The Lord had another agenda. Divine Providence used my plans against my own purpose. And, for my own good, my plans got twisted. After a few confession meetings, Fr. David asked me if I wished to take part in, on the coming Tuesday morning, a weekly meeting, organized in the parish by the priests, with a few lay couples, with the purpose of reflecting on the reading of the following Sunday liturgy. The meeting was supposed to bring some insights to the priests and help them to prepare the following Sunday homely.

It was much too tempting for me not to accept the invitation. Suddenly a new page of our American life had turned. A new venture had started. The weekly group of reflection kept my heart and my mind busy, in straight connection with Catholic Liturgy. I had no the time to be idle.

When in Mid-December 1998 I left Duquesne, I had no other teaching opportunity in Pittsburgh. So, I accepted in January the provisional proposal to teach a six-week course of Mediaeval Philosophy at Our Lady of Corpus Christi, and I drove to Texas.

At that time, OLCC was a small Catholic College, which was recently founded by SOLT, the Society of Our Lady of the Most Holy Trinity. I drove there during the first half of January 1999.

It was an interesting undertaking driving down there from Pittsburgh, crossing the eight states of Pennsylvania, West Virginia, Ohio, Kentucky, Tennessee, Missouri, Arkansas, and finally Texas, all over from Texarkana down to Corpus Christi. The driving was hazardous because I started during a winter storm.

My European background made me unaware of the risk that such weather situation could raise against me. I soon realized that I was not in Europe any more. Fortunately, I had a heavy car and, thanks to Divine Providence care, I was able to go through.

On the first day I drove from Pittsburgh, Pennsylvania, through West Virginia and entered in Ohio where, after a while, in the long straight line of the highway, I had the unusual panorama of a kind of movie scenery: the whole white track of the highway was adorned with cars and trucks everywhere on the road, on the shoulders, and even in the traffic island. It was an amazing spectacle. I was even surprised to go through without major problems…

So I continued my way down to Kentucky. While I was passing through, I had some prayer for the people involved in the many other cars, stopped in the middle or the side of the highway… The road was perfectly in harmony with the past Christmas season with all those blue, white, yellow, and red flashes all around… It seemed I was inside of a huge Christmas tree, illuminated with lightning vehicles: individual cars, ambulances, firemen and police…

When I left Pittsburgh, I did not realize what I was going to drive through this hazardous area. By chance, it went well. When I entered in Tennessee, I was out of trouble already. Then I joined Arkansas through the beautiful site of Mississippi corner, where Ohio and Mississippi rivers meet, in an extraordinary scenery… surrounded by mountains, suddenly followed by high plateaus… It was the discovery of gorgeous rural and wild areas.

Friends followed closely our adventure. They remained near to us with their amiability, friendliness, and support. Without similar human companionship, we would never have had force and perseverance enough to maintain our undertaking and finally get through all the uncertainty and struggle. The correspondence with them during those days of uncertainty and hope shows that it is true that "Nothing is impossible with God" [Luke 1:37].

Among these familiar figures, however, there was the statement of an immigration expert, Carlos Bajo, working in First Street, Manhattan, for 1011, the Catholic Chancery, who after reviewing our situation, said that he couldn't find any way for us to get the Green Card.

We were familiar with the expression: "Never take no for an answer."

Nonetheless there is always a gap between those words of hope and the crude facts. A kind of spiritual wind of trust is necessary and makes the difference. A similar change, however, starts inside of us. It is in our heart that every fight starts and is first winning. Then the facts follow. Above all, we must keep peace in our hearts all along.

The need of applying for the Green Card increased progresssively. It became soon unavoidable. On February 1999, our lawyer, Mr. Jeffrey Van Doren, working in downtown Pittsburgh for the law firm Cohen & Grisby, who took care of the yearly renewal of our seven visas since we entered the States, told us that the visas were provided to us for the last time and they could not be renewed again. If we wanted to stay longer in the States, we needed to get the Green Card before our new visas had expired.

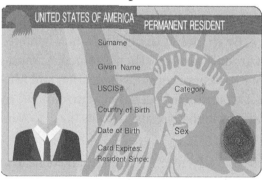

Diverse applications were available. We only needed to select the good one.

It was an engaging endeavor. As I already reported, after consulting an expert of immigration of the diocese of New York and receiving the statement that unfortunately there was no procedure that could work for us, it appeared evident that the Green Card was out of reach. We were supposed to pack again.

When, only a few weeks later, I told Carlos that we already got it, he looked astonished and said that we actually achieved a totally impossible endeavor. I simply replied that he just defined what a Gasconade is: "promising an impossible task and then achieving it." This is one of the thinks that the people born in Gascony are so proud of.

The three Musketeers, who were all Gascon, are a typical example.

Yes, he was exceedingly surprised when, within a month, I told him that we succeeded in our endeavor. Against the evidence of our performance, he confirmed at that time that he continued to consider unaffordable the whole process, due to the new States policy on immigration…

Being an expert, his eyes helped us to understand how true it is that Divine Providence does not know any borders. God has no limitation at all… and he is accustomed to transform every struggling situation in a joyful endeavor.

To say the truth, running towards the Green Card became suddenly dramatic. Too many issues were to address in too short time. Along these weeks, it was easy to find in the morning a difficult issue that definitively jeopardized the whole course of action. Later in the day some unexpected phone call or a conversation suggested us to make a new attempt trying some diverse approach… then, working hard, in the afternoon we had gone through…

While sometimes in the morning the whole process got definitively closed, soon in the evening there was hope again. A clearance was made. Similar courses of events happened several times. For a few weeks, we experienced a kind of Scottish shower, when too hot and too cold water alternatively and successively falls on you.

It would be impossible to describe the many things we did during these weeks. If a movie producer would recount the whole story, he would be considered the author of a pure fiction movie. Yes, in some occasions, reality overcame fiction. Besides, everything in that urgent endeavor was supposed to be addressed in addition to the already busy activity, which is proper to a five children family newly arrived in the country.

Let me recap few flashes on our life through some of the letters I wrote during the period which prepared and witnessed the application and finally the release of the Green Card. I like to stress that we were facing struggling situations, which became soon even more dramatic.

I selected a few in the midst of the letters sent and received to and from our friends during the months of these struggling days, while we were fighting to be allowed to remain in the States. Among them, it emerges first the correspondence with Bruno Venturini, a near friend living in Rocca di Papa, Rome, Italy, at the headquarters of the Focolare movement.

Detroit, on Tuesday 20 June 2000

Dear Bruno,

Two months have passed already since my last message to you. The weeks of May and June went through very quickly. At moments a month looks like a day! It was an intense period for various reasons. First of all, I was involved with an intensive course to teach (six hours a week) on Philosophy of the Human Nature, that elsewhere is called Anthropology. It is extremely demanding for the teacher and even more for the students. The course ends up tomorrow. The students are enthusiastic and they want to continue to share on the topic and to draw wisdom beyond the academic framework. They do not know yet, that all the wisdom they are interested in with my teaching, is coming from the spirituality of Chiara Lubich.

De facto, the study on the person was an occasion not only to discover the intimacy between soul-body-mind, but also to experience together in the threesome human constitution the traces of the same mystery of Trinity. They also acquired a greater awareness and maturity in their own humanity. I could not hope a better result. Our class meetings are moments of contemplation which sometime go on paths diverse from what I was expecting: as an example, a study on Pascal on the complementarity of heart and head, as the two wings of the same flight towards the truth, and as initial conditions of true human growing developed steps towards deep intimacy with God, while the study on Nietzsche, which the luminosity seemed so obvious to me, was less illuminating. Among the text books of the course, I inserted one of Chiara Lubich, in order to introduce the collective dimension of personal development.

To the teaching endeavor we must add internship supervision. Summer is the time of the year when seminarians are engaged in activities of apostolate in parishes, hospitals, prisons, and charity centers of the diocese. The whole "apostolate" activity concluded last week. It was a wonderful experience. At the beginning, I wrote to Sr. Mary Finn, the nun who coordinates the program: "The endeavor will surely be a success because I received from Divine Providence part of her bill to pay: I have kidney stones. By chance, they're not entirely unbearable, otherwise I could not be involved in the program and would even be unable to write a simple letter like this. They are nonetheless painful enough to be a good price to pay."

In fact, that activity completes the other business activities, like commuting every week between Pittsburgh-Detroit – driving 5 hours from home to work and vice-versa, the Focolare meetings that I used to run both in Pittsburgh and in Detroit for the sharing of the Word of Life (an excerpt selected from the Bible that we put in our daily life deeds as an attempt of re-evangelizing ourselves), and so on.

Recently, Fr. Bruno P., a priest of PIME, living in Detroit, came to Pittsburgh to visit the parents of a priest who acts in Africa. While in Pittsburgh, he also visited our house, and his appreciative comments helped us to see our place with renewed eyes, the eyes of Jesus present in the community, "When two or three..." It was a blessing for us.

Then, inside of this frequent to and from, Pittsburgh-Detroit, I got kidney stones. A series of investigations (generalist, clinical tests, ultrasound, Urologist, X-rays) indicates that these renal colics are connected with intestinal calcoli that we are supposed to address when I'll be returning to Detroit, after August break.

Furthermore, the stones belong to a type that resisted the ultra sounds bombing, and they do not seem even appropriate for chemical intervention. For the moment I have been advised to drink a lot of water and take strong analgesics in case the pain is too high. All investigations are suspended during the time I am home, in Pittsburgh. Doctors will address the situation later, after the third week of August, when I'll be back to Detroit.

Since last week, the schools are closed, and all the children are busy in activities where they are allowed to be. Many are the possibilities of work here for the youth, since the age of 14, but our kids cannot take advantage of them until we get the Green Card. Here is why Marie-Therese was induced to refuse a job of hair dresser, that would have been well remunerated. Not being allowed to work, Marie-claire enlisted for summer courses, which will accelerate the number of credits she needs to graduate. Michel is making some search on Internet, which will serve for school. Friends proposed us, a house that they use in Florida. Although the house was for free, we saw that the visit to the amusement parks over there and the gas would have involved imprudent expenses. So, avoiding costly holidays elsewhere, we subscribed to a local pool, where the children can walk from home and gather friends. The swimming pool is particularly appreciated on warm days, and it is a pleasant place. Last Saturday, I was pleased to also play ping pong there, with Marie-Therese and Michel.

In addition to visits to the sick and the elderly of the parish, Chiara animates the small Focolare community keeping contact with those who want to become familiar with the spirituality of Chiara Lubich, organizing meetings where people share personal experiences on the Gospel. She also acts as a volunteer for Europair, following girls doing au pair, domestic works for families in Pittsburgh.

Spiritually, we all are in good shape. The visit and sojourn of Mariateresa, Chiara's mom, was pleasant and successful. Chiara welcomed also home an aupair girl, from Riunione Island, who was temporarily with no place to go. Often these aupair girls come to visit us, for the time of a café, or to spend a few hours. they like to meet Chiara, who offer them her maternal affection, and the advices they need, during their sojourn in the States. Many of these girls, especially those coming from Europe, have difficulty to adapt here, for they do not immediately notice the cultural change. and this may cause them troubles. They feel at home in our place, and they also develop friendship with Marie-claire.

In addition to the friends who come every week to spend time with our children, and often overnight, we also have friends who visit us. A family came from Ottawa, Canada, recently. Many contacts were made. A student of mine came recently, to share some concerns. Last week it was a colleague with his whole family. We are often surprised to discover what tragedy may exist in the life of peo-

242

ple. *Beyond what we are told and what we are able to see, there is much more to discover in people, both in good deeds and suffering.*

Not knowing always the true situations, we eventually prefer to be wrong for exceeding love, than for too much prudence. We do our best and leave the results in the hands of Divine Providence. She knows and guides everything.

Perhaps you'll be surprised to hear this, but through these meetings and sharing, I have discovered the figure of Judas in the Gospel. Jesus always loved him, although he knew as bad, he was going to end up. He loved him so much that Judas had not even the excuse to say that Jesus loved him less than the other. Here is why I try to follow the rule of love more than the one of prudence in our relationship with the people we meet and we are not familiar with. In the Gospel Jesus protected Judas even against possible negative judgment from other apostles. At times, even if certain situations do not seem promising, I know that I have to love, following the example of Jesus, freely and unstintingly.

Sharing love is more powerful than any speech. Each time we welcome people home and share their own endeavors of difficulty and joy, and the quality of our family life increases. This commitment enlarges the panorama of our daily endeavors. There is no doubt that the people of the country show an original civilization. The dynamic configuration of American society presents surprising and fast changes, which sometimes involve proportionate bewilderments. Living the Gospel everyday is the key to behave there. In this context, I found a church where I may have confession every week and I use to bring some kid with me every time I go there. They are happy to come and grow in the intimacy of the Lord.

I admire the way Chiara is able to manage the needs of our family with my own, and unique salary. I do my best myself while driving back and forth between Pittsburgh and Detroit with the amount that Chiara allows me to spend every week. Nonetheless in a few months, the gas price duplicated: a gallon raised from 99 cents up to $2, 15, using the lowest unleaded variety, which actually is good enough for my car. Higher gas varieties get absurdly expensive figures, and the price continues to rise a little more each day. It *is even not the same at Pittsburgh and at Detroit. The difference is consistent, but it would be imprudent to keep the gas in containers from Pittsburgh and use it when I drive at Detroit... There is no other solution, than being wise, and put everything in the hand of Divine Providence, who knows what is going on, and take care of us.*

About the Green Card, our lawyer wrote us yesterday confirming that the application is in process. The government asked more information, which means that the practice is going forward. We truly want to get it soon. The lawyer counts to receive the response during the month of July, if all things continue to go through. I now believe that there is reason for hope and, of course, we pray and our friends pray with us for this. The actual course of action is the fourth application that we make, since the month of September 1997. For some reasons, every other procedure failed.

Here in Detroit, through the Seminary, I was put in contact with a lawyer office, which cares the issues of the archdiocese, which may eventually help in case the process would stop again. As soon as the Green Card is delivered, many things will become easier for us. In this perspective Chiara and the kids get ready to start some jobs. Chiara especially has her Resumé ready to activate some contacts.

Meanwhile the attorney sent various invoices of $800, $900 that were paid. One of $250 arrived today. There was also a bill of $1.000, that I contested, and was withdrawn. I really am surprised, that we have been able to face all these expenses.

Another charge that we have to face, and we want to support, is the health insurance of Marie-Claire. Being now over 18 years old, I cannot have her included in the benefits of my job in Detroit. A new disposition was made in Michigan and, starting this month, I should pay the amount of $200 more every month for her. Meanwhile Marie-Claire took information at her university of Philadelphia, and she found that with $60 a month, the university will cover her for 10 months. For the other two months, July and August, she found a company of Pennsylvania, which will accept to ensure her for the amount of $80 per month. We are going to succeed.

Last summer, we also had to paint the outside of the house. Being in part made of wood, the house needs this kind of maintenance.

A room mate of Marie-Claire, Sindey, has the father who can do the job. At the time, his offer was more convenient than the requests of the companies, which were immediately available. In spring, Chiara noticed that the façade of the house was damaged by water infiltrations, due to the weather. She managed to have the wall repaired, free of charge, by the same company.

I admire the capacity, showed by Chiara, to handle concrete issues. She has a sense of organization which looks typically American. Then a big store was closing in the neighborhood and Marie-Therese was able to get, for a good price, everything she needed, to make a coat of paint on the balcony, the porch, and the shed in the back yard.

We also had to provide small repairs on the heater, in the kitchen, the laundry and a bath. All things concerned water plants, which I am not able to do by myself. Personally, I made some works of manutention for the light and telephone line. Also, I had care for rooms and cabinets of doors, which needed adjustment, or new locks. Every house requires constant manutension. It is rare that I have not something to fix, during the weekend, when I am home. A family of seven people, eight when we have the visit of Chiara's mom, needs a house clean and efficient.

Chiara does an excellent job with the kids to keep the house clean. Those continuous needs of care are mainly attributable to the continental weather, that reaches peaks of hot that border 100 degrees Fahrenheit in the summer and peaks of cold that can get 20 degrees below between January and February. These storms in temperature go with seasonal storms, like the couple of tornadoes, which surprised us last year, and abundant rains, which go everywhere, and make us feel that the house is immersed in an aquarium. If the windows are not properly sealed, the water enters like a run. Thus, these works are normal maintenance. Perhaps that a stone house like those we have in France or Italy would not stand too long in similar weather conditions.

A problem that arose last fall is the roof that needs to be remade, at least in part. We already feared for the last winter. The cover is smashing here and there. Many of the so-called "tiles", which are man-made, were twisted by the weather. We had the roof inspected and we were told that there is no room for waiting longer to do it. The most convenient estimate runs around $5.000, using again all the material which still looks good. At this time, we have not the sum yet, but, somehow, we will go through.

We still are in contact with Fr. Brendan, even if we are not plan-nng to move to Texas yet. His hermit life is typical, and being in Tex-as their own cabins are exposed to the weather. In fact, a storm had recently destroyed part of the house where he lives and they have not enough activities in the community, to make their life in the ranch self sufficient. The offers they receive are barely enough to prevent them to die of hunger. Sometimes I send them money, too, dividing the little we have. I plan to see Fr. Brendan, during the summer, for he intends to visit the hermitage, that he has near Pittsburgh, at Littleton, West Virginia, during the next month of July.

Recently a tragedy struck the family of his sister; while working in his Ranch in Sandia, near Corpus Christi, her husband was killed by a Vagabond, who was caught while stealing in the house. There is however the possibility that with the increasing price of petrol the ranch where they have their hermitages could receive an offer of oil producers to draw some gas from the supposed resources, they have underground. It would help a lot for their activity of support to the poor and of evangelization activity.

When she visited me at Detroit, Chiara wanted to see if there were some places in town, that would be available, in case we would move from Pittsburgh. That would avoid me to drive back and forth, every week, between Pittsburgh and Detroit: a 300 miles trip that I do twice a week. It takes a minimum of five hour per trip. We visit-ed several places, both inside and outside the city, up to a distance of about an hour by car from the college, the Sacred Heart Major Seminary, where I actually teach.

We got some few surprises. For example, we discovered along the lake, before the straight - from which Detroit got its name - a residential area, that shows a richness that I did not thought even possible on earth. It is the area, near St. Claire Shore, where it is forbidden for pedestrians and no car is supposed to stop, anywhere, *unless to enter in some of the gorgeous mansions we found there. The police allowed cars in the area only for transit. It is therefore totally prohibited to stop and have a walk in the beautiful neighborhood.*

In other areas, we found constructions which seemed accommodate huts instead of houses. Nonetheless, the price for those so-called houses was roughly costing more than twice the price of our home in Pittsburgh.

When finally, we entered a district where the constructions looked livable, we found a small house that could have been suitable for our family, but the price was four time much higher than our home in Pittsburgh, in the case we would sell it. Also, food and clothing are more expensive in Detroit. Therefore, for the moment, we gave up with the idea to move to Detroit. Chiara and I, we were both surprised to see how everything is so expensive there, even the gas.

At this time, it is easier, then, for our family to live in Pittsburgh, even if I have to drive back and forth. In any case the kids are not ready yet to change schools. And those of North Allegheny, where they go, offer a teaching of better quality that the schools in Detroit, unless we send the children to private schools, which would increase too much our expenses.

Another characteristic of the city of Detroit invites us to reflect more about the opportunity to move there. It is the usual conditions of daily life. At Pittsburgh our kids are accustomed to walk around to visit their friends up to a few miles away, sometimes up to five miles away. They use to do so during the day or even in the evening when it is already dark, especially on weekends, when the school is over. And their friends do the same towards our home without problems on daylight or on evening. A similar behavior is not conceivable in Detroit. Students here were robbed just outside the fence of the Seminary, and they were said by the police that they were fortunate for still being alive.

A Latin professor, a Jesuit, who had just arrived from Philadelphia, wanted to pursue here, according to the schedule he was previously used, to run every day outside the college along the palisade.

247

So, he started jogging the first morning here, as soon as he arrived in Detroit. He had not done a quarter of the lap yet, when he was stopped by the police, and brought at the station to be questioned.

The police believed, for sure, to have got a thief, who was running out: the outfit of the priest, a sweat suit, and the absence of any I.D. encouraged their suspicion. The police couldn't believe that a mature man, as he was, could have been unaware of the minimum rules of prudence which require to never take a walk alone in that area, unless for a few steps. It took him a few hours, before he was allowed to call someone in the Seminary, and ask to come to the police station, and clear the miscommunication.

Three miles further northeast, around the Catholic Cathedral, it is not unusual to find some corpse in the morning. The police recommended to the Cardinal to transfer the Cathedral in the suburbs. The archbishop refused saying that the Catholic Church must be present where more it is needed from the people. Next year, however, the diocese is going to spend something like six million dollars, to expand a little bit the church, and restore the adjacent streets. I do not know yet what the project is, but it should make possible for people the walk around the building. The situation is similar for a large neighborhood.

One of my peers, prof. Roberto Fastiggi, a theologian who lives with his family only twenty minutes away by car through the regular roads, finds more comfortable, every day, to take the highway and the main roads to go home, which requires fifty minutes to strike the distance. His wife dissuaded him to drive through the city.

Hoping that the Green Card will come, I asked the bishop who runs the seminary, to renew for another three year the current contract that ends in July 2001. He accepted to keep me there in the same conditions, which is allowing me to live in the Seminary during the week, and shuttle on weekend to Pittsburgh. I plan to leave some other year the family staying in Pittsburgh and procrastinating our transfer to Texas. It seems wise, at this time, to offer the kids to complete their school studies there. Therefore, I confirmed to the bishop my intention to remain here for the next four years.

I thank you for the patience you had reading this all along un-

til now. There would be surely more to say and I'll tell it next time eventually. Now I have to prepare a test for the students, and write a couple of letters before I leave for the weekend. If in my letter, you found some inaccuracy, do not pay attention to it: while I was writing it, I had some computer problem. It stopped working a few times, and I had to reboot pulling off the battery, and isolating suspected programs. This misadventure did not prevent me to tell you most of what I wanted to say.

I remain near to you with continuous prayer and renewing every day our pact of unity in the Eucharist. I have a great desire to see you again and I count the days from now to November when you will visit the community of the Focolare in Washington D.C. I hope that you will be available for a short conversation that I'll deeply appreciate. Always yours in Jesus'

Alain

Bruno's reply of June 2000 was to have been included.

Unfortunately, in 2019, some resources came to an end, and we had to move out of the house we had purchased in Pittsburgh, for it became impossible to finish paying the mortgage: the community which had made the commitment to help us while we had the mortgage decided to stop helping.

In spite of our request, those in charge, Magnus, Jesus M. and Maria V. remained implacable. We had to move out. As a result, I threw away more than 10 metallic cabinets containing files of all sorts, including important documents from the Vatican, the Church and the Focolare Movement, some personal letters from authorities and Famous people, like Igino Giordani, and Chiara Lubich.

I gave away more than 2000 books…

Yes, moving from our house in Allison Park, Pittsburgh caused me to lose several boxes of documents.

By chance, during the moving, I was able to preserve the files concerning Moissac.

Pittsburgh, Saturday 8 July 2000

Dear Bruno,

Forgive me for being late in replying to your kind note. I confess that the last time I drove to Pittsburgh, in addition to the kidney stones, which are still current, there were many small things to care with family life and house maintenance that I barely had time to breathe and surely not to rest. Not everything was done when I had to drive back.

Meanwhile I got influenza, which, for two weeks in a row, kept me down, physically and psychologically. It gave me moments of great tiredness. I still remember the suggestion of Peppuccio who, at the international Gen Center, used to consider our common colds as a sign of lack of spiritual commitment. If it is so, it can be the price to pay for 10 months of continuously intense work and challenging commitment in Detroit.

Actually, at the Seminary, everything went well, better than expected. On second thoughts, I can see that there were special graces in my teaching commitment. I know that I'm not supposed to rely in the future, at least not as a natural course of action. This excellent endeavor, fortunately, was not proportionate to my own misery. I dare to say that it was even inversely proportionate to it.

I trust that God will continue to provide this undeserved helpful presence, that makes so consistent my commitment at the Seminary. All of this is surely linked to his plans for us. It is a contribution, I believe, to feed the nascent springtime of the Church. I was impressed by the recent activity of the Focolare in Africa. I was updated on it, both in Detroit and in Pitttsburgh. I'll be happy to talk again on this topic, which increasingly convinces me that we witness a process of renewal of Christendom, that even with the most burning imagination, we cannot figure out what the Lord is going to disclose among us.

Therefore, when I arrived home, in Pittsburgh, there was to deal with minor things, and I collapsed. It is true that living with uncertainty the expectation of the Green Card may transform daily insecurity in a sort of dying agony. Nonetheless, in the middle of precariousness, God's providence is source of growing serenity. You know the picture. I understood better the value of holy indifference towards situations and the necessity to pursue God's will, everyday, in spite of the mediocrity of our common misery. It is a process linked with the mystery of Eucharistic Jesus.

I feel better now. Little by little, the strength comes back. It looks like a fictitious movie, when leaving a long lethargy, an astronaut feels the physical, then the psychic, returning slowly to life. But the soul remains unchanged, in its burning thirst for God. Therefore, little by little, I start to take care again of things that, days ago, I had to leave in God's hands.

Only today, I opened the computer again and checked the mail. Then I took care of some business. Meanwhile Chiara shopped a little bit, in order to see if there was another company ready to repair the roof, under better conditions, but the one we contacted first remains the most convenient, and they will start the repair next Monday.

We also organized a moment with the children, at least once a week, practically on Sunday morning, which is a time of formation. We share about the Gospel before Mass.

Then, always once a week, we also have a general meeting of sharing in the family. We check how things are proceeding at home, and everyone refers about their chores and their spiritual life...

I suggested the children to write a diary or a journal for that, because it seems, sometimes, in spite of very busy days, we are unable to report anything. Furthermore, the society today conveys the patterns of disparate or conflicting values. Meeting to check how we are going, is like using a vacuum cleaner which absorbs the superficiality of the days, and leave us alive, with the worthy endeavors we exert. It is beautiful to be able to evidence good deeds and share proper understanding of our behaviors.

The moment of sharing is therefore a time for cleaning mind and soul together. Sometimes it helps to understand the significance of the suffering of one or another, and show how there is no betterment, without some such process of purification and generous sacrifice.

Chiara and I take care of having once a week, usually on Tuesday, an entire day to spend with one of our kids, hiking together somewhere. It is beautiful to be able to get some intimacy, one on one, with our children. It produces great improvement of our family life.

Marie-claire left this morning to spend a week in the house of one of her companions from the University, at the ocean in North Carolina. She will resume her study at the Community College, doing some baby-sitting services and working as a waitress. Meantime Marie-Thérèse and Marta alternate study and baby-sitting.

Michel leaves tomorrow for Kansas. The father of a school compagnion moved in Kansas City, and wanted to pay for the trip, by air plane and the stay of Michel over there, to thank Michel for the good help he offered during the year, to his son at school. He will stay there until the first of August. When he is back, he will resume its various work commitments.

Chiara and Marta are going to the summer Mariapolis in Allentown, together qith a group of eleven people from Pittsburgh. So next week I will be home only with Marco and Marie-Thérèse. Meanwhile the whole community of the Focolare in the States is preparing your coming in November, with the international Focolare Headquarters in Washington D.C.

Next Saturday we will go in West Virginia to pay a visit to Kent, who lives in a cabin in the woods. In spite of a good intellectual preparation and a large human experience, Kent leads a very humble life. Years ago, when he lived with his family in Washington, parents and brothers were victims of a massacre. He was so shocked that he is almost unable now to behave properly in society. After a period abroad, first in England, then in Ireland, he returned to the States he suffered another mishap which deprived him of all resources. He remained so without means.

Eventually, he was able to trade for a trailer, which is frozen in winter and sultry in summer, and he lives there in the company of animals, mostly cats. He helped me many times in the past, reviewing the notes of my lessons of philosophy at La Roche, or at Duquesne. Asking his assistance for the redaction of some articles is very helpful to me, and he truly deserves the few bucks I give him in return. I gave him, to do so, an old computer, which was a poor device, that he was later able to trade for a better one, that he is now using.

I also asked him to copy or transcribe on paper a few lectures that I plan to use for publications. He does an excellent job in this kind of work.

While driving there and greeting Kent, we will visit nearby the hermitage of Catholic Solitudes in Littleton. For a time, I thought that Kent could have been one of the hermits over there. Unfortunately, John-Mary, one of the priests of Catholic solitudes, has another agenda. He is tightly connected with Thiara and Mirtha, two seers of Monterrey, Mexico, who easily exclude those who do not focus on them, beyond the teaching of the Church.

When Chiara and Marta will be back from the Mariapolis, we will have a picnic, in our back yard for my birthday. We will have it on July 22. It is a good excuse to have a family party with our friends in Pittsburgh. Last year we were around 40 people. We are expecting almost the same number this year.

If we get the Green Card, I will be pleased to travel to France, in August, with some of the kids, and visit my siblings over there, and also, part of us will, probably, come to Rome next Christmas.

I remain near to you, with prayers and thoughts, in the endeavor of our holy journey. Say hello to everyone over there, Chiara, Chiaretto, Oreste, Peppuccio, Enzo and all those living at the headquarters of the Work of Mary. Hope to see you soon.

Alain

Pittsburgh, Tuesday 29 August 2000

Dear Bruno,

Thank you for your last message full of enlightening discernment. Looking to our family with your eyes, help me to see us all under a better light, we better understand God's love for us and are comforted in our earthly adventure.

Talking with our lawyer, this morning, it came out that, because of a recent decision of the Congress, we will no longer be granted the Green Cards after September 30th. I asked if it was in anticipation of this deadline that, just yesterday, the Immigration Office granted permission to request the statute of resident. The lawyer asserted that it would have been the opposite. It was clear that we have to only thank Divine Providence for it.

We must present the application within a week, duly document-ed for the seven of us with specific photographs, birth certificates, bank accounts, taxes receipts, photocopies of the whole of our pass-ports (while two are already expired, and need get renewal in Wash-ington D.C.), various blood tests (in two different medical centers – with timing results of analyses), and finally a medical examina-tion with approved federal doctors - which actually have scheduled appointments up to the mid of November in the best scenario. In one word, to do so is humanly impossible.

After our lawyer call, this morning, I run in town from one of-fice to another, and was busy over the phone. I was also trying to inform Chiara about the new situation, but she was on the road, driving Marie-Claire to Philadelphia University. It is six hours away from home. She had to bring her back. Marie-claire was almost shocked for losing her first week of classes because of the Green Card business.

Today we will be busy the whole day, running between banks, photography studios, medical centers, doctors and hospitals. Tomor-row we will leave together, at five in the morning, driving to North-ern Pennsylvania, in order to be at Erie, at the opening of a medical center which, exceptionally, agreed to try to insert us among their scheduled patients. We have no warranty of success.

When yesterday the federal doctor heard, over the phone, that I was not asking for me only, but for the seven of us, who need a full physical, he refused to accept us. I told him that we will drive there, every morning, and be at the door, when the clinic opens, untill he will find a way he could see us all. It was my decision, and he could not change it. He had just to agree, due to the fact that, after all, it *was at our own risk. We will try again every day until it is done, putting everything in Providence hands.*

Friday, I have to be at the Federal Building, to update taxes information. Sunday, after the Mass, with the family in Pittsburgh - which will be of thanksgiving, I hope. I have to drive the usual five hours to Detroit, and be at a meeting at the university - which was opportunely postpone - and then assure the teaching the following days.

I told you that this year I felt not ready for the courses I teach there, but due to the circumstances all classes will need full creativity. I'll give the students the best of my knowledge. With a similar background, I assume that my teaching will be pure wisdom, and ultimately it will be excellent.

A soon as Chiara and Marie-Claire will be done, they'll drive back to Philadelphia.

We offer the whole intense, and almost tragic, situation, as a living prayer for your coming trip in the US, together with the Focolare Headquarters. We are pleased if we can add our spiritual concern in favor of the commitments that Chiara Lubich took in this country. Following the words of Ignace of Loyola, we do everything as it was depending only on us, knowing well that, ultimately, everything belongs to the hands of Divine Providence. At the end of the day, this evening, with the children we will pray together, according to the suggestions in Matthews 18:19: "when two or three gather in my name to ask something to the Father on my behalf, He will provide it".

I never understood so well a similar suggestion, that in the Latin words of Vulgate start with "consenserint." And Luc 1:37 says that "Nothing is impossible to God." As a result, it would be a disease of not believing it possible. We have nothing to lose. We must try to go through, even if everyone around says we are knocking at and empty door, for it really seems that our endeavor is in no way doable. I understand how God likes us to ask for what he plans to deliver to us, even if it must be a miracle. After all, miracles are probably more common everyday than I foresaw.

Say hello around. Before running out with the rest of the family,

I remain near to you, and to everyone near to you, together with Jesus and his Mother,

Alain

Bruno replied the same day, wishing that the whole situation should ultimately appear like a cloud, a storm, without bad consequences. I wish my computer did not crash in September 11 and everything I had in the computer, including his letter was lost.

Fortunately, I had some material in some portable device which could be saved.

It's impossible to repeat the many situations experienced during the month of September 2000. A Scottish shower, with a fast repetition of frosting and burning water, would probably provide the right feeling. I don't know how many of those intense events are not reported in some letter or note... For some reason they disappeared from my records. I probably wrote so much around, about these events, sharing them with friends that, afterwards, I decided to erase some, and, unfortunately, I erased almost all.

Something nonetheless survived. Some few letters repeat the same situations, but not under the same perspective. It is worth, so, to report some...

Pittsburgh, Saturday 2 September 2000

Dear Luigino,

Our adventure on this side of the sea continues to be eventful above our expectations.

On August 28 the Department of Labour approved our request to apply for the Green Card. The lawyer would call later to inform us about the details to proceed. But the following day was a cold show-

er: a decision of the Congress suspended the delivery of all Green Card of the category we belonged to after the end of the month… And he provided to me a long list of approved doctors who were supposed to fill a governmental form to start the process. We needed a federal physical visit, in order to get the application approved.

After that, the lawyer called me to tell that, we sere supposed to get the Green Card before September 30. I started right away the first step: getting an approved doctor to get the mandatory medical examination.

I soon faced the impossibility to get any doctor appointment for the mandatory medical statement… The Lawyer gave me name and address of many of them. I did not understand at first the reason of a so long list of doctors, residing in Pennsylvania and nearest states. "Why are they so many?" I thought.

When I started to call them for a visit, I understood the situation, and it was a nightmare. All doctors around, from Ohio, on the West, to Connecticut in the East, were all booked until mid November and I needed such a visit right away…

It was useless trying to get an appointment with any doctor in Pittsburgh and vicinity… In Ohio, New York and Connecticut they were all booked until far after mid-November. Finally, I found a Doctor in Erie, who was stretchable about seeing me… To force his schedule I said, "Don't worry we will be at your place tomorrow morning."

A silence responded to me over the phone, then a question came: "Did you say, 'WE'?"

"Yes, we are seven people in the family…"

"Oh! Seven! That is absolutely not possible"

"Don't worry," I replied, "We will come every morning to your place, and we will be at your door, every morning, until the day that you find the time to see us"

It was an offer he could not refuse.

He didn't say a word, for there was nothing to say.

Immediately, I called the family, and I explained the situation.

257

Everything was supposed to be postponed to the medical visit that we needed first. Meanwhile we were supposed to get all medical certificates and vaccinations reports. It was even too late to make any new vaccination. It would have taken too long. But, fortunately, all vaccinations for the kids were in order because of school requirement and we got the report of it the same day.

We also called our previous doctor in Rome, to get vaccinations reports for me and Chiara. The records were wonderfully in order and we got them by fax the same evening.

Additional blood tests were required and we went all of us to Passavant Hospital to get them

Then, just before the bank closed, I was able to get the whole amount we had there: a thousand dollar, to cover the fee for the mandatory physical visit, needed for all of us.

Afterwards, during the night I prepared a folder for each one, with all the documentation, I had. Around five o'clock in the morning we were on the road towards Erie.

Two hours driving were necessary to get the city, then, I hoped we could find easily the place of the doctor clinic. We found it before it opened.

We were at the door, around 7:45. And we started waiting, keeping our hearts at peace...

I was amazed to see how the kids were behaving in orderly fashion.

They understood how serious the issue was for all of us. They were silent, behaving accordingly.

When the nurse opened the door, we told her that I spoke with the doctor, the previous day, and we agreed that we would enter, only when the doctor was available for us, for we wanted not to fill the waiting room, with the family, if he had no time to see us.

"It is not too cold outside!" I added... and she agreed.

Around nine thirty, we were still there, and the doctor came out to see if we still wanted that physical visit. We confirmed our intention, and I provided the doctor all the files, that I prepared the previous night. He was happily surprised to see that half of the paperwork was already done. "Oh! I see that you have already provided all the documentation. How did you know that you needed these documents?"

"The lawyer told me", I replied ; and I immediately went to the hospital and the child clinic with the whole family to get them."

He remained silent.

The more he looked at the documentation, the happier he was with the whole material. His happy surprise was confirmed while ending to browsing the papers: he could find almost everything he needed... There were even the receipts of the blood tests made the previous day at Passavan Hospital...

"You are very well organized," he commented, "and you even did those tests! We only need the results now." He uttered.

"Yes," I said. "We should get the results in two days."

"Wonderful," was his comment, "please, come in."

We entered his clinic at once, moving as a sole person, and we right away occupied the whole room.

Then opening the files again, one by one, he started the medical examination of each one... It took time to go over all of us... but we were so happy, we weren't hoping that the physical could go through on the first attempt... and everything worked accordingly.

We also filled all the papers which were supposed to be signed as soon as he had received the results from Passavan Hospital.

When we get out, in the afternoon, a great joy invaded us: the first obstacle was over...

Actually, some unusual event had happened. I understood the reason why the lawyer gave me so many names in the list of doctors to call. Actually, even the lawyer knew that the process was reasonably impossible, nonetheless, if he wanted to get his fee, he was supposed to hide this and pretend to help us and invite us to try.... his wage was at risk.

This first attempt worked so well that it made the lawyer right: "we had to run! It was the case to celebrate... we drove to a mall to

259

get meal in a fast food. Then, during the meal I told the children what we really had achieved and, as a celebration, we were going to Walmart and they were supposed to purchase whatever they needed and wanted for school.

Out of the thousand I took at the bank, US$ 700 had been employed for the medical visit.

Now I wanted to celebrate, putting the rest of the money available, for the children. It was an incredible spectacle to see the kids around... "Dad, may I have this notebook?" "Dad, may I take this pen?" What a pleasure for once to be able to answer, "Yes, sure!"

It was a true celebration and the kids were so happy to get whatever they needed for school.

The day after, there was no time for rest. At eight o'clock in the morning, the lawyer was at the door. He took us by surprise, coming to our place bringing a large envelop that I was supposed to fill and send right away. It was supposed to be filled the same day and received in Washington D.C. the following day.

One of the issues was to gather all passports, with the list of every entry in the States and eventual trip outside the country, adding every time the proper documentation with the visas...

It was a long work to gather such material and I had been working at home from 8 in the morning (when the lawyer brought me the form to fill) until 3 p.m. when I was finally ready.

Then, I needed to make copies of all and went to Office Max... At five, Office Max was supposed to close and I was not done yet. Exceptionally that day it was open two hours later, because the following day was school opening. That providential circumstance allowed me to complete the documentation the same day.

During the same day I also was supposed to send the whole material by express mail, in order it was received in Washington D.C. the following day. The lawyer had even provided to me, the express envelope, for the expedition...

When I left home at ten to nine Chiara asked me: "Where are you going?"

'I have to mail this letter at the post office." I said.

"But it is closed at this time!" she insisted.

"I know that, but I have to try" I explained

"And if you do not succeed?" she asked.

"This letter must be in Washington D.C. tomorrow, otherwise the whole process is over"

"Good luck, then"

I drove directly to the main post office, which I got the address at the door of our local post office. That principal postal business was supposed to be open up to nine in the night. It was nine fifteen already. I drove there. I was not familiar with the place. I parked nearby and I walked around, not even being sure where the entrance was. I had the express mail envelop in my hand that I was waiving as a signal, as if I had an appointment with somebody there.

Something unexpected happened. Suddenly an officer came out from the building: he took my envelope and gave me a receipt... I was astonished. "How much I owe you?" I asked. "Wow!?!" he said "I cannot accept money from outside and I cannot bring stamps either from inside."

His generous behavior seemed useless, when suddenly I remembered that I kept in the car stamps for the kids when they need them to send a letter to their friends: "I have stamps in the car" I said.

"Go and get them" he encouraged me.

When I came back I had many regular stamps and was not sure if I was able to cover the amount of US $12. that were necessary. Besides they would be too many to put near the address on the envelope. The employee understood my trouble and wiped it away: "Don't worry, let me put the stamps in the back, there is room enough there..."

I was amazed by his availability and his efficiency. I wish I would remember his name to pray for him everyday in gratitude for what he did for us that night...

When I drove back home, I was barely touching the ground, I had the feeling I was flying... not for the speed, but for the joy filling my heart. Entering the house, I looked so happy that Chiara was surprised: "What happened to you. You look like kissed by an Angel!"

"It actually happened" I said.

Thanks, Luigino, to have the kindness to read these notes. I really needed to share our endeavor with you, and pray in thanksgiving for everything does happen.

Cheerio,

Alain

Here follow other letters that I wrote in the following days to Bruno in Rome.

Pittsburgh, Sunday 3 September 2000

Dear Bruno,

It was a delight to read your deep message on problems which are mere phantasms and on apparently terrible events which are only clouds, hiding a radiant sun, upon our daily life. Additionally, wind and rain help grass and plants to grow, which means that we need storms in our lives, to develop accordingly. As an echo to your message, the past week invested us with terrible situation, requiring to employ all our strenghts up to the extreme limits of our forces, but keeping our heart serene in our weakness. I'll drop the details. Too many events shook us. It happened, in a few circumstances, that the whole endeavor, towards the Green Card, looked definitively compromised, then, shortly later, for an unexpected gesture of Divine Providence, we suddenly were again put on track. Afterwards, it only remained the memory of what we had been able to offer, in the moments in which every hope was lost. It was a shaking situation, which is not over, yet.

When every human support is missing, it is difficult to understand what to do. And the required commitment became every time more consistent, like some internet game that follows every success with a more challenging level. Sometimes you are offered a five minutes deeds on internet, and you enter in some expandable programme: after you are said that only a click is needed, you need hours to configure the service in the computer. So was the physical visit required near a federal doctor, in addition to the difficulty, to find one, who was available for such a short lapse of time.

So was the picture process. Same difficult process was gathering all visas and travel evidences.

Meanwhile regular contretemps were present, too. A toilet obstructed. A tap leaked. The television set stopped working after the roof was remade: I had to climb on the top of the house and play with the antenna. These were all regular occurrences in a family house of seven people. At the same time, many electronic messages and phone calls came from our friends, asserting that they prayed with us. It was a great comfort. The whole experience made us more discerned and composed.

Mr. Jeffrey VD, our lawyer, was fighting well for us, in all possible directions. He was also trying to obtain permission to introduce our unusual request to the Immigration Office, here in Pittsburgh, instead of Lincoln, Nebrasca, which was assigned to us. According to him, only if we get the interview, here in Pittsburgh, there are probabilities for us to succeed.

If the application will be accepted in town, I'll have to drive immediately from Detroit. In a few days, the lawyer came three times in our house to bring and take documents. I often was given a large file to fill out, with forms, and enclosures. At times the material was so abundant that I needed almost half a day only to read it all, and I had to rush.

There is such a mass of paper and documents that invades my study that I have taken the habit of calling it now, more properly, my stock. Still is a surreal situation. I would say it ubuesque,

Yesterday, there was another surprise: the pictures that we almost miraculously managed to get for all of us, including Marie-Claire, who precisely came from Philadelphia, of three diverse types, for each one of us, with a fee of $35 by head, well, these pictures were rejected by the federal agent... I was ready to return to the shop to obtain a new production, not being sure how I could *gather the whole family again, when I suddenly had a doubt: we had been very consistent with the official norms, may be the agent should check them better, and I asked the lawyer to bring the pictures back to the federal bureau... eventually, trying to meet a more experienced officer... Very kindly the lawyer took all the pictures back.*

The situation is tragic, too, under the perspective of money management. All this running and deeds involved expenses which are drying up our bank accounts, and I am concerned, in case some inspection found them almost empty: that would be also a cause of Green Card refusal.

Being immigrants, we have no health insurance. Only the physical visit with the federal doctor costed $100 each, in addition to the vaccinations ($60 by head), and the analyses ($40). To this must be added a setback with the taxes and Chiara will go on Tuesday at the federal building to pay what would remedy the situation.

We were told that a large amount is due. Hopefully, there is a mistake there, too.

I needed to take advantage in the bank of a line of credit to deal with all that.

We are so stretched. And to say the truth, Chiara is producing miracles every week to cover all our needs. This is barely supportable. Hope we'll soon be over.

Divine Providence, however, acted very clearly to keep alive our courage. We found sometimes employees or government officers who showed such kindly manners that they made easier to address sensitive situations. Some time it was a simple goodhearted approach. In some situation it was so a significant help, that we seemed to have been flooded by God.

Typical was the endeavor of getting our birth certificates. I could recover my own that I still had in files.

The situation was different for the children: Rome township registry was closed for strike. It was therefore impossible to have them, despite the efforts of Luigino, who went on the spot of the "anagrafe" for three days in a row.

Fortunately, we could recover some, which were recently produced at the Italian Embassy in Philadelphia. And for Chiara's birth certificate, which is still missing, it should come today from Livorno.

Nothing was easily done. Yet it was all, in a sense, providential. I mean that during those difficult days we found clearly Divine Providence next to us. I am now collecting data for another form and I'll be working the whole day. I must also work on the passports, collecting all the visas. I just found them yesterday evening, and I believe all are there. Then I need to make a full report with photocopies. Not everything is in order. We must leave space, even there, to Divine Providence.

At times we wondered if all that immense fatigue was necessary.

Certainly, the green card does not deserve such a painful endeavor even if it causes it! I thought that the travel of Focolare headquarters in November to Washington D.C. deserves some suffering to be offered as a prayer for it. I also considered that the prayer of many is needed in favor of a better health of the Holy Father. For these reasons, yes, I do agree to enter in such struggling steps! It was a luck that this week I was at home, free from teaching. In this manner, I could address many aspects of the Green Card endeavor.

I was so focused on that issue, that I had not organized yet my courses, for the fall semester. I was not psychologically able to do so, from here, in Pittsburgh, because of our residential emergency.

I'll drive to Detroit this afternoon and as soon as I arrive at the Sacred Heart Major Seminary, I'll focus my mind on the courses of metaphysics, Ancient History, Mediaeval Philosophy, and the knowledge of God in Maritain. I think that the best preparation consists first in being at peace, then letting my mind to deal with what I have to do, moment by moment, one thing at a time.

It is not necessary to schedule everything. It is sufficient to address, every time, the issue that pops up in my mind, doing it intensively, but peacefully.

As you were teaching yourself at Luminosa last January, everything depends more on the light we carry inside, than on our actual expertise. Everything we do and teach is mostly related with our capacity of keeping the heart clean and limpid, acting moment by moment, serenely, even in the midst of a storm.

Wisdom does not depend solely on the quantity of data we know, but more on our intensity of love and care towards our students. If I'm really concerned with my students everything will go smoothly, otherwise even the best expertise will never be enough.

In the meantime, the courses are starting. In a sense, this large burden, actually, gives my mind some rest from the Green Card struggle. I'll be too busy there with teaching to have time, then, to be also concerned with the business which is expecting me there in Pittsburgh. I just need to do my best and leave everything in Divine Providence's hands.

While I was home for a week or so, the days passed by like a storm on American soil. Everything was somehow assaulted, sometimes devastated but always cleaned. Then, the desire to survive made our life more genuine. There have also been situations of strong tensions at home, especially among children, from whom we are demanding so much. It seems that the lesson was not enough for all.

Perhaps we will need other thunderstorms to make everyone understand that, at any moment, we know what to do: the permanent duty of every situation is love. Through love everything is properly done. We must learn to act with humility, doing the best we can.

We were so busy that there was barely time to think about our assignments or for scheduling what was the most urgent business to address. I was only facing at every moment the duty that would pop up in the mind, the emergency that would come through a phone call, or found in a piece of paper, which eventually just fell on the floor, or through a person we came across...

Just doing moment by moment the best we can was the key, and immediately after moving to the following call, making another commitment, then another one, and another again, and so on, as a continuous game. I saw that for each moment there is the grace of serenity and opportunity that soon disappears and remain with you as far as you are able to change accordingly, adapting with the present call.

It was not possible during those days to think ahead. I only was able to address the current chore.

I had before my eyes the example of Mary, who does not know how the promise is supposed to happen and humbly follows God's will. She engages herself entirely in the present call, full of generosity and charity. Humility is not an attitude that shows up spontaneously. To get it, we need the help of God, who enters by force in your life sometimes.

I was given courage to go ahead when I thought of the great commitment and suffering of the Pope, and of every ruler in the nations or head of a community. I never considered before how much heroism there is around. How much generosity is present in those who lead us and how easy is it to criticize them! I could see how easy is making mistakes in similar situations and how careful I should be, for the whole process was so delicate. As a result, I justed need to do my best in what I am asked to accomplish.

Another comfort came from the awareness that what I was asked to address in a similar emergency was nothing but God's will. Doing so, it became easier to ask the Lord to help me to accomplish what he was asking me to do.

At the same time, I was supposed to only care for what I was requested to do, and not for its results... all results of our deeds belong to God, and we must leave it that way. It would be useless to believe that we are in charge of a situation, a person, a duty... No, we only are asked to do so and then we must abandon everything to his care. Doing so no burden is too high, everything remains affordable, and we keep peace in our heart.

It is with this attitude that I am returning today in Detroit, caring only of being transparent at any time to the will of God. This fills me with the desire to love and serve each one and every situation I encounter.

At any time, we get an appointment that, I understand, is introduced by God himself in our agenda. I think on that with gratitude even when the agenda looks overwhelming. Then it depends on us to make that appointment or commitment properly addressed. With a similar attitude I see that this would be a lucky time to die. In a similar context, our sins – that never fail to interfere – are almost diluted in the face of our own large misery. Such an understanding and availability helps God to watch us with mercy. It is a curious experience. It is a kind of mercy second, that pervades us all and, enjoying our merciful God, it makes us merciful in turn towards every creature. Yes, in a similar context it would be beautiful to die.

Peppuccio once explained to me that when our soul feels ready to die, it means that God is actually making us, mystically but really die, and He introduces a new presence of Himself in our life. It is actually a process of rebirth, which makes a new configuration of our relationship with the surrounding world. If it is so, everything is welcome.

All the more, it is a tremendous grace, that maybe should be called presence of Mary. I cannot say more. The capacity of living in the present, is a continuous exercise of losing everything else. Being able to do so is a gift. It is the teaching of Chiara Lubich.

The gift is free and incredibly great. For those who have not tested this experience yet, we must call it "capacity to let go". But this title is only a translation. When you experience it, you address the overflowing presence of God, which makes everything else disappear with a disruptive strain, acting as a storm, precisely.

This peaceful weakness may recall the words of Saint Paul talking about his own poor strength in the sense that if we set up the soul, then Jesus commands our life and converts, builds, acts – he operates all things, which we believed were our own deeds when we were freshly converted...

We thought we were making those things. Now, we understand they come from God. I pray the Lord to keep me in this attitude, which is a full Marian endeavor. I understand that this is only the grace of a moment of lucidity. Perhaps, as soon as we emerged from this whirlwind and extreme insecurity in which we are, soon will forget it. I would hope to never forget! But remaining in this genuine behavior is a grace. I seek her and want her.

Forgive the digression. If we get the Green Card, which we hope with all our heart, many aspects of our life will need to be addressed. The good news is that, having the Green Card, every job opportunity will be allowed. It will make a great change. Chiara is very concerned, but we know that the Lord uses to make us want, what *he is going to give us. But this is a topic to be considered tomorrow. For today we must accept that we are in this absurd situation of extreme need.*

Receive many greetings from all of us towards all of you. I am fraternally near to you in every endeavor of yours, together with Jesus and Mary,

Alain

Pittsburgh, Saturday 30 September 2000

Dear Bruno,

You heard from Chiaretto about the good news of the Green Card that was released to us even before we finished all the paperwork. In fact, the Immigration Office gave us the delay of two additional weeks to complete the documentation.

The important thing is that they already printed the Certification of Residence on our passports and for M. Claire and Marta, whom the passport had expired, was issued a provisional document of Permanent Resident, so everything was done within September 30 as scheduled.

All this happened on Thursday evening while I was traveling between Detroit and Pittsburgh. And, at my arrival home everything was already done.

Our joy is great! The serenity that invades us has no comments. You were right to say that those heavy clouds upon our heads were only frightening ghosts. The ability to live serenely the situation in the midst of the hardest uncertainty allowed us to address properly the recent events.

There is no doubt that without the help of the spirituality of Chiara Lubich we could never overcome the recent difficulties. For a while it was like living in a constant utopia. With a joke, Chiara added: "The whole situation was also a good test for the physical. If today we are not dead of cardiac arrest, through these breaking events, it means that our hearts are in good shape!

We are expecting the lawyer home today. He just informed us by phone that he is bringing us back the passports and the provisional certificates. Also, he will tell us what documents are still needed and must be provided within the coming two weeks.

Those who are familiar with immigration procedures are amazed by the events, which characterized our steps towards the Green Card. Even if all that is already done, they don't believe it truly happened. To say the truth, even the immigration inspector we met at the Federal Building last week had exactly the same feeling. First of all, the appointment came up so unexpectedly, that we needed to call and pay another lawyer for the day, and I had to drive especially from Detroit. In fact, Jeffrey, our lawyer had previous commitments for the day, that he could not postpone.

The immigration officer could not believe that all the documentation we were putting under her attention had been composed in less than 25 days. She was continuously uttering, "The procedure cannot have been done in such a short schedule." - "Everything was done too fast!" - "These files should be a fake."And she was inquiring with even more attention and she spoke with the seven of us, one by one, taking almost 30 minutes by person, asking to each one a series of questions... Surprisingly for her, and for us, everything went through. Several times she complained here and there about some document and by mistake, passing home I took the wrong briefcase: instead of the usual bag I took the case including all the paperwork I had been working with the previous days in Pittsburgh. That mistake was providential for, at every demand of her, I had in the bag the proper files to complete the documentation. Even the lawyer was amazingly surprised. What that actually was a mistake appeared to be an excellent preparation: I had everything handy... What a Providence!

When Chiara recounted that series of events to Sara, her cousin, who lives in Washington D.C., her husband, who is a lawyer, was hardly accepting that she told the truth...

He said that many of his clients could not get the Green Card this year because of the same reasons that made us running like racing cars the whole month.

A procedure that easily requires a year or less of hard work, was accomplished in several days, all counted they make a little more than a month! No doubt that prayer works. Yes, we are deeply grateful for your prayer.

For me, I had the feeling that Our Lady was telling me: "You see, Alain, my son wants you to stay in the States with your family!"

Now I'll be even more attentive to God's will.

Yes, I was truly busy with this matter in all recent weeks. I spent on the issue, several nights, too. And I had to address my teaching in Detroit all the same. In addition to more back and forth traveling between Detroit and Pittsburgh, I was used to get barely more than 4 or 5 hours of sleep per night.

Therefore, I will be quite busy in the coming weeks both at Pittsburgh and in Detroit to address all the issues that could not be properly done during that emergency rush.

Today I finally got a normal night of eight hours. At the Seminar, the bishop, and later the cardinal of Detroit, were so happy when they got the good news. The Bishop replied immediately in person over the phone and spoke in Italian: "Congratulazione ed Auguroni!" and he said that he would have spread the news in the Seminary and at Sacred Heart College in Detroit.

I will provide additional information when everything will be definitively accomplished and when I actually have the passports in my hands. Meanwhile, we have a provisional Green Card that stands for six months. We should receive soon, at home, the definitive document (renewable in ten years), that confirms our Permanent Residence.

This is the famous Green Card, which today shows Bordeaux color - I like that color, which symbolizes Gascony, the country which I come from. We got that achievement on September 27, which is the feast day of Saint Vincent De Paul, the greatest Saint of Gascony, whose name I carry as my second middle name. Also, that occurrence made me think about a special protection from above all along the process.

Together with this good news, Chiara found today a part-time

271

job as Italian teacher for a Pittsburgh firm, which runs business, with Italian companies. The pay is modest at the moment, but it allows her to begin working, and helps us to deal more serenely with daily expenses.

Soon, all the children will get in the neighborhood some job, too. That can be done as soon as they get their passport and make application to the office of work. They will have then to pay taxes on it - which is an unusual situation for them!

But we'll see, little by little, how everything works. I will let you known.

Another good point is that finally there are no more obstacles to cross the border. We seriously plan with all the family to visit Rome for Christmas. The boys had no occasion to see Italy again, since we left Rome, during the summer of 1995. In that occasion we will be so grateful, if you and Chiaretto will offer a Mass of thanksgiving, in your place for us. We leave to God's Providence all the details to be done.

Then, the following summer, I wish to visit France, and have a moment of gathering near the tomb of my mother, especially for the fact that I was unable to attend her funeral, for I was not allowed to leave the country during the rush for the Green Card.

I thank you for your prayers, for your constant spiritual nearness, your unity with us during these days, your presence that cheered up us all along. This accomplishment shows the magnificent grace of God. We keep us ready for the next call he will require us to achieve.

One always with you in Christ,

Alain

Postlude for the Tableau on Green Card

1. A few other events happened during the whole period of our rush towards the Green Card, which it was not possible to bring properly in the previous pages. Worth notice was the departure of

Marthe Montazel, my mother, moving into afterlife. I will refer to it, in the next Tableau.

2. After the period of seeking the Green Card was over, I did understand at least one teaching of Adrian Monmayou… A few topics deserve attention:

3. First of all, the whole period told of above was a time of grace from the Divine Providence. It is a splendid example of the manner we must always be aware, all along our life, to behave under its permanent care.

4. Second of all, rushing so hard for getting the Green Card, was, actually, only a training for going swiftly, all along our life, to get Eternal Life, who is expecting us to reach Her. And, we must rush even more towards Her.

5. It is even clearer for me, now, what was the teaching of Our Lady at Lourdes to Bernadette Soubirous. She spoke in Gascon. Many make a huge mistake, while translating Her words into French. Mary never said to Bernadette: "I will not give you, the happiness in this world, but in the other". NOT AT ALL…

6. Our Lady, actually, said: "I will not give you the happiness of this world, but the happiness of the other", which is the happiness from above. And Our Lady gave it to Bernadette during her life on earth.

7. According to Matthew (19:29) and especially to Mark (10:30), the hundredfold that the Lord promised, in reward for whatever we quit to follow Him…, that hundredfold is not for tomorrow, when we go upstairs, but it is for us, now. Yes, we are supposed to receiving it, NOW, while we are still living on earth.

8. Yes, we must get Eternal Life NOW on earth. And our rush must be, at least, with the same care and intensity, that we implied, during that month, to reach the Green Card.

9 The Lord knocks already at the door, bringing our wage…

10. The reward is coming soon.

Mom and Dad

Tableau # 23
Marthe Montazel

AS I WROTE PREVIOUSLY, MY RECENT TRIP IN GASCONY gave me the opportunity to stay with Marthe Montazel, my mother, according the wish she expressed, previously, from her room in hospital, in Rouen, when she said her desire to see me before she died.

All went the manner I recounted in the Tableaus of Montauban and Moissac.

I did not know, during my sojourn in Montauban, that such a trip was giving me the opportunity to meet my mother for the last time.

What was, at first, an excuse for my trip, became its real endeavor. Those days were actually the last moments on earth with my mother.

I need, now, to complete the topic, addressing her departure for heaven, which happened the following year.

She was one of the many witnesses of Espis, and one of the few, who never forgot these events.

Both, my mother and my father, Raymond, they were good friends of Maria and Adrian Monmayou, and they never ceased to comply with the messages of Espis, even if, at the same time, they never disobeyed the Church authorities.

It was not easy to understand how they could accomplish the double commitment, remaining always calm and gentle; pleasing Our Lady with good deeds, and accepting the words of Montauban bishops and priests, who were against the Moissac events, and demanded to ignore them, to never go there any more for public worship, and to never speak about it.

Nevertheless, they did so. And because the public pilgrimages were organized on the 13th of every month, they used to visit privately the shrine, the following day, on the 14th, or sometimes later…

During our sojourn in Montauban, with my mom, I asked her once: "How do you consider the contradiction of Our Lady, urging devotion to Eucharistic Jesus and, on the other side, the Church authorities forbidding to hearing her voice?"

Her answer was clear and simple: "We must comply with both".

"How it can be?" I asked again.

"Our Lady knows everything. She esteems the priests, and the Church authorities, too. Respecting them we please her."

Her few words were an important teaching.

Suddenly many topics came to mind, completing the understanding of the messages coming from Moissac.

God never demands us to perform any impossible endeavors. Besides, as the gospel said, a kingdom cannot be divided, otherwise it would destroy itself. When they come from above, private locutions or apparitions would never go against the Church, which witnesses God's presence, on the opposite, they support the Church betterment.

The shrines of private apparitions are not supposed to replace regular churches, they emphatically support them. It is a lack of confidence in the Lord that finds contradictions, where *de facto* contradiction do not exist.

Augustine's words remain true. He brought great hope when he said: "There is no wrongness that God wouldn't allow, if similar evil does not make possible a better good."

The greater good is still to come. We cannot predict, when it will happen. We know that it will come, and we must prepare for it. Moissac was a warning from above, in favor of greater Eucharistic life inside of Christendom, and more authentic experience of the Gospel. It fails only on the short range for those who doesn't trust it. Our Lord needed to die on the Cross to bring us life, and provide his resurrection.

Each one of us, too, must be willing to die to his or her personal and private beliefs, in order to be ready to be born into the larger garden of the Church… Besides, the Church, is not merely the actual Catholic Church.

In the Gospel, on Holy Thursday, after the last dinner with the Lord, John reported the Prayer of Jesus to Our Father: "That they all may be one..." (John 17:21). His prayer, let us understand, is the call to gather all people into one brotherhood, gathering all believers, even more, the whole of mankind inside the same Church.

The whole panorama is far better than the best perspectives single people may have. For the Lord never makes small endeavors. Whether we know it or not, His testament will happen soon. It seems to me that the next twenty years will undergo the most dramatic changes in the history of mankind. It will be huge fun.

All of that, obviously, will never happen in full harmony with the Gospel. The way remains the one that the Gospel proclaims: The Cross and suffering are the path toward resurrection, otherwise said in American words: "No pain, no gain".

They seem mere words, but they are hard facts.

Bernard de Clairvaux used to stress enthusiastically how "suffering is pregnant with resurrection". Here is why it can be difficult to understand how my mother was able to comply peacefully both, Espis and the Church. For her, it was the same voice, speaking with diverse accents.

She was a perfect example of the statement of Paul, "we know that all things work together for the good, to those who love God" (Rom 8:28).

Meeting the people I knew for having been present in Espis during the reported events, while many had forgotten Moissac, Marthe Montazel, my mother, did not. Mom was one of those who witnessed several events identified by many as true miracles.

Among these I must quote the healing of pilgrims, who were without hope from a medical perspective. There is also the case of my own sister, Marie-Bé, and the one of Colette Rigal, a family friend. Details on those issues would eventually make these pages too abundant.

One famous miracle, was in the sky... on March 2, 1947, as soon as Gilles's family had moved from Bordeaux to Moissac.

Mom has been one of the main sources of information for me on Espis, not only because of what she witnessed, but above all for her wisdom.

With her departure to heaven disappeared the important source of information I used to refer to. It was evidently the last living source I was still able to consult. It is appropriate, then, to give her the homage due to her great help on the story of Monmayou.

Her "*Natus Est*", when leaving earth, on Wed. October 20, 1999, was the actual conclusion of my previous journey to Montauban. Mom was a wise countrywoman, levelheaded and shrewd, by whom I liked being taught.

Throughout my youth, even during my worse days of identity crisis, when I was between 14 to 17 years old, when I would have not the courage to meet my father, I was still pleased to visit home, from time to time, and talk to my mother, while Dad was at work in the Department of Public Environment.

I did not realize in those days that the difficult relationship with my father was reciprocal: he was afraid of my replies back, and how I could argue against his beliefs. I did not know that, and I was unfair: my father gave me the opportunity to make studies that he never was given the chance to, and I was using the knowledge, that I got because of his care, against his own convictions, which where the whole meaning of his life.

Meanwhile, Mom was able to tell me her true opinion without hurting me. It was a gift she had with us all in the family... Sometimes, when I was too angry with my father, she was able to settle me down, in a very simple manner.

One day, I came back home after another terrible discussion with my father. I was trying to draw her on my side, stressing how I was right and how Dad was wrong. She did not fall into the trap. She only said: "Alain, he is your father!"

Those simple words, "He is your father", still strongly resound in my heart. This simple reply of hers directed my mind to essential values: being right or wrong was less important than respecting my parents.

She was right.

It was after a trip from Detroit to Chicago that. at my arrival, I was given the news of her departure for heaven. The following day, being back in Detroit, I wrote this email to Bruno Venturini in Grottaferrata, Roma, Italy, with whom I was used to being in touch and entertained a continuous spiritual sharing. I wrote him how I experienced her departure…

Here is the message I sent, dated Thursday, October 21, 1999.

Dear Bruno,

I'm back from Chicago, where I spent the night at the Focolare center, and get some news about the movement irradiation all over the world and its continuing growing in Gospel experience.

It's almost impossible writing something about my Mom's good departure to heaven and not talking with her, too, right now, while putting down these reflections on the paper. Therefore, these notes reflect more than simple memories.

I hope that any eventual reader, whom you will share this message with, will get, through the pages, the prudence and the wisdom, which my Mom used to spread around to those who met her…

Visiting them in Chicago was the opportunity of enjoying the agape atmosphere at the place of the Focolare. In a few days, Bill will see you, in Rome, and will tell you, how deep were the moments of unity we spent together.

The visit offered me also the occasion to begin reading the book of Chiara Lubich entitled As a Rainbow, *which shows how people blossom, developing through the Cross, in all human dimensions. Reading it, was true gladness.*

Yesterday, while I arrived there, in Chicago, Bill invited me to call home. I did. Over the phone Chiara told me that, Marthe, my mother had left this earth, a little earlier, at Grenoble, France. It was the consequence of falling down, in the house of my sister Christiane, trying to get the phone. She was left alone, and she hurt badly her leg and broke her hip.

After that happened, I spoke with my siblings in France. She died in hospital in Grenoble. Saturday morning her body will be brought to her home, in Montauban, Gascony, where relatives and friends are expecting her.

Then the funeral will be celebrated in Saint-Jean-Villenouvelle parish, where she was used, for years, to attend morning mass, every day, together with my father...

Her remains will be buried in Villefranche-de-Rouergue, 60 miles away, to the northeast, where the whole family has its tomb.

Mom was ready to go. Since my father died, followed three months later, by the departure of Joseph, my brother, she was even expecting to go.

Maybe we, her children, were not so ready to understand it after all.

She was longing to reach my father over there.

Because of her unhealthy conditions, she was given by the bishop permission to keep Eucharistic Jesus in her room. And the permission was renewed by every bishop, in the places where she was moving: not being able to live alone, any more, she moved from a place to a place staying time by time with one of her children.

Similar changes, from house to house, were producing a continuous struggle for her: as soon as she finally adapted to a place, the time had come to move to another place, and start to adapt again to the new situation...

She ultimately would prefer to stay in her home in Montauban, but no one, among us all, the siblings, has been able to leave his/her own place and stay there, in Montauban, with her, permanently.

Even the perspective of a turn over did not work. We would like to do so, but it was not affordable: all siblings were living too far away, with job and family commitments.

It was surely easier for us to have Mom, moving from a sibling home to another. Notwithstanding, being obliged to successively leaving homes, where she finally had just become pleased to stay, were increasingly pushing her spiritual availability to leave earth.

At this point comes to my mind the great commitment that my parents entertained with the Focolare, which was the greatest pledge of their life.

The Focolare community in Montauban area developed because of my parents. My Father looked the most enthusiastic and active organizer, but he never would have been able to do anything, and he even would not dare to, without the strong supportive behavior of my Mom. We understood better that effective relationship between both of them after my Dad departure in April 1987.

Everything started because of a visit that my Father made to a Focolare center, during the summer 1958, while he was in Paris attending a conference business.

In Paris, he met Gino Bonadimani, who impressed him strongly by his peaceful and deep commitment with the Gospel. Then my father invited Gino to pay us back a visit home, in Montauban.

Not having any answer, he repeated the invitation. Later, in November 1958, Renata Borlone and Nuzzomaria Grimaldi came to Montauban and stationed for two weeks in our house, meeting the people who was used to visit my parents at home.

From these almost daily, and numerous, encounters a great ferment of "Ideal life" was born in town, which induced later the Focolare movement to monitoring so intense activity from the nearest city, Toulouse, which is second to Bordeaux in Gascony.

Toulouse is only thirty miles away, from Montauban, driving south.

After the Benedict monks had left Tlemcen, in Algeria, Fr. Emmanuel, from En Calcat Abbey, France, who was a near friend of my parents, was seeking some association or community to handle the buildings and property of the previous Tlemcen monastery.

When she heard about that concern, Mom suggested to making Tlemcen a center for the Focolare movement there. Here is how, during the years 1960s, the Focolare started activity in Algeria, at north of Sahara desert.

Both, Raymond, my father, and Marthe Montazel, my mom, became the first married Focolarini in France...

Their commitment with the Focolare increased dramatically after they organized the journey of several families from Montauban, in Gascony, to attend in Fribourg, Switzerland, the summer

Focolare gathering, known as Mariapolis, during the summer 1960. Their impressive activity for promoting a living community in Montauban area induced the Focolare movement to move to Toulouse the men center they had in Grenoble.

The great hospitality and charitable endeavors of my parents towards the Focolare induced Maras, who was, in those days, the leader of the community in France, to believe that they were gifted with large financial resources, which actually they were not.

Here is why Maras decided to entrust my father with the news periodic paper of Nouvelle Cité, which was the expression of the movement in Paris. But the project did not go through for the effective lack of financial availability of our family.

Maras asked my father to leave his job in Montauban and move to Paris, to work for the Focolare paper. But Maras was offering no compensation in return for such commitment.

In those days, the needs of the family were still high, due to the fact that some of my siblings had still the age of attending school, while the three eldest sisters were already married.

The request of Maras was urging. My parents believed which it was part of their commitment with the Focolare to agree with it.

After a few days and nights of prayer, and a long sharing together, weighing the pros and the cons, our parents went to the only one affordable proposal to the family: the three eldest girls would have take care of the three youngest boys, Marie-Jean, Joseph and Jean-Marc, who were supposed to move from home and go live with them.

Then, our Father was supposed to move to Paris, alone first, starting the job, and, as soon as an apartment would have been found, my Mom would join him in Paris, together with Marie-Bé, our youngest sister.

Then our family house in Montauban would have been sold in order to support their needs.

I was not directly involved in the dramatic decision, because I was living in Loppiano, near Florence, Italy, at the Focolare center of formation for new members of the Focolare. I was independent, already.

I was, however, indirectly involved, due to the fact that my parents believed, either it was true or not, that refusing Maras' proposal would somehow jeopardize my "vocation".

Fortunately, the Lord did not allow that their generosity could damage the whole family. Mom and Dad called for a family meeting at home, in Montauban, and presented the project.

As usual, Raymond, my father, was talking for both. Marthe was silent, but supportive. At first Raymond explained the request of Maras, the details of the situation, and tried to convince the family to agree with the project of generously agreeing to the difficult endeavor... stressing the opportunity of serving the Church through the Focolare, accepting Maras' request in spite of the restrictive perspectives.

The family meeting thrilled. My eldest three daughters, Jacqueline, Annie and Christiane did not accept to see our family falling apart and they supported the unconscious concern of our Mom and Dad to see the family destroyed by such dramatic division. In spite of several attempts from my father to convince the whole family, the project was rejected.

Before this denial, Maras refused to see and talk to my parents any more, and he asked the Focolare leaders in France to behave the same.

Nonetheless, both mom and dad continued to support and be generous with the Focolare in many ways.

My parents suffered very much the situation. It happens, sometimes, that the Lord allows his followers to suffer because of those they love the most... This is why, sometimes, it is the Church itself, which put those who serve her so well to the test.

My parents' generosity was not a fake. My parents always enthusiastically supported my conversion to the ideal of the Focolare and my commitment with the Work of Mary, which is the official name of the Focolare movement. And it was actually Maras, the one who made me go tp Loppiano.

I was totally involved in Focolare matters at that time. In those days I was living in Loppiano, near Florence, Italy, fighting for conversion and taking a pledge with the new experience of the Gospel as proposed by the Focolare.

Even if they did not know my exact situation, Mom and Dad asked my brothers and sisters not to say a word to me on the struggle that the family was going through in order not to disrupt my eventual agreement with the Focolare...

And my brothers and sisters had been consistent with the request of Marthe and Raymond to be silent with me on the difficulties endured because of the Focolare. I heard about these events and the volte-face of the movement towards them long time after it happened.

At the moment the Focolare ignored the struggle of my family and my parents, together with my siblings, were unable to explain the real situation to the Focolare. This was the result of a lack of a clear communication.

Sometimes the Lord allow people to suffer the distance of being rejected by those they serve and love the much. Such miscommunication happens every day in daily life. My parents were good friends of Padre Pio who had been deceived by some expert of the Vatican who made some inaccurate report on him to the Secretary of State: as a result, the Vatican did not understand the real situation of the monk. It is by God's permission that Providence allows similar situations, which ultimately put to the test those which the Lord wants to improve the holiness. It is a case when human imperfection serves supernatural grace.

Miscommunications happen more often than it should. Nonetheless it happens.

Despite the fact that for a mutual misunderstanding, Raymond and Marthe experienced the event of being left alone, for they were excluded from the Focolare, they continued to promoting the movement in Montauban area and to helping maintain there a living "Ideal" community.

From Montauban area, many Focolare members, volunteers and supporters showed up. There are permanent members of the Focolare, the so-called Focolarini, like Patrice Pagès and Nicole

Calmejanne, who are still engaged in the movement today.

Many other members showed as well like Cecile and Alain Pradeau, Gaston Jonquière, André Gleize, Robert Dubéros, Denise and Henri Bonjour, Madeleine and Alain Bonjour, Yvette and Renée Roques, Simone and Rémy Gabens, Henriette and Raymond Berthomet, Marie and Georges Campagne, Mimi and Christian Mallet, and many others who remained faithful to the ideal of the Gospel as promoted by the Focolare.

As an example, my Dad used to organize a monthly meeting that used to gather regularly from 50 to 100 people. For a while, Fr. Abel Salesse, parish priest at St. Jean Villenouvelle, made the church available for the meetings.

These meetings were transformed for a time as a monthly prayer to Our Lady, and were always hold on the first Saturdays of the month. These meetings continued even after my Dad died. They were organized, then, by René Roques.

In addition to the trip to Fribourg, my parents have been pleased to organize similar journeys for Focolare meetings in Toulouse, Paris, summer Mariapolis in Saint-Laurent-sur-Sèvres, near Angers, or even in Grottaferrata, near Rome, Italy. All meetings there, in Villa Maria Assunta, remained a spiritual corner stone to all those who attended. At that time my parents became tight friends of Danilo and Annamaria Zanzucchi, who were in touch with married Focolare all over the world.

A few days ago, I could speak with my mother over the phone while she was already in hospital. She was facing great suffering, but she was at peace, as she always used to be. I asked her to pray for my students who had in those days a midterm exam… Some of them were taking their written examination in class three days ago,., just after that conversation over the phone.

Mom was still asking news about the Focolare movement everywhere, in addition to our family news, here in America. She amazingly remembered all and showed love for everyone.

She and I were very close. She was ready to leave for moving upstairs.

For some months her sight had decreased and it was very feeble, therefore the rosary had become her favorite prayer. In addition to the feeling of great solitude she was going through, she was enduring a high level of physical suffering, due to a cancer of the intestine. Because of it, she dramatically lost weigh. Only in the last two week she had lost 5 pounds. Her weigh went down to barely 90 pounds. Then she fell, breaking her hip, and the accident was decisive in speeding up her departure to heaven.

I am happy for her, because, in heaven, she reached my father, my brother Joseph, my sister Marie-Thérèse and also Nuzzo-Maria and Renata, who remained forever some of their best friends.

I'll be unable to attend Mom funeral in Montauban. My visa and the expecting for the Green Card may not allow me to reenter, then, the country. I would need a specific permission to go and come back. Besides a similar absence from the States during the process of getting the Green Card may jeopardize its success.

Going there would oblige me to make too many deeds in a few days. On the other side I see that my sisters and brothers are following all things very well. There is no reason to be concerned and I'll be there spiritually.

While I drove from Detroit to Chicago yesterday, I halted to a rest area, on the highway, with the desire to call her over the phone. It was near to two o'clock here, so it was eight o'clock of the evening over there. It was a good time to call and talk to her after dinner and before she started sleeping for the night...

Then, while the phone was ringing, I suddenly was afraid of waking her up, from an eventual precarious sleep, and I hanged up.

I knew later, from my brother, that this was approximately the time of Mom's departure to heaven. I am pleased to have had a loving thought precisely at the moment she left us and joined our relatives up there. That moment of loving intimacy keeps my heart warm. I am grateful to God for it.

Returning to the seminary today I found a great solidarity from all, administrative, superiors, colleagues, and students. Various priests, among them, will say mass tomorrow morning for her. Also, in Pittsburgh, where I'll drive tomorrow, after class, some priests will say mass for her, too, on Saturday morning, at 8 o'clock, which will be likely the time of her funeral in Montauban.

Her departure produced great serenity in my heart. For the love that Mom always showed to the Focolare, it seemed to me a good sign that she was offering her last breathing at the time I was going to get a first sight to the Focolare in Chicago.

While I am writing these lines, I receive a call from my wife, Chiara, who tells me to have received a very affectionate and warm fax message from Don Pasquale Foresi. He sent it as soon as he heard the news of my mother's death. Please, tell him how much I appreciated it.

I remain near to him and to you with Jesus and Mary.

Alain

Tableau # 24
Voltaire

VOLTAIRE WAS THE NICKNAME OF FRANÇOIS-MARIE AROU-
ET, emerging philosopher of the time of XVIII century, also known as
the enlightenment century.

Commentators believe that he took a nickname to allow his free
thinking and more easily hide against the toughness of political authorities. He wanted, in fact, to avoid public harassment, due to the
fact that years before, it was the case for Descartes, who was con-
demned by the intelligentsia of the day and forbidden to teach in all
European universities.

All teachers were forbidden to pronounce the name of "Descartes", even when their purpose would be to oppose Descartes' ideas.
Therefore his fear was justified.

The popularity of Arouet, however, grew so fast, that he remained
known under his nickname.

Voltaire was a believer, seeking truth. He engaged in social freedom and liberty of knowledge. Within such a context, he wrote a
philosophical dictionary, which claimed the right to doubt many official beliefs, and which spread his combative purposes, which included fighting against injustice, inequality, disrespect of human rights,
especially despotism and authoritarianism.

This led him to become anticlerical, because of the association of
Church and civil authorities in running political power of the days.
Today the situation is different and his militancy would probably as-
sume a totally different aspect.

His belief in God was based on his observation that the complexity of the world could not exist at random. Voltaire is well known to
have expressed such evidence: "How would be possible to believe that
the world, which is even more complex than a clock, would subsist

without a clock maker?" The same argument had been stressed long before by Aquinas, and will be used again later.

In a similar context, worth mentioning is Albert Einstein.

Concerning the immense entity of God, Voltaire knew that we were facing a mystery that could not be reduced to mere definitions or codes of conduct. Here is why he expressed a deep concern when he said: "God made people to his image and resemblance but then people did exactly the same with God himself!"

I'm not sure how much Monmayou was familiar with Voltaire, but he truly knew the habit of people to reduce the entity of the surrounding world to their own mind and to believe so easily that each individual, including God, was less gentle, generous, and bright than they are. It is a constant endeavor among humans to believe that the other people do not reach their own caliber of perfection. This behavior usually goes with gossip.

Oppositely, Monmayou was constantly opening wider perspectives on the borders, which constitute spiritual entities and had everyone in good esteem.

When at the Sorbonne I had occasion to deal with philosopher Friedrich Nietzsche and his philosophy of masks I understood better how Voltaire was right… Yes human reflections are so easily "Too human" that "Man is something that must be overcome." Here is why, Nietzsche defined people as a bright entity which includes the whole of animal and spiritual dimension. Famous are his words in the *Zarathustra* prologue, "Human nature is like a rope tightened between the beast and the superman."

Monmayou would have been in agreement with Nietzsche on that issue. Many of his statements were against the many believers who claim to refer to a "god" they reduced to their own measure. In fact, how many people are used to say: "If God would exist, he would make the world better…", ignoring that we, people, are involved in the creation process.

Through the toughness of the world, in fact, our Maker gives us the opportunity to show his own goodness, through our own interactive conduct. Our presence on earth is not just to watch, observe, criticize, and rest. Every human being has a task to accomplish. Yes, everyone has a call — i.e. etymologically speaking: a vocation. We are not on earth at random!

Apparently, this inclination to show reductive viewpoints is a common behavior, if not the practice of all those who deal with spiritual issues… unless they get a special help from above. Even heavenly locutions and visions are shadowed by the same capacity of thinking, reflecting, and understanding of the same seers… unless, the grace of visions is supported by a life of virtue and holiness, which depends on the seers in person. Just as a beautiful painting does not make everyone an art expert, not all messages from above make seers perfect. Even in such a case, God respects human freedom. Spiritual experiences help if the one who witness the wonderful pictures of above want to grow consequently.

After my first meeting with Monmayou, I had other encounters with Adrian, especially during the summer, while I was free from school. It happened very often until I was about 13 years old.

Then after I was 14, I almost lost any contact for a few years, until I reverted at 18 to the Catholic faith. Then a few visits marked our friendship. I gladly remember pieces of conversation, which I have sometime difficulty to date with precision. These pieces of acquaintance are clear and present in my mind as immovable stones.

These short dialogs with Adrian, pop up like flashes of wisdom inside of my mind. They come at random sometimes. I cannot say, however, if they stay in my mind or in my heart, for they are strongly rooted inside, and they continue to teach me.

These insights, clear in their utterance, have been sometimes understood later in my thoughts. Some of his enlightening explanations were like seeds, which die in your soul and make roots to produce afterwards better life and awareness.

Some news that he gave me, exploded later at times, unexpectedly, as astonishing disclosures, or precious answers. Many and various are the messages of Monmayou. All, however, move towards a common stream of hope.

Hope is a dynamic and luminous entity. It stands and grows inside of us and splashes around. Being with Monmayou I understood better the meaning of truth: where there is no hope, there is no truth. Where there is no gentleness there no truth either... You cannot provide any truth sharply... It always includes positive outcomes... When a truth brings to you mere disappointment or sad consequences, truth has been mutilated... According to Monmayou this characteristic of truth suffers no exceptions

My father used to call Maria and Adrian over the phone every time we were supposed to visit them at Lunel, in order to be sure that we would find them at the farm. Then, while my parents were driving towards Lunel, they used to say the rosary in the car, involving the children in the prayer. Sometimes, after arriving, we prayed again the rosary together with Adrian and Maria, too.

Adrian and Maria liked the rosary: "The rosary is the bible of the poor," or "it is the catechism of those who can't read," Maria said. Adrian used to add: "The rosary is the simplest way to be in touch with Mary" and he specified: "The rosary is the most powerful remedy..."

I recalled these words, yesterday, while driving near Chertsey, I was passed by a van which showed a label in the back: "When you get angry grab a weapon, pickup a strong one, purchase a rosary". I found it funny and it is actually true, the rosary brings answers to many problems. Raymond, my father, always suggested his friends to pray the rosary every day. One of his friends, Christian, was accustomed to keep a gun in his truck, after long discussions with Raymond he paid a visit to Lourdes where at the confession chapel he bartered his gun for a rosary. The exchange was the start of his conversion.

Usually Adrian had not much to add on the topic. When referring to the rosary with him he would rather invite you to say it together with him. Praying the rosary was surely better than any discourse on it. Often, during that prayer we receive enlightenments on questions or concerns we're struggling with.

Once I dared to ask: "Last Sunday in the church parking lot, I heard that saying the rosary is a nonsense. It is a useless repetition of words".

His reply was nice and warm.

"Do you think that your mother would be bored with you if you kept telling her how nice she is and how much you love her? When you truly love somebody you don't care about the words you say, you just let your heart speak"

His speech had been longer than the usual. Adrian was not used to chatter. He never spoke much. He was accustomed to talk by snatches. His true talking was a continuous inside conversation with the Lord. And sometimes we were given sudden externalizations.

After a day of work in the fields, he used to bring back the tools and stable the horse. Meanwhile, Maria fed the chickens. Afterwards in the cowshed they milked the cows — until they had them — at around 6 p.m. Then, slowly, with the typical slowness of a Gascon countryman he made his way home for dinner. The dinner was a soup meal. He considered his duty to share it with us and it would have been impolite to leave without getting a taste of it.

It is between the cowshed and the house that one evening he uttered to me: "Do you see the trees and the bushes around us?"

"I see them," I said, wondering where he was pointing…

"One day they all will provide food."

He was looking at the courtyard, which was surrounded by bushes and trees. He seemed to see beyond everything that surrounded us. He reiterated: "Someday all these bushes will produce fruits!"

I looked around, trying to understand. "Is it so!?!"

"Yes, their current sterility comes from Adam's stupidity!"

I thought, at first, that he was referring to some neighbor, and asked, looking at few houses between the hills: "What's Adam's house?"

He looked at me with his scrutiny sight to see if I was joking or not… then he answered abruptly: "You do not understand!"

"Yes, I don't," and I insisted: "Please, tell me"

"Did you forget your catechism?" he said.

"I surely do not!" I immediately replied.

"To tell you the truth, Adam made a mistake and because of his blunder we are obliged to work. Fortunately, one day, everything will be over and the fields will produce spontaneously much more than what they provide today after our hard work."

He really got my attention: "When is that supposed to happen?

With a bit of an impertinent tone, he said: "Oh! This! I'm not allowed to tell you."

"Why?" I said in reply.

"It is a secret." Then still with some malicious smile in his face, he asked: "Are you able to keep a secret?"

"I surely do" was my answer.

"I do, too" added Adrian with the same kind of voice, and he left me, immobile and astounded, in the middle of the yard...

After dinner he sat on his armchair in front of the house under the vine, with the dog at his feet. I crouched down nearby and stayed silent for a while; until I dared to recapture the conversation.

"So, when are we supposed to enjoy so many fruits from the plants?"

"Many people are supposed to die first"

I was happy that he answered. It was a good start. Prudently I asked again: "How is that?"

"Terrible days are to come. Three quarters of the whole population will disappear."

I was astonished: "Is it supposed to happen here, at Lunel?"

"Yes, at Lunel and around, and all over the world.

My surprise was growing. I asked "Why?"

"When someone wants to wash his cloths, he starts to throw away what is too dirty and sometime we lose our shirt because it is torn up and we make a rag or a duster with it. It is just good to clean the furniture. It will be the same with people."

I dared to ask for more details: "So, the people who are going to die are like the duster which are only good to clean the furniture?"

"Oh! Even worse! They are wood to be burnt" His answer was a shot!

I tried to figure out the picture, "Will that be to heat the winter?"

"No, many will perish in hell"

I could not understand and nonetheless I prevented myself from asking for more information. It was evident that Monmayou knew things that he was not fully able to recount. The whole picture, however, was clear in his head because his answers were immediate, persuasive, with no ambiguity.

These answers were for me like pieces to add to a large mosaic in which many pieces were still missing. Additionally, many pieces of information I was given were precise answers which nonetheless were difficult to interpret and I almost had no clue where to put them in the map.

So I kept these enlightenments inside, hoping of getting some day other pieces of connection which would make me understand the picture. Meanwhile I only could offer these insights to the Lord and move on.

Adrian's wife, Maria, had care of putting down in writing his utterances in a notebook, which were like fragments of thoughts or aphorisms. The notebook took the name of *Adrian's Manuscript*, which is however silent on many topics.

Witnesses state that countless visions and locutions were received by Monmayou and the young seers at Espis Woods. It seems difficult even to attempt to summarize the messages. A deeper search would be necessary. Among the communications acquired from above, there is the invitation that Monmayou received one day to pay a visit to cardinal Roques and tell him: "Our Lady is happy to see how much your heart is ardently attached to Eucharistic Jesus. Please continue to do so." The circumstances are not clear, but Monmayou met the cardinal one day in Montauban and transmitted the message. The cardinal's response was almost predictable, and brutal: "But... I already do so!"

For the cardinal there was nothing new in the communication. A similar answer however, shows that the message received by Monmayou was true concerning the cardinal's homilies, but evidentaly the way it was reported to the cardinal did not produce what maybe Adrian was expecting.

Was the embassy to the cardinal another test of Monmayou's trustworthiness? Was it another test of the ability of Adrian before he was entrusted with a more important mission? Maybe such an approach to the cardinal was for Monmayou a first training of doing what he was asked, to encourage his fidelity in whatever circumstances, and give him some familiarity with a prince of the Church.

With some sense of humor, my father considered that bringing amessage in the name of Our Lady, Monmayou was not supposed to get a better answer from the one who in Montauban would represent Jesus in those days. Our Lady remains Mary, Jesus' mother, the one whose presence, at Cana, was determinant for the miracle that Jesus worked at the wedding. Even there, Jesus gave a harsh answer to his mother before performing the change of the water into wine.

Cardinal Roques was well aware of the fact that the Eucharist makes the Church and that the Church makes the Eucharist. Each one produces the other in a virtuous circle. More likely he would have barely accepted any comment from someone, like Monmayou, he would have considered as incompetent in such a matter... And it was difficult to know what was the feeling of Monmayou afterwards.

"But... I already do so!" was the Cardinal answer, and Monmayou left. According to the observers of the audience he was publicly humiliated, Yes, all along, and especially afterwards, he had to lower his head before the cardinal, but inside he was more likely proud for having accomplished his chore. He was supposed to bring the message to the cardinal and the mission succeeded. Concerning the result of his visit to the cardinal, it was not his business any more. As a good servant he had the delight for performing the will of the lady. This did include neither the fact to be heard, nor to be immediately understood.

In the Gospel it is not the son who says "yes" and then changes his mind, but the other one, who says "No" but accomplishes the will of his father afterwards, who is the faithful one. It is not sure what impact such a communication had on the cardinal, not even how much the cardinal did share the issue around. His immediate answer suffices for stressing the authenticity of the messenger.

While I was a professor at the Gregorian, I asked once to Fr. Joseph de Finance about the dependability of the messages received by private revelations. His reflection was consistent: "when a seer speaks about messages from above, the mind of the seer always interferes with what he or she really saw or heard."

One of the purposes of heaven coming down into Espis woods and speaking to Monmayou and the other seers seemed to stress the consistency of Eucharistic Jesus. It looked like that the invitation of Mary to her people was "Eat my Son. Be another living Eucharist Jesus." This was also the invitation that Monmayou received and was entrusted to spread abroad.

Meanwhile the number of pilgrims visiting Espis woods was growing exponentially. As a local authority and member of a public administration, my father was entitled to organize public manifestations and ask the police to coordinate the flood of the crowd visiting the places of apparitions, regulating its entrance and outlet. According to the same request of Our Lady, a special celebration was held every month on the 13.

It is obvious that when the Eucharistic Jesus gathers the members of God's people from the extreme borders of the earth, to build the whole Church in one unique family, where Jesus speaks, like in Espis, many people come together. Also the variety of people who visited the woods, along the local road 695 at the eastern exit of Moissac, during the following years bore a large amount of situations, feeling, experiences and needs. The crowd reflects the characteristics of the place: many are the messages from above, too. Espis expresses through the multiplicity of visions and locutions the same fertile variety of the treasures which compose the complexity of the people living the same unique mystery of the Church.

The number of pilgrims was growing so consistently, at every celebration that, soon, Montauban ecclesial authorities had to make some decision about a similar unusual event.

At Espis all the seers talked of the Eucharist. Sometimes there was some confusion in their talks. Once I asked Monmayou: "Is that true that to be ready for the difficult time to come we are supposed to store food?"

I saw immediately in the eyes of Adrian that I was touching an interesting question.

"Do you think that the Lord may ask people to gather food in their own basements when a large amount of the world population is starving?"

I was silent. His reasoning was clean of defect. And the reflection was moving even beyond any of my eventual suspicions. He saw that I was expecting his discourse to be completed... "No! It is not mere food that we are supposed to make reservation of. The food that we have to be sure that we never are missing of is the Eucharist."

Another silence followed.

Then he insisted: "Espis does not contradict the Gospel. In the Gospel and today, Jesus is still Jesus, who wants to feed us and save us."

"Yes the food we need the most as provision during struggling times is the Eucharist, not indiscriminate mere food that may perish."

My second question was connected: "And what about the water?"

"Aren't we supposed to gather shipments of water, too?

"Yes", he said, "Talking to the children of Espis, Mary asked them to tell everyone to hoard a large amount of water." His smile indicated that he was going to reveal some unexpected news... so he continued: "People understood that they were supposed to stockpile a large supply of containers in their home for the tough days to come."

A short silence followed.

Then he provided anew some typical of his enigmatic questions: "Do you think that reservation of drinkable water may avoid a flood, an earthquake, a massacre, a war?"

"Well," I said, "I agree, that the eventual solution doesn't fit the trouble".

"And do you think that Our Lady would be so stupid not to see so?"

Again his reasoning was perfect. I couldn't do nothing but consent: "Surely not!"

"Besides, in the history of the chosen people, God provided water when it was needed, as well as food. So he surely would not suggest people to seek what he can easily disclose to us." I remained silent, waiting for the final explanation that was supposed to follow.

I was right. After another moment of silence, Adrian continued: "What is the water the Lord refers to in the Gospel? There is a moment, meeting the Samaritan, when the Lord spoke about his eternal water, the Divine Grace, which we should keep in order to survive. Do you think that at Espis the Lord would have changed his mind? "

The answer was obvious. To be sure, however, that I grasped the concept I concluded: "So when Our Lady or the Lord asks a seers to make reservations of food and of water they indicate that the only way to survive tough times is to be filled with the Eucharist and live in God's grace. Is that so?"

It was so simple that I wasn't even too sure of it.

But Monmayou was already out in some other daydream… Probably, there was no need to be concerned about my questions any more… so he felt free to move away with his mind. Every important insight had been released…

I had, however, more to ask. *De facto*, I brought more question to him throughout the years. Little by little, Monmayou answers composed a kind of fresco in my mind. Sometimes the same questions were asked two or more time as if I wouldn't be able to understand at once his answers.

I understood later, studying philosophy, that "The art of learning", as Bergson said, "is the art of asking the right questions". Notwithstanding, to do so, we need previous and progressive enlightening. Not all Monmayou answers could have been given at once. I'm providing in these pages some of his explanations, which I witnessed while he was talking to someone among the family or the friends, or even directly to me. These explanations struck me strongly enough to remember them even if sometimes their meaning came later.

During one visit to Lunel I heard my father asking a question I was not able to understand then: "At Garabandal, the seers said that ac-

cording to Our Lady one day the mothers would kill their babies..." The answer came sad and bitter: "Yes. It will be terrible. A large amount of mankind resources will be suppressed. Many sources of hope will be killed: engineers, architects, politicians, scientists, artists, geniuses will disappear in the womb of their mothers. When that discussion was held, neither Monmayou nor my father knew about the concept of abortion, yet.

Once I had a delicate question: "There is a seer that said that one of the priests attending the celebration in the woods should become the next pope. Is that true?" Monmayou looked alarmed and got like an involuntary start. His attention was again fully present. "This is strange," he finally uttered, "I'm afraid the child who said so misspoke Our Lady's words", he said.

"How was that?" I asked.

His answer came very slowly, as if he tried not to hurt anyone but also wanting not to be heard wrong: "It may happen that a seer tells you that you will be the next pope... This does not mean at all that you are supposed to go to Rome and be elected by the cardinals in conclave... Excepting the fact that Rome will not exist forever... When you are said so it simply means that you're supposed to run the Church. But do not misunderstand me. It is similar with the mystery of Eucharistic Jesus, who is the center of the whole world. It is actually the Eucharist, which keeps the world in existence. Where there is the Eucharist, here is the center of the Church. When you celebrate the Eucharist you are another Jesus, another Christ on Earth, another Pope. Here is the full mystery of Eucharist."

A silence followed; then he concluded abruptly: "Never say to someone that he will be the next pope. It can provoke a terrible mistake!" The tune of his voice was imperative. Then, out of a moment of contemplation, he said: "Every Christian carries on his shoulders the burden of the whole Church, because of the intimacy with Eucharistic Jesus. Everyone is called for holiness"

This was really enlightening.

After his accounts, I understand today what it means when in some place the Lord says that from that very place he is supposed to save the whole world. Supposing that the Lord spoke in Kerizinen, Pontmain, Garabandal, San Damiano, Dozulé, Medjugorje, Monterrrey, Kibeho, Naju, Emmitsburg, and every other place where we heard of private revelations, when the Lord asserts that "the place is the one which he will save the world from," it means nothing but the fact that his own presence is salvation. That very place is his Eucharistic presence. And where the Eucharist is, there is the place where the world starts to be saved. This is also due to the fact that we, people, think in time and space, while the Lord lives in eternity. Eternity is continuously present to every place on earth. Supposing the Lord speaks somewhere, his words confirm the teaching of the Church. Monmayou was well aware of that. It is what he taught me.

Adrian was happy that time for having been able to provide explanations that usually are not so easily expressed out of his mouth. I never was quite sure when was the best time to raise another question. I added nonetheless: "I have another concern, even if now many doubts are little by little knocked out. Many topics make sense".

That day offered a very pleasant conversation already, so Adrian continued: "Please, tell me…"

"Well… I'm not sure how to ask… but… what about hiding… when difficult times come, how do we know where to go, and for how long we are supposed to hide?"

Adrian smiled again. "Don't worry, the Lord wants you not to run away, he just calls you to look for him and not to go back for our belongings. We must live the present moment the way we are".

A silence occurred. Then he said: "just stay at peace, where you are, and let Providence work. Being at peace hides you better than any wall or woods…"

I understood that there was no need to hide anywhere for the

Lord will save us whenever and wherever we are, unless we are short of "His food and His water." Here is the secret of the end times. Since the time of the apostles the Christians were concerned with end times. Since then, the apostles suggest that we behave and stay every day at peace in God's will. When the Lord dwells in our hearts we actually hide from evil. Here is the true hiding place to keep.

Another time, Monmayou gave me some interesting insight to know every time what to do. "Use your mind and your heart and behave with good sense" he said. "Wisdom lies there."

In front of my surprised and inquiring face he added: "Never allow your feeling to overcome your decisions, use your mind to mitigate it. All the same, never follow just your mind, true discernment involves both mind and heart. Do so and little by little you will train you conscience to proper discernment. Conscience develops while using it"

Later I read St. Francis de Sales saying: "Everything that may trouble your heart is not of more worth than its peace… and does not come from the Lord…" Therefore, "Drop any concern that does not improve your inner peace" added Juan de Yepes, alias St. John of the Cross.

My parents were wondering why society is made with so many diverse people together and interacting to one another, rich and poor, sophisticated and childlike, skilled and inexpert, courteous and rough … At first Adrian tried to explain that this is the departure point where we find our situation after the wrong turn of Adam, "But," he said "it is not diversity which causes social injustice but a lack of friendship among people," and he tried to explain that justice follows the mystery of life; its diversity is more to contemplate than to explain.

Adrian tried to show how diversity improves society when relationship expresses respect, courtesy, and love. Busy as they were in the conversation with Maria, my parents didn't pay attention to his attempt to explain. Meanwhile, Adrian left the room for a walk. I left the farm following his tracks.

"Look at the countryside ahead, do you like the scenery?!" asked Adrian. Actually, I was not sure if it was a question or just an invitation to observe the beauty which surrounded us.

The hills across the valley displayed diverse colors in a combination that would delight and inspire the most talented painter... It would provide some beautiful model to compose... The land offered actually a unique picture. Sometimes, I thought, nature surpasses fiction.

"Oh yes! 'It's marvelous" I said

"Do you think it would be as nice as it is, if all trees were the same!?"

Once, before I got married, I visited Maria and Adrian at Lunel. I came with the one I was engaged to, Chiara, who is now my spouse and the mother of my children. When Adrian saw us he immediately understood that Chiara had some terrible disease that we were not aware of yet and we discovered soon after we married. That day he gave us a prescription or, if you wish, a remedy that people of the country are familiar with. I never dared to use it with Chiara, but later on I used it once with one of our children who in despair needed relief, and it worked.

The recipe is simple, so simple that it is even difficult to believe in it: "it only requires, he said, to look at the disease as a point of darkness and look at the nearest light, the sun or whatever enlightening source we get, as a source of healing and compare the two, knowing that darkness cannot stand the light and saying so." To eventually make more sense, he also suggested that the part to be healed should be bathed with dirty water. It is then suitable to pray that the darkness of the disease will disappear into the light which irradiates. It is simple. It seems too simple to be true, but it worked for me once. My brother Marie-Jean used it also once to release my mother from varicose veins. It worked out well, even if he, actually, was not comfortable with that kind of behavior. He made it work, even if he always pretends not to believe it.

Oh! America. I came here hoping to rest, but another business jumped on me.

Tableau # 25
Ask Your Guardian Angel

ADRIAN WAS FAMILIAR WITH PADRE PIO, A CAPUCHIN PRIEST FROM ITALY, born in 1887, who during his life surprised his fellow monks and visitors by his intimacy with heaven, which caused wonders, like his capability to read inside of people hearts their thoughts, their needs, their wishes and even their secret demands.

Padre Pio also amazed more than a few with his moving around the world as if the earth had no borders for him. The pilgrims, who visited his Monastery, in San Giovannni Rotondo, near Manfredonia, Italy, were enlightened in charity, hope, and faith.

No one reported to have come with a question to him, and had not been answered.

It happened sometimes that Padre Pio provided the answer even before the question was asked of him, or even before he had read the demand.

Typical is the case narrated by a religious sister, who came back to her convent saying that, while she tried to transmit to Padre Pio the letter from her superior, she was told: "Oh! I already answered this one!" When the perplexed superior opened the envelope containing the letter that she wrote to Padre Pio, great was her surprise to find, together with her letter, Padre Pio's response to it.

Like his fellow Franciscan brother, Anthony, he showed the ability of moving at the same time to different places with his body. Most of these extraordinary bilocations were accomplished through the ministry of the Angels, he said.

Once, in Adrian's living room, Raymond, my father, moved to sit in the armchair.

"Please don't sit there" Adrian said.

"Why not?" my father replied.

"Don't sit there. That's where Padre Pio is sitting."

I was, silently, witnessing the situation.

It was true: Padre Pio used to pay visits and share with Adrian heavenly business. Padre Pio did teach Adrian about several issues. He was his tutor on several topics.

Padre Pio died on September 23, 1968. He was declared saint by Pope John Paul II, on June 16, 2002, in front of huge presence of people filling Saint Peter's and the streets around.

It was twenty years after Adrian had left us for heaven. During his life, Padre Pio liked to visit Adrian, as many other friends on earth. Sometimes he was just there because he needed some rest.

My father asked the reason for Padre Pio's presence in that chair.

The reply of Adrian was quick: "He likes to sit on it when he comes to visit me."

There was no more to say.

The topic that Adrian loved to talk the most about, after Eucharistic Jesus, was Our Lady.

His familiarity with Our Lady could fill an encyclopedia.

It was sufficient to name her, to excite him with gladness and fervor.

For Adrian, where Jesus stays, his mother stays.

Together with Jesus' Mother, the Angels are present, too.

When we pray the litanies, we invoke Mary as Queen of Angels.

Dealing with Angels, we address the kingdom that Mary encompasses.

Angels belong to heaven neighborhood, which Adrian was familiar with.

Adrian used to make clear that: "Heaven is not a place. It is another kind of world, truer than ours, but present here, too,

He was in fact pleased to say: "Heaven is here, but many cannot see it."

The true presence of Mary and the Angels in our life was tightly connected with the business Adrian entertained with Padre Pio. Both had a common familiarity with Mary, and were surrounded by the Angels. We are, too, even if we barely are aware of it.

To say it properly, talking about Adrian without referring to the Angels who surrounded his life, would be like talking about a fish without referring to the sea or the rivers.

It is an obvious issue, which can never be missed. The Angels formed the normal environment in which Adrian lived. They always surrounded him.

Fr. Emmanuel de Floris, a theologian from Bordeaux, who used to be a friend of Adrian, told me once that according to St. Thomas Aquinas, God never acts directly on earth: when someone says so, he/she means that God always works through Second Causes, which the Angels are.

The Angels are God messengers. They are those that Aristotle used to call "gods" when referring to the forces who move the whole universe.

This means that the Angels are not merely God's ambassadors, for they are his direct executors and the managers of the world …

Endless conversations kept us absorbed with Adrian on the pure spirits, which Angels are, kept us totally absorbed and enthralled.

"I am afraid of the Evil", I said once.

"Don't worry Alain; Satan is only an Angel who took a wrong turn."

"He cannot force any deed upon you, unless you allow him to do so."

"What does that mean 'Unless I allow him to' ?" I asked.

In those days I was not aware, yet, how the friendship with Adrian had already introduced me to the heavenly realm, and that such familiarity with things above was preparing an important meeting, which became the most frightening of my life. I understood only later how being associated with Monmayou was a serious endeavor.

You cannot become familiar with the Angels and have not your life involved in a dramatic adventure.

The whole undertaking jumped on me in a very curious manner.

I was 14 when this familiarity with the mystery of God got a sudden turning point.

I was living in a boarding Catholic school, called Diocesan School of the Sacred Heart, and I wanted to get out. I clearly understood the need of a better acquaintance with the culture of the days.

Yes, I wanted to have a better confrontation with the outside world.

Curiously, living in a Catholic boarding school was intended to prevent me from doing so, in order to protect me during my educational process. This is why I wanted to get out.

I actually wanted what superiors at schools and my parents tried to prevent me from meeting.

I had the feeling that there was a better presence of values in the world, than inside of the walls of the school, which was supposed to offer us a comfortable cocoon of beliefs and behaviors.

I wanted to breathe a better air, but nobody agreed with me, neither the priests running the school nor my parents.

I understand that the familiarity with Monmayou, and with the seers of Moissac had put deep roots in my heart, together with a strong desire of values that the shell of the school did not allow.

Here is why I wanted to leave.

I was fighting badly, provoking troubles of any kind in the institution, to the result that I accumulate the largest number of penalties, excluding the one I was looking for: the expulsion.

In good faith, the superiors of Sacred Heart Minor Seminary and my parents knew that my reactive behavior was the result of a spiritual fight. They were right in their analysis. Nonetheless, they were wrong with the prognostic.

As a result of the situation, my father used to come every week to the school, in order to pay the damages on books, benches and desks, painted walls, broken doors and windows, and so on... The more they were keeping me prisoner, and the more I was rocking the boat.

At the end of the academic year there was the usage to go to confession and confirm our intention to come back the following year.

I clearly said to Fr. Yves my intention to leave the school. He said that he could not give me the absolution if I did not change my mind. I understood, his behavior was consistent with decisions from above.

When I left the confessional, I waited in the church for him to come to me and give me the absolution.

Fr. Yves came several times inquiring: "You have changed your mind. Haven't you?" In front of my sign of denial, he was moving back to his place without further comment.

Not getting a positive answer, he was turning back to confess other students until the whole school was done with confessions.

Fr. Yves came again, still asking me to wait for the forgiveness rite, but to change my mind.

I did not.

Finally, the evening was getting dark and, lucky me, Fr. Yves had other business to deal with.

He finally gave me the Lord's forgiveness, stressing the need for me to reflect again and, eventually, change my decision to leave. He insisted that I should communicate to him the change of my decision, right away.

I never changed my mind. Then I, definitively, left the school at the end of the semester.

During the summer I went once to watch a movie: *The Buccaneer* with Yul Brynner.

I am sure that many can see that movie for no other purpose than to enjoy a delightful action adventure.

For me, it was a providential meeting: I was deeply touched by the scenario. Jean Lafitte jeopardized his own life and the lives of his pirate company to save an American city. Later he was apprehended by its citizens, who had been just saved from death, and nonetheless accused him for ransoming a boat of their city.

The scene happened, actually, a week before, when the boat was attacked by one of his captains, who disobeyed his orders… I was shocked first by the event, when those, who got their life just saved by him, turned back against him.

Then, there was the incredible behavior of pirate Jean Lafitte, who took responsibility, for the wrongdoing of one of his man…

His high sense of value struck me. The movie made me understand that values count more than success, and comfortable life. It pulled me to put values at the center of my life… Such circumstances revealed to me the distance between what I actually was and what I was called to be.

I came back home that night crying…

I knew that this movie had awakened a vision of the values to which I wanted to dedicate my whole life… Mom saw me and asked: "What are you crying about?"

"It's because of the movie I saw this afternoon," I said.

"You should select better the movies to watch," she said in reply.

"No, Mom, you don't understand, it was a beautiful movie and it moved me because of the fact that my life is not good enough."

She left the room, without a word...

I felt that I had to make right away an agreement with the Lord.

It was night when I got out. The sky was filled with bunches of stars as happens only in August in that area... I walked for a little and I found myself at the edge of the garden, in the back yard, where my father used to grow strawberry plants.

There, I spoke with the Lord. It was that sort of intense encounter, when you know the Lord is listening.

Obviously, I also knew that the hole I had inside was because of him.

My prayer was an answer to his call. I had the feeling that I was talking with my Father, even if I said: "O Lord, I put my life in your hands. Please, do what is needed to make my life consistent with what you want".

It was the kind of prayer that the Lord never leaves unanswered.

The Lord heard me well. He answered, however, in a way far different from what I was expecting.

A few months later I met the Focolare movement.

In November 1958, Renata Borlone and Nuzzo-Maria Grimaldi visited my family in Montauban.

Nuzzo, took a moment the following morning to talk to me. I was surprised that a friend of my father would like to share something with me. He started referring to the project of human blossoming, which he saw that I had posted on the door of my room. He stressed that we cannot improve, with no more than the strength of us alone. We blossom in interaction with the people around us. He finally ended up with the sentence of Matthew: "When two or three are gathered in my name, here I am."

For sure, many may have heard that sentence, without changing anything in their lives.

For me it was a sudden shock. I understood, through the Focolare, that in every community, I was in the presence of God.

The discovery required a new life adjustment. The evidence of God's closeness frightened me to death. The same day, I decided to leave home. I wanted to avoid another confrontation with Nuzzo.

I needed however to hide that escape. I immediately found a good excuse: I justified the sudden departure arguing that I had to go camping under the tent with two friends, as if it was a programmed training ordeal with the Boy Scouts, like a winter test of resistance to the cold weather in a wilderness survival camp.

Then I convinced two friends, Alain and Eric to come with me. I intended to make the trip into the Forest of Montech. The following morning the two returned home and left me alone in the woods.

Under the circumstances, I could survive alone only another day.

Then I returned home, too.

But when I arrived home, I was surprised to see that Renata and Nuzzomaria were still there.

I had not escaped. Their sojourn in our family house was longer than I previously thought. I understood, at that time, what a tight connection there was between my parents and the Focolare. So, I determined to leave home soon definitively.

Meanwhile, my parents managed to arrange for their many friends to meet with Renata and Nuzzo, too. It was the beginning of the living community of the Focolare in Montauban and the surrounding area. Later a Focolare Center was moved to Toulouse to accommodate such a large community.

As regards my own endeavor, I do not remember exactly when I left home. The process developed progressively but fast. There was a battle inside of me. I was torn between the admonition of Nuzzo to adjust my life with a full adhesion to the Will of God in the present moment, and leaving home in order not to be challenged so hard again.

Nuzzo was almost winning the contest in my mind.

I understood the need to reflect more deeply on it. With the best purpose, I decided to sit down, in my room, at home, and address the issue once and for all.

It was simple: I had to decide about God's existence.

If God was real, my own life would be changed. Otherwise, I had to leave and look for another option.

Meanwhile I could not stay home, for my personal struggle would have produced trouble in the soul of my younger siblings. I knew that I had a strong influence upon them. Honestly, it would have been unfair to share my struggle with my siblings before offering them another solution. The whole family would have been so disturbed by such behavior that our sprightly, but peaceful, family life would have become soon a true field of open war.

Ultimately, moving out would have been better for all, them and for me. It would have been impossible for me to go through this ordeal without gaining some neutral ground.

Yes, everything started with the best intentions.

l purchased a notebook. I sat in my room. Then I analyzed the question, whether or not God does exist. I did not know, at that time, that God's existence is not a speculative issue, but an existential one. I begun to write down some sort of essay on the topic: "Does God Exist?" The introduction was easy to make, it was my sincere and true inquiry. Then I gathered one by one the evidences of God's existence, in the balance and richness of nature, in other people, especially in their love, in the meaning of the whole life, in the complex organization of the world...

Little by little, I was getting more and more confident that my torments would be alleviated by the result I was going to find: the evidence of God's existence. It was with clear sense of liberation, and almost comfort, that I started the conclusion.

Here came the disaster. It suddenly popped up in my mind the obstacle of wicked people, natural disease, intermittent disorder, chaos, pain and suffering in the world. This was a strong objection, which I couldn't get over. The presence of evil in the world was the evidence of God's absence. I had to accept it and live accordingly.

Here is when I left home. I was not happy to do so, but I had to.

I was committed to find the alternative issue, which would have made God's existence an obsolete question. I do not remember clearly, now, the way I did survive for two years, or more, living alone on the street, hiding, time to time, to some occasional friend's house.

I was finding a different place to stay, every two or three days, in order not to let anyone understand what I was going through.

I changed residences constantly: one day, I was asking to a classmate: "Where do you live?" At the answer I used to say "Oh! I have to be in the neighborhood early tomorrow. May I stay in your place tonight?" And so on.

Meanwhile I was selling stuff at a moving store, which was attending fairs, every other day, in the area. It was a way to raise money for surviving. And in order to avoid too much trouble with my parents, I was still attending school almost regularly.

Actually, my father used to come to the school, once or twice a week to check on me. Once, the principal asked me: "Why is your father coming so often to see if you are here?" But above all: "Why does he not even ask to see you?" I replied that we had different schedules and would barely meet at home. This is the way I finished school and got the diploma and started study at the University in Toulouse.

Even today I have difficulty remembering the way I survived for those years until I was 19.

I do remember, however, that once a week, especially on Saturday morning, while my father was at work, I used to pay a visit home after lunch time. As soon as my mother identified my routine, she managed to cook more than they needed for lunch on Saturday. In that manner, she eventually started serving me a couple of steaks and a mountain of French fries. That was my favorite meal. Afterwards I used to take a nap in what was previously my room, and leave, as soon as I woke up. I happened, sometimes, that I didn't wake up till the following morning.

The meetings with my father at home were never peaceful engagements at that time. Once the fight was more fierce than usual. I tried, later, to share my views with my mother. I attempted, then, to display my reasonings.

Once when that the fight had been particularly poisonous, she stopped me: "Alain, he is your father. Remember it".

A similar reply soothed any bellicosity of mine: she was right and I was wrong not to consider it.

But the fight inside of me was even more dramatic than my life was.

I was living a growing nightmare.

My refusal of the Christian faith destroyed my confidence in the truth too. Not believing in God, I successively lost my trust in the truth: I lost confidence with every book, every teaching, every discourse, every thought…

At first it was a book that I put in doubt… then every page of the book… later on, even a sentence was doubtful and, finally every word of it. Yes, the definition that I found later in Nietzsche that "Every word is a prejudice" became my daily thought. It was not only the question if an author tells the truth. Or even, does he believe what he says? Or else, do I understand him properly? My thought was in trouble: does that make sense?

Little by little, I got trapped with the Nietzschean aporia that losing God, who is the arbitrator of every though, everything becomes arbitrary.

That was my experience. I was living a horrible nightmare. I had become unable to trust anyone, any thought, any reflection, even my own… I did not know at that time that such a terrifying situation had been, properly, the one of Nietzsche as well. With his words, in *Gay Science* §125, "God is dead", Nietzsche is not uttering a cry of victory, but the opposite: he expresses the discovery of a terrific deception, the perspective of the full breathtaking nonsense of the whole world, and the whole life…

In those days, my own life consisted of a permanent farce. The methodical doubt of Descartes was even obsolete in comparison with my inside torment. When I was alone, I was lost, without any ground to stand on.

I was permanently putting a mask on when staying with other people, hiding the turmoil I had inside. I didn't even realize that, in response, the other people were keeping me alive. Their interaction was challenging me and giving sense, even for a blink of time, to my life. In a word, I was a true Sartrian existentialist even before I knew Jean-Paul Sartre. Years later, when I read Sartre's *Being and Nothingness*, together with his other writings, like *Durty Hands*, *Flies*, *No Exit*, and *Nausea*, to name a few, I had no surprise at all. I had a clear feeling of knowing him very well, and of being familial with him because of my sufferings during those dire days.

The same happened later on at the Sorbonne, when I met Friedrich W. Nietzsche. I knew that I went through his craziness. His words like "You Christians you should look more saved, if you want me to believe in your Savior", or "You should look more happy, to make me believe in the Good News of the Gospel", or again "If you Christian had truly showed love to the world, the whole earth would be, now, fully Christian already" resounded like calls for help.

It was the same calls that I was despairingly uttering during my days of searching, while people around only understood that I was fighting against the Christian faith. Oppositely, with every cry, I was pushing buttons to see if there was, at least one, that would work. But no answer came out for a while.

Sometimes, God likes to hide, in order to make our search more serious, more accurate.

I was not at all surprised to hear Nietzsche say: "The cadaver of

Christendom is stinking up the world." All these desperate cries were calls for help. They recalled my own experience. The whole situation did indeed challenge me.

The growing eradication of any belief was also accompanied by a psychological destruction of the person. The increasing untrustworthy steps were also afflicting me deeply.

Little by little, the lack of interest, made me lose the capacity to pay attention to anyone or anything. Then too, the mistrust of any topic made me lose my proper capability to reflect and concentrate on any issue. Finally, I lost the faculty of memorizing. Somehow there was a systematic course of devastation that was attacking me from every side, at every human level.

I truly attempted to provide sense to my life. But those attempts fell short. It was a kind of continuous conflict with all surrounding people and things.

As an example: at the university, I could not accept to walk in class through the corridors and doors which were an abuse of constrictions from some architect or even worse for some engineer who did not even followed architect's plans. This is why I used to entering class from the window, climbing up outside through the gutter. My class mates were laughing at my idiosyncrasy, but, kindly, they used to open the window from inside to allow me to squeeze through.

Every physical obstacle was, for me, an additional occasion to check whether or not I was alive.

During that period of time, I risked my life many times, for no good reason, except the need to overcome a challenge, like jumping from a 500-foot bridge over a river, with an electrical line to go through, in order to fall where the water was barely there. So I was struck twice — by water and by the ground; and remained almost paralyzed for a week…

The situation was getting worse every day. After every daredevil challenge, I obsessively craved to find a bigger one. Many of them could have gotten me killed. To say the truth, so many times, a friend was there to save my life. Once, it was Alain Roques at the entrance of College Saint Théodard, who shoved me against the wall to avoid my bashing brutally into a boundary marker on the Cours Foucauld, while I fell from the external wall that I was trying to climb. A similar situation happened at a church, near Léojac, while I fell from the tower, which I was climbing from the outside. Again, someone kept me from falling further onto a big jutting rock, which would have surely killed me.

At that time, I was resigned to surviving the day only if I could force myself to overcome some risk. Often, I most definitely would have died, if I had not been stopped by somebody.

Fortunately, God never ceases lavishing his benevolence upon his creatures. Because I was sincere in my search, God never allowed the Angels to diminish their assistance, even while I was running along wrong ways or openly fighting his views. The conflict was still raging inside and my capacity for resisting the grace of God was slowly but surely mitigated a little more every day, until I finally gave up.

I was 19 when I capitulated.

The Lord won the contest. He took me by surprise, even if it happened naturally. It was like a ripe apple falling in the hand of the gatherer.

It was the first Saturday of December. A new member of the Focolare, Nuccio Santoro, visited my parents' house in Montauban and

expressed the wish to see the whole family. They introduced him to my siblings. He soon realized that someone was missing and my father explained why. Nuccio insisted on meeting me.

My father said, "Today Alain is running a moving store at the fair in the market place in Montauban downtown." Nuccio became acquainted with the fact that my father never gave up on me after my departure from home and was continuously aware of where I was, what I was doing, and how I did. Now I even suspect that some of my good clients where so enthusiastically purchasing my stuffs because of him.

"So let's go to visit him," said Nuccio in reply.

The afternoon was over and the end of the fair was near. I was at my One Franc Stand , an equivalent of a movable Dollar Tree, when I saw two heads which were not following the randomly move of the crowd, they were standing on the same line of perspective. I looked more attentively to see if they were leaving the square or coming to my stall. They were coming. So I looked better to see what they would eventually be in order to possibly foresee their taste for purchase. To my surprise one of the two was my father... I did not know the other one, but he surely would be a believer, otherwise he would not be in company of my father. "It may be a member of the Focolare" I thought. And it actually was.

When they arrived at the stall my father introduced Nuccio as a philosopher. I immediately smelled that he was a priest, so, right away, I attacked him: "I like and have esteem for Jesus, but I dislike Christians and especially priests."

He replied in a way that surprised me: "I like Jesus, too!" -

"But Christians and priests are terrible," I said

"Well, it is in order to become less terrible that I try to follow Christ!" he said.

Such a humble and realistic observation took me unprepared. Besides, Nuccio suddenly answered the inquiry on evil that I had been unsuccessful seeking for years... I unexpectedly realized that Evil was not a value as such, but a missing good. Evil is something that I am supposed to erase like darkness must be erased by light. I would complete the need of good with more intimacy with the Lord. A similar view made sense. For the first time, evil was put in its proper perspective...

The conversation continued on light issues about Christendom. I didn't want to hurt him, so I tried to avoid uttering my usual tricks against the Church. During our exchange he invited me to visit him at the Focolare center in Toulouse, "which is not far from the University," he said. Then came the time to fold up the store and put all merchandises back onto the truck.

The owner of the shop came with the truck and I started to load it. Nuccio and my father moved to help. I was concerned to see that no too-heavy tray of goods came into my father's hands. So I was selecting the lighter ones for him, saying that the one he was going to take was supposed to come after. He was kidding, saying that he did not understand my technique: "why do you load the heavy one directly onto the truck if it was supposed to come after?" A good climate of friendship developed among us and when the truck was ready to start, I told the driver that I would meet him at the next fair as usual.

Meanwhile Nuccio and Raymond were wondering what would be the next move. I assuaged their doubts saying: "Let's go home!"

"Where, exactly?" asked my father knowing the few possible places for me to stay.

"No, let's see Mom!" I said.

And we walked together to their car and I went home that evening. Mom was so happy to see me: "Are you staying overnight?"

"No, Mom, I'm just passing through, but I wanted to say hello!" I said in reply.

It was a nice evening. The following Monday I had a History class at the university. It was about the history of Japan and the death by *Hara-Kiri*, a ritual suicide, of the hundred samurai, which gesture made possible the political, social, and cultural changes which improved the country. The teacher's conclusion was a sophism: "Because they got killed, all improvements were made possible!" He was supporting the idea that we must be ready to kill those who oppose the revolution we want to foment in society in order to make the necessary improvements... I vehemently disagreed and immediately stood up. Notwithstanding, I understood that it would have been easy for the professor to reply to any of my arguments and thus make the whole amphitheatre laugh at me. The other students knew my stringency on values. I did not want to compromise my good reasoning that the teacher could turn upside down. I was wondering what I could say to show my disagreement and his mistake… but it was hard to find a good sentence to say. My mind was spinning. Meanwhile I was walking towards him until I found myself at his desk. But no good sentence was there to say yet. So I walked round the desk and confronted him right in face, but still without a good argument to provide. The whole amphitheatre was silent, wondering what would be the end of the challenge. At that very moment I saw a door behind his chair and I took it. At this point quite obvious that I could not show up again in his class.

Just outside the door, there was another history teacher, probably waiting for the end of the class, for a little chat … I had a few repartees with her and I left, wondering then what to do for the rest of the day. Here is when I decided to pay a visit to Nuccio at the Focolare center in Toulouse.

When I arrived in Neal Street, I knocked at the Focolare door. Riccardo opened and went immediately to call Nuccio for me. But nobody came back. After a while Riccardo showed up again and led me through the apartment, until the end of the corridor. He opened the door to a small bedroom, which could have barely b room enough for a bed and a chair. He told me to wait there.

Nuccio was still not coming and I was wondering that it probably was time for me to go, when Maras, alias, Alfredo Zirondo-li, showed up. He was a priest, too, newly in charge of the Focolare in France, and he had just arrived in Toulouse from Rome. He introduced himself and sat on the bed, leaving the chair to me. Then he kept silent. He was silent but he clearly was open to make a conversation with me, he was just leaving it to me to start the talk. And I did. I was talking nonsense and tossing in a few jokes that usually provoked people to laugh. Maras did not laugh and was still silent. The situation embarassed me and, slowing, without even noticing it, I started to talk and explain the cultural and spiritual situation I was going through. The more I was talking about my personal confusion and quest for truth, the more he looked interested. It was the first time in years that I opened my heart and my mind to another person.

Maras was clearly interested and he spoke about Loppiano, a school of the Gospel where I could find what I was looking for. My reluctance against Christian issues was not over yet.

"I will never go there!" I said

"Why?" he replied.

"Because I'm not old enough. I need paternal permission to leave the country. My father will never allow me to go." Then, I added another excuse: "I still need to finish the university year." But I finally told the truth: "I do not want to revert to the Catholic Faith!"

Maras looked not at all uncomfortable with these assertions.

"Well", Maras finally said, "Concerning the first two difficulties, we'll find a way get around those. But concerning the eventuality of going to Loppiano, you have to be consistent: you go there for six month and if you do not convert within that time, you are afterwards free to move out and go wherever you want."

It was inescapable. It looked like a bet and we more or less agreed to the following: "You go there and you will convert" while my answer was, "I'll go, but I'll never convert." "OK, but you promise to stay six month! After that time you're free to go"

The wager was settled. We only needed to organize the departure…

We agreed that I was supposed to leave right after Christmas. It was not at all obvious how such a departure could be arranged in a few weeks.

Tableau #26
Loppiano City

TOO MANY THINGS HAPPENED IN THE TWO WEEKS BEFORE CHRISTMAS to be reported here. I only want to stress how everything worked accordingly. It was as if everything was led from above. It was, actually, even if, at that time, I was not aware of it.

I refused to talk personally to my parents about the project of going to Loppiano. I explained that, it is very likely, that they wouldn't believe me. Then I asked Maras to do so.

He agreed to speak with them, personally.

I asked "when are you supposed to see them?"

"I'll go to see them at Montauban tomorrow." He said.

"Morning or afternoon?" I asked

"First thing in the morning," he confirmed.

"Well, I'll be there at noon to check in!

The following day I was home around noon. My mother couldn't hide her joy to see me. But it was clear she was not aware of my departure yet.... So, I asked:

"Did Maras come here?"

"Yes," she said, "he is talking with Dad upstairs"

I moved upstairs, waiting next to the door of my dad's office. I was not sure about the result of the conversation between Dad and Maras. And I could barely restrain my eagerness to know. When they came out through the door, my father was silent. He looked shocked, I thought he had disagreed... But Maras reassured me: "It's OK," he said. Nonetheless, I was wondering why my father looked so uncomfortable...

My parents couldn't actually believe that the one in the family who was most in opposition to their own experience of faith and to Focolare, and who was unwittingly leading all my siblings into taking that hostile position.... was also the one who, in a few days, was leaving to attend the Focolare formation center of Loppiano, Italy. The surprise of this too-good-to-be-true news, left my father speechless for several days...

Then my mother invited me to stay for lunch.

"No, Mummy, I have to go. But please, don't say a word to my siblings. I'll tell them at Christmas during the "Réveillon"." In Gascony, we call "réveillon" the meal we have at Christmas, when we come back home from Midnight Mass. It was then, two days before departure, that I planned to make my siblings aware of such a dramatic change in my life.

The result of my sharing my decision with the family on Christmas was a catastrophe. I did not realize that my sibling consider my endeavor against my parent's practice of faith, as a first defense against the kind of Church totalitarianism experienced in our home. When I told them that I was leaving, they expressed an unexpected disappointment. My father suffered from the situation more than I did: he saw my disappointment but he did not know that, after all, I was not expecting to be cheered up. It was, however, a good idea not to leave my parents with the responsibility to convey the news. My siblings would have made my parents responsible. When they heard from me about the decision to go to Loppiano they only considered me a traitor, but with no anger against my parents... It was still a better result.

On the 27th I was taking the evening train from Montauban to Nice, where we were to arrive the following morning. There I should get, on the nearest track, the train to Florence, which could be reached in the afternoon. Finally, in Florence, I could get in the local area the train to Incisa Valdarno.

That evening of December 27, all my siblings gathered in the upper room of my parents' home, which was the bedroom of Christiane, my third sister. They were expecting the time of my departure to go with me to the train station. It was their understanding. A few minutes before leaving, I climbed the stairs to the third floor in order to greet them, one by one. I did it to say goodbye, due to the fact that no one told me that they planned to drive with me to Villebourbon, which is the name of Montauban train station. I said "Bi" to each one. It was difficult to move from one body to another, among the ten people, who packed the room: I had to reach each one on his/her chair, or on one of the two beds, without pushing or disturbing anyone else. No one was moving towards me or giving me room to ease my greetings to the neighbor. My struggle to kiss everyone goodbye was a real performance. The atmosphere in the room was of such a sadness that, after I left, they all fell asleep.

At the moment I was leaving, Joseph, one of my younger brothers, came down to check if we were ready, and he walked back up to call out our siblings. He could not summon the courage to enter their room. He just called them from the landing. No one replied, they were all fast asleep. Getting no answer from anyone, he believed that they had decided not to come with us to the train station to see me off.

He came down crying. I tried to cheer him up as best I could during our trip to the station and then on the platform while we waited for the train to arrive. All this was causing my parents to suffer terribly. I knew that going to Loppiano was my personal decision. It was a commitment with the Lord, whatever was the situation at home. It seemed that my siblings had made the decision to leave me alone. This was actually pushing me even more into the arms of Our Lady.

Days later I received a letter from Joseph. When he was back home, he had run up to Christiane's room to tell them his disappointment. At his arrival they woke up:

"Is it already time to go?"

"No, I already called you before going to the station and nobody answered....

Then they accused him of not waking them for a last goodbye at Villebourbon.

Such confusion was another joke of the Divine Providence. Not being able to say a proper farewell to me, they wrote me afterwards, and some communication between us that had died was revived. The contact among us was restored.

I would have been very surprised if I had been told then that the main reality I would encounter in a few days in Loppiano, would be the existence of Angels. It is true, actually. (More about angels later.)

I arrived in Loppiano in time for the beginning of the semester of formation. I was living in a little house there, which had just been built. We were seven people in a small prefabricated house, including three bed rooms.

I arrived in Loppiano almost by mistake. Normally, at that time, the people who were allowed to come there, were supposed to be already experienced in the Focolare life, and ready to engage their lives at the service of the Gospel, in the Work of Mary. They were supposed to be all willing to engage inside of the Catholic Church, through the Focolare movement.

When I arrived in Loppiano I still needed to convert. At that time, I did not even believe in God, in Jesus, in nothing actually but myself. And such "trusting myself" was not properly consistent. I could identify myself exactly, in some book of Sartre, Camus, Gide, Kierkegaard, or Dostoyevsky. So, saying that I believed in myself was even a euphemism, everything was considered through a dramatic perspective...

As soon as I arrived, I was surprised to see how the people I came across were always so happy... I was looking for the reason of such happiness. They had a way of welcoming me, which provided me a great discomfort: being an existentialist I was trying to keep away from any close relationship with anyone. They were doing the exact opposite. While I was trying to put a barrier between me and the other people, those inhabitants of Loppiano, were greeting me beyond that barrier.

I was shocked. They were able to touch my heart, while I was barely moving around, keeping my distance. They were not deterred by my aloofness. They, on the contrary, were so friendly, that every distance was lost... was erased. This was my first impact, and the first surprise...

The second surprise was the lack of food. There was actually very little to eat at meal time: a baked potato, a slice of cheese and an apple. That's all. I had the chance to sit just in front of a large German, Hans, and I was convinced that he needed more food. I repeatedly asked for additional meal, saying in the few Italian words that I quickly learned: "Please brings more food for Hans, I am hungry." On the first evening I thought that so little food was due to the fact that my arrival had not been announced. But the lack of food was the same the following day both at lunch and at dinner. And not only the quantity was poor, but it was exactly the same meal every time. The cooking was poor too.

At this point I began to be concerned for my survival and observed carefully the other people, my companions in misfortune. With amazement I observed that they were happy, and no one was complaining about the lack of food, not even criticizing its monotony. Additionally, they all looked in good shape. I really was in a peculiar place. I was forced for the moment to accept the situation, and try to endure it.

The presence of gladness was strong all around. It was easy to see the great joy that everyone was showing... I soon understood that, at Loppiano, the whole life is regulated by the fact that each one wants to follow the Gospel. The impressive gladness, which every relationship irradiated throughout the day was a direct consequence of the Gospel. Additionally, every week, an excerpt of the Bible, mostly from the Gospel, was given as the motto of our behaviors.

In this place, the Gospel was not mere material to study; it was the soul of our demeanors. My Italian was too poor the first week to understand fully the teaching we were given. I understood, nonetheless, that not only did we need to know the 26 letters of the alphabet (actually only 24 in Italian) in order to read and write, we also needed to know the words of the Gospel in order to act as a Christian. The idea was clear. I understood that living, day after day, the Gospel's words were the first step to take, in order to enter into the mystery of the city. The Bible passages to live by, were different every day, during the first ten days or so. Later, every week had its own motto.

On the first week we were given these words of Matthews: "To those who love me, I'll show up.": I took seriously that motto to guide my conduct, especially in the afternoon, during working time. In fact, Loppiano's schedule was simple: study in the morning, work in the afternoon, and share in the evening. The fee for our morning study was covered by our afternoon activity. Along the day I was repeating the motto of the week: "I'll show up with those who love me" as a kind of key to open to me the mystery of the place. Somehow this constant behavior brought me nearer to God. But I still was far behind on the road.

Once, coming back from work in the evening, Ezio, an Argentine, shared with me how unbearably heavy he felt those metal beams to be, which we were carrying all during the day. It made me proud at first, because I had been able to do the job, together with him, who was twice my size and my weight. He said: "At a certain moment I was going to drop the beam. It was too heavy!" - At this point my pride was at its pick.

But his sharing continued and amazed me: "Then I thought about Jesus carrying his cross to save us, and I was ashamed of not being able to carry a simple beam to help build his city." That really opened my eyes: I was doing the job to prove I was not inferior to anyone, but all those people had no care for personal performance, but just being obedient to a call from above. It was evident that their life had more sense than mine.

The second week, our motto was taken from a sentence of Saint Teresa of Avila: "Nothing counts, but loving thee", or if you want: "there is nothing to do, except to love you, oh Lord!" In the field, the clay was still impregnated with the abundant rain of the previous days. I was helping the construction of a prefabricated house. As a start, we

were bringing on site all construction material. At a certain point the four of us were carrying a pack of four doors, when my left boot got stuck in the mud. Hans told me to loosen my grip and get my shoe, and he was going to coordinate the time for all of us to let the pack fall. I though "Nothing counts but loving you oh! Lord!" and I replied, "Absolutely not, if I drop the pack you will too, and all doors will get muddy." I knew how the hours of work were precious and I did not want to be responsible for losing hours to clean muddy material that could even be damaged. I continued, then, helping to bring the doors to the construction site.

I continued to think, "A boot doesn't count, loving you my Lord counts!" It was logical in the perspective of the city. When we finally were able to drop the pack, there was a breath of relief in everyone. Then Hans went out into the field to fetch my boot... And we all got surprised when he turned the boot upside down and emptied the water as if my boot were a bottle filled with water... "Did you have that much water when your foot was inside it before?" We all laughed loudly. We were having a good time.

This nice event made me feeling like one of them for a moment. It was a lucky day. We all worked happily up to the evening. When they left to go home, I stayed a little longer to reflect. Yes, the whole city was the evidence of the Gospel. That was my thought. Suddenly it popped into my mind that in the next house there was Giovanni P. 's who was sick. He had hurt his leg with the chainsaw the previous day. I remembered from my childhood, in Montauban, how I had witnessed my father visiting the sick in hospital. I thought, then, that loving the Lord may include a visit to Giovanni. I took off in the direction of his house. While I was climbing up the stairs, I had a doubt: "It could be that my visit will disturb him". Therefore, I immediately went down: "Well, maybe visiting him is love" I thought, and I climbed again. In the middle of the stairs, I stopped: "I'm not sure what love is. I should go and check. If my visit doesn't please him, I will leave right away." With this in mind I entered the house.

I did not know what room was Giovanni's, so I called from the entrance: "Is anybody home?" From the last room, in front of the entrance came out Alberto Sasso, whose huge stature was covering the whole frame of the door. The presence of Alberto indicated that Giovanni was not alone. I concluded that he did not need my visit any more, and I moved to get out, but Alberto stopped me: "Why are you leaving?"

"Well, I came to say hello to Giovanni, but I see that he is busy," I said.

"Please, Alain, come in," he insisted.

I stopped in the entrance, not being sure of what to do. From his bed Giovanni couldn't see me. He called me: "Alain, where are you? Would you like to enter?"

"If that's what you wish, I'm pleased to come in."

His answer was positive. A few minutes later I found myself near his bed, while Alberto sat on the other bed. Almost immediately the conversation turned to my spiritual situation: Giovanni and Alberto were wondering whether or not I believed in God... They asked me: "Do you believe?"

"No!" was my answer.

They looked at each other, with a visible expression of disappointment in their faces:

"Poor guy," Alberto said.

I heard that. I was not at all offended. As a matter of fact, I knew they were right: my own life was actually poor and I saw that everyone in Loppiano had a richer life than mine, for their deeds were consistent with their faith. It was not the same for me, my own life was pure nonsense.

Suddenly Alberto made a suggestion to Giovanni, which I barely understood. He was referring to an excerpt from Matthews (18: 19): "Where two or three are gathered in my name, here I am in their midst" and "As soon as you gather, whatever you ask the father in my name will be provided." They asked me if I agreed to pray with them to the Father for what I would need. I had no objection to do so. Immediately, Giovanni started: "Heavenly Father," Alberto and I repeated after him: "Heavenly Father..." - He continued: "in the name of Jesus among us". We repeated: "in the name of Jesus among us." He said "We ask you" - We repeated: "We ask you..."

At this point Alberto took me from the collar of my shirt, almost tearing it, and brusquely asked me: "what do you want us to ask him?" His grip was so strong that he was lifting me up in the air. It was surely not the time to disappoint him...

With great hesitation I said, "let's ask that I meet him, that I see him…"

Immediately Giovanni continued to pray "We ask you that Alain may see you, may meet you." And we repeated afterwards "We ask you that Alain may see you, may meet you." then he said, "Oh! Mary! Take care of our prayer" and we recited after him: "Oh! Mary! Take care of our prayer" . Then he concluded starting a Hail Mary that we recited with him. The Hail Mary was barely over when Alberto took me again from the collar and asked me with a kind of anger: "Do you believe now?"

"No! I don't!" my answer was. It was almost an act of courage to answer in a way that was not meeting his expectation. He released his grip on me, and I could turn on my feet.

Again, Alberto looked at Giovanni. Both had a typical face some people have when they smell some stinking cheese. They said again: "What a poor guy!"

I was shocked. Not merely by the prayer, but by its simplicity: "How those people could pray to the Lord so easily? How could they do so in a room when there was not even a spiritual picture on the walls?" Actually, the house was new and no picture at all had been put on the walls yet. When I left the house, I was confused. I couldn't believe that we actually prayed the Lord together: "How those people could manage to talk to God in such a trifling place?" My stupefaction had no answer: "How could God hear us in a so simple demeanor?" It was a true astonishment: "How so frugal a room could allow us to meet God and talk to him?" Notwithstanding, I trusted them, which made me even more perplexed.

I moved down the stairs and begun walking in the field. No road had yet been traced to get to the house. So walking through the field was the only way home. The night was dark, with some wind, and with the lights of many stars in the sky. I suddenly stopped there and looked up. It was, somehow, a similar situation to the entertainment I had one evening, five years ago, in my parents' back yard, in Montauban. Again, I had the feeling of being utterly alone… Nevertheless, I persisted in behaving as though there was somebody with me.

It was evident that, the way people lived in Loppiano, was the result of God's existence. From what I saw, it was the implementation of the good news, provided in the Gospel. Yes, it was so. Besides, all people in Loppiano were expressing their experience of faith in their every deed. All was so harmonious and good that there was no other option for me than to agree with it. And so I said it: "Yes, God exists!" I said it slowly, as if it was a blasphemy.

Notwithstanding, after I said it, nothing happened. That apparent indifference of the sky to my words surprised me. Therefore, I cried them out again: "Yes, I believe in God!" I uttered as loudly as I could, and I repeated it: "I said that I believe in God!" Still nothing happened. After I decided to accept the reality of God, it came to my mind, that it was not sufficient for me to say "Yes, I believe in God." I inquired: "What is happening here?" And I cried out a last time: "Yes, I believe in God." Nothing replied to me. I still was an atheist, even if I knew that God exists.

It was a strange situation. The world had not changed around me. A great silence surrounded me. I knew that God exists, but I still behaved as if he did not. I dramatically understood that many atheists are those who say: "I know that God exists, but I don't care." Actually, I did care. I was truly concerned. I wanted to believe. I wanted to get a relationship with the Lord, but I did not know, how to enter into intimacy with him: God was still a stranger to me. Somehow the cry of Jesus on the Cross came from my lips: "Lord why did you forsake me?".

I did remember that afterwards Jesus said "Father I commend my soul into your hands." Such a confidence was too much for my senses to bear, and I did not consider saying those words. But slowly, as coming from far away, a new compulsion arose inside me, inviting me to say "God, I believe in you!" No, that was too much to say. I refused to say it. The impulse inside was growing. I rejected it again. But the pushing was so imperative that finally I said so: "My Lord, I believe in you!" And, immediately, a storm exploded inside of me. I felt like a new house, freshly built, having no door and no windows, but holes in the walls. The house was dirty. The words: "My Lord, I believe..." swept away the dirt.

Then a lot of considerations emerged inside, fighting against my recent attitude: "You are rejecting five years of conflict, and denying the whole philosophy of your life!" And also, "You are rejecting all that you fought for and left your parents' house for when you were 14." All that dirt needed to be swept out and I said calmly "My God, I believe in you!" But, again, other considerations invaded me : "You are giving credence to those people, here, who believe that they are right and you are wrong."

And again: "Well Giovanni and Alberto will believe that their prayer is working! Are you supposed to let it go?" These considerations were mere human consideration, just poor human respect; they were driven by the fear of the likely judgment from other people. I wiped these thoughts away, saying again: "My Lord, I believe in you." Similar words were like putting myself in front of him, like kneeling in his presence. Yes, by saying over and over again, "I believe in You", I was entering His presence. Similar words changed my inner attitude. I was aware of how fragile I was. I immediately run to San Vito, the little church on the top of the hill, which providentially on this particular night was open, even though the church was usually locked during the night. I entered the church and before the Eucharist I said: "Jesus, here I am. I did what I could, now it is your turn to take care of me, and everything else!' And I left the place. It was the eve of January 25.

When I woke up the following day, something had changed inside of me. Curiously, I was not an existentialist any more. Up to the day before, everything was a struggle inside and outside of me. The whole of reality surrounding me then was altogether in conflict with myself. I used to see all things as in conflict with one another. A house was an obstacle which prevented me to see the trees behind it. A tree was an impediment to see the grass behind it. The grass in the field was a barrier preventing me to see the ground. And so on. Entering a house, I felt constricted by the structure of the house, which obliged me to enter through the door, and most of the time I was entering by the window. Even, at the university, in Toulouse, I used to do so, and my friends, who were used to my eccentricity, would open the window for me, even when the class was on the third floor, and I got there by climbing along the gutter... My oddity was the result of the need to behave in conflict with the obvious and ordinary. To say it with one word, my whole life was a continuous nightmare!

334

The following day in Loppiano, everything had changed for me. The whole chaos of the world had suddenly disappeared, and there was even peace in my heart. It was something that I was not accustomed to feel any more. It had been sufficient to talk to the Lord. I immediately became a believer. I started to feel his presence as a Father. Suddenly all the people around me had become more than friends, they were my brothers. We all were sons of the same father. And the whole world was creation, not chaos. The whole world was an expression of his love. That new feeling was not the result of reasoning. It was the existential result of an act of faith. That morning I saw harmony everywhere. The chaotic sensation of the previous day was over. All my life had changed. Waking on the streets of Loppiano, I looked up toward the sky and, spontaneously, I said "Our Father who art in heaven…" But I could not continue reciting the rest. Even that simple prayer had been erased from my memory…. Nonetheless, these words, "Our Father" expressed my feeling that morning.

I knew that in the morning all the people of Loppiano used to go to San Vito for mass. I never joined them before. Not having been able to complete the prayer "Our Father, who art in heaven… " I decided to share the celebration of the Mass, that morning. Nonetheless, the many disturbing arguments, which assailed me the previous evening, moving against my reverting to God, were still partially there, providing the strange feeling that I had been trapped. Therefore, I was hanging my head and keeping the tail between my legs when I entered the church.

Entering the old church, while the Mass was being celebrated, I was surprised to see Alberto and Giovanni in the back, as if they were expecting me. Actually, they went to Mass that morning with the same low profile that I had, because they believed they had failed with me, and they were afraid that they pushed me too far. They did not know the good result of our "Consenserint" prayer together the night before. When they saw me, they got surprised, too, and to hide their happy surprise: they pretended to push me out with some ugly grimace, which made me laugh. Laughing in church released me from any anxiety. I felt free again. I understood that: "No, they did not drive me away. They pulled me into freedom, instead." And a great sense of peace invaded me.

After so long years of spiritual nightmare and existentialism, I had the free feeling of breathing again. It was like that, during the recent years, I had been expecting for this sole day. It was the beginning of a new endeavor, in which the world was a friendly village, and the natural surroundings was a landscape. Everything I saw, was composing a harmonious place, made by God. All people had suddenly become familiar and amiable. I, spontaneously, began to follow the rules of the Gospel, which run daily life, there, in Loppiano. I could not imagine, that morning, how I had entered into a series of amazing discoveries, connected to that full immersion in Loppiano life.

At the end of the day, I also shared, for the first time, evening prayer, together with the people I was living with inside the house. Each house was organized as a family group, which in Italian is said "Focolare". Great was my surprise that evening when I heard the people of my Focolare praying to the Angels. They recited "My guardian Angel, I pray you to protect, to lead, to comfort me, because I was entrusted to you, to be helped in my daily life, in my earthly life." I was really surprised, for I never considered that believing in God also includes believing in Angels.

At that time, I thought that Angels were reminiscence of Greek folklore. I decided to remain silent that evening and check the issue the following day with Fede, who was in charge of the whole school center. It was not easy to wait, for the issue disturbed me most. I thought that Angels were mythological creatures, or some entities invented by people, I never thought they were real beings." Therefore, I thought that praying the Angels was heretical. But I didn't want to bring trouble into that Focolare... I was not sure about what steps I should take.

The following morning, I knocked at Fede's office. He was in charge of the whole Loppiano community. I introduced my argument as slowly as possible, trying not to make waves. A sentence like: "By chance, do you know, if Angels do exist?" would have been too much in my opinion. I wanted to avoiding referring too clearly to the fact that the previous evening, my Focolare had prayed to the Angels... or Fede might punish them for engaging in forbidden practices. I had no intention of betraying them. I would not even say, "Would it be possible that, here in Loppiano, there might be someone who prays to the Angels?" I was convinced that those people would have been ordered, then, to leave Loppiano immediately because of some sort of fanaticism. "*After all*, I thought, *"they are at Loppiano to convert and learn Gospel tutelage, as am I."* It was obvious to me that coming to Loppiano was similar to going to school: you have to lose acquired biases and learn a lot of new material.

So during the conversation, I brought up the issue with a low profile and said: "Oh! Fede, tell me, ah, ah, it came to my mind some really strange ideas, you know, I think they are called Angels. Obviously they don't exist, do they?"

His answer amazed me: "Oh, for sure, they do exist"

He added then a few statements: "You know, Alain, Angels are good friends of ours..."

"Oh! Really! Are you sure they are real? Are they existing creatures?"

"For sure they are. Don't you remember Gabriel, who visited Mary and asked if she wanted become the mother of Jesus?"

"Oh yes, that's right." His answer relieved me.

"And don't you remember Abraham, when he received the visit of three Angels, who predicted that Sara, his wife, was going to be the mother of his son?"

The relief increased. "Oh yes, that's right," I said again.

"And, don't you remember Raphael, who led Tobias to his fiancée, Sara, that he delivered from a deadly danger, and how he later cured his father, Tobit, from blindness?"

"Oh! That is right, too. So, you're right! Angels do exist!"

"For sure, Alain, they do exist. And they fought hard to help you and lead your steps in order that you might come here. And they did a lot, during the last days, to help you meet the Lord!."

"How wonderful it is," was my last reflection.

When I left Fede's office, I went to San Vito Church and I stopped before Jesus in the Eucharist. I asked him for more information about the Angels. While I was praying before the tabernacle, I got a sort of enlightenment: I suddenly saw how between me and God there was not a total empty space, a total absence of beings, as I used to think before.

"Before" meant, actually, only up to a couple of days ago, for two days before I just reverted, and I discovered the presence of God in the world. Right now, I just made another marvelous discovery. I understood the presence, the role, the necessity of Angels as an integral part of the world. All at once, I saw what a wonderful equilibrium there is in the world amongst creatures.

I knew that God is now, actually, in the process of creating everything. God is present to everything now, because God did not create the world just many and many years ago. We depend on God's love now, too. We depend on him now in our life, in our existence. It was so obvious that God creates us now, and he is now putting me in the wonderful countryside that I see around me. It is a wonderful surrounding, made by material items like stone mountains, roads, houses, i.e. everything I can see, I can touch, I can hear...

God is also placing me among living things like trees, grass, vegetables, which provide beauty, gladness and food. There are also animals, that is to say, the creatures which are living beings and also have sensitivity. Beyond that, I am surrounded by people, men and women, as a large family of mine.

Then, I could finally understand how we, the people, are not the summit of creation. Above us, above people, there are pure spirits. Pure spirits are called Angels, and they are those that Aristotle considered as secondary causes, i.e. the forces that run the world. A similar activity includes help to support and lead us along our daily life in order to behave, to follow Christ, to love more one another...

That looked to me to be a wonderful panorama. With the presence of Angels, the whole world configuration took on a marvelous harmony. After the discovery of God, which included his love and his will, and changed my life, the discovery of Angels became the most wonderful and comforting discovery. I was not alone in front of God, all Angels wanted to support, to ease my life, and lead me according the call of God. In his mercy, the Lord was calling me to share his love, and his Angels were supposed to lead me along the steps towards him. What a marvelous configuration...

At this point I was ready to start the true training of the Focolare in Loppiano, near Florence, Italy. Loppiano was the name of the farm where the Focolare intended to build a "Marian City," a "Mariapolis", which was implementing the role of Mary on earth. As Mary was the one who perfectly lived the will of God on earth, fulfilling her call, which was to deliver Jesus, the Word, the Light, to the world. Identical was the call of Mariapolis.

Actually, the Focolare used to organize every summer some kind of gathering to foster among its followers the experience of a provisional Mariapolis. But there was, in Loppiano, the project of making  a similar experience permanent. So, the Focolare Movement had the project of building a permanent Mariapolis on every continent. Loppiano was the first permanent Mariapolis.

There, people are subjected to an actual 24/24 hours training program. Living there includes work, study, and prayer and the many moments of similar commitment, following the example of St. Benedict's rule defining prayer as the work of the soul and work as the prayer of the body, while the mind is sharing both through study. It is a consistent and continuous commitment experienced throughout the day in every activity.

As a worker, I was assigned the task of driving one of the few cars in the city, which usually entailed picking up the teachers at their residences and taxiing them to the hall where they used to teach. Performing that duty afforded me a familiarity with Giulio, who taught us sociology, Peppuccio, our philosophy professor, don Stefano, teacher of the history of Communism, Michel, teacher of Church history, and so on.

The liberty of movement that I had from the usage of the car gave me also the occasion of serving as a nurse for them, but only for minor care, like injections and so on.

One day, don Stefano Vagovitch read a trace of trouble on my face. He asked me what was disturbing me. Yes, I was in trouble for something which I was not able to express. My spiritual life was shadowed by a concern. I did not tell anything to anyone, because I was afraid to share what I was suffering inside. But that morning, while I was helping some people who needed medications and preparing in the kitchen the material to give them a shot, Don Stefano stepped in the kitchen and asked me "Alain, you've been looking strange these last few days. You are less joyful than usual. What's happened to you?

I answered "there is nothing so serious that is worth talking about."

"No, please, tell me" he insisted.

I was surprised and asked: "how do you know, that I'm having some struggles?"

"I see you sad, while normally you are so joyful. There are clouds in your life." He said.

"Oh," I answered, "it's not really in my life, it's just in my mind."

"And what is it happening? Please tell me." He insisted.

"Well, you know… I'm afraid about the demon."

"Why?"

"I understand the demon is a real person, and I would like really… I understand that previously my past life was under his influence… Many times, I followed his steps. I would like to be sure of not taking after his ways again. And, really, I don't know what I have to do to avoid him from running my life again. I'm so afraid to go down, to regress through the former experiences I had before. I want not to become again the way I was when I arrived here in Loppiano."

His simple answer amazed me: "if you truly do not want to have anything to do with the demon, you will never have to deal with him on your paths. You will never meet him. You will never be influenced by him."

"How that is possible?" I asked.

Don Stefano explained: "The demon is a pure spirit. He is an Angel, but he is an Angel who refused to stay with God, so his name is demon. Nonetheless, he has the nature of an Angel. As with any

Angel he cannot have a relationship with you, if you do not want to. When you do not allow him to get any connection with him, he cannot relate to you."

"Oh! Are you sure of that?" I asked again.

"Oh! Yes! Because pure spirits are not communicating through sounds, voices, writings, like we do, like all human people do. Pure spirits communicate directly." He said.

"Wow! What a discovery! How marvelous reality is!" I concluded.

Don Stefano made me understand that it was sufficient for me not being concerned about the demons, and I never had to deal with them. Here is why I understood how it is useful to know the Angels. Knowing the Angels, I also would understand what I have to do in order to never ever meet the demons in my life, and to always have a good relationship with Angels in order to receive help from them.

Obviously, not having a relationship with the demons does not exclude attempts by some demon to induce me into temptation. But he could do that only externally, by observation and supposition, not by a personal and direct knowledge from my soul. For example, seeing that I was putting a lot of effort into sports and body-building, the devil can put, before my eyes, pictures or situations that could induce me to pay too much attention to the care of my body, and neglect prayer or regular chores... Temptations remain, but they come from outside, as an external action on us that we can easily stop from inside, when we close the doors of will, mind and soul to fallen Angels.

The discovery of the whole field of creatures, which includes the Pure Spirits, was a comforting enlightening. The scenery of my life got suddenly breadth and scope. It was like a large bay window had been opened, and gave to my soul more room to move, a large panorama to consider. There was actually an immense panorama, where before I met only darkness.

It would be impossible to relate how a similar discovery enlightened my human endeavor, and embellished the adventure of my whole family. Saying so, seems to me, so far beneath the facts... Actual experiences express better who the Angels are. It is in the case of an emergency that the angelic presence is most vividly revealed. To

341

say the truth, it is also in similar needs that we properly refer to them.

Since Loppiano, the Angels have been on friendly terms with me. In emergency situations, even the simplest ones, I had in front of my eyes the candor of Adrian, talking with the heavenly beings without cowardice… His example helped me more than once, to make such familiarity explicit. For example:

I was studying philosophy both at the Sorbonne and at the Catholic Institute. One day, when I had to organize a meeting for the Focolare community in Paris and I needed to urgently purchase material from an office supply store, I was driving through the "*Quartier Latin*." Latin Neighborhood is the name that even today the Parisians call the city area surrounding the university. I was in a hurry. I drove several times around the square of Saint Germain des Près, unable to find a place to park the car in order to get the material I had to purchase in one of the stores open in the square…

What was I to do? I started talking to my Guardian Angel: "Please, take care of this predicament and help me find a place where I can park my car." Immediately I saw places to park, but they were far away and by the time I could get there, the places would already have been taken by some other cars. The traffic was too intense to take the risk to move there in vain… I told him that: "I thank you for showing me these places I didn't notice before. But they are too far away."

I insisted: "Please, show me a place that I could afford.!"

At that very moment, the car in front of me stopped without notice in a split second. I almost crashed against it. I became upset: "I asked for help and look at what you did, I almost crashed. This is not the time to play games… I asked you to give me a spot to park… Please do so!"

While I was complaining about the lack of help, I looked at the entrance of the store, just in front of me, and a spot was free, right there. Because of the stop, I had been obliged to make, I was in the perfect position to enter there first…"

"By the way," I said to him, "Forget what I said before. I was out of my mind. But thank you for your help! I really needed it, you know!"

Tableau # 27
End Times

THERE WAS IN THOSE DAYS SOME HEARSAY AFFIRMING THAT THE WORLD WAS SUPPOSED TO END within a year, almost like previously there was a warning for the 21 December of the next year...

When I asked Monmayou about it, he laughed long and hard. His laughing was similar to a successively inextinguishable series of falling water running from the mountain... and, between two laughs, with tears in his eyes, he asked me:

"Why do they want to wait so long?"

I did not know what to say. While I was silent, he continued: "It could happen right now, while we are talking together, or tomorrow morning before we get up!"

I was surprised by such clear assertions. Not being prepared to address the issue, I was speechless...

"In the Gospel," he continued "Jesus told us that nobody knows the time, not even the Son of Man! And now somebody would like to put a date for an appointment we have with eternity. They even would care to prevent us from being ready for it. If they say when it is supposed to happen, we will never be ready. For we are supposed to be ready now, not tomorrow or in a few weeks"

I understood again that we are supposed to be preparing for the event, and not predicting it. It will be the glorious moment when the whole of creation will come together again in full harmony. And it will happen in a manner that will please those who trust the Lord. There is no need to run here or there. Leave to the loving Lord the choicest time and place for each of us.

"Are you afraid of it?" I dared to ask.

"Well, no more than when a storm is coming and I see the sky darkening," he said, "the time to meet God in heaven will come to

343

every one of us, anyway."

His assurance and evident hope comforted me. I understood that, everything will happen, not in a different way than this precise moment, while I write these words or you, the lector, are reading them.

"But my parents told me that there will be days of trouble" I asked again.

"It's true! And we will never stress enough the need for us to get ready for the difficult times which will come before! Then the way everything will happen is all in God's hands! He knows everything and he wants to save us. If we want to be saved, too, and live accordingly there is nothing to be afraid of" He said all like in one word…

Again, his confidence made his own words truly convincing …

"But what about the troubles of the end times I was told about?" I continue to ask.

"Are you sure that our days are free from troubles? Everything will surely happen, but again, there is no need to make plans to avoid them or to more easily go through. This is an issue that comes from above and it is only in proportion that you belong to the above that not only they will not harm you, but they will be the proper crowning of our life. All human plans are obsolete already. And you must make reservation of food and water as Our Lady said…"

"Well I know, (and I completed his sentence) we must drink the water of the continuous intimacy with the Lord, which is the water of living in grace, feeding ourselves with Eucharistic Jesus, the only true food, keeping us in permanent prayer…"

Adrian had a large smile that enlightened his face of a countryman, marked by years of hard work in the fields… He finally concluded: "You know then what to do…"

Knowing from Fr. Emmanuel that God acts in our lives through "Second Causes" makes me aware of the Angelic presence in every spiritual activity. It means that our relationship with Mary, with Jesus, operates in the center of the celestial court. Even the relationship between Jesus and his Father goes together with the fullness of Angelic presence.

Adrian Monmayou used to repeat the prayer that Padre Pio recited every day as a favor for all those who asked him for help... He was pleased to teach that petition to those who wanted to increase their trust in the Lord...

> *O my Jesus, You have said, 'Truly I say to you, ask and it will be given you, seek and you will find, knock and it will be opened to you.' Behold, I knock, I seek and ask for the grace of...*
> *Our Father... Hail Mary... Glory be to the Father...*
> *Sacred Heart of Jesus, I place all my trust in you.*
>
> *O my Jesus, You have said, 'Truly I say to you, if you ask anything of the Father in my name, He will give it to you.' Behold, in Your name, I ask the Father for the grace of...*
> *Our Father... Hail Mary... Glory be to the Father...*
> *Sacred Heart of Jesus, I place all my trust in you.*
>
> *O my Jesus, You have said, 'Truly I say to you, heaven and earth will pass away but my words will not pass away.' Encouraged by Your infallible words, I now ask for the grace of...*
> *Our Father... Hail Mary... Glory be to the Father...*
>
> *O Sacred Heart of Jesus, for whom it is impossible not to have compassion on the afflicted, have pity on us poor sinners and grant us the grace which we ask of You, through the Sorrowful and Immaculate heart of Mary, Your tender mother and ours. Hail, Holy Queen...*
> *St. Joseph, foster father of Jesus, pray for us*

It was in San Antonio, Texas that I started reflecting more precisely on the Angels, guided by the teachings of Adrian Monmayou.

I was visiting my daughter Marie-Claire, who was struggling through some difficulty at work. I was not sure I understood what the causes of her problems were... Nonetheless, I saw and I heard her suffering and I did my best to share it, or to offer a positive presence that could help her to address her situation with more serenity.

The Gospel does not require us to understand. It requires us to cry with those who cry, laugh with those who laugh, and pray for those who cause our troubles [Rom. 12:13]. And I did so.

Being near to someone who is struggling is, probably, the very best situation in which to invite us to intensely pray the Lord every-day for help, asking whatever he wills, including miracles... I opened my heart telling him to come inside, to read the sadness of my soul and fill it with joy and the waters of eternal life... the ones of the end times.

When you are far from home, you are easily lost. You miss most of the tools you are used to, when you are home, your library, your notes, a car, a store, even a church nearby... During my stay over there, I put my roots in the Lord, repeatedly, every day, every morning, every eve-ning, every hour... alternating the continuous trilogy:

"God have mercy, Christ have mercy, Lord have mercy,"

With the traditional praise to the Guardian Angel,

"Angel of God, that thou art my guardian, enlighten, guide and govern me, who has been entrusted to you by divine mercy."

I also used to repeat the prayer of the Russian Pilgrim:

"Jesus, the only Son of God, have mercy on me, a poor sinner, and hasten to assist me."

It was a confusing situation. I came there to support her, to offer fatherly friendship, and let her choose the decisions she considered the best. My days were a continuous dialog with the celestial pres-ence... I was busy helping her pack her belongings when she returned from work, during the time when I was running two online courses of philosophy in Pittsburgh. I kept constantly uttering ejaculations, especially those of Nicolas de Flue, Patron of Switzerland:

"O Lord, I am nothing, you are all."

Which he liked to synthesize as:

"Nothing---All, Nothing---All, Nothing---All...."

I was also repeating his other prayer:

"O Lord, take me the way I am,
and make me the way you want".

... and again:

"Nothing---All, Nothing-==All, Nothing-All...."

And talking with the Angels: "Everything is yours"

"Thanks for your help", etc.

These utterances flowed out with my every breath. At each exhalation, "NOTHING..." At each inhalation. "ALL...". I tried to have my whole life rooted in celestial company. While walking down the stairs I would pray, "Thank you. Our Lady and dear Guardian Angel for the gift of gravity and balance." or climbing up, "Again, thank you, Our Lady and good Angel, for the exercise." or I would keep in my mind Jacob's Ladder that everyone is supposed to ascend... or the steps of the spiritual life according to John of the Cross from the enthusiasm of the first call, through sensorial purification, illumination time, mind purification, up to unitive life...

Yes, the stairs of Marie-Claire house, that I had to go up and down several times a day, where a good occasion of physical training and of providing a symbol of our earthly journey... raising up my heart to celestial concerns and going down to pick up earthly facts or struggles... The difficult moments of sharing her ordeals became an opportunity for intense prayer and intimacy with the Lord... I was gathering up all her concerns to bring them to the upper floor... My physical endeavor was just the symbol of a more important spiritual adventure... that I will be totally aware of in moments of Beatific Vision...

I tried to share this experience with Marie-Claire, but she confessed that she had no intimacy with the Angels, no intimacy at all.

As a result, I prayed the Angels to provide...

One morning, she was supposed to report to her job later than usual. During breakfast, I shared with Marie-Claire the experience I had in her home there in San Antonio. It was the occasion of an interesting conversation.

AS - Do you believe in the Angels, Marie-Claire?

MC -Yes, Daddy, I do.

AS - Do you talk to them. Do you pray to them?

MC - No I don't. I only pray to the Lord.

AS - When I mention the Angels, what do you think about?" She thought that question over for a moment. Her reply surprised me:

MC - Sometimes you and Mom called one another "my Angel," It also happened, many times, that Mom or You, Dad, called me or one of my siblings "my Angel," and we knew how this lovely word shows your affection for us. "Angel" is a nice word to show love to someone, to a child, to a spouse, or to a fiancé. This way to speak, sometimes, is more expressive than anything else. Maybe only when at night you came to say "Good Night," and you added, "I love you". These were surely stronger words, we got from you and Mom. Giving us the nickname of "Angels" shows a kind of poetic analogy, which involves beauty, goodness, harmony, warmth...

AS - Interesting, indeed!

But she continued:

MC - Today, there are a lot of paintings of Angels all over the place. We find pictures, publications, commercials, articles referring to Angels. That popular fascination with the subject of Angels surely shows the need of people to reach for more spiritual issues in our materialistic world of supply and demand, of "do ut des", of business and trade. Our physical world is prisoner of tangible topics, and time seems so imperative, every day we must cover our bases on the jobs, every week is scheduled so tightly that referring to the Angels gives us some breathing room.

The comfort that a mere reference to them brings in our lives is so evident that it pleads by itself in favor of their existence, their consistency. It is so pleasant to believe that they are near to us, in daily circumstances, that knowing they exist makes our lives better...

Well, they are reported with confusion sometimes, I remember reading a book on the Angels, in which Sophie Bernam presented Mary as an Angel, and she said that Mary is one of the greatest

Angels. This is, obviously, a mistake, due to the fact that from the point of a view of theologians, Mary is not an Angel but eventually she is the Queen of Angels.. Nevertheless, the confusion shows an interesting issue: there are several apparitions or visions of Mary in the world, and these celestial interventions are similar to Angelical interventions.

Many Christians, mostly Catholic people, suggest going to Jesus through Mary, and the fact that Mary appeared in some place like Lourdes, Fatima, Medjugorje or Kibeo, in Rwanda, induces the people who are not familiar with Mary to confuse her with Angelic figures. Actually, at Fatima, for example, the apparition of Mary was preceded by the apparition of an Angel. Or in Rome, when our Lady appeared to the Jew Ratisbonne, in Sant'Andrea delle Fratte, she showed up on the altar of Saint Michael. There is a tight connection between Mary and the Angels. We must distinguish them and Mary, but they still remain connected. Don't you think so?

AS - Interesting indeed! Yes, confusions are common in this field of investigation. One of the greatest experts of spiritual life, Juan De Yepes, also known as John of the Cross, says that we can make great mistakes in revelations, especially when they come directly from God, because, we are living on the Earth, and our capability to understand is really quite poor, in comparison to the enormous richness and consistency that these revelations bring to us. The confusion you referred to between Mary and the Angels is just an example. More confusion can arise between Angels and other apparitions.

MC - I also read some other interesting information about the Angels. They are contingent like every creature is; and at the same time, they are pure forms, because in them the form does not activate and shape a body, the form exists independently of matter. An angel is only form, only soul, only spirit. The celestial bodies that their forms actuate are not physical, but just spiritual imitations. If I think of the soul of an Angel, this soul is totally the Angel. The Angels are pure spirits, because they are not involved with matter in their configuration.

You told me the other day that Aquinas makes some analogy

here: while physical entities may have the same form of the same species, as we have many dogs, many cats, many wolves, and many individuals of the same species, which reproduce the same form, in which we recognize a species. The Angels do not reproduce diverse forms... because each unique Angel is identified totally by its form, and has all its individuality in the form. There is for every form only one species, that is to say only an Angelic individual. The Angels are different depending on their form, that is to say on their species. In Thomist language, each Angel is from a different species, and so we have as many Angels as we have spiritual species.

You also said that because a pure spirit is not limited by matter, he possesses in fullness and by himself all that comprises the nature of his species. There is no other limitation in the fullness of his nature. Each Angel realizes the fullness of his own nature. He doesn't share his nature with any other... There is no incompleteness in him, therefore the medieval question of the sex of the Angels is overcome: they have no sex, they do not need any specific relationship with a he or a she to blossom. They are already blossoming in what they are, instead of what is happening on the earth with all living beings.

And also, you explained to me that an Angel does not know through the mediation of senses, because he has no senses. And he ignores all that is connected to senses, like: feeling, emotion, sensitivity, moods, or opinions. A pure spirit is also pure intelligence. All his nature consists in being intelligent and wishful. The Angels know what they are. Their first act is intelligence. Their way of thinking is not through concepts, judgment, and reasoning, like every human person. They do not need any discourse as people do. An Angel knows directly what he looks for. We would say that he knows intuitively all of reality through the essence of things. As soon as something does exist, Angels know it.

Because an Angel is not limited by senses or matter, he does not know progressively but immediately. Every pure spirit has in fullness the knowledge of nature, and of the whole world, including who he is. The work of God in which an Angel recognizes God is himself. By knowing who he is, an Angel recognizes himself to be a creature of God. The pure spirit knows God immediately. Starting from the moment he exists, he does know, and he is aware of the fact that he exists as a creature of God. He understands that he is the one who is receiving right now his existence from God. A similar awareness remains for ever: even the twisted Angels, the Demons, are believers. They do not suffer doubts.

AS - Wonderful! You truly impress me, Marie-Claire! I would like to stress what you say about the difference between human and Angelic intelligence. A human knows God through the mediation of senses, his/her awareness is progressive and never totally complete; which means that it is possible for a human to commit a mistake of knowledge. Oppositely, Angels do not commit any mistake of awareness, because there is in them no limitation imposed by the senses, all their knowledge is perfect and immediate. An Angel knows everything, including his own person, exactly the way it is... No mistake of understanding is possible for a pure spirit. The presence of God, as the cause of his own existence, is fully ascertained. An Angel knows that God exists as surely as he knows his own existence.

I would also like to underline that all the activity of a pure spirit is only intellectual. This means that all his life is spiritual only. The Angels do not make improvisation, they never guess... They do not need or make any reasoning, supposition, expectations, assumptions... They don't even need words, language, abstraction, interpretation about reality. They know reality directly, exactly as it is. They know themselves and each other exactly as they are. They also know us for what we are.

We spoke about the intelligence of the Angels. We have to say the same for their willpower, for their will, for their activity in willing. An Angel is pure intelligence. He is also pure willing, because his will, his capacity of deeds is not limited by senses. An Angel loves himself directly with a pure act of will and intelligence. An Angel is a form or spirit with a specific degree of intelligence and will. He is gifted with determined power of penetration, of comprehension, of decision. The Angels are recognizable to one another by their way of thinking and willing. They are not identical.

They immediately move with their will toward the good they know by their intelligence. It is an unique act. They have a perfect *will, that is to say they are totally master of their knowledge and their willing. They do exactly what they want to do, and they know exactly what they want to know. They are perfectly self-mastered, and the decisions they take are always perfect and in full freedom, and that is also the reason why Angels are totally responsible for what they do.*

I like to insist on the fact that because they cannot make a mistake, the Angels choose always the same choice they did the first time, they did it freely, because they have total knowledge without any mistake, and so they cannot change their choices. This expression, "they cannot change," is not very fair about the Angels. It would be better to say, that the Angels never, they never want to change their own decisions, their judgments, their determinations, their will, because they can never make mistakes in knowledge, in ascertainment and willing. They are perfect knowledge and perfect will. A similar perfection includes a definitive choice in everything they do. Similar perfection is also valid for the dethroned Angels, or fallen Angels who are the Demons. Never, never again do the Demons want to change their mind. When they made the wrong turn, they already knew all the consequences…

At this point, we may ask in what way the Angels act in the world. Because they have no sense, no sensitiveness, no physical contact, they do not move things, powers, wind, planets pushing them like a human person would do. Being pure spirits, pure willing they act directly into the things. They move things by their direct will. Because an Angel does not have a body, he cannot act externally on things, but because he is pure spirit and pure will, he does what he wants to directly.

As people we are distinguished, separated and united by our bodies. We communicate through our voice, by reciprocal sights, by shaking hands. The Angels, who have no bodies, are connected to one another directly, just by their will and their knowledge. They communicate with us the same way: just by an act of will and intelligence. The pure spirits communicate with each other directly without any obstacle. The spiritual world is a world of communication and celestial interpenetration.

The first outcome is that pure spirits move physical bodies in a way that no human being can observe, can notice, because they are not acting from outside. When the Angels act, they do so directly inside of the things, and this move is noticed because the things move. Again, the action by which an Angel operates is just their will.

MC - Wow! This is beautiful to hear! I sort of knew it, but I was not too sure... And how do we communicate with the Angels?

AS - We also communicate with the Angels by simple act of intelligence and will. By intelligence we understand with whom you are in contact, and by will we do communicate with them... The Angels are pure spirits, they communicate with reality directly by their will, and we, too, communicate with Angels by our own willpower. It is sufficient to say "Hi", internally, to speak with our Guardian Angel. It is sufficient to say "Help me" to immediately be connected with the Angels who are already anxious to help, to protect, to support, to promote us for the glory of God. Obviously, we act in pure faith, because we do not see or hear them. However, the results of our prayer show that we truly communicate.

It is by their actions that the Angels manifest themselves to people; they serve them, and they become known. They are not recognizable by their presence, unless they want to be. They manifest their presence near to us through their action in the things, the situations, the places we are dealing with. The Angels, in fact, are present where they act. It is difficult for us, to understand clearly, the fact that they do not have a body, and that their movements are instantaneous... They act so fast that people say that they are flying. Here is why usually we represent artistically Angels with wings.

MC - Would it be possible for an Angel to be in two places at the same time?

AS - Well, the Angels act so fast that even if they are not in two places at once, it is likely the same for us as if they are. Reading the experts on the Angels, like Augustine, Thomas Aquinas, Catherine of Siena, St. Teresa of Avila, John of the Cross, Gregory, there is no indication that the creatures that Angels are can stay in the same time in two different places. The answer is usually "No, that is not possible, because the manifestation is unique in every one of their acts, because they have only one form, one intelligence, and one will, and so in one time they act only one way.

MC – Some saints were able to bilocate. Why don't the Angels?

AS – Well, bilocating does not mean to be and act actually in two places at the same time. When Saint Anthony, from the pulpit in the Church of Padoue, moved to Arcella, and made the homely he promised to the religious Sisters, there, he was seen both, in the Church and in the Convent of Arcella at the same time, yes, but at that time, he was acting, preaching, only to the Sisters, while at the same time, he was silent in the Church. We say bilocating, to indicate the capacity to move, immediately, somewhere else. But actually, in a situation of bilocation, the saint, who ever he/she is, Anthony, Don Bosco, Padre Pio, Gemma Galgani or someone else, is acting in only one place.

Or at least, that is the way I see the situation. Only the Lord, after his resurrection, was able to be in several places at the same time, as Saint Paul said. Maybe at the End Times, when space and time will be restored in their one unique nature, such double presence will be possible for us and, obviously, also for the Angels.

MC - I understand that their own configuration makes them invisible to us. So how could they show up at times?

AS - I agree with you. The Angels are normally invisible to us. The reason why sometimes the Angels do reveal their presence and speak with people is simple. When they want to be manifested to our senses, they need to take some form of matter to make their presence sensible, and that is the reason why normally theologians consider that when the Angels want to be visible, it is just because they took some provisional physical aspect to manifest their presence.

Theologians say that they take a borrowed body or a transitional aspect. Because they actually have not any body, they act in physical entities, in order to produce visible forms and sounds to manifest the voice, the form that people would enjoy according to the mission they are performing to us... In similar situations the Angels take a temporary shape just to be seen and heard by people. But similar appearance is not specific, it is an accidental, transitional situation, which only shows the capacity of the Angels to manage

354

with the sensorial world.

Regarding our personal relationships with the Angels, it is characterized as an outcome of their nature of pure knowledge and pure will, so it actually depends both on what they want to do and our own particular sensitivity... A relationship is possible to have with the Angels every time, everywhere, just as we want to. It develops then as every true relationship: the way we deal with a relative, a friend, a colleague, or other people depends on us and on them. Every relationship is unique and personal. It is the same with the Angels and because of their typical ethereal consistency it can be actuated so rapidly and differently.

We know that we truly can deal with the Angels. That does not mean that we are able to see them immediately. Even when people are not able to see the Angels, the relationship exists as soon as people ask for their presence near to us. Besides, we have also to consider the fact that the Angels are already present in our lives and always intervene, act in our deeds. It would be sufficient to look at any city traffic to understand how it is possible that so many misbehaviors produce so few accidents, And the Angels are present in our situations, ease our struggles, direct our endeavors, alleviate our sorrows, support our efforts. They always are anxious to serve people, to serve us more than we desire their help. Even more than we dare to ask.

Therefore, we can stay at peace and behave, doing whatever we have to, with serenity and care... The Angels are present in any case and they always help, support, suggest, and protect us every day, everywhere. The explicit protection of the Angels depends on them, but it depends on us to ask for and, especially, to become familiar with them, in order to recognize their presence in our life. We must take every occasion we can to thank them for their many deeds.

MC - Thanks, Daddy, your words, confirmed what I read and made it even more understandable.

AS - I see that you are impressively knowledgeable about the Angels. May I understand that you are familiar with the Angels, too. You are, aren't you?

MC - Are you trying to scare me?

AS - Not at all. I just wanted to quote Juan De Yepes and his invitation to be prudent in our investigation about the Angels in daily life. In order to be able to enter in the spiritual consistency of the Angels, we need first to get the spiritual nature of people. In other words, we need to discern the difference between a ghost and an Angel. They are not the same, even if they look similar sometimes.

The body of a human person, man or woman, exists as a body only because it is matter animated, organized, structured in a person. A body manifests the presence of the soul, which organizes the body. In every situation, the body is the physical expression of the soul, as well as the mind is the speculative expression of it. But the soul itself is the spiritual expression of the other two.

The traditional distinction between body and soul, which came to us from India through the Greeks, is not sufficient to explain the consistency of the person. All together, body, mind and soul are one. They are the physical, speculative and spiritual expression of the person. They are not part of it. People are not machines. Each one is a person in his/her physical, speculative, or spiritual endeavor. The person is one and shares the three dimensions of the macrocosm, which actually are the physical world, the speculative world, and the spiritual world. They are the three worlds composing the whole of creation.

The soul is present in everyone, and you can distinguish but not separate the soul from the body, or from the mind, otherwise you do not exist as a person any more, you are merely a corpse. In Latin, the word for soul is anima, *which means animator, developer, organizer. The soul is the heart of the whole person. It organizes the whole configuration of the person. When the body is losing its own organization, we say the soul has left the body. The expression is, actually, improper, because the physical expression of your soul, that the body is, does not exist anymore when you die... The whole physical entity of yours has disappeared and what is left of your body is following the natural laws of decomposition to return to the ground, dust to dust. The corpse we see is only the souvenir of what the person was. A corpse represents what he or she is not any more...*

Here is why at the Sorbonne, Jean Daujat and Jean Guitton

used to tell their students: "When I see you, I see your soul."

MC - What do you mean by that?

AS - I mean exactly what I just said: the body is the physical expression of the soul. Your way of walking, talking, thinking expresses yourself in a unique way... every behavior expresses your soul. Therefore, "when I look at you, Marie-Claire, I see your soul." If I was not able to see your soul, I would only see your cadaver... Because you're alive, I see your soul.

When I say "I am my body," I automatically express that I am a soul incorporated, or vice versa, I am a soul with its physical expression, the incorporated body. We are so accustomed in our present society to defining ourselves merely by our sensible expressions, which our bodies are, that we finally end up conferring upon the material part of ourselves all the attributes that are leading our ways of living, our ways of speaking, our ways of writing, our ways of sleeping, and many times we do not even remember that all our material consistency expresses what is organizing all of that, that is to say the fact that I am and I am a substance ensouled.

MC - Is that reality of Body-Mind-Soul the characteristics of people only?

AS - This is actually an excellent question. The Greeks use to make a permanent analogy between the small and larger entities in the world, calling "MICROCOSM" the small entities and "MACROCOSM" the largest ones, indicating that each one reflects the other: which means that the configuration of people (microcosm) reflects the same configuration of the universe (macrocosm).

MC - Does that mean that the universe, too, has a soul?

AS - Actually, yes, the whole universe is obviously material, as everybody likes to see it, but also speculative, in its own complexity, and especially through people, but also spiritual, through the presence in it of the Second Causes... The Angels are part of the spiritual dimension of the universe.

MC - How do you define each aspect of material, speculative and spiritual entities?

AS - This is another interesting question. In his teaching at the

Catholic Institute, a disciple of Jacques Maritain, Jean Daujat, used to distinguish every diverse entity by their own configuration:

Material Things are supposed to be consumed when in use, like food, paper, notebooks, pens, and so on. When you use some soap for the shower, I can use it too, if there is some soap left. But I cannot use the same soap you used. And if new water is available, I may also later on, take a shower. But the water you already used is not accessible any more.

Speculative Entities do not decrease nor increase, while they are in use. For example, you can read the whole newspaper today, and I can read it also, after you. Nothing is consumed during the reading...

Spiritual Entities increase while they are shared. I may tell you about your mother in Pittsburgh and our conversations, and while I do so, my friendship with the whole family increases; and while you are listening, your own quality of life is being likewise enriched.

MC - O, wow! But what about the soul of the whole universe?

AS - As with every person, who is a microcosm, the macrocosm, too, needs its spiritual dimension to exist!

MC - So only with my soul am I alive.?

AS - Yes, you're alive and everything you are and everything you do is an expression of your soul. It is, then, correct to say: "When I see you, I see your soul..." And because the soul is the organizer of the body, supposing you were going to exist again, the soul would organize you in exactly the same manner as you are now... Here is why Plato's metempsychosis, i.e. the reincarnation of the soul, is impossible in another shape than your actual presence on earth... When the soul incarnates again, it will organize matter exactly the same way it already did to produce its physical representation that your body is.

MC - So a Ghost is the provisional status of a Soul while it is expecting the End Times when, through the event known as resurrection, it will be allowed to activate again on earth its true body. Is that what you're saying?

AS - Yes, it is.

MC - But why in the Gospel does the Lord say that at the End Times we will be like Angels?

AS - The expression of Jesus in the Gospel according to (Mark 12:25) "When people rise from the dead, they will not marry anymore, and they will live like the Angels in heaven." Actually, the Lord does not say that people will be Angels, but they will behave like them, i.e. they will be complete in their own configuration and will not be in need of another one to be fully a human being. Today a human person is a male or a female. He or she needs another person to blossom in their human nature

In the present situation, every human being has a sex, which means he or she is divided inside, from the bottom of the feet up to the top of the hairs. The whole person is incomplete and needs another one to make himself or herself complete. Those who do not marry complete themselves through the community they belong to. Such a completeness is first of all spiritual, the physical aspect helps, but is not essential. Everyone who has been in love knows the difference between "having sex" and having a conjugal intimacy. Without love, even sexual intercourse brings failure... It is just a physical intercourse it does not help people to blossom.

A similar handicap will not return when at the End Times people raise again with their true bodies. Everyone will get his/her body in the fullness of its entity. It will be not the incomplete body that we have now. Every soul will activate its body from "the new earth and new heavens," which means that the body will be free from of the dichotomy of space and times, free of the physical pain, free of sex configuration, in one word: free of the consequences of the first sin.

At the End Times, our initial human ingenuity will be restored. The earth will get its true entity, too, without the restriction of space and time, which is the one that we suffer now. Every person will be free. No one will be in need of someone else to be in fullness who they are. It will be a celebration of the whole human community and the whole personal blossoming, when everyone finally gets the fullness of his/her personal relationship with God and the whole world....

The Angels do not receive the advantage of the time of mercy that people get between the first sin and the End Times. Because of their physical composition people may go by steps, they may repent and change the course of their life. Angels do not. Here is why: Since the moment they exist, the Angels know who they are, whom they belong to, what business they are in charge of, and the call to freely agree with it. Their decision is taken with full awareness and no other information can be provided afterwards so there is no reason, no opportunity to repent or change their mind. Whatever their decision is, it is final, already. Here is why the Angels and the Demons exist from the beginning of their own existence.

MC - So, when we people receive a visit from above it could be from God in person, from an Angel, from a Demon, or from a Ghost. Is that true?

AS - Yes, these are the options. And what you call a visit from above is just an additional deed to the permanent course of action of afterlife. The spiritual dimension of the macrocosm never stops to impress the physical world: actually, physical entities exist because of the spiritual ones... Without the Angels the world that we know, as the physical world, would immediately disappear.

The presence of the spiritual in our lives is always God's presence. He keeps us in existence and manifests himself to us, through creatures like Angels, Demons, and Ghosts.

That presence, however, is not only visually manifested, it can be a thought that pops up in our mind, a suggestion, an intuition, an act of love we receive from a neighbor... Our own life swims in spiritual features, we are spiritual inside and we move, act, speaks, listen to the whole spiritual field that surrounds us and that we belong to.

MC - A Ghost is a visitor from the dead, right? And the Demons are those Angels who twisted their vocation and, because of it, they change the whole nature of their behaviors: they are not Angels any more but demons. Is that correct?

AS - Very good!

MC - If the Angels have natural power, what happens to the tasks that the Demons were previously in charge of?

AS - Twisting their own configuration they twisted their deeds, too. In his mercy, the Lord continues to provide existence to the pure *spirits even after they twisted their own behaviors. If the nature of a twisted Spirit was to take care of some physical business, such a responsibility remains. If it was canceled, the whole existence of the Spirit would be canceled, too. As a result, the Demons remain in charge of what they were supposed to care for as Angels... but now, concerning the field of competence which belongs to their control, they no longer support its proper operation. Demons bring what they are as such; their own configuration remains. They are the cause of struggle in the natural world. They cause disorder where they were supposed to bring support and order. They provoke natural disasters, Tsunami, hurricane, earthquake, disease, sickness, accidents, and so on...*

MC - Why did you compare the connection between body and soul with the connection between the physical and spiritual world?

AS - The connection is the same. The microcosm of an individual reflects perfectly the macrocosm of the whole world... The concept comes from the Greeks. Macrocosm and Microcosm got the same sophisticated configuration. The soul does not exist before the body, it makes the body to exist at the same time it shows up. Look at the wood chair you sit on. Can you separate the wood from the chair? No, because it is a chair made of wood. The wood of the chair can be separated from the chair only when you destroy the chair... in such a case you get the wood which was the chair, as a corpse is the body which a person was.

When the wood loses the form of the chair it becomes simply wood and follows the natural rules of determinism that apply to every piece of wood. But without the wood of the chair, you cannot have the chair. In the same way, you cannot separate the body from its soul, you can rationally distinguish them, one from the other, you cannot separate them, because they belong to the same substance, the same entity, the same object for the chair, the same person for the body.

MC - When we die the soul exists without the body. Isn't that so?

AS - This is a difficult issue: The soul is the organizer of the body. It is what organizes the body. It is what makes the configuration of the body, makes it alive, and keep it alive. Philosophers say that the soul is the form of the body. Technically, the soul should exist only with the body, as a form exists only with what it gives its shape...

As a result, the soul would not exist without the body... and nevertheless it does... We face a mystery here. How is it possible for the soul to exist without the body that it is the form of? It is like saying that the chair can still exist without the wood... Well, it can exist in my mind... as an idea... So maybe the soul can exist, too, in another kind of existence...

Because people are made in the image and resemblance of the Lord they do exist forever.... They are not eternal, only God is eternal, but they are immortal, i.e. they have a beginning as creatures, and then they exist forever... In fact, people are capable of immortal acts like knowledge and love, which is evidence of their immortal nature. Immortality is a gift that people share with the Angels...

To tell the truth, we must also stress that people are superior to the Angels inside of the work of creation. Death, which is our human weakness and fragility, can ultimately become a condition which puts us above them: people are capable of dying for love... The Angels cannot die, not even for love, as Jesus did... "No one has greater love than this, to lay down one's life for one's friend" (John 15:13). A similar condition is the sign of our higher connection with all things in creation.

People may also reproduce themselves, the Angels do not... People are fecund while the Angels are only efficient... According to Aquinas this is the main reason why a few pure spirits disobeyed... Demons refused to kneel before people. In the involvement of creation people are in charge of bringing the whole universe back to God. The Angels want to help people in their incredible commitment. It was because of Adam that the whole world became twisted; it is now the task of people, after Jesus' act of redemption on the Cross, to bring the universe back on track.

People are called to bring the whole world back to Christ. St. Paul says that the whole world depends on people, but people belong to Christ, and Christ belongs to God... Under similar perspective the Angels serve people as they serve the whole world. The Angels keep the world in existence, but the destiny of the universe is in people's hands.

MC - Daddy you're going too far... We were talking about immortality....

AS - "Immortality" is the nickname of the soul. The business of the soul is to bring life, to organize itself in the world as the physical entity that we call a body... It configures and animates the whole person. Aquinas says that the soul is my own act of existence. The soul does make someone. We call the soul the organizer of the person, but it is more than that, the soul is the person itself.

Because of its connection with the physical dimension of the world, the actual body is perishable, the soul, which produces the body, is not perishable. What is the soul is the source of existence and life. There is nothing in the soul that does not raise vigor, strength, activity.... We say that the soul does exists to always express itself in a body. And, now on earth, the body is an accidental expression of the soul, for, at this time, the whole universe endure the catastrophe provoked by the First Sin, which separated time and space. Such a dichotomy is for our days, it does not exist in Eternity. The present situation remains accidental.

MC - You said "accidental". Why?

AS - Because the soul is much better than what it can express today. It's like a race car driver who might happen to be driving an old jalopy... He would not be able to show off most of his racing driver skills. It happens similarly with our soul presently on the actual earth, which the disease called "original sin" made sick, incomplete, provisional, and perishable. As far as we live in the dichotomous condition of space and time our souls are handicapped in their capacity to actuate the person. They cannot express in fullness what they are. Their capability of providing life is restrained and provisional as the same universe is. In other words, living in a handicapped world our souls activate and shape handicapped people....

Body, soul and mind are the threesome configuration of the one person. It is not proper to say "I have a body," as if the body was an acquisition. People use to say so, but it is only partially true. Following the words of the existentialists, we should say "I am a body."

363

After Aquinas, the Catholic Church defines the soul as the form of the body. It means that the soul is form, that the soul is not part of the person, as well as the body is not another part and the mind the third part.... The soul is not a part of myself as well as my body is not either. When I say "I", I refer to the soul, to the body, and to the mind, which exert the full expression of who I am. The three are only different perspectives of the same person.

When I say "I am a student," I identify myself with the fact that I am studying in some college or university and my entire self is involved in the endeavor of study, sport, readings, listening to courses, meeting other students, eating at the cafeteria, running from home to school and from school to home... All these different aspects are included in the fact that I am a student. In the same way, I have to say "my body shows what I am and expresses my characteristics, i.e. the characteristics of my soul.

Body and soul are two aspects of the same person, who is also mind, i.e. speculative. Soul, mind, and body are not three components of the person, but three diverse expressions of the same person, like sunrise, midday and sunset are three phases of the same day... Soul, mind and body express the capacity of a person to be related to spiritual issues with the soul, to speculative topics with the mind and physical entities with the body.

I am a person. It is a fact that involves in space and times all the many aspects of my being: physical, speculative, and spiritual. I behave with all of my being through my physical connections. Everything I do involves everything I am. When I shake hands, I do not say: "my hand shook the hand of my friend." No, I correctly say "I greeted him", or "We met." Actually, through our bodies, we do meet. That means that "I am my body." And I am my mind, too. Identically, when we say "it popped up in my mind" we intend to consider some idea that we personally had. I am myself with all my mind. When I think, I commit an act of the whole person. Similarly, we are fully in our spiritual endeavors: prayer, love, generosity, mercy, friendship, and so on.

The threefold configuration of the person is almost like being a pedestrian, a driver, and a traveling passenger, all in the same day... They are three successively diverse activities of the same person. These activities are part of a day's business. They are not part of the same person. They do not compose the same person: they express it. It is the same person that acts as a pedestrian, a driver, a passenger... The same person exerts three diverse endeavors, which identify him or her as a pedestrian, a driver, and a traveler... These diverse identities are three diverse configurations of the same individual... It is the same for acting spiritually, with our soul, speculatively, with our mind, and physically, with our body. We are a triune being. The three faculties exist at the same time as the exertion of the same individual.

Technically, without the soul, the body does not exist and vice versa. In fact, the soul is the organizer of the body. Without the body the soul does not organize anything, therefore it regularly cannot exist on earth anymore. When I talk about the body, the soul is included, and vice versa. After we die, we improperly call what is left a body... But a corpse is not a body anymore; it is only matter in decomposition. After I die, what was physically me returns slowly to unorganized dust, according to the process of natural laws. It is not a person any more even if it keeps for a while my configuration. Body, mind, and soul are one. Yes, body and soul include the mind in a threesome configuration. We are persons, i.e. physical, speculative and spiritual as one. If one of the three dimensions is missing, the whole person is missing, too.

Looking at the whole world, the macrocosm reflects the microcosm of individuals. In the macrocosm, the Angels represent its spiritual dimension. What the soul is for the microcosm of a person the Angels are for the whole macrocosm. They keep the universe in existence. The Angels are its spiritual power... Technically, they are not "pure spirit" for actually only God is. They are mere spirit, which means that they are will and mind, which organize the world. When I say that they are will and mind I mean that they are spirit. Willpower is included in the fact of being a spirit. They are all what are included in a spirit, understanding, simplicity, serenity, communication, activity, freedom, organization, promotion, and source of existence. As a result, the Angels do not use reason to think, they get directly the intelligence of things. In the Angels, ideas come from the awareness of things that exist, not through sensorial information, which they animate. They know directly everything in fullness and perfection.

At the End Times, the whole universe will get back its own harmony. Physical entities will not be handicapped any more. The drama of time and space will be over. The whole universe will enter in its afterlife.

MC - So the End Times mean the death of the universe?

AS - That is a proper definition of it. We people die because we belong to a macrocosm which is supposed to die. Death is part of the adventure of the world. It happens for individuals and for the whole society. The macrocosm is sick as well as every microcosm inside of it. Such sickness was called by theologians "original sin." The whole universe carries the traces of that mistake which made a breakage in the earth that will finish with the End Times.

Afterwards the whole universe will have started its afterlife. The spiritual dimension of the macrocosm, which the Angels are, will keep the whole world in existence. It will be a new consistence of everything. Existence will be free from the disease of the first sin. It is the business of people to bring back the whole world to Christ in order that Christ can restore the configuration of the world.

MC - What is death?

AS - Death is nonsense. If death is the event that causes something that existed in the past to cease to exist in the present, then there is nothing to understand any more. What does not exist cannot be known. It cannot be understood. Only what does exist can be comprehended. If death is the end of human life there is nothing more to say and the discourse is closed. Notwithstanding, philosophers like Socrates, Plato and Aristotle define death as a change of status. If that is true, then there is still something to know. Here is why the question of death needs a proper reflection.

In our current civilization, death is usually disregarded, denied or set apart from our thoughts because death is so troubling. Death is damaging our reflections concerning ourselves and our world. Nobody likes to consider his or her own death. Most of the time people flee away from contemplating the inevitable prospect of death.

Considered under the perspective of the present world, death is utter nonsense because it is the extinction of someone who does exist. It is sufficient to see how strong is the effort of people to deny death in their life to understand how death is an event of absolute finality. Accepting the challenge to confront death, puts us in the perspective of an afterlife, and establishes in us the process of our eternal birth.

Under the perspective of our earthly journey, death is nonsense for it is our meeting with nothingness. It makes our life not to exist: it is the event which effects our non existence. Death is the most radical change of our life. Death is absolute. From the point of view of this life, death is life's negation. In this endeavor there is no answer to questions like: "What happens after death?" or "What will I do, then?" or "Is there something after death?" Death is the event that marks the end of this kind of life. It is the definitive termination of what we are. Death is real. Death is full abolition of our present consistency. Through death nothingness absorbs our being. We can only accept death as the ending of everything we know, everything we love, everything we want. Whatever diverse perspective to the contrary would be wrong.

Notwithstanding, if we consider death under the point of view of the definition given by religious accounts and philosophical reflection, it figures as a totally different phenomenon. It is defined then as a change of status. "Death is establishment of an amazing endeavor." Actually, it is not the beginning of a new endeavor, for that new situation knows no time and no end.... The old picture described as "the separation between soul and body" does not reflect the facts, because the body does not exist any more. With death, the body is destroyed. It no longer exists after what people improperly call "the departure of the soul." Actually, death is not a separation between soul and body, it is a change of status, that from the perspective of time can be called "departure", but under the perspective of the access to the fullness of life, should be identified as a blossoming. If we explain death as a departure, we affirm that there is something which disappears, and something else which starts.

Departure means change. Departure does not mean total death. As a departure, death means a change of schedule in our traveling. It is the end of our provisional body and of its limited endeavor on

367

earth. Such a mindset is, however, not fully consistent. It ignores the real dimension of death...

Under a philosophical or religious point of view, death is not comprehensible, if we do not take into account the intertwining relationship between eternity and time. The afterlife stands outside of time. After death, people share the experience of eternity. It is not, however, a totally new exertion. While living on earth we already became accustomed with sparks of eternal life. Love, thoughts, values, prayer, concern develop behaviors that transcend the conditions of space and time.

Space and time are typical of the present life. Space and time are, however, written in another context, which makes their own consistency. Animals have no notion of space and time, because they live totally inside of it... Being aware of space and time is a typical human characteristic. It shows familiarity with that larger context in which space and time exist. People have familiarity with eternity during their own journey.

Every time two people say that they will love one another for ever, they do overcome space and time. People are capable to make a promise, animals do not. Every time I make a promise, I sign a contract, I go beyond mere reality of space and time... Similar circumstances share the context which extends beyond the limits of death. In other words, people start to live in eternity while they are on earth. With the event of death, every part of us that belongs to this world is canceled, but we continue to live in eternity, with what we were able to share beyond.

Theologians give the name "Soul" to the part of us that survives. But it would be a mistake to believe that the body stays and the soul goes. The body does not remain, it disappears, under the manner in which it now exists. At the event of death, the body is not a body anymore. And the soul, which is the organizer of the person, needs to continue to animate what we are in order to exist... Because in the afterlife we live in a totally different context, the person exists differently.

From an earthly perspective, death is just the end of life. From eternity's point of view, death is a process of delivery, of getting the freedom that characterizes eternal life. Such a delivery, such a departure, such an entrance proceeds in proportion to how much of eternity we have been capable to understand, to love, to know during our earthly journey.

We are often blind in front of eternity. We are much too negligent, indifferent, and insensible to the truth. Eternity does not begin only at the moment we die. We will be able to recognize and experience eternity in proportion to the familiarity with the afterlife we will have developed during our daily endeavors on earth. How much we overcome the limitations and determinations of physical laws and achieve a spiritual participation in eternal life prepares us to access the afterlife.

Inside of the limitations of space and time, we are able to gain the freedom of the spiritual life; and the more we do, the more we enter eternity even now. The more we enter now in eternity the easier will be the process of our death. Christians have a typical expression that says: "Here and now we are building the house we will live in hereafter and forever."

Death remains incomprehensible if we do not already radiate love, intelligence, beauty, knowledge, wisdom, piety, and familiarity with spiritual entities, including God. Each of us is like a chrysalis in the process of transformation, the process of dying. When the larva in the chrysalis, as it were, dies, it revives revised and emerges as a butterfly... Time is the chrysalis, the preparatory phase of eternal life. Eternity is the awareness of the knowledge which starts in the darkness of this world, with limitations of space and time and precariousness of things. We live in blindness on earth. Saint Paul says that over there we will see the truth face to face, we will meet God face to face... We will enjoy the presence of the celestial court where dwell the Angels we are now unable to behold. We will enjoy their presence over there. Eternity has already started for us. Eternity starts all through our common life on earth while we experience love, promises, serenity, prayer... There is something in us that never dies... It is what philosophers call the soul.

Every experience of love is a beginning of our experience of eternity. Such experiences will blossom when we die. That consistency

369

that we are which is called soul, is what experiences life everlasting.

MC - What is the soul?

AS - Our body exhibits a spiritual configuration, a spiritual consistency that makes it alive. The body expresses the spiritual action that organizes it. Such spiritual action was given the name "soul". Soul is not a mere entity; it is the source of life from which our body proceeds. That is the reason why we are so afraid of death. We understand that, when we die, we totally disappear. When we die, there is no room in the world for us any more. Nonetheless, because the soul brings life, it cannot disappear and continues to be. However, entering the afterlife, what we improperly call the soul shares the exertion of eternity. Actually we should say "we" for "we are" the ones who shares the experience of eternity. Eternity is present to time at once. Every moment of time, past, present, and future is transparent to eternity.

But there is something more to say about the soul. The soul is a piece of eternity, if we are allowed to say so. There is some paradox when speaking about the soul. It has a beginning and nonetheless it belongs to eternity, which has no beginning and no end. Eternity is continuous present. We surely can put inside of time the date for our entering in eternity. In time we have dates in eternity there is no beginning, no end, everything exist and happens at once. Eternity is full process, and full action. When we say that the soul is a piece of eternity we say that the soul belongs to eternity, which it finally reaches after its time of gestation and growth on earth. It is as if the soul needed a long delivery, a long journey, in order to enter the place where it belongs.

In the days of the first Christian communities, people used to call the day of their death "Birthday". On the tombstone they used to write in the language of the day: "he was born on..." In Roman language they wrote "natus est..." with the date they entered eternity. That means "This one was born into eternity at this time." But because eternity is eternal presence, full presence of everything, we cannot describe properly what eternity is, what is it that the soul belongs to. Eternity overcomes time and the soul does too. If we were able to say in time what eternity is, more likely the "so called eterni-

ty" would not be eternity. Through our death, we change our status in life, and we enter into a kind of life which befits the soul, which is a context where the soul continues to exist, where WE continue to exist. To say it by way of an analogy: When we play with numbers we do arithmetic, when we play with figures we do geometry, when we play with the stars we do astronomy, when we play with corporeal bodies we make physics, when we play with living bodies we do biology, when we play with substances we do chemistry, and so on. It is the same with the soul. Inside of the physical world the soul organizes my person through my body. Inside of eternity the soul organizes my person as a spiritual entity... It makes me live a reality out of time and space... It is a context that I belong to. And all along my earthly journey I constantly live beyond physical entities. And because out of time there is nothing but eternity, time proceeds from eternity. I already live in eternity during my journey on earth, exerting a life of space and time.

Some theologians like to stress the absurdity of death as a diabolical. They speak about the structures of sin which embody our lives. It is a devil's point of view on life. Death is absurd in perspective of human life and raises concern, struggle, and fear insofar as there is no hope. No good endeavor is produced by fear, unless it is the fear of God. The great mystics, from St. Bernard, through St. John of the Cross, up to Marthe Robin teach that nothing is done from negative concerns, which produce sadness or struggle. "Nothing that comes from God causes trouble in our heart", said Francis de Sales... He also says, "Whatever troubles your heart's peace is not worth that peace." In other words we must raise our sights with hope and trust, and everything, even death, will make sense.

From a heavenly perspective, death is only one of the many metanoia, conversions, blossomings, which mark our spiritual life. The separation of the soul out of the body is not such... It is not separation of the two, for they cannot be separated... It is our earthly death, when we stop living under the rules of sin, under the structures of sin. When we die we lose our earthly configuration and continue living in eternity... It is the start of a new configuration, which is the continuation of what we started on earth to understand about eternity. A certain way of life stops. We stop living under the re-

371

striction of space and time. *This rupture, this breaking puts us suddenly and totally in the fullness of eternal life. So, instead of being mere death, our death is the beginning of our freedom in total life. While under the panorama of time death is negation, is destruction in every sense, at the same time that total negation makes us enter into the fullness of life. It is the perfect illustration of the parable of the seed: "If the seed does not die it does not produce fruit..." Yes, death as such is totally absurd, because it is not the end but a new beginning. St, Bernard used to say that "The Cross is pregnant with Resurrection!"*

When we feel that death is absurd, we have a good feeling, because time and eternity meet there. And the many deaths of our lives prepare us to that great moment when we finally are born, "natus est," into eternity. Philosophers call the soul that part of us which enters into eternity after our earthly consistency has disappeared. But it is an improper language, for it is not a part of us which goes, while another part stays... Actually the whole of us disappears on earth and the whole of us enters eternity. When you prepare a cake, all that you put in the oven disappears to become afterwards cooked and deliciously edible. The cake is totally different from the dough and the many ingredients combined within it. We are not concerned about the many grams of wheat and the many eggs lost. We are interested in the cake... Time does not understand death, because it does not see the cake. It does not see what we are in eternity. It is actually a provisional situation, while we are waiting to get our resurrected body, which will be our actual body, not the handicapped one we had on earth. I mean, we will not live as a broken physical entity any more, we will live in the fullness of our physical capabilities. The perfect example of it is resurrected Jesus: he can eat, he can speak, he can be touched, he moves through walls, he can be in different places at the same time... as Saint Paul says. At that point, obviously, we have entered the mystery of the Christian life that we now share through faith.

In other words, the soul is us as the shrine of the Holy Spirit, where we continuously meet Jesus and together stay in worship of the Father.

MC - If the soul is a shrine what about the many churches and shrines around the world?

AS - They all are precious places to pray. People are not only individuals they also are one, as a community, as a society.

MC - What do you mean that people exist as one?

AS - It reflects the mystery of the trinity. People are at the same time one and many. Many individuals make together the only one mystical body of Christ. It is like the Eucharist, every piece of host is Jesus, the same Jesus present for us everywhere at the same time. It is not the quantity of hosts which make Jesus present, as it is not the numbers of individuals that make the society. Individuals make a crowd not a community. Nonetheless, as far as individuals become persons a community starts to exist. Augustine says, as far as "every individual becomes another Jesus", we all become a community, a society, the whole body of Christ. Eucharistic Jesus' purpose is to make us one. He is the one who is pulling the whole universe towards the global world. Pierre Teilhard de Chardin said that if hypothetically, for a while, there was no Mass celebrated on earth any more, the whole world immediately would collapse. The Eucharist is the one who keeps all the Angels in action. The Eucharist is not mere spiritual issue. It is not even mere anthropological issue. The Eucharist is a universal and natural issue, which includes all other perspectives. Eucharistic Jesus works physically, speculatively, and spiritually.

Speaking of shrines: in everyone we meet we also meet the Lord and Our Lady, his Mother. But above all the shrines around the world, the most important shrine is always inside of our heart. The great shrines all around the world, like Lourdes, like Fatima, like Medjugorje, like Kibeho, like Jerusalem, like the neighborhood church, they are there to stimulate and wake us up to the reality of the true permanent shrine where Jesus dwells inside each of us.

MC - And that is the soul?

AS - It is what philosophers call the soul. They are us, living inside of the celestial court. In the presence of all celestial entities that we roughly call the Angels, because...

MC - Why are they "roughly " called Angels?

AS - Because every Angel is such a unique entity that a single name does not give justice to so many various and amazing creatures composing the richness and intensity of heaven.

It is easier to think about life than about death. Actually, there is nothing to think about death unless it is not totally death. Yes, because we have to think life, and we will speak now about life. We have to investigate about the life of people after their time on earth, and about the life of Angels who are already now living in its fullness. Life after death is exactly the life that Angels know, and which is usually called supernatural life. What we call natural life, it is just a first step, a preparation of our being to be transformed in eternal life. We should not be surprised if already in our life on earth, we are capable of foreseeing, of perceiving the presence and intervention of celestial entities, who act upon earth from eternal life.

What the Angels do, acting on earth while living in eternity, invites us to do likewise. While we act during our journey on earth, we are invited to progressively share eternal life. Death is only the last commitment we have with eternity. It is our main appointment with eternity. It comes at the end of the many deaths we are supposed to go through during our journey. Every death is an invitation to share eternal life at every moment of our earthly life. When we go to a drive-in theater, the screen shows the direction to take. It is an indication for us about the direction we have to put the car in order to see the movie as soon as it starts. It is the same way with death. Death is today the indication to keep our soul oriented towards what is expecting us, the life to come. Death also tells us that every pain, every difficulty, every disease has to be addressed with the whole strength of our soul, because suffering is the door we go through to enter into the life to come.

Montaigne used to stress that death has to be the main preoccupation of everybody life. He invites us to continuously think about death to properly behave: it is the main training to exert as the most important school for life. Yes, we have to learn how to die if we want to be ready when we actually die. We need to become familiar with death and learn how to die.

Many occasions of self-denial prepare us for death. Every suffer-

ing is like a little death. We have to address them with care. Every invitation of withdrawal from instincts, affections, sensorial goods prepare us to become spiritually ready. Chiara Lubich calls a similar endeavor of overcoming sensorial goods, affections, interests, "the art of losing". In other word "suffering makes us free." It leads us to overcome the limits of this life to progressively exert spiritual growth. Here is one of the meanings of Jesus' words: "They live in the world but they do not belong to it." We must address our earthly journey as living dead, being a living transparency to spiritual values. In this context, we achieve our commitment to our journey by living a continuous friendship with the Angels.

MC - You said before that without its body the soul does not exist. Is that true?

AS - I think so. In fact, even the body does not exist anymore without the soul. These two terms, body and soul remain improper. Here is why there is some confusion about them. When we die, the whole person dies: physically, speculatively, and spiritually. When we die we do not exist anymore on the earth. Now the question remains: do we continue to exist elsewhere, in what philosophers call afterlife?

MC - How can you affirm human immortality then?

AS - This is a totally different concept. It is important first of all to affirm the fact that there actually is a spiritual dimension of the world. If someone claims that we should demonstrate that Angels exist, this one shows that he totally disregards the spiritual values of the macrocosm. It is a question of good will: you see the spiritual dimension of the world only if you want to. When St. Thomas demonstrates the existence of God, he does it for believers, not for non-believers. He wants to show the believers the rational confirmations of the truth they trust and believe in. He stresses how understandable it is to believe that God exists. A similar demonstration is not for those who still need to meet God.

I think it should be the same with the Angels. We must meet them first. Then we can speak about them. So, supposing that you never heard about the Angels, it would surely not be my intention to convince you of their existence, but to help you to eventually meet

375

them. Actually the desire of the Angels to meet us is stronger than our own desire to see them. Additionally very few people on earth deny the existence of values, of the quality of friendship, love, beauty, justice, intelligence...

Afterwards all the reflection on immortality is easy: Let me start with an analogy. How do you communicate, Marie-Claire, with native Romans who still live in Rome?

MC - I go to Rome and I speak Italian with them. Or I call them over the phone.

AS - Very good! It is exactly the same with the Angels. In order to enter in communication with them, we need to behave according to their own spiritual nature, for they are spiritual beings only. They communicate with one another by intelligence and will. This is the way we will communicate with them in the afterlife. But we can also start now and communicate with them by intelligence and will.

MC - Does that mean that intelligence and will are immortal behaviors?

AS - Yes, they are. Pure spirits do not share the precariousness of physical entities, nor the precariousness of human beings which ares involved with the physical world. Pure spirits have nothing in their configuration that is supposed to perish, they are quite the opposite, they are the forces which produce life in the whole world. Their spiritual status makes them immortal. We share their status by what is spiritual in our own human make-up. Actually, being able to communicate with those who are immortal requires us to share somehow their own immortal nature. The simple fact of thinking about them, who are immortal, shows our capacity to move beyond time to reach them.

MC - Could they be mere imagination?

AS - Feuerbach, Marx and Engels say that spiritual issues are fruits of imagination. Actually, spiritual entities cannot be a simple construction of our mind, especially when we have evidences of their presence in our life. Imagination works on the field of sensorial issues. It does not go beyond physical issues. When we identify forces acting in the universe, without sensorial aspect, we show our capacity to move with our mind beyond the physical world. Think-

ing about pure spirits shows that we are able to share that level of existence. Speculative activity works beyond time. Sensorial activity can be involved, but speculations go beyond senses. When we deal with arithmetic or mathematics, we are not subject of time. When in philosophy we deal with being as such, its whatness, what is traditionally known as universal, we address facts that will never perish.

MC - So you say that intelligence activity is a spiritual deed?

AS - Yes intelligence is spiritual. It is therefore immortal. And it will shows immortality, too.

MC - How is that?

AS - Gabriel Marcel says that when I make a commitment, I overcome time. But the strongest immortal activity is love of friendship. When I love someone, it is forever. Time is overcome by the lovers. A marriage is a commitment that is made to stand forever. Every true friendship, every marriage involves our life with a commitment, that goes beyond time. Every suspicion of provisional relationship is not friendship, is not love. True love is unconditional.

MC - Does that relationship of will and intelligence work with the evil angels, too.?

AS - It works the same with the demons. Here is why when we want to have nothing to do with them, it is sufficient to ignore them and want not to have relationship with them. Intelligence and will is the way to communicate, or to refuse to communicate with pure spirits.

MC - Are they totally unable to read what is in our hearts? Are they truly disconnected if we want them to be? Can they use another process to know what we feel? Do they ignore what we think?

AS - Actually they can't read inside of our mind and of our heart unless we allow them to do so. Nonetheless they see what we do, how we behave, so they can interpret our behaviors, then provoke situation where they hope we will be tempted.

Days ago, when he met in San Antonio, Claudio reminded me of something Chiara Lubich said: "The best way to keep the demons away is to have always a smile on my face." As far as the demon sees happiness on my face and on my lips he remains confused for he cannot read anything directly inside of me. His success is our sadness: when we are sad, we are exposed to his suggestions, to his lures, all situations and discourses he may provoke to induce us into failure sinful behaviors.

MC - Some people say that the existence of God cannot be demonstrated. Is that true? Do we know that God exists only by faith?

AS - Absolutely not. You cannot believe by faith the existence of someone that you do not know by experience whether he exists or not. We need some evidence of his existence to understand where the message of faith comes from. It was Descartes, first, then the idealism of Kant who stated that people cannot know God. Fortunately, during the following century, in 1870, the Council of Vatican II showed more trust in human intelligence. The Council stated that everybody has the evidence of God's existence as everyone knows a cause by its effects. When you find a letter in your mail box you know that the mail deliverer has passed by, even if you do not see him or her. The fact that it is not the property of a letter to come by itself to your mail box, its presence there is the evidence that the mail deliverer has passed. Once in Texas I knew there was a bobcat on a nearby ranch because I saw its tracks outdoors in the morning. The same can be said about human tracks on the beach. Because it is not proper to the sand to show these tracks, they evidence the passage of somebody. It is the same with God.

Aquinas explains that the existence of people, out of human precariousness, shows the presence of a prime mover to cause them to exist. That prime mover is the one that religious traditions call God. A train car does not move by itself. It needs another car to pull or push it in order to move. The movement of a series of boxcars cannot be explained unless there is a locomotive. The longer the train, the stronger must be the locomotive. The locomotive does not act directly on every single car, but by moving the first car, all the other coupled cars in the whole train move as one. This obviously is a poor image to show how God keeps in existence the whole world through the Angels, who act as second causes. It is insane to believe that the movements of the one can be explained by the movements of the many: The physical world itself is made up of a conglomeration of

378

dependent phenomena, but it does not explain their existence.

The spiritual dimension of the world explains its own existence and the inhabitants of such a dimension act in it as second causes. We know that God exists by simple observation of world precariousness and appropriate reasoning. Every honest investigation on the configuration of the world agrees with the famous quotation of Voltaire: "The world is similar to a large clock that cannot be accounted for without its clockmaker." Similarly was the statement of Einstein: "Such a sophisticated world surely depends on a higher intelligence."

The same must be said about the Angels. Many examples of the presence of the Angels in the life of people can be found in everyday life. All we need do is look at the evidence. Just by reading the biographies of Saints, we can learn how to deal with the Angels, how to thank them for their daily presence. Spectacular examples are found in the lives of Angela Merici, Don Bosco, Teresa of Lisieux, just to name a few.

Every heavenly manifestation happens through the mediation of Angels who are the ones who are naturally invested with the business of human relationship with the spiritual realm. Saint John of the Cross says that we can make great mistakes in the understanding of visions, locutions and revelations, especially when they come directly from God, because, we are living on Earth, and our capability to understand messages from above is really very small in comparison with the enormous profundities these revelations bring to us. His invitation is to be prudent. It is actually a great warning to follow in our investigation into the reality of the Angels in our daily life. The simpler we behave the nearer we move towards the facts.

MC - I have difficulty considering death as just the end of this life, without other insights.

AS - You're right, Marie-Claire! Actually, death is the beginning of eternal life. On the tomb of the first Christians, their relatives and friends use to write along with the date of their departure: "Natus Est" – which means he/she "is born" to Eternal Life…

And death is the symbol of life physically (our own skin remains young in proportion to its cells' capacity to die and then be constantly replaced by new cells, which requires us to clean, by showering or bathing every day). Death is also the symbol of life psychologically (if you do not live in the present, being always free from our past, we are never fully alive), and spiritually (we must constantly abandon our past to the mercy of God, and the future to the Divine Providence, in order to live always IN the present in His Presence till we are able to enter the Eternal Present. Many philosophers, after Michel de Montaigne put death as the goal and purpose of life. Montaigne suggested to live having always in front of our mind the fact of death...

MC - What does all of that have to do with the Angels?

AS - Here is the point: we are our souls! Supposing that from the afterlife someone wanted to manifest his/her presence to somebody here below on earth: He/she does not have a body anymore; he/she is a ghost, i.e. a soul in a provisional situation of suffering the absence of its body and waiting for its restoration at the End Time.

When a soul comes from afterlife, however, it shows itself with the resemblance of its previous body, because whatever is the material that the soul is able to organize, in order to manifest itself, it always has the same shape. Here is why a ghost resembles the body it previously possessed. Obviously, it also manifests the true body that we already get, in the Eternity of after life, which is, actually, our true body, the one we would have had without the original sin, and will be renewed on earth only at the End Times.

Here on earth, we will never insist enough about the unique entity of the person. I used the expression "we are our souls," because it is true. But we also are our bodies as well as we are our minds. A person is one, acting in many ways. Each one of us is one person whom the soul organizes in all dimensions, physical, speculative, and spiritual, including psychological and emotional. Yes, we are a threefold entity, one and three at the same time, for we are a creature, which reflects the mystery of the most holy Trinity.

AS - Here. Actually, comes a deeper consideration. Let me ask: "Do you believe that it would be proper to say that God knows what you will do, at this time tomorrow?"

MC - Yes, naturally!

AS - Well, de facto, God does not live in time. He is Eternity –

Actually, He does not live in Eternity, for He cannot be in something else other than Himself. So, we should not say that "He knows everything that will happen – NO, for God knows NOW what we are going to do tomorrow. Past and future belong to His eternal present. Eternity does address everything, past, resent, future, right now. For Eternity is now.

Then, we must also consider the nature of our new, true body, which, in Eternity, our soul gets now. Our person continues to exist, soul, mind and body. But in Eternity, we already get the eternal body, which is actually our true body, the one we would have had since we came into existence, if we were without the limitations produced by the First Sin, the original sin. That same body will be known on earth at the End Time.

But there is more to say.

While I was in Loppiano, I heard Chiara Lubich, who explained that when we die, we Christians, something else also happens. Because we have been feeding our body almost every day with the Eucharist, transforming us, during Communion into another Christ, this transformation does not remain sterile, but it prepares all of us to enter the afterlife with a particular strength from above; and such nourishment from above produces also a similar miracle on earth: that body, transformed by the Eucharist, produces an additional event on earth. Leaving behind our own body, we make of it a gift to the earth: our "Eucharistic body" is a seed planted in the earth, it accelerates on earth its capacity to become new, to transform itself, in the new earth and the new heaven.

If the seed does not die it does not produce fruits... Actually, giving our perishable body to the ground we sow there the seed of the transformation of earth and heaven at the End Times. The body remains always a sign of the person, and even after we leave the earth for the afterlife, our body remains still an ultimate presence of our soul, of our person on earth.

Meanwhile, our soul continues to exist, providing the organization of our true body, the resurrected one, which is already present in Eternity but, in time, will show up at the End Times.

When I die, I will see the difference. I will see that the material part of me is losing its unity. At that time, all its entity is progressively disappearing; all its consistency fades, all its configuration perishes, and so on... Even when I say that "I will be a cadaver," that situation will be only a temporary position because really my corpse, my cadaver. is a provisional issue, it is already in the process of returning to the cycle of matter and it is already following the rules of material dust.

MC - What do you think about miracles?

AS - What are you referring to?

MC - I'm thinking about the inexplicable healings and other good things that happen that science cannot explain.

AS - Well, science has expertise in explaining about the way the earth works today in its precarious and provisional conditions. In such an environment, miracles are nothing but the manifestation of the natural presence on earth of spiritual entities. If the earth was not under the disease of the first sin, miracles would be the regular activity of things.

Today, miracles show the overflowing presence of spiritual life. They actually are mere anticipation of what will be the rule of all after the event of the End Times, when the earth and heavens will have been renewed and we will have a natural connection with the whole world.

The perfect conditions of life that people had in the first Eden will have been restored.

Tableau #28
Regina Mundi

THE PONTIFICAL INSTITUTE "REGINA MUNDI" WAS A COL-
LEGE AFFILIATED TO THE GREGORIAN UNIVERSITY, located on the
Tevere River in Rome, in front of St. Michael Castle, also known as
Castel Sant-Angelo. Regina Mundi Institute was erected in 1981, under the care of Card Pierre Paul Philippe, to offer university studies,
which would be available to religious sisters, belonging to congrega-
tions, existing all over the world.

Soon, 150 nations were represented among the students. The
Institute included five sections of study: Italian, Spanish, German,
French and English. The students were supposed to follow a four-year
course to prepare a Master Degree in Religious Studies. I was teaching
there in the French section, from 1988 to 1995.

Often the conversation with the students continued for a few
minutes after my philosophy class, outside the classroom. I particularly remember one of these informal meetings, which was intense.
As usual, a few students greeted me in the hall, at 4 p.m. I was un-

acquainted that day with the fact that just one year later I would be living in America.

Suddenly Sister Basil, from the Middle-East shouted:

"Why did you talk about the Angels during your metaphysics course? Why waste time talking about them? They are useless. What need could there be to refer to entities that have no business with us?

AS – Actually, Sister, the opposite is true. I agree with you that there are people who consider the Angels no more than beautiful figures that, ultimately, have no more utility than embellishing the horizon of our lives. Fortunately, such a perspective is far from the facts. The Angels are more present and necessary than the air we breathe. They are even more effective than the air.

I paused for a moment of silence to stress my statement.

Then I added:

A scrupulous investigation into all aspects of the reality sur-rounding us cannot exclude the presence of the Angels. We cannot disregard the pure spirits who have a precise place in the universe, and a specific impact on our lives. In a prophetic way, Jean Daniélou wrote in 1963 that the question of the Angels was ignored, while atheism was raging all over Western culture. He also predicted a re-turn to God, which was going to make atheism an obsolete ideology, adding: "Being an atheist today, means being behind in the course of history." He also indicated that "Such a return to God is not a return to Christ, but a generic return to deity as a supreme power. It is sim-ilar to a kind of new paganism." In such an environment, there is a return of interest in the Angels as spiritual presences around us all. But, in such a new mental view, their identity is confusing.

And Sister again:

If they are pure spirits, and almost nothing can be said about them, why are we supposed to waste time on such a lost issue?

I replied:

I'm sorry to contradict you again, Sister. Not only are we able to identify and know the Angels, but they play a significant role in the configuration of the world. Additionally, being pure spirits means that they are pure powers, pure actions, pure deeds, the results of which can be checked at any time. The Angels compose a prodigious presence, which keeps the world in existence and makes it properly proceed on. For what I remember, Sister, you are an expert in physics., aren't you?

Sister B. – Yes, I am.

AS – What would you say to someone who would affirm that physics is a useless topic to deal with?

Sister B. – It would be insane to say so.

AS – Well, curiously, you affirm the same nonsense when you say that the Angels are useless. They are integral part of the world. Denying or disregarding their existence would handicap our understanding of the configuration of the whole universe.

While looking at the cosmos, it is insane – to use your own words – to consider only minerals, vegetables, animals, people and nothing more. A serious investigation is not allowed to stop at the level of human life, disregarding spiritual entities, which are part of the whole creation, and even representing the most interesting part of it.

A materialistic mentality prefers to ignore anything is not physical, corporeal, solid, or tactile. Such a perspective calls tangible only what is visible and touchable. For centuries people have been trained to disregard spiritual issues, which the Angels belong to. It was not an easy endeavor, nonetheless it was done. And it increased the opinions that what is not solid is useless. This caused the conviction that the Angels are rarely seen or met, while the opposite happens. The Angels are so present in human life that we meet them continuously, even when we deliberately ignore the fact and direct our eyes elsewhere. Just because we look at the sea does not mean that the mountains do not exist.

Sister B. – If we were able to ignore the Angels for centuries, maybe we do not need to deal with them anymore. Do we?

AS – This is not a good argument. Centuries of ignorance do not cancel a topic. For a few millennia, people never traveled by air; it does not mean that planes cannot fly. Most people do not pay much attention to lung functions, but they still breathe. They don't care about the air we live in. Nonetheless, if there were no air, they couldn't breathe. Our need of the Angels is similar.

The presence of Angels in our life is just as natural as meeting animals, plants and other people. The world is maintained in its existence by the permanent action of God's creation. God is acting directly as the Creator now. Hypothetically, if God stopped thinking of us for an instant we would immediately cease to exist. When we say "Stop thinking about us," it also means "Stop loving us." We exist because of the permanent loving care of God.

According to Aquinas, God acts on earth through second causes. God intervenes in the world through his messengers, his gofers, who are the Angels.

The Bible refers only to some exceptional deeds of the Angels, with Abraham, Jacob, Tobias, and so on. These events are like the emerging tip of the iceberg… Their action is permanent. It happens sometimes that the Angels make more explicit the work of God. The Scriptures are full of such spectacular interventions of the Angels all throughout the story of the people of God, from Abraham to Jesus.

We live today between the first ad the second coming of Jesus Christ. It is a time of intense angelic activity. The Catholic Church in 1615, inserted into the Roman calendar the liturgical feast which is now celebrated on the second day of October, when we recall our Guardian Angels, a few days after the celebration of the three Arch-angels, Gabriel, Raphael, and Michael. The Guardian Angels have the mission, among many, to act near people, protecting, guiding, and encouraging Christian followers to instill apostolic zeal and get souls closer to God.

Again, those figures are the emerging tip of the iceberg concerning the pure spirits, for the Angels are not mere messengers, or nuncios, for they are the ones who actuate what they announce. Sometimes they are called "supernatural" to stress their spiritual exertions. To tell the truth, such supernatural presence is still part of creation. We naturally need help to do what is proper for us to accomplish.

We need help to understand and exert the action God requires us to perform in our life. Faith is a grace before being a virtue; hope and charity are a grace from God, before being the virtue of every Christian. When we believe it is our business to do so, we forget to put our whole persons under the care of God through his Angels. When we believe or plan to change something in the world, even for the good, we miss the most important commitment: to let the Angels move us and help us for the good.

Sister B. – I'm not comfortable with the issue of the Angels.

AS – Well, Sister, you grew up in the Middle East. Over there, the Christian Community is surrounded by the Ummah, the Muslim Community, which follows the Ko'ran that, according to the words of Muhammad, was dictated to him by the Archangel Gabriel.

I may understand that in a similar context, when every day the Mohadjin utters, several times, from the minaret, the Mosque tower, "God is God, and there is no other God than God." We tend to ignore any other entity between God and people. Actually, those who Aquinas called Angels are the same as those Aristotle called "gods", who are the forces running the whole world. In a similar context, I easily understand that you are not comfortable with the topic of the Angels...

Sister B. was comforted by these few words. Later on, she asked further explanation....

Sister B. – How do you explain Mohamed's revelations?

AS, – "Well, I'm not sure. Nonetheless, as a general statement, Saint Augustine says that "God never allows anything to happen if this cannot serve for a better good." And saint Paul, "Everything works for the good of those who love God" (Romans 8:28). Actually, Muslim wars in Western Europe during Middle Ages increased consistently the expression of faith and charity in Christendom. Additionally the suspicion of Islam that Christian people would worship three gods challenged the authority of the Christian Church, which elaborated better through several councils the configuration of the dogma of the Holy Trinity. Christian populations better understood the identity of three persons in one divine nature. The Church was forced to grow up because of the many heresies of the days. Before he died, Augustine counted more than seventy heresies during his days. The number may be the symbol of the seemingly infinite variety of doctrinal diseases like Arianism, Pelagianism, and so on.

As a result, Islam played a special role in the growing Christendom.

Sister B. – How did that happen?

AS – Genesis (16:7-12) recounts how the Lord sent an Angel in the desert to take care of Hagar and Ishmael, the son she had from Abram, and saved them from death. God never does anything at random and, as usual, everything is done through the Angels. The event shows the care of the Lord and the mission he gave to Ishmael and his descent.

In the Acts (16:6-8), the New Testament recounts how in two occasions the Holy Spirit prevented Paul and Timothy to move further East and North. This event is reported without comments. The fact was reported to explain why the evangelization trip of Paul, among the gentiles, remained confined inside of specific borders. It shows that the Holy Spirit wanted to concentrate the first wave of evangelization in the area of traditional Greek settlements, and of the Roman Empire.

To tell the truth, from the V to XII century, Islam forced Christendom to develop in the same area. Islam was a barrier for Christendom to move further east, towards Asia. Card. Jean Daniélou stressed that Christendom developed in the cradle of Greek and Jews culture, which started in Alexandria of Egypt around the III century AD, not long before the emergence of Islam in the Arabian Peninsula. The barrier of Islam obliged the Christian Church to grow and consolidate its own identity before addressing the old civilizations of further east and west from the Renaissance and later…

Sister B. – How can you affirm that those persecutions had been beneficial? Today, Christian communities are shrinking in the Middle East. Aren't they?

AS – Yes, it is an historical fact. For centuries Christians were captured along the borders of Mediterranean Sea and persecuted by the Mamluks, the Ashashins, the Ottomans, the Mores… The roads towards the Holy Lands were closed.

To free their friends and relatives, Christian communities were *forced to give away personal belongings to raise the money, some-times melting sacred vases and even the bells render precious metals in order to pay the ransom. In that manner, for more than a century, the whole Western Christendom was ransomed... Some congrega-tions, like the Trinitarian Fathers, were born with the specific goal of freeing the Christian people, who had been forced into slavery in Middle East and North Africa areas. The result of such long harass-ment is surprisingly comforting. It makes the Gospel true: "Give and you will receive," or "To those who love me I will reveal myself," or else "Blessed are the poor..." (Math. 5:3), and especially: "The one who perseveres to the end will be saved" (Math. 24:13).*

At the end of the Middle Ages, Europe experienced an incredi-ble process of development while the whole Muslim domain was in decadence. To make a long story short: centuries of devastation, of destruction and pillage obliged European nations to exert charity, hope and faith, in order to survive. Around 1450, such positive ac-tion pulled Western Europe into the process of the Renaissance.

Meanwhile the borders of the Mediterranean Sea of North Afri-ca and Middle East, populated by those who got easy money sacking and spoiling European people, had become a large desert. What a joke the steps of history made! What a teaching for those who love God! It confirmed that beatitudes are consistent even historically. History gave the warning: those who exert human power without discrimination and plan to run the whole world because they have power lost everything. Meanwhile, those who are humbly persever-ing in charity and hope around the world got everything as a re-ward.

Sister Rina, from Yugoslavia, tried to help Sister B.

Sister R. – Don't you think that the situation is similar today?

AS – Do you have some example in mind?

Sister R. – Well, the present situation resembles what the Middle Ages were. A lot of European money is moving to the Middle East, because of gas. Isn't it? The price of products increases constantly be-tween the steps of production and when products are on sale. Don't they? All that abuse of economic power should provoke a change in the world economy. Shouldn't it?

389

AS – "You're right. The whole population on the planet is hostage to those who run the economy. New privileges have been established. Western Democracy is a fake, because most of economy and politics endeavors are handled by a few bankers and business operators. Notwithstanding, to address present situation our concern should be not the present situation itself but the present values to be consistent with, the needs around to address.

Good is always stronger than evil. Spiritual issues build. And again, spiritual issues are the nickname of the angels... Looking at the good is the best manner to help it to show up. Then everything will follow accordingly. Matthews (6:25) gives the warning: "Do not worry about your life" then he says (6:33-34) "Seek first the kingdom of God and its righteousness and all things will be given to you besides. Do not worry about tomorrow. Tomorrow will take care of itself. Sufficient for a day is its own evil."

The reason of it is that the world is not evolving according to an automatic process, but it is ultimately run, by spiritual values. Spiritual values are not mere ideas. They are the actual forces of the universe. What counts is to be consistent with them. But, such a fidelity to the good needs improvement.

Here is why we need humiliation and purification to move near true values. A spiritual experience follows a regular process of joy and pain, warm and cold, day and night... The growing process is not at all casual. Think for example at the last time you suffered a very difficult situation... You know, this kind of situation, which is apparently insoluble...

I refer to the conditions when you can only pray, and sometimes you can only suffer... Nevertheless, whatever it is, after a while you experience the unbelievable solution. The problem is over. Sunshine has come. On the day light, you totally disregard the former darkness. It is impossible then to teach you anything, for your own experience tells you how the Angels are near to you when you finally understand what you are: the last one in the universe... When you finally understand the nothingness that you are, you are ready to let the Lord dwell in your heart and let the Angels be at work...

Unexpectedly, the conversation took another turn.

Sister L, from Rwanda, stressed situations of harassment, violence, persecution, power abuse in several areas on the planet. She was right: "I'll send you like sheep among the wolves. Be prudent like serpents and simple like dove" reads Mathew (10:16).

"Blessed are the poor, they will possess the earth..." and "Blessed when you are maltreated because of me..." I had suddenly the feeling to attend a surreal situation. I saw the whole meeting under a new light, within entirely new surroundings...

The angelic simplicity of the sisters pulled me into a celestial arena... I had the feeling of being surrounded by the angelic choir of Christmas: "Peace on earth for those of good will..." Suddenly, the angelic presence looked more real to me than the crowd of students, gathered at random in the hall we were walking through. It was not even in a specific room. We were moving between the classroom and the department auditorium, as we called it, although it was no more than a large meeting room. We were talking about the Angels... but it seemed to us that we were actually witnessing their visit. Yes, the Angels were present, not allowing that our good will and deeds could be lost.

I added a few words to make explicit what everyone was implicitly experiencing.

AS – "We need to pay attention to the graces we receive either in darkness or in shining days. We must always express our gratitude to the Lord, whatever the situation is. Every experience is a gift from above. Keeping our soul alert, we understand how everything is mediated by the Angels, in our relationship with God. In every situation, there is always something or someone which intervenes in our life: it is the action of Divine Providence."

Sometimes we are able to understand the events, other times we are not. Spiritual reality involves us even when we are not aware of it. It is always sufficient for us to know that the Angels are present in our life. It is a fact. They are really present. We need to know it and keep a continuous conversation with them.

Sometimes we do not feel them, and sometimes we do; and immediately our own relationship improves. Slowly but surely our eyes will adapt to the whole of reality. This capability to see what reality is consists in the gift of piety. It comes from above and grows while all virtues grow in our life."

Little by little, we understand what is going on. The present days are surely moments when the presence of Angels on earth is critical. Besides, the business of the Angels will improve while we are moving towards the end times. That event will be their apotheosis.

Sister Marie-Claude showed a sudden interest:

Are the Angels living only in heaven, while people are living only on earth?

AS – It is not like that, Sister! Heaven is not a place. It is a condition of life. As a place heaven can be everywhere, even in this hall right now, while we speak.

Again, Sister Marie-Claude:

Are the Angels near or far from us?

AS – A friend of mine, Peppuccio, would say that they are nearer to us than our own clothes.

Well, because they are pure spirit, it cannot be depending on a physical perspective. Actually, it depends on us to have them near or far. They share time and space in a manner which is not ours. It is proper, however, to state that they are nearer to us than any of our neighbors, friends, familiar or relatives. And, nevertheless, they are also distant, far from us...

It is our doing that makes them nearer or farther. But it is not what we do which regulates the distance, but the way we do what we have to do. According to their own nature they are more remote than the most distant galaxy. Notwithstanding, they are here with us right now, while I am talking to you. It is a true fact.

When we think on the Angels, we cannot put any distance between us and them. It happens now, while I say so. It is not like now and in a few minutes. No, it is true now, before I am finished speaking, when we are speaking with each other. As Bonaventure said, it is not the words that count, but only the intent we have in our heart.

Sister Marie-Claude – How is it possible to say that? Your words seem contradictory.

I did not reply. Sometime a silence speaks more than a few words.

Sister Chantal, the head of the French Department, was listening to the conversation.

She entered the discussion very appropriately:

Ma Soeur, Prof. Sauret, explains that they are spiritual, not physical. That's all!

Her insight interrupted the conversation for a few minutes. Each of us was reflecting on her statement. Then I added:

AS – Yes, this is the key: Angels are far or near to us in proportion not of an objective space and time, recognizable by technical tools or evaluations by science. This distance from us depends on our spiritual attention to them, in the moment of our life... To put it another way, it depends on us if they are so near, or so far away, right now, from us. They are spiritual creatures and we can meet or reject them only by our spiritual behavior, which means, by the quality of our heart.

Sister MC – What do you mean, exactly, by spiritual behavior? It is just if I live more... highly?

AS – You may say so, Marie-Claude! Actually, it is simpler than that. It just means that it depends on my inner attitude to meet them or not. They always are nearby. It only depends on our concern to approach them or not. It is, in other words, according to our capacity to love, to love unconditionally."

Sister – Are you kidding?

AS – Absolutely not!

Sister MC – Please, speak clearly. I want to understand.

At that point, Sister Chantal saved us from a long explanation. As the person of good sense she was, Sister Chantal said:

I am sure that, Professor Sauret, will be happy to explain that next time in class, because the question may be of great interest not only for the few of you here, but also for the whole class. Isn't that so, Mr. Sauret?

It would have been impolite not to take the hand she offered...

AS – I do agree. It is true. And that is exactly my purpose. So, please, Marie-Claude, prepare some questions for me to raise at the beginning of our next meeting in class. Your questions will help me to enter immediately in argument. Would you like to do that for me, please?

Sister MC – Oh, yes, I will do... I will speak also with Sister Michèle on that topic... I know she is interested in the topic, too. And she has very good questions, too, to ask you.

Tableau # 29
Back in Heaven

THE INTERRUPTION, MADE BY SISTER CHANTAL. GAVE ME A CHANCE TO GO HOME, where I had to replace the baby sitter attending my kids. While I was teaching, in the afternoon at Regina Mundi, after the work of the morning in the Vatican, Chiara, was teaching at the township elementary school of Gianturca beside the Pantheon.

I left Regina Mundi and made my way home. I was on my bicycle, along the Tiber River, protecting me from the sun, already hot in April in Rome. I was enjoying the shadows of the great maple trees of Tor di Nona riverside. It was a beautiful promenade on this side of the river.

I stopped a moment to reflect on the conversation I just had. Spontaneously I looked up to the sky and invoked the presence of the Angels in my reflection. While I was looking up, my eyes were regaled by the statue of St. Michael, just above his Castle, on the other side of the river, the wa-

ters of which reflected the massive figure of the angel atop the massive walls. I started a moment of intimacy with Michael.

Michael is the leader of Angelic troops in their actions in favor of our deeds. I knew that Michael was already present with the other Angels, some minutes earlier, during our short but intense conversation focused on the pure spirits... Looking at "Castel Santangelo" I remembered the story of the Castle and how centuries ago, Saint Michael with his followers saved the city from a terrible plague... As a commemora-

tion of his intervention for the city, his statue was put on the top of the castle. That same statues seemed to smile to me as an answer to my reflections in his favor.

I continued, then, the reflection by myself.

Suddenly I realized that I was not biking back home. De facto, I was flying in heaven: the previous conversation, in the corridors of Regina Mundi after-class made me enter the universe of the Angels, who were surrounding us in heaven. Even when arriving home, I was still flying around the house, near the kids, they all looked less real than the place of bliss I was really moving through. The whole heaven was surrounding me like in a beatific vision: I had the feeling of moving alone in God's love, under his blessing, where I met the whole world.

Yes, we cannot say that people live on earth while Angles live in heaven. Earth and heaven are not two separated places, like my home and my car: being both material things they can be attached, when the car is in the garage or detached when the car is on the road.... Heaven, however, is not another place in the world. While earth is effectively somewhere in the universe and is a part of it, heaven is a spiritual fact.... Actually, we do have to consider heaven as the real consistency of earth.

Heaven is the effective support of the earth. It keeps earth in shape. What is spiritual is more consistent than what is material. When you give some coins to a poor person, you may do so to empty your pocket, or because you love that beggar and have no better possibility at this time to show concern for him or her. When you love, all behaviors are integrated. Otherwise, it would be just a kind of animal reflex, with no consistency or value.

The spiritual part of creation supports its material part. It is the spiritual world which keeps earth in existence. Heaven and earth are connected to one another everywhere, every time. Every being is evidence of a similar connection: As a person, my body stands because of my soul. It is the same in the world. The earth stands because of the spiritual forces which make it stand. Here is why Angels are not at all strangers in our lives. They are so near to us than we never can be separated from them.

You know, it is not sufficient to be aware of the existence of the Angels to be able to comprehend who they are... When you know that they exist, it is a first step, but you almost know nothing yet... Only when you relate to them, the Angels become real in your lives, and they openly act in your daily chores and deeds.. Knowing and meeting them is more than the logical consequence of what they are. It is a living endeavor.

Behaving in accord with the Angels follows a training that we learn while we exert it. It is a living process of education, rich in events, examples, teachings, and experiences. While too few pieces of information are given about the Angels today, they want to be part of our life and inform it beautifully. We improve in our actual relationship with them — as it happens with every human relationship. Every human relationship is unique and irreplaceable. It happens the same with the Angels: they are people whom we come to know, through proper and unique connections. Try this: start to talk to them and ask them to talk to you. Such a relationship is a blossoming process.

Every spiritual endeavor involves the deeds of the Angels. When their deeds become noticeable to us, it is an amazing adventure. In the

Bible, Hagar and Ishmael received food from an Angel in the desert, because the Lord heard their cry for help.

Saint Joan of Arc changed the course of history because of them... It was the cry of a whole nation that the Lord heard and he chose a young girl to show that her deed came from above.

Saint Catherine Labouré, who is the one who received, from Mary, the Miraculous Medal, recounted how she was introduced to Mary by her Guardian Angel... She was led by her personal Angel to the appointment with Mary, from her dormitory of Rue du Bac, Paris, on the night of July 19, 1830. Catherine explains:

He was moving standing always on my left side and beautiful rays of brightness were emitted everywhere he was passing through". She said that her Guardian Angel looked like a child 4 or 5 years old, but he was gifted with the fullness of the most powerful human strength in his own movements and words: "He came to me", she said, "and introduced me to Mary, the Mother of Jesus, because I had prayed him a lot for that!

Saint Angela Merici was used to communicate to his spiritual director through her Guardian Angel, who actually was transporting her letters to him, and vice versa to her so swiftly that the communication itself was faster than the time she or he needed to write those letters...

When Don Bosco was in danger of being murdered by some criminals who wanted to stop his charitable ministry, an Angel came in the shape of a wolf, and protected him from the wicked thugs.

While he was alone in the desert, Saint Anthony was brought half loaf of bread every day, and when he got a visitor, some Angel, in the shape of an animal, provided a full loaf.

Saint Benedict was about to eat some poisonous meal, provided by some jealous man, when a crow took the meal out of his hands and saved his life.

All these examples show the care of the Lord for those who love him… and his prompt intervention through the Angels. Acting always through second causes.

Years of love and intimacy with the Angels, made me aware of the consistent field of creatures they represent. I am pleased, occasionally, to share this patrimony of knowledge. Actually, talking about them is the opportunity to know them better. The more we spread around the news concerning the presence of the Angels in our lives, and the more they act efficiently to enlighten, guide, support, defend, and govern us. Because they are living persons, talking about them makes them efficiently alive among us.

Teaching metaphysics in Steubenville, I had the opportunity to refer to the prevalence (consistency) of spiritual values in the world as part of the macrocosm, including the fact of spiritual entities, like those that Aristotle called second causes and he identified as pure spirits.

Occasionally, I shared with students, how the pure spirits refer to those that our religious behaviors call "Angels". I stressed how most people, today, are unaware of what Angels are. Such a statement raised the interest of a few who developed, at times, interesting conversations outside the classroom, while I was leaving the University campus, or in some coffee shop nearby.

The whole conversation on the Angels continued without interruption for months with the many after class talks at the university. Here below are samples of responses from the complete panorama of questions the students posed. Permit me to refer to a few:

Q. Did you say that pure spirits and Angels are the same?, Mark asked.

AS – Yes, they are. But the two names indicate a diverse relationship with the same identity. They are the same but not approached from the same vantage. When Aquinas refers to the Prime Mover, the one who, according to Aristotle, is the source of every being and activity, Aquinas has care to avoid any confusion between philosophy study and religious worship. He says: "The Prime Mover is the one that religious traditions call God." He does not say the Prime mover is God, which would be a kind of mistake... or improper definition. He more clearly affirms that the one we study in philosophy as the ultimate cause of everything is the one that, in religious behavior, we call God."

While philosophy is a work of reflection, the Prime Mover is understood as the source of every existing being. A similar source is the one we meet and relate in religious pursuits, which include interaction and worship. Through philosophy we understand better who is the one we call God, and to whom we are related.

Pascal was right to see a difference between the "Eternal Bachelor of the worlds", as he defined God under the point of view of some philosophers, and "The God of Abraham, Isaac, and Jacob" of whom we speak from a religious perspective. The two attitudes are distinct but interact to complement each other. Likewise, we call pure spirit the actual forces present in the universe, which we like to refer to in the context of our spiritual life. The identification of pure spirits with second causes, according to Aristotle and Aquinas, helps us to understand who the Angels are.

Q. What do you mean by second causes? Mark asked again.

AS – Second causes are the forces which run the universe. Our materialistic mentality tends to believe that matter moves by itself. It is true that matter shows properties, the same properties that belong to the forces which keep it in existence and movement. All physical and chemical laws developed the concept that every power of change is inside matter, almost like many disregarded the souls which govern our bodies.

According to Aristotle, matter itself is only "capacity of change". It is the same capacity of change that produces a chain reaction. Capacity of change belongs to matter, but the power of change comes from another source. On the track of Aristotle, Aquinas assigns all actual changes on earth to the second causes. "God does not act personally on creation", he says, "God acts through second causes". The whole universe exists and moves by means of the spiritual side of its own configuration.

Q. Why are angels are so popular today? Lizbeth asked.

AS – Talking about Angels was for a long time almost taboo in our western culture. Recently, however, probably after 1960 or so, many cultural and religious movements made them popular. These waves of popularity inside of Christian circles, from the New Age movement, or the Jehovah Witnesses, speak about the Angels and our relationship with them. A few years ago, entering a bookstore and looking inside the religious publications section, you would find a lot of volumes regarding the Angels. When you opened one of these books, however, you would find the testimonies of people pretending to meet the Angels. But absent from those pages was a systematic presentation explaining what the Angels do, who they are, in what way you can meet them, how you entertain a relationship with them.

It is not enough to know that Angels exist. It is not even sufficient to know that they are near to us, if we have no information about the way to deal with them. We need to identify who they are in order to understand better the way we can maintain a continuous relationship with them. They barely indicate the manner to ask them for help in our daily life.

According to these works everything goes at random, while nothing works by chance with them. Fortunately, many examples of the intervention of the Angels in the life of people can be found in the Bible and the accounts from the lives of the Saints, like Augustine, Gregory the Great, Anthony of Padova, Rita of Cascia, Angela Merici, Gemma Galgani, Don Bosco, to name a few.

Then, to answer your question on the reason why the Angels are so popular today, I dare to say that in our civilization, the cultural development goes by waves, almost the way we walk, having once the body too much unbalanced on the right leg, and later too much unbalanced on the wrong (pardon!), on the left leg. It is a discursive process. What is right cannot remain hidden forever. After centuries of disrespect of the Angels, the growing process of science shows its own limitations, and interest is given again on the unknown. It is natural, then, to enter the current of great interest in the Angels, who have been so long ignored.

Q. What kind of beings are they? Joshua, who was passing by, wanted to know.

AS – The best way to understand what they are, is to meet them in person. Being open to the possibility of their existence is a first step in our approach to encountering the reality of the Angels. We are talking about entities which are not simply things to look at. They are living creatures, who are more present to us than we are to the people around us, and exert more activity than we do.

Talking about the Angels, we refer to persons who are near to us every time we mention them. They actually are nearer to us than the physical bodies we can see, we can hear, we can touch. They meet us directly inside of us. They help us to think, they give us strength, they provide insights, desire to grow and capacity to behave.

For more than half a millennium, most people did not deal properly with the Angels. Loss of interest started with the Renaissance, when people were focused on new discoveries of lands, products, art expression, social behaviors. It continued at the time of Descartes, or so, when the general interest for positive sciences distorted the attention to spiritual values and disregarded the presence of the Angels in our lives.

For centuries people were totally ignorant of them. Rationalism, positivism, pseudo-pragmatism, scientism developed a civilization tending to consider the whole world as mere matter. The role of Angels inside of the world was substituted by a so called "Mother Nature." The lack of awareness, towards them, persisted until WWII. It was a long period of ignorance of spiritual values, which ironically took for a while the name of "enlightenment".

During that long period of decades, the whole cultural vocabulary filled everything with mineral, vegetable, animal, and human items, but the whole glossary concerning pure spirit has been missing for a while in our civilization. Teilhard de Chardin provided an excellent example of how it worked for centuries... "During those years," he said, "when a scientist entered his laboratory, he used to leave outside the door together with his umbrella, his hat, his coat, also his faith. No wonder if after years of a similar practice we have a science language which provides a civilization, in which any experience of faith is disregarded or considered as an oddity or a foreign behavior." The evidence of the Angels in our civilization is a recent introduction.

Now, you know the environment we belong to. It is then, through our experience of faith, that we are able to explore the mysterious nature of the Angels, and actually meet them. Meeting them provides experience that is even more enlightening than meeting regular people: yes, everyone is different, everyone is original, everyone is unique. This is true for people, and it is truer for the Angels.

Q. Why did you say "pseudo-pragmatism" about the human behavior of rationalism and scientism?

AS – I deliberately said "pseudo-pragmatism", because true pragmatism should be related to the facts, without discrimination. The Angels are part of the facts. They are real and work efficaciously. True pragmatism would leave them room enough to act openly in our daily endeavors. When you have a problem, a trouble, a doubt... You're not alone... Spiritual theology calls ?answering prayers" what we usually call "prayer of petition".

Q. How's that?

AS – When we ask the Lord for something, we actually are ask-

404

ing to help us in the situation we are experiencing and which was provided by God's Providence. So, our so-called "prayer of demand" is a true answer to God's Providence. It is obvious then, that what we ask is what the Lord wills to disclose to us, and was the reason why he put us in similar conditions. Those conditions are supposed to push us to ask for what he really wants to pour into our lives.

Q. What do the Angels have to do with it?

AS – I cannot prevent myself from repeating that, Fr. Emmanuel de Floris, the hermit who was my spiritual director, until he died in March 19, 1992, used to tell me that, according to St. Thomas Aquinas, the Lord never acts personally on earth, but he acts through second causes, which means through his messengers, the Angels. Whatever you ask, when you ask you are provided for by the Father, who reaches you through his Angels.

Because Our Lady is the Queen of Angels, she is present, too, at every moment as his graces are delivered. This is why Pope John-Paul II called her several times "mediator of all graces", in the sense that she always takes care of us in a manner that brings us back to her Son, who is the only one mediator, the Redeemer.

Q. So the interest of our civilization in them is a recent event. Isn't it?

AS – Thank you to pull me back on track. Well, referring to the Angels in daily life is a very ancient behavior, which seems to have been lost for a while. I would say that the long period of ignorance of spiritual beings, would be from the Renaissance up to WWII. Before that, angels felt at home in human society.

Western history reports the connection with the Angels, made by philosophers like Socrates, Plato, Aristotle, to name the first ones. According to his disciples, Socrates used to refer to a demon that at times provoked him, encouraged him to reflect and dig deeper in his search for truth, justice, beauty, piety, understanding, virtue, value, facts, and so on. In Anabasis, *Xenophon recounts the courage and determination of Socrates to save the moral of the Greek corps, during the campaign of the ten thousand Greek soldiers, who had been abandoned in Persia and had to walk for 1,500 miles, through unknown land, towards the sea. He recalls typical episodes of celestial meeting in Socrates' life which strongly impressed him. Xenophon reports the surprise of the soldiers seeing Socrates immobile, during the afternoon, standing bare foot in the snow and keeping the position all the evening while they hardly endured the cold temperature.*

Their surprise increases over time, seeing that Socrates did not move for the whole night and they still discovered Socrates standing in the same position the following morning... until he shook his head, in a way of agreement, and reentered his tent, to start his regular regimen of a soldier's day, addressing his chores as usual. It is reported that when some of his companions asked him, "What did you do last night?", he answered: "Oh, I had to talk with my demon." Socrates was talking regularly with his Angel and he simply related that later to his friends or his disciples.

Plato, too, reports a similar example at the beginning of the Symposium, *when the disciples decided not to interrupt Socrates, in spite of the impatience of the guest, in order not to stop "his conversation with the demon". .Socrates' friends understood that when Socrates was struggling with some issue, he would stop all activity until he got what he was looking for. Then, when he finally was happy with the issue he was seeking, he was ready to go back to regular business, and able to address people and normal chores.*

In his Dialogs, *Plato speaks about reality as the perfect world of ideas, of which our sensorial field is just pale reflection of its pure consistency.*

Later on, Aristotle addressed the topic of pure spirits. Aristotle is the first thinker speaking clearly about them as pure spirits. According to his writings, they are pure will, pure intelligence, and pure understanding. Aristotle explains that the whole world is moved by mere forces, that he called pure spirits. Pure spirits are in the Physics *real entities, which appear as the strengths, as the different powers, which are running, moving and leading the world. To be true, the main works of Aristotle, those concerning logic (Organon),*

Physics, *and* Metaphysics, *deal with these entities, which are an integral part of the universe.*

At the beginning of the Christian era, when the two traditions, the one coming from the Jews and the other one coming from the Greek merged into one, in Alexandria of Egypt, they produced Christianity. In this context the Angels are recognized as the pure spirits. This understanding, however, emerges slowly in Christian culture. It is especially during the Middle-Age, with some philosophers like Albertus Magnus and Thomas Aquinas that there came a new and clear interpretation of the thoughts of Aristotle. Then they understood that the pure spirits whom Aristotle spoke about were exactly the same ones who were well known amongst Jews and Christians under a different common name. They are the ones who are reported in the bible under the name of Angels. Then the topic of the Angels became common during Middle Ages. Actually, the awareness and understanding of the Angels came out progressively.

After WWII, they began to be popular again. Philosophy, theology, literature, poetry, arts started to deal with them anew.

Q. If they are so present in our civilization, why don't we see them?

AS – The answer is very simple. Can you see the north side of the city of Pittsburgh from Mount Washington when you look towards the south? Can you observe a biological cell by looking through a telescope? Can you see the configuration of your house looking only at the woods and the grass of the backyard? Can you observe the nightingale that you hear in the morning from the trees, while looking on the other side of the yard?

Q. Obviously not, but… is that your answer?

AS – We do not see them for we are not looking at them. How can we pretend to see the Angels today when we seek them, under some sensorial appearance. When a scientist wants to observe a cell, a specific preparation is necessary, because a cell can be seen only by a specific approach. Why would people like to see the Angels without the appropriate perspective? Additionally, it could be that they show up today in a different manner than yesterday.

Q. *How would that be?*

AS – While I was living in Italy, I met a scientist, Piero Pasolini, who was a man of faith, engaged in the Focolare movement and working at the rehabilitation of the township of Fontem, a wild area in the large forest of West Cameroun. We had insightful conversations together. Various expressions of his speeches are still mysterious to me. Once, in my house, in the Cinecittà neighborhood, in the south-east sector of Rome, we talked about the Angels. They were characters he was familiar with.

To my surprise, Piero included them among the UFO's, that people were talking about in those days. "They are the same thing," he said: "In such an industrialized society as ours is, there is not a more decent way to show up." During the conversation, he explained the miracle of Fatima as if it were an extraterrestrial intervention. I do not dare to say more about his perspective on the miracle of the sun, for he described it in a way that combined his scientific views and his religious understanding. There would be too much to explain in order to relate his views in a proper way.

On that occasion, he told us how he had, in Africa, the visit of a UFO, that stood all night long in front of his window, without a word, without any other communication than standing there as a mysterious calling presence... We were all impressed by that silent call. For some reason, that story prompted me to think of a call from heaven, as a visit, similar to what Francis of Assisi named sister Death. I was not at that time aware of the fact that a few months later Piero would travel to Africa and would return to that place, where he would actually die.

Q. *Do you believe this?*

AS – The reference of Piero is just an example, and it can be taken as such. The example shows the capacity of Angels to enter our lives according to the way they consider more opportune to raise our attention. We recognize an angelic visit through the message which is left. Nobody shows amazement when in the bible an Angel takes the appearance of a human traveler, to introduce himself to Abraham, or Tobias. We also know that such appearance is provisional. There is nothing to be surprised about, if today an Angel takes the form of an alien traveler. As pure spirits they have not a specific form, they provisionally take at times the one they consider mot opportune for what they intend to accomplish.

Q. So there is not a specific way to represent the Angels. Is that so?

AS – According to Aristotle the pure spirits are not merely contemplative entities but forms of power. They are forces, who maintain the world. At the start of Christian era, new philosophers in Alexandria, Egypt, reflected on the thoughts of Plato and Aristotle, interpreting the reading of the Bible according to Greek teaching. Later, Thomas Aquinas discerned that the second causes, of whom Aristotle spoke, were exactly the ones, who are reported in the Bible, and are known as Angels in Jewish and Christian traditions. In the Bible, the Angels are the messengers of God. In this case, "messenger" must be understood in its highest sense of "actor", "executive operator", "manager", etc. These messengers are the executors of the messages they bring. The "word of God" is never mere speaking. Always, God's word is action.

We find the Angels all throughout the Bible. The book of Genesis tells how God asked an Angel to keep the gates of Eden closed after Adam and Eve have been kicked out for their misbehavior. Later on, all during the history of the chosen people, from Abraham until the coming of Christ, the Story of Salvation is bearing witness to the continuous deeds of Angels. Through them, God visits his people. He speaks with his people. The Angels bring them the Word of God. A similar intervention is always an event. Bringing the word of God, the Angel does what he says. We listen to his words, the action he enforces. When the Angels spoke to Abram, he becomes a father. When he is sent as a divine messenger, Jonah speaks, and Nineveh is saved. When Raphael speaks, Tobias' spouse, Sara, is released from the deadly demon, and Tobiah, Tobias' father, gets back his sight. When Gabriel speaks to Mary, she becomes pregnant with Jesus, the Son of God. Bringing the Word of God, the Angels are the most efficient actors in the world.

As a result, giving the Angels the name of "Messengers of the Lord", means that they work, build, save, convert, and govern things and people. Matthew (8:27) says that the Apostles were surprised to see the wind and the sea obey the words of the Lord. His words are feats, indeed. All the same, the Angels, His Messengers, are divine workers. The examples I cited show only exceptional assignments... But, what about the many Angels who keep the world running as a regular business?

Q. What do you mean by the "regular business" of the Angels?

AS – The Second Causes in Aristotle and Aquinas, primarily refer to the forces running the actual universe. Aristotle understands that planets are not agents, but masses, and the forces between masses, which Newton refers to but does not explain, are the Second Causes.

Q. Do you mean to say that all physical laws refer to angelic actions?

AS – This is what Aristotle and Aquinas say. Our materialistic society ignores the soul of people and disregards the spiritual presence, which is the source of forces in the universe, or it includes such forces among physical property without any indication to whom the natural forces belong. It is true that my body shows specific behaviors. And it is correct to see in bodily activity a natural process, because it is so. But it would be incorrect to deny the presence of the soul as the spiritual dimension of the body, as well as the mind as its speculative expression. It is surprising to see how many Christians believe in the presence of the soul in people, as the organizer of the body, and disregard where the natural forces come from in the world. Well, ultimately, they say that everything belongs to creation, therefore it belongs to God. For some reason, however, they disregard the spiritual dimension of the whole of creation. Creation is not merely physical.

Q. Does Aquinas say so?

AS – Yes, he does. This is the traditional teaching of the Church. But as usual, the teaching becomes successively and growingly understood. Our civilization proceeds by waves. Christian people become progressively aware of the patrimony of knowledge of the Church. Not everything is immediately appreciated. We surely understand more today than in the last century; and, nonetheless there is still a lot of issues that we need to become aware of today. Most of the comprehension concerning the Angels needs to be uncovered.

As soon as a new question has been identified in Christendom, it enters into the liturgy. Concerning the Angels, we celebrate the feast of the three Archangels, Michael, Gabriel, and Raphael on September 29 and soon after, on October 2, we celebrate the presence of the Guardian Angels in our lives. Then we celebrate their deeds in the life of saints and especially in the history of salvation, at Annunciation, Christmas, Easter, Ascension, and so on.

Another feast should be introduced. Just as we have the feat of All Saints, we need the one of All Angels. But a better understanding of what the Angels are is needed inside of the people of God, before such celebration is introduced in Roman calendar, unless the Angels are already included in the observance of All Saints. De facto, the Angels are Saints, too.

Q. Are the Angels different from one another?

AS – Oh! Yes! The variety of aspects, deeds, and figures among the Angels is extremely richer than the variety we see in the physical world. The physical world includes mineral, vegetable, and animal kingdoms; and every kingdom includes two genders, and each gender include various species, and every species includes categories of individuals.

In the Bible there is not a specific teaching about the Angels: they are just part of the History of Salvation, with the exception of just one, the Angel of the Lord, who seems to be the Lord in person. Later, with the Fathers of the Church, Christendom counts nine choirs of Angels, elaborated in twelve main series. At the upper celestial hierarchy, they classify those who are involved with the worship of God, like Seraphim, Cherubim, and Thrones, the second choir in-

411

cludes those who care the large process of creation like Dominations, Virtues, and Powers, and finally the third choir refers to those who attend individuals by continent or geographic mainland (Nations), by nations or historic community (Archangels), and by group, family or individuals (Angels). This classification, however, remains approximate. The sources of information, are not unanimous in that regard.

Q. How many are they?

AS – Nobody knows the exact number. The theologians who are familiar with the issue count many more identities among the Angels than physical entities. The spiritual world is more various than the physical one. The Angels are defined by their roles – they are what they do. So, this confirms that there should be many more than physical individuals. The Angels take care of individuals as single, as groups, as species, as genders, and under their physical characteristics. Every category of action has its own caretaker, who organizes the proper process. The forces acting in the universe are many more than physical entities.

Q. Is that a fact?

AS – Well, we're talking about pure spirits. They are entities that we cannot see, unless they want to be seen and take forms that make them visible. They are entities that we can understand, but not imagine: imagination works with sensorial entities, which they are not. In the language of Aquinas, pure spirit is synonymous with mere power. There are not physical entities, but power entities. You don't see the wind. You do see, however, its effect on trees. leaves, houses, roads, and so on. It is the same with Angelic Powers, we do not see them, but we clearly see what they do.

Q. How do they communicate?

AS – They communicate through what they are... Being only thought and will, they act by love and mind. They truly act, indeed .They communicate the same way both within one another, and with human people. However, if humans deal with them only *by mind and will, they often take a human appearance to become fully observable by people. They need to adopt a human semblance to raise the attention of people, and make us ready to listen to what they have to tell us.*

Q. What do you mean?

AS – The whole difference between the way we behave and the way they behave consists on our dependence on sensory activity and their own independence from it. According to Aristotle, "there is no knowledge in our mind that was not first in our senses." which Aquinas confirms with: "we have no knowledge of what we have not experienced." In other words, our capacity to think, to produce ideas, sentences, starts from sensorial activity.

Our senses produce images in our mind. These images come from our five sensors: touch, smell, taste, sight, hearing, which are the only five doors through which people are connected with the surrounding reality. All together the cybernetic activity of senses allow us to identify objects as animal do.

People, however, are gifted with intelligence. Etymologically, intelligence comes from "intus legere". Intelligence is the capacity to select, to read (legere) inside of things (intus) what they are (being, ideas, concept). Intelligence is the capacity to read the whatness" of things, what they are, what is universal inside of things. These universals, that people read inside of things, are the ideas, the concepts, they get from it.

*The one concept, one idea produces a universal abstraction of what things are. Human language starts from it. Then, two ideas (or two words) form a proposition. Then, two propositions form a reasoning. And so on: all reasoning steps together form a discourse. Every human discourse is always **partial** — (it has to be done somewhere, sometime, addressing things step by step), **successive** — (a sentence is uttered after another, they never go together at the same time. Sentences are related to one another), and **progressive**. The whole reasoning is driving the mind to a synthetic understanding. During a human demonstration, reasoning (going by steps) and intuition (global comprehension) go together. Intuition lead the rea-*

soning, and the reasoning makes the intuition grounded.

Angels think differently. Intelligence does not work discursively for Angels. They do not think the way we do. They do not proceed by steps. They just know. Because their thinking is not subject to senses, they know immediately what something is, without the long process of investigation that people need to go through.

Q. Does that mean that they talk to one another without even speaking?

AS – Yes. Exactly: by mere thinking they communicate. By mere willing they ask and answer. No word, no uttering, no reasoning, no sentence is necessary between each other. Their relationship is immediate, is occurring at once.

Q. How do they know, though?

AS – As soon as something exists, they know it. If there are conditions to rain, they know that rain is coming. As soon as a baby does exist, they know it. They know a baby as soon as it is conceived. Notwithstanding, because the conception of a baby is the result of a free, conjugal action, between two people, the Angels do not know that a baby is going to be born, before parents actually make it conceived. Nonetheless, as soon as a baby is conceived, it already exists, and the Angels know it. Such awareness comes far before scientific and medical devices tell the mother that she is pregnant. Nonetheless, the Angels know nothing about what does not exist yet, and would be the result of free human actions. The Angels cannot know what is more than the mere result of natural laws...

God knows it. They do not, unless they are told by God, like in the case of Gabriel at Annunciation. But, at the Annunciation event, the birth of Jesus is not effective before Mary says "yes, I agree, I am the servant of the Lord." Then, and only then, after her "yes," the whole process of incarnation begins. Gabriel showed a great humility when bringing the message of the Lord that needed the agreement of Our Lady to put it in force... The agreement of Our Lady made Annunciation "operational", to say it with our human words.

To summarize the Angelic knowledge I like to stress that the Angels know everything that exists and everything is supposed to exist as a natural consequence of it: growing, development, further happening, as far as the successive events are the regular consequences of the natural laws, which they are in charge of. That's all.

Which is not written yet, they do not know. Most of the future of people is still open. It only depends on human freedom and Divine Providence. Both are causes that do not depend on natural laws. They produce the unpredictable future. Therefore the Angels do not know it. The future of people belongs to the secret of the Father. In the Gospel, Marc [13:32] says, about the end times, that "nobody knows the day and the time, not even the Angels in Heaven, not even the son, only the Father knows, and those whom the Father wants to reveal it..."

Here is why every announcement concerning the future, even approximately, is suspicious. Any discourse on the future is not credible, unless it is conform to the teaching of the scripture: "Be ready now", "Prepare yourself, for you do not know when." The Bible speaks about the future only to make us ready now to meet our maker. All the rest is fantasy, is useless, or false thread. We must reject both those who say that there is time before that and cause distraction or those who announce that the moment is imminent and cause another kind of distraction due to emergency. Both divert us from living properly the present as we must. We must act accordingly, operating as if everything was depending on us but knowing that ultimately everything depends on God. This was the suggestion of Saint Ignatius to his followers: "Take care of everything as it only was your business, knowing that after all the Lord is in charge."

Q. Are the Angels always available?

AS – They are much more effective than merely available... They always want to improve our lives. The Angels continuously are ready to perform what we have not even asked yet... They already know what we want for. When we need help and ask the intervention of a friend we must go through the whole process of contacting our friend, being convincing, and allow him the time he needs to help us effectively... We have to wait for the necessary steps that a sensorial process requires… Angels are ready far before we ask, and they want us to demand in order to free them to perform. Our present desire to get help is already foreseen by the Angels, especially by our Guardian Angel and by all the Angels who are involved in the situation we are in…

Do not hesitate to talk to them. Being in touch with the Angels is the way to release them. A simple though, a desire, an intention is sufficient to be connected. There is not even the requirement to talk. If we want to, we are in touch with the Angels. And engaging a connection with the Angels allows them to move on. When you share your sadness with the Lord, they are the ones who bring your need to him and beg him earnestly for you… The whole process is faster than the time I need to describe it… It is immediate… Suppose you ask your computer what time is it … You just need to look at the screen. Even so a rapid action requires time. Well even the faster computer is slower than any Angel course of action, including getting your sadness, hearing your needs, referring the situation to the Lord and bringing back the solution you need… The Angels are not subject to physical time, all their business is faster and more efficient than we can imagine… Their behaviors emerge as soon as our needs show up… "Oh! Lord! I am not worthy of your help, but say only a word and my call is clear."

The only mistake we may commit with the Angels is to be slow for asking them to prevent our needs and to arrest our struggle… The Lord wants our happiness and he knows us better than we do. Why are you afraid of asking what you need? Why are you slow to request what you intimately desire? Why do you delay a request that the Lord is just waiting to receive in order to unleash the Angels who are in charge of taking care of you and those you love?… Only your lack of trust is the obstacle to the Angels' action. The betterment of our present situation depends only on our free expectations. The immediate improvement of my present conditions depends only on the trust I show… The more I hope the attendance of the Angels and the more they effectively perform their job… As soon as I believe they can, they actually do… Oh! Lord! Increase my faith!

Praying the Father makes us enter in the Trinitarian process of the prayer with the Son. When we pray, we are included in the relationship between the Father and the Son, and we move inside of the Holy Spirit. And we do so at the presence of the whole celestial court. All the Angels are present when we pray and they support our prayer. As soon as we utter our love to the Lord and express some demand, they are ready to act according to the graces the Lord is already disclosing towards us… When a prayer is heard, the Angels are involved. When graces are provided, the Angels are involved. In every relationship with the Lord, the Angels are involved. Actually as soon as we exist, the Angels are involved. Whatever we do, they are near to us…

Asking the Angels for help is like opening a faucet and getting water… A faucet is made for delivering water. Opening the valve, we release the water… When we connect with the Angels, the process is faster, for it works immediately, and it is made with our own will… Desiring Angelic help, activate their skills. Talking with the Angels make them free to proceed with their own business… Being in touch with them, make them happy and allow them to make us happy… It is a virtuous circle.

That dialog brought me into conversation with the Angels. Leaving the students that evening left me alone with the angels. I continued to converse with them during my drive home in Pittsburgh. Oh! Please! My good Guardian Angel, proceed accordingly! All good Angels around, please, accomplish everything I need, even beyond what I may be aware of. O Lord, come and dwell in my soul and introduce me before the celestial court. I want to be with you, now and forever.

Knowing that God acts in our lives through the "Second Causes" makes me aware of the Angelic presence in every spiritual business. It means that our relationship with Mary, with Jesus, operates in the middle of the celestial court. Even the relationship between Jesus and his Father goes together with the fullness of Angelic presence.

Tableau # 30
Pope Pius XII

THE OLD SEAT OF THE ROMAN EMPIRE, ROME, HAS A NAME that in Latin and Italian (*Roma*) can be reversed as "*Amor*", which means "Love". Such reversal exemplifies one among the many symbols the Christians have been proud of since the first centuries.

A journey with Gilles to the city of the first Christian martyrs was the next assignment of Adrian Monmayou.

At departure, the parish priest of Lunel suggested to Adrian that he contact the French Seminary in Rome for help in managing the logistics necessary for him and Gilles to complete their mission in the eternal city.

At the French Seminary, Fr. Marcel Martin, the library keeper, decided to offer his help.

The Seminary building is a solemn palace, even if it is nothing in

comparison with the splendor of the Vatican. Adrian was tall but he looked even taller next to Gilles. It is not by mistake that the child is known at Moissac as "*le petit Gilles*", the little Gilles. Both made a strange pair, easily identifiable in the streets of Rome.

Fr. Martin received the two pilgrims in a parlor of the institution on the first floor, near the large hall entrance, in front of the cloister. After listening to them, he was torn between total incredulity and some open doubts about their story. There is only one thing Fr. Marcel could say with certainty, and that was that Gilles and Monmayou would never enter the Vatican, unless some providential event were to occur.

He wanted, nonetheless, to offer some accommodation. Then, if it didn't work, it would be easier to dismiss Adrian and Gilles. So, in their presence, he decided to make a first try, and called the switchboard of the Vatican to find out what they would say.

At the Vatican phone center, Sister Anna, a new sister, is serving at the switchboard. When Sister Anna recognizes the French Seminary as the source of the call and hears the request of her interlocutor to request a papal audience, she immediately pushes a button, but instead of connecting the Seminary with the papal audience department, she accidentally connects it to the Secretary of State!

Immediately she realizes her mistake and tries to correct the mishap, but it's too late to adjust: someone on the other end has picked up the phone and says: "*Pronto, Segreteria di Stato!*"

Fr. Martin tries to explain the situation to Fr. Bellini, the Secretary of Msgr. Giovanni Battista Montini, who has at that moment entered the room to get a file. Bellini explains the request to Montini who immediately picks up the receiver.

Montini recalls well the little child who, four months ago was introduced to a public audience with pope Pius XII. All the newspapers in the city reported the event.

Montini's reply is immediate, and amazingly clear: "Please send them in the late afternoon, around four, at the Bronze Gate and I'll see what I can do"

Fr. Martin is overwhelmed by this surprising answer.

Msgr. Montini is the highest authority in Vatican after the pope. Fr. Martin had barely occasion to talk to somebody at the Secretariat of State before, and surely not with Msgr. Montini. He doesn't know what to think.

His pale face and speechless behavior makes Monmayou think the phone conversation was a failure.

Gilles remained silent; he knows that everything will proceed according to Mary's plan, whatever happens in between... *"The command of Our Lady brought us to Rome, now she will lead the endeavor even more closely, step by step"*, he thought.

"There is no doubt that everything will go through. We both did exactly what Our Lady asked for: she putt Monmayou in charge of every decision to be made during the trip. Following Monmayou's decisions means obeying Our Lady's orders." Whatever decision Monmayou decides to take, Gilles will follow.

After a moment of hesitations, Monmayou takes Gilles' hand: "Let's go..." he said.

Fr. Martin stops them: "Not so fast, the appointment is for this evening."

Monmayou and Gilles froze in place, half sitting and half standing, looking at Fr. Martin with an expression of huge surprise, their wide eyes looking as though they're about to jump out of their sockets, as if they had been struck by lightening.

Finally, they sit back down, and Fr. Martin explains that they are expected at the Bronze Gate in the afternoon.

Fr. Martin showed them how to get to St. Peter's Square, but they will have to walk alone, for some other previous business prevents him from walking with them towards the Vatican Gate.

Everything was moving way too fast... and he was wondering if it was ultimately a good thing...

Meanwhile they were invited to have lunch with the seminarians in the refectory.

During this conversation, the expression of surprise on Monmayou's and Gilles' faces has changed into a vision of happiness and peace, which made them curiously attractive.

The events, however, are moving almost too fast even for them.

During lunch they sit and eat in silence. But their peaceful and happy behaviors excites the curiosity of the men sitting near them at the large table.

When a seminarian asks them what they are doing in Rome, Gilles answer, "We're going to meet the Pope" leaves all the students suspicious, and nobody dares to ask any more questions.

Those two characters are unwanted visitors in the French building, and some consider them a little bit strange too... After the reply of Gilles every one turned back to his personal reflections... Nobody in Rome would say, "I'm scheduled to meet the pope." They would usually say, "I'm going to see the pope", which implies attendance at some public audience. Gilles, however, was expressing the certainty of a private audience.

After lunch they went to their rooms for a few minutes. A knock on the door: it is Fr. Martin asking if they needed anything special before they left. It was clearly an excuse to greet them one last time.

Some previous commitment has prevented Fr. Martin from leading them across the streets towards the Vatican.

But they cannot miss it he tells them:

When you get out of the building, you go left. Then, in Piazza Santa Chiara you turn left again, taking via di Torre Argentina, until you reach Corso Vittorio Emmanuele. You turn right there, and walk forward for a couple of kilometers. There are about twenty minutes to go until you reach the bridge with the angels on both sides of the tower bridges.

After crossing the bridge, you enter in Via della Concili-azione, on the left. At the bottom of Via della Conciliazione

you'll see the Vatican Basilica. From there to the Basilica it will take about 45 to 50 minutes. The Basilica is always open. You may stop there and pay a visit to the Blessed Sacrament before reaching the Bronze gate, where you are expected.

Looking at the Basilica from the entrance of the square, the Bronze portal is on the right, at the very end of the right side of Bernini's colonnade. You will not miss it.

It was at least the fifth time that Fr. Martin had explained the way to get there.

The three of them were moved by the wondrous events.

And everything was proceeding so fast!

That phone call with the Secretary of State had changed the whole dynamic of the circumstances.

Everything had moved from a deep uncertainty to a sudden appointment.

Yes, it is true that for God nothing is impossible.

Even Father Martin, who was accustomed to the convolutions of Roman protocol, had difficulty believing that he was awake and that the whole story was really happening.

Monmayou did not express his deep emotion… As a countryman he was accustomed to follow the events, without asking why…

There was just one thing to do: Adrian took the hand of Gilles, and led him out of the room, along the corridor, through the monumental stairs, across the hall to the big entrance and, yes, they were already out of the Seminary.

They walked on the left in Santa Chiara Street, towards Santa Chiara Square… Both were silent. Gilles was totally confident in his huge companion, and in the Divine Providence…

The walk proceeded as Fr. Martin said.

When they reached Saint Peter Square, it was too early to walk to the Bronze Gate, so they had all the time they wanted to pay a visit inside the Basilica…

The solemnity of the monument prepared their souls to the solemn audience they were about to have…

When they left the Basilica, the clock on the top of the church frontal, the one on the left, showed it was a quarter to four. It was time to go.

At their arrival at the Bronze Portal, however, the entrance was closed.

This was a blow to their hopes they had not expected. For an instant they felt lost: how could the door be closed when their arrival was officially scheduled?!?

Looking around, there was no sign of a doorbell.

Almost spontaneously, Adrian, started to bang on the door with his massive fist with all the energy he could muster. He put all his strength into it.

This unusual behavior proved even more effective than expected: the loud knocking resounded on the metallic door and echoed down the monumental corridors and walls which formed an excellent resonance chamber.

A Swiss Guard, inside, was startled by the unexpected booming and was not even sure where the sound came from… He opened the gate to check outside and saw Monmayou, with his fist in the air ready for a second round of pounding.

The Swiss Guard raised his halberd to stop him.

"What are you doing here? What do you want?" He asked in Italian with a strong Swiss-German accent.

Adrian replied in French: "We are here to see the pope!"

Monmayou's incredible answer was no less unexpected for the Swiss Guard than was Adrian's unusual manners.

Immediately, the Guard called the two or three Italian policemen on duty in Saint Peter Square, who were already on their way, attracted by the unusual noise.

At that very moment the telephone in the Swiss Guard station started ringing. The Guard at first ignored the call; but the phone kept ringing, so he finally he answered..

Immediately, his whole demeanor changed from an expression of anger to a look of surprise and finally to a gesture of full obedience, with a brisk military salute and a click of his boots.

Apparently, it was the pope on the line, asking if two unusual visitors were there for him: a little boy and a huge man.

Many times afterwards, Monmayou took delight in recounting those event.

In less than the blink of an eye, the whole situation had changed.

The Italian police released the two immediately, even before they fully realized the whole course of events.

Then, the Swiss Guard led them towards the stairs leading to the San Damascus Court that they were supposed to walk across in order to reach another flight of stairs leading up to the Apostolic Palace. They followed the directions.

After Saint Damascus Court, the monumental steps were open to them.

Those stairs were too big, too steep and too many for the short legs of Gilles.

Monmayou took him into his arms and he continued to climb, when a kind of solemn fright came over him by surprise… He wanted to stop and go faster at the same time, but he could not change the too-slow ascent of the stairs.

He continued to walk up with a kind of august reverence, overwhelmed by the awesome context of huge walls, stairs, rooms and doors…

He looked like a huge Saint Joseph carrying a small Jesus in his arms.

So impressed was Msgr. Gianbattista Montini, Secretary of State, as he gazed in admiration at them from the top of the staircase: "It is a biblical figure" he thought.

It was only when the two chosen ones had arrived almost at the top of the flight that they saw him.

In these sublime surroundings, even the small stature of Montini looked gigantic.

Msgr. Montini ushered them into an antechamber. There he asked Gilles, in fluent French, if he wanted to keep Adrian nearby during the audience. Gilles and Adrian looked at one another.

Suddenly it became evident to them that what looked like a dream before, had become a fact: the audience with the pope was about to take place. They would be granted what Our Lady asked in Espis: to allow Gilles to talk to Christ on Earth. Yes, the audience was truly scheduled and the Secretary of State knew who was the one that the pope was supposed to meet: it was not the man, but the little boy.

Adrian declined the offer to stay with Gilles: "I was entrusted with bringing you here. My business is done. Yours starts now." With a docile endeavor Gilles took the hand that Montini offered to help him enter the audience chamber.

Inside the audience hall, Msgr. Montini took a chair and put it near the papal throne.

Then he took Gilles up in his arms and set him down on the chair.

He entertained Gilles for a few minutes, and said: "Please remember this small Monsignor of the Vatican when you have occasion to talk to Our Lady again".

Gilles would remember well his humble request.

Finally, the pope, Pius XII, entered the room, and sat on his throne near to Gilles.

He immediately recognized the very little boy who had come to him five months earlier during a public audience in December of 1949.

It was the same little boy that many Roman newspaper referred to as the "Messenger of Our Lady".

In December, however, the boy did not say nothing relevant to the pope.

The pope bent down toward the child.

Their eyes meet, and Gilles saw the profound sense of love and intense inquiry in the gaze of the pope.

"Bonjour Gilles", the pope said…

"She did not die… " Gilles uttered…

The pope asked the boy to repeat. He was not sure he had understand his words clearly.

He asked: "What did you say?".

Gilles started again: **"The beautiful lady told me to say that she did not die but went to heaven with her soul and her body"**

Everything was said, the message was transmitted. Gilles was happy.

The pope remained silent for a long, long time…

These words, from the mouth of a 5-year young boy, were the answer to a question he had been widely asking for several months already.

He planned, in fact, to declare the dogma of the Assumption of Mary and had questioned the bishops of the entire Church about the consistency and the opportunity of such promulgation. The advices was not always consistent — some were in favor, some opposed

He still needed further confirmation to fulfill his inquiry.

He was expecting something more compelling.

Nevertheless, he was not sure, about what sign of assurance he was still waiting for.

As a matter of fact, he was still in need of a true answer from above…

That answer had come suddenly, now, here, in his home, without precedent.

He was almost shocked, and he needed to digest such sudden evidence.

On November 1, 1950, Pope Pies XII will promulgate the dogma of the Assumption of Mary, which states that, at the end of her life, the Virgin Mary was taken up into heaven, with her living body… She was assumed body and soul into heavenly glory.

The promulgation was made with his Apostolic constitution *Munificentissimus Deus*.

The eastern and Oriental Orthodox churches agree with the dogma through their traditional belief of Dormition of the Theotokos, i.e. the process of getting asleep of the Mother of God, and her amazing

Assumption.

After the promulgation of the dogma, the Assumption of Mary is celebrated on August 15 in the Roman Calendar.

More recently, Pope John Paull II, made at Lourdes, for the celebration of the Assumption of Mary, on 15 August 2004, the assertion that the scriptural bases for understanding the dogma stands in the excerpt of John 14:3, asserting "If I go and prepare a place for you, I will come again, and will receive you to myself, that where I am, you may be there also."

Considering that Mary is the one who fulfilled the words of God, such a statement was a promise, which she fulfilled first.

It is interesting to notice that the feast of the Assumption of Mary, celebrated on 15 August, is a public holiday in many countries, including Belgium, Chile, Ecuador, France, Greece, Italy, Lebanon,

Malta, Portugal, Poland, Spain, to name a few.

A similar devotion to Our Lady and the beautiful understanding of her performance on earth, as an example to every human being, is not achieved without appropriate suffering and humble endeavors.

Chiara Lubich was familiar to a similar process in Focolare life. "When you look at a tree," she said, "you see the foliage which is proportionate to its roots."

There is no virtuous endeavor of heroic virtue that has not sprung from the roots of suffering.

It is the same as driving a car, the more we burn gas, the more we go. Chiara expressed this idea beautifully: "there are no thorns without roses." Suffer the thorns properly, and the roses will decorate your life.

It is a beautiful endeavor, when every pain, offered to the Father through the Son, transfigures our life every day.

Many would be inclined to think that as a result of their trip to Rome and their amazing accomplishments there, Gilles and Monmayou's life would have become much easier...

Quite the opposite happened.

Reading the Gospel, I was surprised, once, to discover that Jesus was not tempted by the demon before his baptism, but afterwards. It was after he was baptized that Jesus had to face the demon.

Similarly, after Espis was somehow baptized or confirmed in Rome, with the papal audience, persecutions increased in Moissac, especially from the diocese of Montauban.

While I was teaching philosophy in Rome, at the Gregorian University, a few minutes walking from the French Seminary, where Gilles and Monmayou sojourned, and where I like to remember them, while meeting Fr. Marcel Martin for a while, I used to tell my students: "We'll always have to pay for the good things we do."

Actually, every good deed produces changes in the society for which we must pay the price.

Every improvement in the world has a spiritual price, and a disciple is not supposed to act differently from his master. "Those who

430

want to walk after me, must carrying their cross." All Christian people provide improvement on earth through their participation to the redemptive work of the Lord. Jesus redeemed us through his trial, suffering and dramatic death on the Cross.

We cannot claim and act differently.

I do not say, only, "more easily". Thinking in that manner, would be like considering the cross a wrong way. The cross, accepted as the pregnant step of resurrection, is the shortcut to the kingdom.

As Jesus followers, the best gift we may be entrusted is a sharing of the suffering of Christ on the Cross.

Planning to follow Christ, we must be ready of behaving accordingly... and carrying the cross.

Expecting of getting only joy and pleasure from our good deeds, would be not a Christian behavior.

The more we behave properly and the more we are tested.

Nothing less did happen to Gilles and Monmayou after they return home.

Nonetheless, in those days of great victory, they never cease to show peace, joy and happiness in the middle of struggle.

Being their friend, I learned that "we actually rejoice in the middle of suffering" as Saint Paul said.

They even incited me, to get great hope, in the middle of the darkest situations.

God is never second to provide comfort, joy, happiness, and such blossoming goes with purification, as we prune a tree to enhance a better harvest of fruits.

I leave the details on the outcomes of the good deed in Rome of Gilles and Monmayou to another occasion.

It seems that such a divine economy explains why the Church is supposed to test those who are bringing improvement in Christendom. Padre Pio was a recent evidence of it. Chiara Lubich and Don Pasquale Foresi showed another one.

The community of the Church, around those who are in charge

of leading the community of believers, they all saw the exertion of purification on the members of the faithful who had been familiar to Espis.

The story is not over yet.

Meeting Monmayou was one of the greatest events of my life.

It was probably for that purpose that I had the chance to never witness anything about the visions that many had in Espis woods. I consider it as a privilege.

Another great chance has been meeting Chiara, who became my wife and the mother of our five children, and now twelve grand-children.

While we were living in Rome, both of us met Chiara Lubich who transfigured our human journey.

She straightened our lives beyond scattering situations…

The friendship of don Pasquale Foresi was an additional blessing…

The Catholic Solitudes in Texas and in West Virginia are another example of holy adventures, which moves the world towards its betterment.

It is sufficient to share these few endeavors to understand the whole picture.

There is no doubt that we can see only the tip of the iceberg.

Tableau # 31
Chertsey

ON SUNDAY 7 NOVEMBER 2010, I DROVE THE WHOLE DAY, for 12 hours, to cover 700 miles from Pittsburgh, Pennsylvania, to Chertsey, Quebec, and to meet my friend Vito, who hosted me for two weeks.

Up there in the mountains, where his chalet emerges, on the shore of the lake Beaulne, a fortnight was the time I needed to put down some details of the story.

It was, actually, the lapse of time I got, as a break from university.

"Seize the day" use to say many of my students after Epicurus.

Visiting Vito was a double opportunity: it was a moment of friendship that enriched both of us, and a quiet area to reflect and write…

That day, after a long journey since I left Pittsburgh, I had to drive across the metropolis of Montreal. I always am concerned with the high density of car traffic in that urban area, and with the eventuality of getting trapped in some traffic jam for who knows how long…

I was lucky this time to go along highway 40, following East, and moving across the whole agglomeration... Going through that city from South to North and from West to East calls to mind Canon III of the Mass when it is said that the Lord will gather all people from North to South and from East to West ... Yes, such a long drive is somehow biblical.

I was very proud this time for being able to go across the city without getting lost. (Thank you, Guardian Angel.)

It was when I felt happy to have gone through unimpeded, that I started wondering which way to go next; but at that very moment, I saw the signal indicating route 25 to Chertsey.

"What a lucky break!" I thought.

Well, as a matter of fact, it was too early to sing victory. Almost one hour later I was totally lost in the middle of the mountains, the rivers and the numerous lakes of that large area... I didn't even remember the name of the road - #335 - that I was supposed to take to get from Route #125, after passing the third intersection to Rawdon.

When I was positively sure I was lost, I caught sight of an isolated coffee shop on the side of the road, which was still open at eight o'clock at night. It was not too late actually, but I already had no sense of time anymore. It could have been midnight already for all I knew. Anyhow, I stopped there to call Vito.

To my surprise Vito said that he lived just a few miles away. To avoid any more trouble for me, he came to pick me up with his 4x4 drive. It was easy, then, to follow him to his chalet.

Upon arrival, I did not remember what a beautiful house he had, which he built by himself over the years, when he was able to spare some time on week-ends. The joy of being together again made me forget my fatigue and anxiety. We started a conversation, which continued long into the night.

During the conversation, he asked me about why I needed a special quiet place to write a book, and what kind of book it was to be. At first, it appeared difficult for me to explain the project, which was the story of my family, involving the impact Monmayou had made in my life. I was unable to synthesize, at the moment, and get the few words I needed to tell him what I was supposed to say, in 300 pages or so...

Wow,! Suddenly, talking with Vito, the light came on and I understood finally the reason why I had come to his home. Actually, I needed silence to reflect and write, a silence that I could barely get in Pittsburgh in the middle of family business and university activities.

But I also needed a strong atmosphere of friendship that our old familiarity would support, in order to express what our society needs the most: a familial climate, which might be implemented by the subjects I was going to write about in the manuscript.

Two weeks was the break I needed to gather several notes, organize them, and start this endeavor.

A long drive away from home was also what I needed, to leave every commitment I had in Pittsburgh, take a break from constant phone calls, clean my mind for bills and commitments, and get my heart and my head ready to start writing.

My friend's house, a huge stone house built in the mountains, at around 80 miles north of Montreal, along the lake Beaulne, was more

than an excellent retreat. This castle was like the shell which hid and protected my reflection.

Descartes used to call the small room in the tower where he wrote most of his philosophic compositions his "Stove". The nickname came from the huge stove he had at the center of the room. If I too had to provide a nickname for the room I used in Vito's castle, I would simply call it "Monmayou." In the room, in fact, where I lived and wrote for 14 days, I experienced an especial intense encounter with Adrian, who emerges above all other characteristics of the room.

No, I had no vision, no revelation, no locution, but, somehow, I was graced with even more. Gathering the notes I had collected for this work, I understood better the impact Monmayou had on my life and how everything is currently following the wave of his spiritual influence. Actually, it is as if Monmayou was in my life an alarm clock, ringing to awaken me to the possibility of a better life. He woke me up for a life in Christ. Christ is now a permanent presence.

Then everything came back to me accordingly: my crisis of identity at 14, meeting Chiara Lubich and the Focolare at 18, meeting Chiara V. and getting married with her at 30, then having our family life enriched by five children. All is a process of intimacy with the Lord. Then writing down Monmayou's teaching and deeds filled me with the presence of the One who had changed and transfigured his life.

Staying here in Chertsey was a true retreat. I could in a few lines provide the schedule of my days, for it was a monastic life. Living there, a two-mile away from the shrine of Our Lady Queen of Hearts,

I had the chance to get mass every morning at 7:30. After this starting time of intense prayer I would spend up to twelve hours of study, or thirteen if I stopped for lunch. When Vito is home, he liked to fix

lunch for both of us; and he would calls me when it was ready. Otherwise, I would walk down to the kitchen and prepare the meal by myself.

After lunch, 15 minutes of siesta follow, then a walk in the woods around the house. I walk every day toward a different direction for 15-20 minutes... Then I return home for study, study, and study. I call study what others might call work. I call study the composition of the book, which discloses such a teaching for me that it is barely work and it is a continuous enlightening.

At times, some recollection of Adrian's words or deeds pulled me up into such a moment of contemplation that I had to leave my desk and pray in thanksgiving an Our Father for the inspiration in drafting contents or in request for graces for some people or situation I was made aware of by the remembrance. Here is why I call "study" the time spent in front of the computer. It is exerting an experience in the middle between memory, reflection, and inspiration ... in which writing is just the expression of an overflowing admiration.

It was during the summer 2007, that Michel, my son, and I decided to start putting down on the computer a few issues that we had occasion to talk about… we reduced to a few pages days and nights of conversations. In addition to my notes on Monmayou, these elaborations are the material we started with. While reading them and organizing them by topics I was impressed by the nearby presence of God's governance in our family life. Yes, our physical life is merely hiding the true consistency of the whole world, which is spiritual.

I understand better today what spiritual life is. Years ago, a joke a friend told gave me an interesting definition:

DS – "Do you know what sugar is?"

AS – "I'm not sure".

DS – "Sugar is that white matter, which provides a bad taste in your coffee, when you forget to put it inside!"

Thus is the spiritual life. It is what ruins your life when it is missing. Here is probably one of the greatest insights from Monmayou: God loves us so much that everything we cherish and strive for is like a candle in comparison to the sun of God's gifts. There is no reason for fear. God knows and provides. Fear, however, is like thirst: it helps to more enjoy the water we drink to quench it. And while I am composing these notes, I understand that this message of hope is so rich that I'll probably have to write a few other books after this one, to complete Monmayou teaching with additional endeavors and practical insights.

A few years ago, along the lake, I organized a gathering of people who came in the evening and sat around the fireplace in the yard and shared philosophy issues. They decided to call a similar gathering "Philosophy on the lake."

I understand that the Lord never does things at random or out of the blue. The gathering of insights and deeds of Adrian, is no more than a proper continuation of our philosophizing on the lake. This, book is the first volume of a small number of writings intending to walk on the shore of philosophy.

After a few days in Chertsey, I wrote to Chiara:

I came here with the purpose of writing some notes on Adrian Monmayou.

At the start, the project included 10 chapters. But only four days later the endeavor includes 20 chapters already, of which 8 are already done. The contents are spreading out of the mere figure of Adrian, they span the whole of our life and endeavor and involve more philosophical reflections than I anticipated.

Everything is proceeding beyond the best expectations.

Chiara replied enthusiastically, encouraging me to stay longer in North Quebec if I so wished, for she considered that it could be useful to complete the work. I wrote back to her with the following words:

I thank you, Chiara, for the offer to eventually remain here longer. But I wish not to abuse your patience. Also, I do not want to take advantage of Vito's hospitality. Besides, in the middle of next week I'll have finished going over with all the notes I carried with me. I have more back home in Pittsburgh that I need to consult.

Until now everything worked better than the most optimistic expectations. During the first two days I gathered all the notes I brought with me, organized them thematically, and reviewed the story schedule.

Since then, I wrote, and wrote, and wrote again all through the days, stopping for ten minutes at every hour to gather firewood in the woods or to put logs in the furnace. This alternating of physical activity with mental concentration worked extremely well: I was able to put down three chapters a day for the following three days. Thanks to Michel who helped me, two years ago, to work on this topic, some of these chapters are true masterpieces.

I only had to review what we wrote together to see if it was still consistent with the perspective of the present undertaking. Then I had to slow down, and needed inspiration to get going again. When Vito is here some evening, especially on the week-end, our conversation provides my mind the breathing I need.

Yesterday I spent the whole day on chapter 9. It was very difficult to go ahead with it. I hope I'll be able to complete it within this morning in order to address and finish chapter 10, within the night. Then with some luck I should be able, tomorrow, to work on Chapters 11, 12, 13, and complete them. Wednesday I'll compose Chapters 14 & 15. Thursday I'll do 16. Then Friday and Saturday I'll have to address 17-18 and a lot will be done before I leave.

I'll only need to review the whole manuscript, check eventual details, and submit the manuscript to someone who will make his comments on it. Michel offered to give the book the right format. The whole volume will be ready then to be sent to the printing house. I'll tell you on Friday how things stand.

On Sunday afternoon I plan to visit the Focolare at Montreal and spend the night there. On Monday morning. I'll be on the road towards Pittsburgh. If I need more days, maybe I'll postpone the departure until Tuesday but no later than that — I hope — because on Wednesday there will be a lot of traffic on the roads for Thanksgiving eve. And, I truly want to be home on Thursday and celebrate Thanksgiving with you and the whole family.

This morning, Vito left home around 4:30 and he should stay overnight in Montreal. It will be a very busy day for him and for me.

I wish you an excellent time and I'm eager to see you again.

Actually, the writing did not flow so easily... but, somehow, I am actually pleased I did not complete it all before I left Chertsey, because more reflection was needed to completely disclose Monmayou's message.

During my stay there, I received a note from Patrick, a French writer, who is interested in Monmayou and his history. I willingly replied to inform him about my work:

It's at Chertsey, Quebec, in the northern vicinity of Montreal, that I have the joy to receive your message. It took me the whole day of Sunday for covering by car the 700 miles, which separate this place from Pittsburgh.... I am here for a few days, in the chalet of Vito, a friend who built a large house on the mountain on the edge of Lake Beaulne, far from all — but with access to the internet.

I'm trying in the silence and the fabulous echoes of the wonderful wildlife, to gather the few notes I brought with me on Monmayou. I'm putting them in a manuscript, as a first volume about him. I would like to publish all in order to share with other people the amazing insights he provided. As a philosopher. I consider Adrian one of my masters.

There is so much to say... This time, I try to gather from Monmayou everything that may be a word of hope and trust in Divine Providence. But how would it be possible to repeat in writing the beautiful face of Adrian, his radiant conviction and his convincing words. There are teaching behaviors that can be transmitted only in person and they will be provided between the lines.

Here is the reason why, when Michel and I started, a few years ago to pick up some of his words, we decided to include a few facts as examples of his teaching: and what better example could be selected than our own adventure of coming into the States!?

Communication through language is a typical human endeavor. The problem, in effect, is that often we say some words and then

440

something else is understood. It seemed to us that so flexibility must be used for the good, almost as a delicious cake in a bakery window tantalizes our taste buds. We needed first to depict how Adrian's teaching influenced our life, and the rest would follow. It is that simple.

As usual, however, to be simple is what is what is most difficult to achieve. Oppositely, it is so easy to be complicated and obscure. Being simple requires intelligence and wisdom. Besides, one of the keys to providing good teaching is disclosing facts, leaving to others the freedom of making their own interpretation. This was, actually, the purpose of Plato's dialogues. Maybe that sharing of our own experience can show how divine providence worked within our family.

In such a context, Adrian's words become more understandable. It's almost like writing on a blackboard: you need to clean the board first. The cleaner and more homogeneous the board is the better does it show the new writing. So was our purpose: the exertion of our own trust in God would clean mind and heart and would make us more receptive to Adrian's message. If it worked for us, maybe it would be helpful also to everyone who would read it afterwards.

As a result, I'm trying my best, as if everything depended on me, knowing that ultimately all results depend on the Lord, as Ignatius of Loyola would say. In a word, the best is to keep close to the narration of the facts, with eventually good anecdotes that arouse interest and allow better understanding.

Hope I am right to start the endeavor with such concern. But to say the truth, I flounder. I cannot better describe the situation than by using the words of Saint Francis about human deeds in connection with Divine Providence: "If our action contains flowers, they'll flourish!"

Somehow, your questions correspond in an unexpected way to my research. You offer me the opportunity to write something together. The opportunity of sharing a similar endeavor would involve and appeal to me a lot. We surely must witness what we saw and experienced. Obviously, it is the job of the Lord, then, to decide about the results of our commitment.

What you recounted about your visit to Espis Woods does not surprise me. It is wonderful that you could find in that place some answer for you, your spouse and your friends. What will be disclosed to you will be surely beyond your actual expectations. It is a fact that the Espis Events marked my childhood to the point of enlightening my own life, and it is impossible to separate these events and the story of my own family here in the States.

You also expressed your concern of making Espis known... I support your project with peace in my heart for the Lord, who is the one who came there to provide us insights, desires to disclose his deeds even more than we do. There is always some mystery connected with God's deeds. The first step is to be consistent with God's words, and act in order to remain consistent with them, otherwise we divulge information on events that never happened. Here is why Psalm 127 reads: "if the Lord does not do the job, useless are struggles and efforts of the workers." I truly believe that the best way to disclose the Espis message is by being consistent with it, inside of our own life, then all the rest will follow accordingly. Here is why we must do what depends on us with peace and intimacy with the Lord. We are messengers only; we do not own the message.

Typical in the Bible was the adventure of Jonah: he brought a message which was producing a result different from what he thought. He was actually bringing a message of salvation, while he thought he was entrusted with words of wrath and death. Because the people of Nineveh took him seriously, they converted and were saved. Afterwards Jonah was the only one complaining: "why did you send me to tell them that they will die, if actually they did not."

Here is why, spreading the words of Espis we must keep our heart consistent with the Bible and Lord's teaching all along, otherwise we may convey words that are not from God but come just from us. We are not supposed to bring our own interpretation on Moissac events. We must spread around the hope, the gladness, the comfort, the happiness we experienced there. Repeating literally what we heard and saw should be sufficient.

According to Saint Teresa, there are circumstances that belong to our secret intimacy with the Lord and should remain unspoken. We must, however, spread the joy coming from it. The risk of being *caught by the events in human interpretations is permanent. Here is why we will be able to speak properly if our present life is a continuous conversion to Divine Providence and Mercy.*

Twenty years ago, I heard in Brussels, an interesting homely in a Jesuit parish: "When a rabbit eats a carrot," the priest said, "the carrot becomes the rabbit..." Then he pushed the analogy further: "But when we eat the Eucharist, it is we who are processed and become another Christ."

Eh! Well! This is what should occur each time we deal correctly with the things of God: if we really deal with God's words, our conversion is involved. And it would be a mistake to believe that we must do this or that, run here or there, while we must only make a spiritual move inside of the kingdom, staying where we already are and let things follow appropriately. It is difficult to say it, but every time we have the feeling that we need the support of time, money, and friends, it is probably the sign that we follow a personal schedule. At this point it is better to stop, pray, and let the Lord speak.

Among the notes that I am sorting out, there are surprising events... What I was able to deal with, at this time, seems to be just the tip of a gorgeous iceberg. I am in the middle of it. Do whatever you think is appropriate. God gave us the gift of intelligence, and he is expecting that we make good use of it. He encourages us, in the Gospel, to put at the service of his kingdom the intelligence that others bring to the service of dark purposes.

The novels that have success today are most of the time composed of several stories, whose storylines Intertwine... It became spontaneous with the events of the woods of Moissac, to develop the story, with a few endeavors, that actually intertwine, too. These anecdotes will arouse the attention of those who are curious about the seers of Espis, as Monmayou was. I'm sure the reader will give thanks for the love that God shows through these facts. Not all of what happened is said. And, it is proper to do so.

Sometimes, saying less we say more.

You're right to grow in prayer. It is a gift coming from above. Be in continuous thanksgiving. Saint Augustine was pleased to stress that the desire that God has to enter in our life is even greater than the desire we have to know him. There is a similar sentence in the Ku'ran: "God is nearer to us than our own jugular vein."

The prodigious humility of the Lord, who came down, and spoke with us in the Espis woods, must match a prodigious creativity in the presentation of the appealing events that developed from it. Moissac revelations did not stop in the 1940s, because God is the eternal present! There is certainly a reason for the vacuum of information that accompanies the endeavor of Espis. We must involve all our intelligence in the project, getting our intelligence to act with peace and wisdom, and make a cradle in which God speaks. This behavior requests also a great transparency.

Pope John XXIII had a fantastic expression to explain a similar attitude: "Let us behave the best we can, have hope, and let the birds chirp. "

I wish I could continue my sharing a little more with you, but I have to put more logs in the fireplace. We are at the gate of the great north and temperature is low outside. Please share with your spouse and friend my sentiments of esteem and friendship,

Alain

My brother Jean-Marc sent me a long article, to which he gave the title of "*Monmayou's Paradigm*". To put in a few words his ten pages of reflection he said: "Monmayou is the evidence of what hope is and may produce in people. When hope resides in us, it irradiates around, and its radiations spread joy and happiness around, starting from our own life that is made splendid."

I replied the following:

Some believe that the precarious situation of our days, even the critical context in which everybody is fighting, in our present world, leads towards a disaster, and that afterwards… everything will be better. This perspective opposes Adrian's teaching. A similar thinking disregards the proper configuration of the world and neglects the immensity of the love of the Lord.

A disaster does not improve anything. It is a temptation of the

444

mind to want an end of our present suffering, with a general catastrophe. Only a constant and daily effort, in the many details of our own life, may achieve improvement in the world. The Gospel says that those who are faithful in little things will get a great commitment. A disaster threatens present situations, aborts any attempt of repairing and processing to development… a revolution can only endanger the movement of kindness and embellishment which supports the world, i.e. may destroy the little spots of good that resist here or there… No! Strikes, demonstrations of discontent, expressions of being fed up are acts of war; they only oppose the positively grounded movement towards the establishment of a better order…

And, yes! Your admiration for the mercy, simplicity, indulgence, leniency, patience, friendship, benevolence of Adrian confirms the Gospel words: "The world belongs to the meek". It is the Prince of the World who likes to see mankind stumble in bankruptcy, and fail in a disaster, in order to increase the despair of people, and expose them more easily to his tricks.

It is typical of announcers of incoming disasters to suggest then of hiding and hording food, as if material things could save us from an eventual calamity, coming from above. If the danger would be spiritual, only a spiritual behavior is needed. The Lord does not need us to hide in order to save us. God works with the good. It is the exertion of Marian virtues of patience, perseverance, fortitude, and love that will save the world.

Gianpiero, who was in Washington D.C. during those days, was inquiring about the reasons for my stay in some "nowhere in the north". He kindly provoked me to share the true experience of these days. I soon replied as follows:

It is a gift to stay here, near Lake Beaulne, on the Laurentide Mountains, enjoying the silence of the wild country and the gorgeous neighborhood of splendid fauna and flora.

This morning, Fr. Giacomo, from Montreal, celebrated Mass. We had a short visit afterwards. When he heard that I am a philosopher he suddenly asked me how I am able to communicate the presence of God among us in my philosophy classes. I was unable to answer, even if he formulated his question including the answer... "How do you manage to bring your students near to God, while teaching values..." "Well, it does not work that way," I said.

The real situation is otherwise. As a teacher it is my task to teach... not to manage any conversions... Conversion comes eventually as a gift from above. My business, if I may say so, is to provide a true teaching... and if the teaching is accurate, there is room for God to teach himself and enter personally in the process. When we induce students to see the world as it is, the whole world may show its created identity. It is that simple. The more we hide in words our real life, the more we speak of it.

Chiara Lubich used to say that "People are the shortcut to meet God." "In every neighbor you meet, here I am" says the Lord in Matthews 25. "Where two or three are gathered in my name, I am in the midst." says Matthews (18:19). As a result, living in the middle of society we are in a continuous presence and contemplation of the Lord, that we encounter in everyone we meet, as far as we want to.

Contemplation, which for centuries was considered only an inner process, can be also done in the middle of the crowd, with everybody we encounter. In a world moving towards becoming a global village, suddenly heaven also is moving into it. What was an inside endeavor during the last centuries has become again a living presence, as he was, when he lived among the people in Palestine.

There is no need to talk about God, unless we have to do it for specific reasons. God himself, who is everywhere his creatures are, will do so in due time. If we want to, we meet him through all creatures, in every place we are, in everyone we meet. As a teacher it is not always our business to speak about him, but it is eventually more important to behave in such a way as to make it possible for other people to hear and meet him. Then the development of such a relationship depends on God himself and on those who seek him... Relationship depends on both sides. And the desire of the Lord to meet us is greater than our own want to meet him.

Wishing that today you might receive his visit.

When Vito was home in the evening, after dinner, we used to stay a little longer in front of the fireplace and share. Our old friendship allowed us to utter everything that came to mind without discrimination. Vito was good at starting conversations. A simple reference to some event of the day would help. Most of the time, he liked expressing his thoughts provocatively. He knew that would get me to argue. The topic this night was about chaotic ambiance in society and speculation.

He got me going. I started slowly an interesting conversation that I could summarize as follows:

"Monmayou spoke a few times about the way society should improve. Today, because of the lack of relationship between people, we need tolerance to sustain relationships and money to regulate a proper relationship among all. Money, however, is only a provisional issue. In times to come, society's life will not be regulated by money. There will be a society without money."

"How that?" asked Vito.

"Monmayou saw many things with certainty, but out of the human context… I am sure his purpose was not to predict but to prepare us for the times to come… One day, scientific discoveries will make energy free to everyone. There will be no need to produce energy, and then to sell it, the same for water and all basic products, including food. It will be so abundant, that money will become obsolete."

"I'm too old for this kind of story. I'll never see it," was his comment.

"I'm not so sure about that. What I know for sure is that the Lord lives inside of each one of us and wants to emerge among us as the true bond between people. What today is almost an option in social relationship should become the rule," I said.

Vito, who was becoming almost drowsy, suddenly woke up, "What do you mean by that? Are you referring to a society in which Christ would be the king?"

I tried to explain, "It's all said in the Bible. In his letter to the Romans (8:8), St. Paul said "You owe nothing to one another but love." when we accomplish a love of relationship, we build a family and, later on, the whole society becomes a community. There is no need for money to regulate relationships inside of a true family." Afterwards, my conclusion was simple, "In every one of us the Lord dwells and wants to make it actual" I added. "That will occur at the right time. It will happen even before we know it."

After a silence I continued: "When I was teaching in Rome at the Gregorian University, I was told by my good friend Fr. Joseph de Finance, that Jacques Maritain, before he died, was working on the project of a society without money. It was a Maritain's friend who found, after Maritain's death, his notes on the project on the side table. The project of Maritain was an impossible utopia. Nonetheless, the attempt for a similar project made me think. Yes, it is true that money is today an obstacle for the growing of the society, especially due to the fact that people who have money invest in order to get more... This is a nonsense. Work should eventually provide money, but not the banks. Similar abuses are unacceptable."

Slowly, but surely, we continued to share. A few times, Vito raised the quality of our discussions, with jokes... He spoke about the obsoleteness of products in the market: "Industry today is able to produce, at low cost, bulbs that never fail. But the unions asked the companies to pay searchers to help fix bulbs that fail after 2000 or 2500 hours, in order to keep the market running. They cost more but they are perishable. And the market needs it. In that way the whole organization of economy is kept fixed. As far as we keep all products obsolete, the market will continue to exist."

Another silence followed his statement. Then I said "Yes, all associations and authorities are afraid of change. They want to be in charge. they need the poor to govern them. They are afraid of a free society. They truly prefer to keep the market as it is. Nonetheless, the tools exist already, and they can change the whole configuration of economy."

During the talk, our common reflection agreed with the fact that, willingly or unwillingly, the whole endeavor towards a society without money is progressing. That society will come independently of our capacity to prepare for it. On one side the whole structure of a society built on gain and thief will fail. The whole system of making money on public goods like water, light, cooking energy, fresh air on summer and heat on winter, will fail, too.

Scientific discovery has already made available free energy for everybody. But without a human climate of friendship nothing can be implemented. A climate of charity is necessary. Somehow our days are making true the words of Saint Paul: "Hope and Faith will disappear but Charity will remain forever."

We had enough to think about for the evening. I left the room in silence, and went to sleep upstairs. Vito used to sleep on the bench near the stove, which he regularly fed with large logs during the night.

After lunch, on Tuesday, Vito and I made a drive to Rawdon. I was curious to see the Maxi store over there. I was looking for some croissants that I wanted to offer Vito for breakfast. When Vito heard my intention, he said abruptly, "I don't want to have them." It was typical of him to be contradictory. Actually, even if Vito liked croissants, his first reaction to every issue is to start a fight. He likes to affirm his independence first... and it is also his way to tell me, "Do not spend your money. It's not worth it," then he feels free to accept what he previously rejected, just to save his freedom, but happy to enjoy these touches in our relationship.

We were talking about it... as a senseless conversation, when we were stopped by an old gentleman: "What a nice surprise! It is pleasant to hear people coming from Pennsylvania who speak French".

"How do you know that?" I replied.

"I saw the plate on your car," he said.

"So, you're able to read..." Vito added.

An interchange of a few jokes kept us in the parking lot for a while when, during the conversation, we discovered that we were in the presence of a retired parish priest 81 years old...

It surely was a pleasant surprise. Immediately the quality of our conversation rose up.

"How do you maintain your spiritual life?" I asked sharply.

"I keep it alive through the internet" - he said.

Our surprise increased even more: "How is that?" we asked.

Fr. Bruno explained that he found on internet several gathering of people sharing on prayer, contemplation, and spiritual issues and this interaction keeps her soul alive and even challenged him. You would never think that internet could have such a good impact on people. We greeted one another as old good friends and returned to the chalet.

Coming back, the evening was moving to the night and the wood was happily burning in the stove... Vito broke the silence: "What do you actually think Monmayou would like to say to us today?"

This was a sudden provocative question. I knew it looked strange but I was sure that Vito was hiding there a personal inquiry. I took it seriously, then. I had to be consistent. I remained silent for a while, willing to get some good insight, finally I said: "It would be nothing special, "Monmayou liked never to hurt anyone and his desire is surely to help... I would dare to say that if Monmayou had the book in his hands he would recall Saint Paul's suggestion: "read all with care, try to enjoy what you like, and drop the rest."

Vito looked stunned, "Is that so?"

When we met, the following morning I finally showed up with the croissants that Vito pretended not to notice, trying to make me think that he surely was not intended to have them. While he was serving the coffee, I casually put them on the table, and casually he took one of them. Another taste of our friendship had come through.

One evening, near the fireplace, I told Vito about the story I recounted in the previous pages and about the prophecy of Monmayou concerning the End Times.

"Do you believe him?" Vito asked me.

"Yes, I do!" I said firmly in reply, "I know it will happen as he said, but I do not know when, neither exactly how. Nonetheless we must live in a way to be ready for it."

"What does that mean?" He asked again.

"Well," I said, "let me answer with a short example. Some biographer reported that once, when St. Aloysius Gonzaga was about 12, the school director suddenly asked to the students: "Supposing you heard that the end of the world was coming in less than an hour, what would you do?" Many diverse replies came up: "I would go to confession" said one, "I would go in the chapel to pray" said another, "I would reconcile myself with my friend that I just disrespected," added another one, and so on...

The director replied: "Please do so, right now".

Aloysius was silent.

The priest asked directly to him: "And you, Aloysius, what would you do?"

His reply was amazingly simple: "It is now time for recess... Therefore, I would continue to play, in order to stay in God's will"

Vito took a big breath and finally said, "The End Times are to come and we must behave accordingly. The End Times, however, bring nothing that we are not already aware of, and there is no need for any special undertaking. We have nothing better to do than to continue doing what good we can, without rush and disquiet."

He was right.

The fireplace was burning high while we were silently wondering...

Tableau # 32
Global Warming

Thursday July 19, 2018

I AM VISITING ANNIE, MY SISTER, AND HER FAMILY AT LA CARREYRIE DE VAUREILLES, near Le Gas, in the Department of Aveyron, France, which is an area in the old Gascony. We were talking in the yard, under the porch… when Olivier, one of the neighbors, spoke about Global Warming.

He is complaining that "politicians, today, make it a business: forcing people to provide differentiated garbage, and pay for it, but in the end, all authorities take advantage of it".

He is insistent: "People are forced to pay for giving away their trash; the municipalities ask the citizens to deliver in conformity to strict ordinances and in proper fashion what they do not need any more, and they also demand people to pay for giving it away!"

No one around had the courage to tell him that, yes, he was right, not even I. His reflection was shared by all, but it was too politically incorrect to openly agree with him.

That reminded me of something Monmayou said to me when we were in his front yard years ago: "You see all these bushes? Today they are only bushes, one day they will produce food for everyone."

"What bush?" I asked.

"Each one!" He uttered.

"What kind of food?" I insisted.

"You cannot even imagine what nature is hiding inside!"

I was wondering what time in the future Adrian was referring to.

Concerning the whole of nature, it was easy to consider the many ways people harm the whole world. It would be sufficient to refer to injustice, social abuses, shameful acts of killing, especially abortion…

and other crimes that abound, that people often believe remain unpunished.

They do not. It is sufficient to consider the many manners in which the earth suffers today, so many changes in the weather, like global warming, earthquake, irregularity of seasons... They are, for Adrian, the consequences of sins. He said so.

Tuesday 8 January 2019

A series of adverse events put our family into a very serious situation of need.

I know from experience that to be in need is a sign of God's predilection. It is a call to look up.

As I used to tell my students at Franciscan University, "God keeps his friend in precariousness, but never in misery".

Such is the sign of the presence of God in our life: when we are poor. That is the opposite of the popular consensus that "every gift is a sign of blessing; rich people are the blessed ones". Actually, the Gospel does not support such a belief.

Yes, every gift from above is a blessing, and poverty is one of them.

At Christmas just a few days ago, we celebrated the Nativity of the Lord, when God who became flesh in the womb of the virgin Mary entered human history in a stable in Bethlehem. The mysterious but real events of the Incarnation and Birth, God's coming on earth among us, took place in extremely poor circumstances.

All through his life Jesus never denied such a teaching: he remained poor. Nevertheless, he was never miserable. His poverty was an expression of His Presence among us, with nobility, majesty, beauty, kindness, goodness, and truth.

Wednesday, 9 January, 2019

The teaching of Adrian Monmayou makes me think of the words of Pope François at the beginning of his pontificate: "God forgives always, people do sometimes, nature never forgives!"

At the moment I heard this, I did not immediately, understand it.

I though of the pope as a friend of ecologists, but it is much more than that.

While I was driving between home in Northern Pittsburgh and Steubenville University, Ohio, to start teaching at Steubenville, during the winter 2017/18, we had uncommon days of cold (after maybe uncommon days of warmer temperature during the fall). I was kidding, "This cold is undoubtedly a sign of global warming", and all the students laughed in class.

There came to my mind the words of Our Lady, at Garabandal, in the '60s: "Days will come when people will have no respect for life, they will even kill their own babies" At that time abortion was virtually unknown among people all over the world. "As a consequence of such a human barbarianism, she said, "the whole of nature will rebel, and cause natural disasters" like storms, alteration of seasons, unexpected changes in temperature, hurricane, earthquake, etc.

At the time when those revelations came out, many scientists were happy to contradict Our Lady, saying that there is not any alteration of seasons… Yes, in those days, there was not yet such alterations, but today there are, even as common events. Meanwhile, those words have been forsaken…

When people behave against nature, nature itself rebels against people. Monmayou was aware of this and he said so to those who were ready to listen to him.

Thursday, 10 January, 2019

Some flashes of conversations with Adrian continue to pop up in my mind, maybe at random, maybe not.

I said so already, but it could be that it will never be useless to say it again, and to continue to repeat it…

We were in the yard, in front of his house: "Do you see all these bushes? One day they all will provide food for mankind"

How that? – I asked.

Monmayou did not answer my question. But he continued to explain his vision: "One day the whole of nature will be happy with people, and it will provide whatever people need".

I understood that it depends on us to restore the whole world to health.

That same day he did not say more to me.

After the days spent at Chersey, Quebec, as a rest, in the chalet of my friend Vito Merla, I let the manuscript of Monmayou waiting in my computer. Something was missing in the recount. I was not sure what... Actually, there is much more to say, especially concerning Monmayou's teaching. I was five, the last time I met Monmayou, and nevertheless, it seems like just yesterday in my mind.

Tuesday 19 January 2021

Since last December a PANDEMIC is raging in the world. It got the name of Corona Virus, or Covid-19.

It made me think, immediately on the Black Death that, between 1347-1351, was a calamity which perverted all over the world: according to the area on the earth, from ⅓ to ½ of the population was decimated, destroying the whole structure of the society of that era.

After 1351 it was not possible to continue living according to the previous social structure of human life. And such a change on earth marked the end of Middle-Age civilization.

Then started, at new, a fresh system of social development: Renaissance was born.

Amazingly, a totally new age in history had begun.

I hope that the present pandemic will produce a similar fantastic phenomenon.

We do not know, at this time, what that will be. But it is certain that something else will arise, erasing the present notion of "economy", which contradict the definition of Aristotle in his letter to Nicomachus. For Aristotle, Ethics involves unique individuals like Vito Merla, Politics is the ethics for a specific area, while Economy was the manner to address ethics among people at large, of which, money is proper to be used for the goods people need, i.e. serving the whole society. He agreed with the perspective that money is a good servant, but a horrible tyrant. In one word, economy is supposed to be what we could call CONVIVIALITY, a sort of permanent serendipity.

Today, economy has become the standard manner of dealing with people in every endeavor. This situation is against the nature of human being.

I wish that the present pandemic would restore a proper society.

It is, however, impossible at present to imagine exactly what that will be before we see it.

Sunday, April 4, 2021 – Easter day

It is the most significant day of the year. Everything happens before or after Easter, in a proper perspective. Before Easter all behaviors perceive the imperfection of human life, and we address it expecting Redemption. After, we face the marvelous deeds from above, continuing to carry our cross and to make successful such endeavors of the Lord...

Today are resounding the words of Bernard de Clairvaux: "Every suffering is pregnant of Resurrection." Such is the teaching of Easter.

Much more should be said regarding Adrian Monmayou and the events of Espis. Notwithstanding, at least the roots of his discourse have been given.

The PANDEMIC is still raging in the world. In some places it already changed the manner of living people were used to enjoy. Lock downs, masks on the faces, reducing business activity are a few of these changes.

All these changes remain expressions of Love from above, upon each of us.

The nine choirs of the Angels surround us, and do not let us go on without some improvement

After Easter, every Sunday is again Easter Day. Let's celebrate again and again the endeavor of Redemption and the care of the Angels as we proceed in the process of producing the new earth and the new heaven, until End Times come.

Tableau # 33
Farewell

WHEN I WAS ASKED TO WRITE DOWN YOUR STORY, ADRIAN MONMAYOU, I knew I was in trouble. I lost my breath and felt dizzy for a little while. It took me days, even months, while becoming aware of it, to make me capable of doing so.

Several years have gone by since your death, Monmayou, and the people who could provide me with the details I needed to tell your life are dead too!

Among these potential sources of precious pieces of information, I must count my dad Raymond, my mom Marthe, my brother Joseph, their spiritual counselor, Fr. Emmanuel de Floris, hermit in the Alpes mountain, in the woods of Montmorin, several other near friends like René Roques, Georges Campagne, Fr. Marcel Martin, and finally a few other people in Vatican (like Msgr. Jacques Martin), or in Moissac and vicinity, and a few diverse places in France. When, finally, I decided to start, it was already too late then to get information from anyone. Actually, in spite of the evidence I had about their familiarity with the events I referred to, many of those whom I asked for information claimed they did not know or they did not remember or they never were personally involved with Monmayou… etc. Was that true? The fact is that even after so many years, they still are frightened to talk about these events…

My heart is sad to death in front of such a disaster for the loss of so many good references and sources of acquaintance. Suddenly, amidst such disarray, I found comfort in the Bible. Opening it at random, my heart began pounding with the good news: "If the seed does not die it will not bring any fruit." What a comforting surprise: such a death was pregnant of resurrection! I understood that help was supposed to come to me from new sources, from connections that I was not aware of yet. And this is what actually happened!

Yes, my Lord, death is a disaster. Death makes for missing so many people, friends and personalities, together with their bursts of gladness and their sparks of wisdom, to say nothing about the patrimony of information and the potential of life, creativity, and solutions that death makes disappear with them. Nonetheless, O! Lord! You put death and suffering at the service of your Kingdom, which everywhere brings peace, life, and wisdom.

Referring to Monmayou himself, it never happened that someone would meet this countryman in vain. You may not be aware of it at the moment, but nonetheless, you are full of hope afterwards.

All during the time I was writing about Adrian Monmayou, I proceeded by flashes, or tableaus. The chronology follows more or less the events, which include the endeavor that brought us onto this side of the sea.

Somehow Monmayou prepared me to address during my journey diverse spiritual experiences. There was first the one of the Focolare when I met Nuzzomaria Grimaldi and Renata Borlone in November 1958 at Montauban, and after that, when, through his Angels, the Lord in person changed my life: against my own decisions, he moved me to Florence and Rome first, then to the New Continent.

St. Augustine was right: "God does not allow any evil if it is not for a better good."

After walking together with Monmayou, I understand that all of us are born to die and then rise again forever at the End Times. The teaching of such an understanding, makes us capable of dying every moment to every one of our own concerns, being aware with Saint Bernard that "every suffering is pregnant with resurrection."

Every morning I get up with the immense joy of facing a new day of love… ready to die, if the Lord should ask me to leave. Those who want to come after me must renounce themselves and carry their cross. And we must die physically, affectively, psychologically, speculatively, spiritually. Death is the key of every life.

Yes, everything we do each day is undertaken as if it were our last deed on earth. This is the only way to stay open to the afterlife, and to keep us ready, right now, to meet him upstairs: if we do not behave in order to be ready now, then, when the time comes, we will be not be able to reach that occasion properly: seizing the day is imperative.

With the help from above, I must address every situation, as if it were the last one: it is, actually, the last occasion for me to deal with my wife, Chiara, my children, M-Claire, M-Thérèse, Michel, Marta and Marco, and my 12 Grand-Children (starting with Mica, Marcel, etc. up to Zephan), my students (all of them), my neighbors, and everyone else.

Every day is the last time in my life that I drive to Franciscan University of Steubenville... and then back home in Pittsburgh... Every day I teach my last class of Metaphysics, of Anthropology, of Methodology, of Ethics...

Every endeavor is always the last one we do, like the fact that we had to move out from the large house on Guyton Road, where each of our children and some of our grandchildren grew up. Our financial situation would not allow us to stay in the same large and comfortable house. Some of our children cried at the prospect of losing such a loved home. I was surprised, nonetheless, to learn that during those same days, some religious communities in Pittsburgh, men and women of the same Movement moved to a larger house. For the first time, each member got a room of his or her own. They were able to communicate more easily with Zoom, and take advantage of other conveniences unavailable before. Everyone must adapt to the circumstances that Providence prescribes ...

Now, let's go back to the chores of our current business. It is then and there that his words become life.

Still vivid is the moment when Adrien told me about the time when people will be free again and the whole of nature will enjoy the fullness of its productivity: "You see, Alain, all these bushes? One day they will provide food for everyone in the world".

For a while I have been wondering what he really wanted to say...

I finally understood that he had received a vision of the End-Times...

But there is more. The End-Times, for each one of us comes when we die.

What happens then is contradictory: we enter the afterlife, which is true life, while we make the gift to the earth of our perishable body, the one which has been nourished almost every day by the Eucharist, and goes underground, as a seed, to accelerate the renovation of earth and heaven. It was actually a concept that Chiara Lubich liked to emphasize: "When we die, we provide a last gift to the earth, we give it the seed of renovation of the whole universe, for when the End Times will come." It is the seed that will die for the new heaven and the new earth.

Meanwhile we get our true eternal body, the one which was ours from the beginning of time.

What a marvelous moment, to end our life making a gift for the whole world, in order to help its restoration into its proper true nature, and at the same moment, entering into eternal life, having possession finally of our eternal body.

This is not the end, but only the roots of a bigger story, which needs to be completed...

Yes, it will be told...

Other Books by Alain Sauret

PALMERO & METAPHYSICS
Contemplating Everyday Mystery

MARCEL & CIE:
On the Human Person

CHIARA
and the Foundation of Ethics

Made in the USA
Middletown, DE
23 December 2021